The Collected Works of Chökyi Nyima Rinpoche

Volume II

RANGJUNG YESHE BOOKS • www.rangjung.com

PADMASAMBHAVA: *Treasures from Juniper Ridge* • *Advice from the Lotus-Born* • *Dakini Teachings* • *Following in Your Footsteps: The Lotus-Born Guru in Nepal* • *Following in Your Footsteps: The Lotus-Born Guru in India*

PADMASAMBHAVA AND JAMGÖN KONGTRÜL: *The Light of Wisdom, Vol. 1, Vol. 2, Vol. 3, Secret, Vol. 4 & Vol. 5*

PADMASAMBHAVA, CHOKGYUR LINGPA, JAMYANG KHYENTSE WANGPO, TULKU URGYEN RINPOCHE, ORGYEN TOBGYAL RINPOCHE, & OTHERS *Dispeller of Obstacles* • *The Tara Compendium* • *Powerful Transformation* • *Dakini Activity*

YESHE TSOGYAL: *The Lotus-Born*

DAKPO TASHI NAMGYAL: *Clarifying the Natural State*

TSELE NATSOK RANGDRÖL: *Mirror of Mindfulness* • *Heart Lamp* • *Empowerment and Samaya*

CHOKGYUR LINGPA: *Ocean of Amrita* • *The Great Gate* • *Skillful Grace* • *Great Accomplishment* • *Guru Heart Practices*

TRAKTUNG DUDJOM LINGPA: *A Clear Mirror*

JAMGÖN MIPHAM RINPOCHE: *Gateway to Knowledge, Vol. 1, Vol. 2, Vol. 3, & Vol. 4*

TULKU URGYEN RINPOCHE: *Blazing Splendor* • *Rainbow Painting* • *As It Is, Vol. 1 & Vol. 2* • *Vajra Speech* • *Repeating the Words of the Buddha* • *Dzogchen Deity Practice* • *Vajra Heart Revisited*

ADEU RINPOCHE: *Freedom in Bondage*

KHENCHEN THRANGU RINPOCHE: *Crystal Clear*

CHÖKYI NYIMA RINPOCHE: *Bardo Guidebook* • *Collected Works of Chökyi Nyima Rinpoche, Vol. 1 & Vol. 2*

TULKU THONDUP: *Enlightened Living*

ORGYEN TOBGYAL RINPOCHE: *Life & Teachings of Chokgyur Lingpa* • *Straight Talk* • *Sublime Lady of Immortality*

DZIGAR KONGTRÜL RINPOCHE: *Uncommon Happiness*

TSOKNYI RINPOCHE: *Fearless Simplicity* • *Carefree Dignity*

MARCIA BINDER SCHMIDT: *Dzogchen Primer* • *Dzogchen Essentials* • *Quintessential Dzogchen* • *Confessions of a Gypsy Yogini* • *Precious Songs of Awakening Compilation*

ERIK PEMA KUNSANG: *Wellsprings of the Great Perfection* • *A Tibetan Buddhist Companion* • *The Rangjung Yeshe Tibetan-English Dictionary of Buddhist Culture & Perfect Clarity*

The Collected Works of Chökyi Nyima Rinpoche

Volume II

Indisputable Truth
and
Present Fresh Wakefulness

Translated from the Tibetan by Erik Pema Kunsang
Compiled by Marcia Binder Schmidt
and edited with Kerry Moran

Rangjung Yeshe Publications
526 Entrada Drive, Apt 201
Novato, CA 94949 USA

www.rangjung.com
www.lotustreasure.com

Copyright © 2022 Rangjung Yeshe Publications & Chökyi Nyima Rinpoche

All rights reserved. No part of this book may be reproduced in any form or by any means, electronic or mechanical—including photocopying, recording, and duplicating by means of any information storage and retrieval system—without written permission from the publisher.

1 3 5 7 9 8 6 4 2

First editions published in 1996 & 2002
Printed in the United States of America

Publication data: ISBN13: 978-1-735734521 (pbk)

Title: *The Collected Works of Chökyi Nyima Rinpoche, Volume 11*
Chökyi Nyima Rinpoche (b. 1951).
Preface by Kyabje Tulku Urgyen Rinpoche.
Translated from the Tibetan by Erik Pema Kunsang (Erik Hein Schmidt).
Edited by Marcia Binder Schmidt

Indisputable Truth & Present Fresh Wakefulness.
1. Mahamudra & Dzogchen. 2. Vajrayana Philosophy — Buddhism.
3. Buddhism — Tibet. I. Title.

SECOND EDITION

INDISPUTABLE TRUTH

The Four Seals That Mark the Teachings of the Awakened Ones

Chökyi Nyima Rinpoche

Preface by
Kyabje Tulku Urgyen Rinpoche

Translated from the Tibetan by Erik Pema Kunsang

Compiled by Marcia Binder Schmidt
and edited with Kerry Moran

CONTENTS

Preface	1
Meditation	7
Change	31
Emptiness	49
Experience	65
Pith Instructions	83
Rigpa	105
The View	119
Indivisibility	131
Recognition	145
Key Points	165
Wakefulness	177
Nirvana is Peace	191
Acknowledgments	207
PRESENT FRESH WAKEFULNESS	209
Preface	211
Introductory Teachings	213
A Spiritual Person	223
No Samsara Apart from Thoughts	237
Divorce	253
The Lamp that Dispels Ignorance	269

Release	283
Means and Knowledge	293
Small Freedom	305
Renunciation	317
Devotion and Pure Perception	331
Not Meditation but Familiarization	347
The Heart of the Practice	361
A Permanent Vacation	375

Preface

To gain comprehension through the use of words is intellectual understanding. To bring the meaning of those words into the realm of actuality is experience. We may hear that all composite things are impermanent, but to let that remain as mere words is to stray into intellectual understanding.

It is an indisputable fact, an obvious truth for anyone who can see and think, that composite things are impermanent. There is absolutely no doubt about it. Equally indisputable is the fact that everything defiling is painful. By 'defiling' I mean primarily the ten unvirtuous actions, which most certainly are the direct causes for experiencing pain and suffering. The statement that 'all things are empty of or devoid of identity' refers to the nature of emptiness itself. The result of spiritual practice is called nirvana, literally 'passing beyond suffering'. Nirvana is the state of great peace, the attainment of liberation and enlightenment, the omniscient state of buddhahood.

Nirvana can be understood on different levels: attaining the state of liberation is conditioned nirvana, while the omniscient state of buddhahood is unconditioned nirvana. In the literal sense, 'passing beyond suffering' means to transcend the pain of cyclic existence, the samsaric wheel of life. Please don't think it simply means 'passing away' as in dying. Conditioned nirvana means to be reborn into an extraordinary pure land, with no regression back into samsaric states. It means to be liberated from samsara and to reach a buddhafield. The omniscient state of buddhahood, on the other hand, means that while one is in such a buddhafield one traverses the remaining portion of the path and awakens to true and complete enlightenment. Thus, the word nirvana implies both liberation and omniscient buddhahood.

There is a famous aspiration that includes this line: "Neither straying into existence nor dwelling in peace, may I liberate all beings equal in number to the infinity of space." To "stray into existence" refers to samsara. To "dwell in peace" means to remain in the passive state of stillness. This is why you often hear that one doesn't awaken to enlightenment through shamatha alone. We must transcend both samsaric existence and passive peace! In other words, one may go beyond the samsaric existence of the three realms, but it is still possible to stray into a *shravaka*'s or a *pratyekabuddha*'s nirvana of passive peace. This is not the true and ultimate state.

To go beyond both existence and peace does not only mean to transcend the causes for samsara, the three or five poisons. It also encompasses being free of the attachment to a serene feeling of tranquility while aiming at being able to liberate all sentient beings. That is the true path to the enlightenment of a buddha.

You can truly be said to have transcended both existence and peace once you have attained the twofold accomplishment, which involves purifying the twofold obscurations — emotional and cognitive — and realizing the twofold embodiment of enlightenment, the two *kayas*. To reiterate, the peaceful nirvana lying beyond samsara's three realms which is attained through the path of a shravaka or pratyekabuddha is not the final state. Some portion of the path remains to be traversed before you reach true and complete enlightenment. If you truly wish to go beyond both samsaric existence and nirvanic peace within this very lifetime, this is possible through the Vajrayana path, which offers a means of eliminating the very subtle cognitive obscuration of dualistic fixation. You must realize that the path of a shravaka or pratyekabuddha doesn't fully clear away this cognitive obscuration. The shravaka or pratyekabuddha's path consists of retraining one's concepts of an observer, something observed, and the act of observing. This is exactly what the Vajrayana path related to the third empowerment aims at transcending.

To phrase this in terms of the Sutra path, there is something called the 'sublime *ushnika* empowerment of all buddhas'. In it, the rays of light emanating from the protuberance found at the crown of the head of all buddhas touch the top of the bodhisattva's head, and through this he or she is conferred the ultimate empowerment of fruition. Until this point, the bodhisattva is said to still be slightly veiled by the cognitive obscuration.

Someone who, within this very life, wishes to not only avoid straying into existence but wants to also avoid dwelling in passive peace, must gain recognition of the genuine view and train in it with true diligence. When one is able to thoroughly do so, there is no portion of the path remaining that he or she needs to go through in a buddha-field. It is possible to traverse the entire path in this very lifetime. If that is not the case, it is still possible to take rebirth in a pure land, such as the uppermost realm of the Blazing Fire Mountain. Here, through the third empowerment of the Vajrayana path, you can cover the remaining part of the path and awaken to complete enlightenment.

To summarize, within the Sutra teachings there is nothing more crucial than these Four Seals of the Dharma which are described in this book.

I have one more comment about the words defiling and 'undefiling'. Undefiling refers to the state of true samadhi attained after having renounced the ten unvirtuous actions. In the Vajrayana context, undefiling actions means to visualize the deity, recite the mantra and train in samadhi. But honestly, these actions in themselves can be either defiling or undefiling. The difference lies in our attitude. A spiritual activity becomes undefiling the moment it is embraced with bodhichitta. Conversely, any so-called good deed becomes defiling the moment you forget the precious attitude of bodhichitta. In fact, any action which is embraced by samadhi and compassion becomes the true path of enlightenment. If you lack the understanding of true samadhi, at least try to motivate yourself with genuine compassion and the precious attitude of awakened mind.

• • •

To conclude, please take to heart this book that condenses the vast and profound teachings of the Buddha into pithy advice.

Spoken by Kyabje Tulku Urgyen Rinpoche
Nagi Gompa, 1995

The Four Seals that Mark the Teachings of the Awakened Ones

Everything conditioned is impermanent
All defiling states are painful
All phenomena are empty and devoid of self-entity
Nirvana is peace

Meditation

All the 84,000 types of teachings given by our compassionate teacher Buddha Shakyamuni can be condensed into the Four Seals of the Dharma. In this book I will explain these four seals to the best of my ability.

Before I begin, I'd like to define the qualifications for the Dharma teacher and the Dharma student. I will talk about the different types of teacher we can learn from and the need to integrate learning and reflection within meditation training.

The teacher, who is sometimes referred to as the 'spiritual friend,' should possess numerous great qualities. In brief, he or she should have gone through the proper training of learning, reflection and meditation involving the view, meditation, conduct and fruition of each of the vehicles. The master who possesses confidence and experience in the view of emptiness will never err concerning the meaning of the teachings. Although some minor mistakes in the phrasing might occur, someone with stability in the view will be able to immediately correct such inaccuracies.

The spiritual friend should, of course, be perfect in learning, reflection and meditation, but we, the students, also should never separate these three. Learning alone is not sufficient: what has been learned should be firmly established within one's being through reflection. What is meant by the word reflection? It means to investigate and examine the teaching. So please discern what is said and what is meant. Investigate what the words and the meaning indicate. Understand the purpose as well as the benefit of the teaching — really work it over and ponder it. This kind of reflection clarifies our understanding of what we study.

Without some degree of study and reflection, our devotion to the spiritual master and to enlightened beings is inconsistent. Likewise, our love and compassion for others tends to be fickle and transient. Especially concerning the view of the ultimate nature, without study or reflection it's very hard to be really stable. Without a proper basis in studying and reflecting, we can easily be interrupted by doubts and hesitation. Maybe we don't get completely wrong views, but subtle wrong views can easily sneak in. Therefore, it's very important to gain some intellectual comprehension of the teachings through studying and reflecting upon them. However, if we simply leave the matter with learning and reflection we are still mere intellectuals. There is no doubt that we need meditation training. Meditation here means the process of bringing what we have learned and reflected upon into the realm of personal experience.

When speaking of spiritual masters, there are four types of teachers that we should follow, all of whom are indispensable and can bring us great benefit. Later on in this book I will go into greater detail about these types of teachers, so here I will just briefly mention them. The first of these four categories is the 'living lineage teacher,' an actual physically embodied master who belongs to a lineage. The second type is the 'teacher who is the scriptures of awakened beings,' which includes the words of the Buddha and statements made by accomplished and learned masters of the past. The third type of teacher is called the 'symbolic teacher of experience,' our personal experiences gained from living in this world. To fully grasp the Buddhist teaching which states that samsaric existence should be discarded, we need to comprehend what the nature of samsaric existence is. By understanding the characteristics of our own daily life experiences we come to realize that samsaric existence is futile and unreliable, not something in which to put our trust. In this way, ordinary life becomes our teacher. It instructs us in futility and impermanence. That is what is meant by the symbolic teacher of experience.

We need to meet, follow and take guidance from these three types of teachers. Ultimately, however, there's only one true teacher. This is our enlightened essence, the self-existing wakefulness within ourselves, also called the 'ultimate teacher of the innate nature'. All sentient beings within the six classes of living creatures possess this enlightened essence. Among these six classes, the three inferior types — hell beings, hungry ghosts, and animals — also possess an enlightened essence, a buddha nature. But because of their unfortunate circumstances or, in the case of animals, their stupidity, they are unable to put it into practice and realize it. However, anyone who experiences and realizes this enlightened essence does attain complete enlightenment. No matter how miserable or how deluded we may be, if we can bring our buddha nature into our experience and train in it, we can be enlightened. On the other hand, if we don't experience and realize this enlightened essence, we will not attain complete enlightenment. To meet and realize this enlightened essence, we must utilize learning and reflection; most importantly, we need to practice meditation.

This ultimate teacher of the innate nature is present in everyone, all beings, without any exception. Although this is so, we don't acknowledge it; we don't recognize it. That is why it is said to be shrouded in a veil of ignorance. We have to use that analogy, speaking as if there was something hidden which we need to see. Since our innate nature is locked up inside an encasement of dualistic fixation, we need to destroy this dualistic experience. Now, let's examine whether this statement is true or not.

In terms of destroying this encasement of dualistic experience: unless we use some method, some technique, it just doesn't happen. The best method is of course effortlessness, but effortlessness cannot be taught. Even if we try, we do not become effortless automatically. Effortlessness just doesn't seem to spontaneously take place. But this encasement in dualistic experience falls apart the moment we simply let be in a nondualistic state. Another way to look at it is to realize that every moment of ordinary experience is governed by habit, by conditioning. Our present habit is dominated by deliberate effort. We have therefore no choice but to use our present habit of being deliberate and using effort in order to arrive at effortlessness.

When loving friends want to console or to relieve another's pain, they say, "Relax, don't worry." This is really one of the finest statements that a person can make. Relaxation — especially mental relaxation — is something basic and extremely beneficial. It is human nature to strive for material gain, sense pleasures, a good reputation and appreciation from others, often in an intense or even desperate way. Unless we can relax and not be so caught up, our relationship to enjoyments and wealth becomes hollow and substanceless, almost as if we were robots.

When someone whose heart is troubled and worried is, out of true affection and kindness, told "Relax, don't worry," this statement helps and can make a big difference. Telling someone to let go and relax can instill a sense of peace. This holds true not only for human beings but also for animals. When you show a genuinely loving expression on your face and kindly stroke an animal with your hand, these actions help it to feel at ease. Most important is to behave with love and compassion, expressing these feelings by being gentle and affectionate. The opposite of this is to act out of anger and to be aggressive towards others.

This is why the perfectly enlightened one, the Buddha, said "Rest calmly." In fact, teachings on the practice of shamatha sound very much like "Relax, don't worry." When we tell each other "Relax!" the power of just that one word has some kind of deep impact. Most people using the word don't really know the true depth of the meaning of "relax." We say "Relax!," but that which prevents us from being relaxed is, on a coarse level, our own disturbing emotions. On a more subtle level, that which prevents an utterly relaxed state of mind is subconscious thought activity, an almost unnoticed undercurrent of conceptual thinking.

When the Buddha said "Practice shamatha, rest calmly," he was giving affectionate advice. He was telling us to try to be at peace with ourselves, to remain like an ocean unmoved by the waves of disturbing emotions. We must realize that the degree to which our mind is occupied by disturbing emotions generates a corresponding degree of pain, of feeling unsettled and upset. If there's a medium degree of disturbing emotions, we feel that degree of pain. Even when there is simply an undercurrent of concepts, a subconscious flow of thoughts, this still prevents us from feeling totally at ease and remaining in the peaceful state of shamatha. So, the Buddha said, "Rest totally free, completely without any disturbing emotions, without any thought activity." This practice is called shamatha, and in the Sutra teachings it is taught in incredibly great detail. All the practices of shamatha can be condensed into two types: shamatha with the support of an object and shamatha without any object.

For a beginner it is difficult to simply be at peace, to rest calmly and free from a mental focus. This is because all our activities and ways of perceiving are dualistic, due to the habit of holding an object in mind. Therefore, the beginning practice of shamatha is to keep some concept or object in mind — not a complicated point of focus or multiple ones, just a single simple one.

The most widespread and generally accepted form of shamatha with focus involves placing the attention on the movement of our breath or on an object like a pebble, a stick, an image of the Buddha, or the like. Focusing our mind on one simple object prevents it from being occupied by anything else. We are not planning the future, reacting to some past event, indulging in being upset about this and that or pondering some choice object of love or hate. By concentrating on just one thing, it is possible for a feeling of peace, relaxation and comfort to take place.

Imagine a monkey locked inside a small box with four openings; it is really restless. It sticks its head out one side after the other, so rapidly and repeatedly that someone observing from the outside might think that there are four monkeys. Our present state of mind is very much like that restless monkey. It doesn't linger in one place from one moment to the next. All the time our minds are busy, constantly thinking. When we practice this form of shamatha, focusing our attention on just one object, we become accustomed to this new habit after some time. That is how it is possible to attain stability in a calm state of mind, in shamatha.

Compared to a state of mind that is occupied by nervous, restless thoughts, it is much better to be in a focused, relaxed state of peaceful attention. The benefits of this can be seen immediately: the very moment mind is simply focused on one object, the waves of disturbing thoughts and emotions are absent. Spending a session meditating in this way is like taking a break. It becomes a time of peace and calm, of feeling comfortable with ourselves. When our attention begins to stray away, when we are unable to keep an object in mind, we get distracted, and the feeling of being at ease also disappears. Then we remember the object of attention and continue as before, and the feeling of being at peace reoccurs.

At this point of meditation training, please don't believe that dualistic fixation is absent; it hasn't collapsed yet. Yet, the moment of resting calmly with focused attention is free of gross disturbing emotions; it's free of anger, attachment, and dullness. Say we're focusing on a vase of flowers. We're not involved in reacting against the flowers, in aggressively disliking them, which is anger. We are not attracted to them either, thinking how nice they are, which is attachment. Neither are we indifferent to them, which is dullness. Although the mind is free from the gross expression of these three types of emotions, there is still some sense of focus, of "me," "that," and "I'm focused!" As long as one retains such concepts of subject and object, dualistic fixation is not absent. In this way, it's not yet the perfect type of shamatha, and it is definitely not the awakened state of mind. Nevertheless, compared to an ordinary disturbed state of mind, shamatha with an object is much more preferable, because it's free from gross disturbing emotions.

As beginners, we should stay focused on the object of attention. And yet we need to understand that as long as the mind stays focused on an object, something is still incomplete. Deciding "I will rest my attention on one thing" is quite beneficial. But it would be even better if we could simply rest our attention free from focus, in a total openness free from reference point. This is the second type of shamatha. As long as we remain focused upon a particular object, we retain the idea of "that" and "I," meaning the one who focuses and the object of focus. There's still some degree of fixation or grasping occurring. In Buddhism, grasping or fixating on duality is considered the root cause of samsaric existence. Thus, to practice a meditation that is an exercise in retaining dualistic fixation can't be called perfect. Still, it is a stepping stone. If we don't learn our ABCs in first grade, we'll never start reading. In the same way, once we grow accustomed to the practice of shamatha with focus, it becomes very simple to learn how to rest calmly free from focus. When our attention remains totally undisturbed by emotions, thoughts, and concepts, free from all reference points, and free from focus, that is called objectless shamatha.

Having cultivated this state of shamatha, the next step is to embrace it by clear seeing, by *vipashyana*. The practice of shamatha, of being at peace, is by itself insufficient to obtain liberation from the three realms of samsaric existence. For this reason it is extremely important to carefully study the teachings, to reflect upon them and to become clear about how to practice. If we don't do this, if we simply identify the ultimate meditation state with shamatha, even though we may become very stable, we may never go beyond a samsaric state called the 'formless meditation gods'. We may remain here for a very long time, but when the experience eventually wears out we end up back in other samsaric states. So it's very important to be careful, to see clearly.

We should understand that shamatha practice has both pros and cons, a good side and a bad side. The good side of shamatha is that it is free from any disturbing emotions, free from the agonizing thought activity of the three times. The bad side of shamatha is that in itself it does not lead to liberation from samsara. It only becomes a cause for liberation when embraced by vipashyana. The realization of all the buddhas is described as the unity of shamatha and vipashyana, never as shamatha by itself.

To reiterate, first of all, when we're not involved in disturbing emotions and thoughts, there is an immediate sense of peace, of relief from suffering. The state of shamatha is unspoiled by thoughts of the past, present or future. By not thinking of anything in these three times, we are free from disturbing emotions. In addition to shamatha, there is also the practice of vipashyana, which means 'seeing clearly'. The basic nature of our mind, our innate nature, is a wakefulness in which emptiness and cognizance are indivisible. Unless there is some clear seeing of this innate wakefulness, to merely rest calmly in a state of stillness is to essentially be ignorant. We need to do more than simply be free from disturbing emotions and thought activity. Excellent as it is, a tranquil feeling is not enough to clearly see our innate nature. Self-existing wakefulness, the unity of being empty and cognizant, is totally free from any fixation on subject and object. To rest evenly in that is called the unity of shamatha and vipashyana. So, straighten your back. Stop talking, and don't force or control your breathing — just let it flow naturally. The realization of all buddhas is the unity of shamatha and vipashyana.

The Buddha gave different levels of teachings aimed at different types of persons, so we should apply whatever teaching fits us. If you know how to practice the state that is the unity of shamatha and vipashyana, then you should do that. If you feel that you are better able or more ready to practice the state of shamatha without object, you should do that. And if you feel that's difficult, that you must focus on an object in order for the attention not to waver from one thing to another, then practice shamatha focused on an object. We should practice according to our individual capacity, which is something we ourselves know. It doesn't help to fool ourselves, thinking we can practice something that we don't really understand. Be honest and practice in accordance with your own level. Then the session is not wasted.

Meditation training is the opposite of the ordinary conceptual state of mind that thinks "I am here, the world is there." Because it's so different from our ordinary state of mind, it's vital to study and reflect in order to eradicate any lack of understanding, misunderstanding or doubt that we may have about the correct view, meaning the correct understanding of how things are. If we, after arriving at certainty in the correct view, implement that in meditation practice, even a short period of meditation will have a great impact. On the other hand, if we don't gain an authentic understanding of the view of the innate nature of things, the effect will not be that great no matter how diligent we are. In short, don't separate learning, reflection and meditation, because these can clear away all the faults of not understanding, misunderstanding, and doubt.

Having covered these introductory points, I will now address the main topic of this book, the Four Seals of the Dharma, which are embodied in four short sentences that summarize all the teachings of the Buddhadharma. They are phrased as follows:

> Everything conditioned is impermanent.
> Everything defiling is painful.
> All phenomena are empty and devoid of self.
> Nirvana is peace.

The word 'conditioned' in the first sentence means anything dependent upon causes and circumstances. All our experiences — visible forms, sounds, scents, what we taste and the textures we feel, in short, the whole world — are conditioned. Even the tiniest atom is conditioned. The entire universe is first created, it remains, it disintegrates, and becomes void. Everything that comes into being — mountains, plants, trees, flowers, sentient or insentient — is impermanent; there is nothing that lasts. Everything is impermanent; that is a fact. The Tibetan word for impermanence, *mitagpa*, 'not lasting,' means subject to change, perishable, fleeting, passing — like a bubble on the water. The Buddha said that when we look at a bubble in the water it looks like it is there, like it exists, but then the next moment it is gone. Everything is like that; every single moment is changing.

Most people never question their day-to-day experiences. They accept whatever is felt and perceived as real. Without examining anything we will never penetrate beyond this illusion to see the actual state of affairs. Instead, we will regard everything that is impermanent as being permanent, what is unreal as being real. What an unfortunate, superficial and mistaken way of perceiving things! Actually, the whole world, all the people and beings, and on an inner level what we feel and think, all our pleasure, pain and indifference, is changing every single instant. It never remains constant. This is a fact; this is truly how it is. To regard something that is impermanent to be permanent is to be mistaken. To acknowledge what doesn't last is to be unmistaken. The frame of mind that apprehends things to be permanent while they are not is confused. It is an incorrect attitude.

All phenomena by their very nature are impermanent, unreal and illusory. To simply acknowledge that is to be undeluded. To briefly sum up the difference between these two viewpoints, the former is faulty, defective, incorrect, wrong. The latter, that does not regard things as being real and permanent, is correct, flawless and genuine.

When we understand that all conditioned things are impermanent, we feel at a loss to find anything that we can hold on to. We feel we can't find anything that is a reliable support. Therefore, our habitual fixation on things as being permanent and real starts to fall apart, and this falling apart of fixation leaves room for being unmistaken. So in short, if something is conditioned it is impermanent.

Moreover, whoever is born will also die. Meeting is followed by separation. Everything gathered will eventually be used up, spent. In the same way anything fabricated or made, anything achieved like a good reputation, fame or fortune will sooner or later be used up, disappear, vanish. In short, it is impossible to find anything conditioned that will last.

We have this foolish habit of believing that things last and are real. But things are neither permanent nor real, so our idea is mistaken. It does not relate to how things are. Things in themselves are impermanent and unreal. Through analysis we can understand that everything is impermanent. Apply this to everything, including yourself.

Good health is impermanent, we can get sick anytime. Sickness is also impermanent; we can recover. Life is obviously impermanent. The worst thing is that death is certain. Death has a nasty name and a nasty meaning. There is nothing worse than to tell somebody "Drop dead!" People find nothing more repulsive than a dead body. A very important or good-looking person who is getting close to death is really pitiful. Dying or dead, the body is really disgusting. And it is one hundred percent sure that this will happen to us.

What will help at the moment of dying and after death? We should be really clear about this, as it's already our habit to prepare for the future. Don't we devote our thoughts, words and deeds to ensure that later on we will have a comfortable situation? Don't we employ ourselves as servants in the aim of comfort, pleasure, and happiness, to being secure later on?

Some people they feel that if they can just have a good reputation it does not matter in the slightest whether they are poor or have delicious food. Then when their fame is destroyed, they have a heart attack and die. Each individual has some kind of vision of happiness. Some people aim at being appreciated by others, others at having material luxury. Nobody needs to learn or acquire these tendencies; they come naturally. We are happy with material gain, being praised by others, having a good name and pleasure. We are unhappy when the opposites of these four occur. These are called the 'eight worldly concerns'. Most people are totally under the power of these eight worldly concerns for their entire lives. They employ themselves one-pointedly and with great perseverance in the service of these eight worldly concerns. During this lifetime they never seem to be able to go beyond this hope and fear. The drive to achieve something that is lasting and real is based on the idea that things last and are real. This mistaken idea makes us grab after something hollow and illusory. No matter what we try to achieve, it will never last.

We try to be in charge of our situation, to take control of our sense pleasures, reputation, and material possessions. The result of all this effort is that we are never really in control. In the end, we can't even take charge of our own body. Ultimately, fire or water will take it or insects will eat it. Forget about everything else — money, enjoyments, clothes, good name — there are no exceptions here. It is not that some people can succeed in controlling these and others can't. The situation is the same for everyone.

There are problems in this life, things that don't work out exactly as we want them to, and we may complain quite a bit. Yet we do have a lot of freedom. Maybe we can't say we have one hundred percent free will, but we do have a lot of choice as to how we act. This kind of freedom will continue until our last breath. When we die, however, there is no certainty as to where and how we will be reborn. What assumes control then is our previous karma, our disturbing emotions and habitual tendencies. The situation after death is not like right now, when we can decide where to go and what to do. It is not sure at all where we will be after we die, how many arms and legs we will have, and what we will eat. The only thing that will help us then is something we have the ability to do right now, at the present moment. Right now we are able to understand and identify the difference between what is good and evil. We can understand and gain some clarity about our disturbing emotions and what we do, and we are able to change and overcome our negative tendencies to some degree. We have a certain amount of control and power right now. If we don't use this power now, while we have it, then the situation will definitely be more difficult when we are powerless.

There is an old saying: "Life runs out while we are preparing to live, so better prepare for the next life." What this means is that it is human nature to always arrange to be happy and comfortable in the future. We spend our whole life trying to do that, but while trying to prepare for later, our life runs out and we die. Our preparations are all left behind; they are never finished. So if you want to engage in preparations, it makes much more sense to prepare for your future life.

When, where and under which circumstance we will die are totally unpredictable. It is well known that people die from being sad, but some people even die from being too happy. Of course people die from being poisoned, but some also die from medicine. People die from starvation, but some people die from overeating. Some people die in miserable circumstances, but others die while everything is going very well, while enjoying themselves. Some people die in mountaineering accidents, falling from great heights, while others die from falling down just two or three steps. How and when we die is completely unsure.

The Buddha taught that the one billion worlds contained in this portion of the universe are all impermanent. All the people and animals who are together right now on this planet are just like a flock of birds who have temporarily landed in the same tree. This world we are in now was first formed within space. Having remained for some time, it will eventually disintegrate, until finally it is totally void, without even a single atom remaining. Traditionally it is said that the world is destroyed by the 'seven suns and the one water'. The *Abhidharma Kosha* explains how long it takes for the world's oceans to dry out, depending upon how deep they are. Plants and trees dry out almost instantaneously, but the ocean takes a long time to dry out. The end result is that nothing is left behind whatsoever, only utterly void space. By then, all the sentient beings living here will have transmigrated to other universes.

The Buddha couldn't show us anything conditioned that lasts, nor can we find such a thing. We speak about different kinds of impermanence, coarse and subtle. Coarse impermanence involves the four stages of formation, subsistence, disintegration and voidness of the universe. There is also a more subtle type of impermanence which, being subtle, is harder to understand. For example, people won't say we have aged before a lot of wrinkles have collected on our face. Actually at every moment the wrinkles are sneaking in, increasing slowly but steadily. But until they all show, people don't call us old. That's why we don't acknowledge that a youthful, vibrant person is aging. We don't say "Wow, you are really aging, you don't look young anymore. We wouldn't like to hear that said to ourselves. It is unavoidable and somehow we all know it. So we try to avoid aging; we rub cream and lotions on our faces to make sure it does not happen too quickly. We don't want to age; we don't like impermanence. However, whether the shape or surface of the skin changes or not, our bodies are in fact still deteriorating. We cannot change the fact that our life span is slowly running out. To merely attempt to alter the surface is hollow. The fact that we like youthfulness and we dislike aging is due to our aversion towards the fact of impermanence.

Although we don't want to die, we are still unable to avoid it. At the moment of death we cannot bring anything with us; our mind travels on by itself. Our consciousness will then depend on its good and evil tendencies. If a mind has only a little negative karma and disturbing emotions, then it is called a pure mind, a noble mind. If it has a lot of disturbing emotions and negative karma then it is called an evil mind. An evil mind produces a lot of misery. A pure mind does not suffer much. Isn't it true that if we have a very enjoyable, pleasant day, we have quite undisturbed dreams as well? Whereas if we have a lot of anxiety and fighting in the daytime, then our dreams can be really troublesome at night. That is called the creation of habitual tendencies. Our disturbing emotions and actions create a habitual imprint in the 'all-ground' (*alaya*), the basic consciousness. This disturbed frame of mind must be quickly purified, because everything is impermanent, there is nothing that is stable or sure. We can tell ourselves "I will quiet down my busy mind tomorrow or later," but there are different types of tomorrow. One kind of tomorrow looks quite a lot like what we experience right now. Another tomorrow is to find ourselves in a completely different place after having died during the night.

The statement, everything conditioned is impermanent, is a fact we need to acknowledge. There is some benefit from this. When we understand that nothing composite lasts, our normal tendency to be obsessed with material gain, pleasures, fame, and praise loosens. When the fixation on things as being lasting and real becomes less intense, our mind becomes more free and easy. It's true that the more desperate the attitude, the stronger or tighter this obsession with things as being lasting and real is, the more misery a person has. The less grasping we have, the less busy and speedy we become.

As our attachment and clinging to the pleasures of this life decrease, we start to gain some taste for understanding the real nature of things, which in Buddhism is called ultimate truth. Hence we will begin to engage in spiritual practice. We will be interested in the Dharma and will acquire a taste for it through learning, reflection and meditation — not merely engendering a fickle minor interest, but a strong interest. A real understanding of impermanence ensures that we become unshakable; we will never turn back from Dharma practice. Our disturbing emotions, our anger and desire, all diminish, because we begin to think, "What is the use, nothing lasts anyway, so why bother." We start to have the idea that nothing mundane is really worth striving for, since it is all pointless and futile. This kind of attitude will gain force over time and is very beneficial for realizing ultimate truth. So, reflecting on impermanence has many purposes. First, through it we develop some taste for the Dharma. Then strong interest in the Dharma arises and we really start to practice. Finally, it is the best tool to use to perfect the practice.

I have just explained the first of the four maxims or indisputable truths of the Buddha: "Everything conditioned is impermanent." Reading this is the learning aspect. Next, you should ponder it by asking yourself, "Is everything impermanent or not? What does it mean?" This is the process of reflection. Finally, the meditation aspect is to apply the recognition of impermanence to ourselves personally. The result of this is that we start to feel acutely "I don't have that much time to waste!" People have at most eighty or ninety years, but even that is not sure — we can die any time. When not giving much consideration to the fact of impermanence, one procrastinates. When clearly seeing the fact of impermanence it becomes completely impossible to postpone spiritual practice. The traditional examples given to illustrate this point involve a coward who sees a snake in his lap and a vain girl who discovers that her hair has caught fire — both will jump up immediately, without the slightest hesitation. I cannot stress how important the understanding of impermanence is, although admittedly it doesn't sound nice. It sounds much better to say everything is permanent, everlasting, that there is no death, there is no sickness, no pain. That sounds great, exceedingly pleasant, but unfortunately it's completely false. We do get sick; we get hurt and suffer; we die. If something is conditioned, it follows that it is impermanent. Think about this. If you find something that is both conditioned and permanent, please tell me.

STUDENT: The three disturbing emotions that you mentioned, Rinpoche — are they also the three mind poisons?

RINPOCHE: Yes, we say three poisons: anger, desire, and stupidity. If we count five, the additional ones are pride and jealousy. When we count six, we add greed or stinginess. These can be subdivided further, until there are 84,000.

STUDENT: When we have received a Dharma teaching, is it better to contemplate the teaching alone or to discuss it with others?

RINPOCHE: You can do both. Sometimes you can sit and reflect upon what is said all by yourself, that's very good. It's very good also to sometimes discuss it with others, but it's not good to argue about it.

STUDENT: When you were talking earlier about shamatha and vipashyana, I was wondering if shamatha naturally turns into vipashyana or does one need to learn and study about both?

RINPOCHE: It doesn't happen by itself. You need to receive instruction. In addition to shamatha, we need to learn vipashyana.

STUDENT: Does one need to learn one after the other, sequentially?

RINPOCHE: Definitely.

STUDENT: Could you explain how to make shamatha and vipashyana go together in practice?

RINPOCHE: Vipashyana, clear seeing, in this context means resting in basic wakefulness. It is also called the wisdom in which the qualities of two types of supreme knowledge are present: the knowledge of knowing the nature as it is, and the knowledge of perceiving all that exists. Shamatha, on the other hand, is simply resting calmly, undisturbed or unruffled by emotions and thoughts. Compared to the normal state of mind, which is completely disturbed, it's at least forty or fifty percent clean. However, when measured against the state of a buddha it's not that impressive; it's somewhat obscured and dull. How do we combine or unify shamatha and vipashyana, stillness and insight? First of all, in the case of shamatha, we train in resting peacefully, undistracted by thoughts and emotions. In this state, we are not occupied by any coarse dualistic fixation, but there is still a subtle notion or feeling of there being something upon which we dwell and a dweller. There is something that notices or abides peacefully. There is no coarse abider in this state of peace; and it's precisely because it's not a gross state that it feels nice. But there is some subtle sense of dwelling. Now, what is that state? Is there anything that really abides in peace? Is there any tangible stillness? The general state of shamatha involves some subtle fascination, some subtle attachment.

It's very good in the beginning to develop a sense of stillness. Having accomplished that, we need to destroy it, to make the dwelling on stillness fall apart. The only way to do so is by seeing clearly through vipashyana that there exists neither something to dwell on nor someone who dwells. Nothing else can really uproot such a subtle fixation.

STUDENT: What is the actual practice of vipashyana, since it is not a conceptual training?

RINPOCHE: Our basic state, our innate nature, does not require any effort on our part. We can call that buddha mind. Buddha mind is free from dualistic experience, dualistic perception. There is no "I". The clinging to the idea of an "I" has disappeared or subsided. But there is still wakefulness, which is the unity of emptiness and compassion. Without that wakefulness, the qualities of the supreme knowledge of buddhahood wouldn't be possible. On the other hand, the normal tendency of ego-clinging, which holds the notion of "I," is dualistic experience. Where there is dualistic experience, there is attachment and aversion. When there is attachment or aversion, there is also like and dislike, joy and sorrow, hope and fear. Why is that? We can call it a natural quality, we can call it a defect, but all these result only from ego-clinging. The opposite of that frame of mind is in Buddhism called egolessness. Egolessness is the state of enlightenment or omniscience. That state also has some qualities. If it was totally devoid of qualities, there would be absolutely no point in us putting any effort into attaining enlightenment. The state of buddha mind, our innate nature, is beyond the reach of the intellect, beyond concepts. It is also completely effortless. But in order to realize it, to arrive at that state beyond concepts and effort, we need to use the intellect, we need to use some kind of deliberate method.

It is only possible to mistake a fake to be the real thing if the real and the fake look alike. If they don't, we will not make the mistake. Similarly, within our minds there is something that is real and something that is fake. Because we can't really see the difference, we mistake the fake for being real.

What you should realize is the state that is totally free from concepts and intellectual effort, the buddha mind that is not an object of dualistic mind. This is the real thing. There is also something that looks like it, that is very close to it. This is a state of mind that is free from concepts, in which we are kind of spaced out, absent-minded, vacant, oblivious, free from thought and emotions. It is an incredibly great mistake if for some reason we believe that state to be the true state of enlightenment. That's one of the major reasons why we should study and reflect upon the teachings.

Think of it this way: when we go shopping, it is very important to know what is real and what is an imitation, right? If we know the difference between a real and a fake before we reach the store, then it's not a problem. It's because an imitation looks like the real thing that we can make a mistake and deceive ourselves. So the vital question now is this: what is the nonconceptual state really like? These days there are so many books on Buddhism. We can read about how the innate nature is, how the buddha mind is. It is beyond concepts, it's inexpressible, inconceivable, indescribable, and so on and so on. Merely to think "All right, the buddha mind is beyond concepts,' is not enough. We need to know this personally and for a fact. Okay?

STUDENT: Is there a difference between awareness, self-existing wakefulness, and the vipashyana that you have just explained?

RINPOCHE: At first glance, there's no difference, but when you get down to the details, the nitty-gritty, there is some degree of difference. When you really get down to refining the core of it, there is some difference. I think it's too early to address that now; let's return to it later.

STUDENT: I cannot distinguish between shamatha without reference point and vipashyana. Please explain.

Rinpoche: Briefly put, the difference is clarity. Shamatha without object doesn't have enough clarity; there is some dullness. There is no disturbing emotion, so it's good, but the dullness makes it imperfect. To arrive at the unity of shamatha and vipashyana, that inertness needs to be cleared up. The clarity that is necessary to clear away the dullness is unlike the clarity of normal intelligence, which is always dualistic. The brightness of undivided shamatha and vipashyana, the unity of the two, is not dualistic. Vipashyana means seeing clearly, a sense of brightness — being awake without dullness or obscuration. Because it's not being covered by the dualistic brightness of normal state of mind, it is beyond any worldly or mundane state. That's it.

Student: When practicing, will one sometimes flick back and forth between shamatha and vipashyana?

Rinpoche: In the beginning, yes, but after growing more accustomed to the practice, there is no flicking back and forth. There are of course many types of shamatha, but the one called inert shamatha is definitely no good. It's almost like becoming a potato.

Student: I believe that all experience is conceptual, so therefore experiences and perceptions obscure the truth of the innate nature. I wonder can experiences and perceptions also function as helpers for realizing the innate nature?

Rinpoche: Yes indeed, conceptual experience can either help or prevent understanding and realization. It is an either or situation. The key is that experiences in themselves do not harm or prevent anything. It is our clinging, our attachment to the perceived, that makes the problem. Simple perception without any attachment or fixation is not harmful. In the higher vehicles of Buddhism, experience is given other names, such as 'expression', 'display', and 'adornment'. At first glance, that might seem very strange, but when we start to understand further, this point becomes very, very interesting. There is a way of pointing out that all experience, whatever is perceived, is mind; that the mind is empty, that this emptiness is beyond constructs, and that unconstructed emptiness is self-liberated.

Traditionally there has been quite a lot of discussion about whether or not perceptions and the perceived objects are both mind. The perceived objects are considered 'expressions' of mind, but they are not the mind itself. Each different system of Buddhist teaching, if really understood correctly, becomes incredibly beneficial to reach realization. If we say whatever is perceived is mind; mind is empty; and emptiness is beyond conceptual constructs; that is a very reasonable and practical way to follow. On the other hand, when we start to understand that perceptions are mind but that perceived objects are not, that they are the expression of the mind, this too is very practical. Perception is a word we use based on something perceived, referring to perceptible objects. But without a perceiver, how would an object be perceived? What would perceive it? You also can't have just a perceiver without anything to perceive. It all comes down to the fact that it's a seeming combination of factors that creates experience. There are seemingly objects, there are seemingly sense organs, there is seemingly consciousness, and these all must coincide to allow experience. Then we can say "I see, I hear. I like this; I don't like that." As long as we don't investigate this too closely, it seems like it's really taking place, that there are real objects, sense organs, and consciousness. It seems like these interact and experience really takes place. We feel that without them coming together there would be no experience possible.

Once we start to examine this process in detail, though, we never find any real meeting of the three separate concrete entities involved — objects, sense organs and consciousness. The truth is, none of these entities really exist anywhere. Yet, at the same time, no perception can take place without their meeting. This is the very reason why the Buddha said everything is like a magical illusion, like a dream. As long as we don't question or examine, then everything seems to actually take place. Through the eyes, our consciousness meets visual objects and we see them. But through close examination, we find that this apparent meeting is not so. The experiences such as "I see, I hear,

I touch," are all superficially real — they are relative truth. This is called dependent origination, perception that appears in dependency, through one thing's dependence on another. Without a mind, with only the objects and an eye, there would be no seeing.

When we look from the perspective of that which is truly real — the ultimate truth — there are no such factors as outer objects, sense organs or a mind that connects. The fact is that once we discover the nature of the superficial, the relative truth, that in itself is the ultimate truth. There's a famous quote by Nagarjuna, "When conditioned phenomena do not exist in any way, how can the unconditioned be said to exist?" He said this in the *Mula Madhyamika Karika*, an extremely reasonable and very interesting text. We could go into more detail about this later.

STUDENT: You talked about avoiding disturbing emotions, and I'm wondering how to go about this. For ordinary people disturbing emotions happen all the time. It seems that I can only do one of two things. Either I can carry out whatever comes into my mind, like beating up people and saying nasty things when I get angry. Or, I can try to suppress and keep down the disturbing emotion of anger. Neither of the options are very appealing. What is the best approach?

RINPOCHE: We can certainly all relate to getting angry. There are actually four possibilities. The worst-case scenario is when we are angry inside and we act it out. Or perhaps we control ourselves outwardly but are still angry inside; this is not so bad. In a third case, we're not really angry inside but we act like it. This is really quite rare. The best situation is to neither display anger nor to feel it. How to discover true nonaggression is something we'll get to in the next few days of teachings.

STUDENT: Is the practice in all the Tibetan religious traditions the same?

RINPOCHE: All of the different Buddhist traditions teach both shamatha and vipashyana. There is some difference in terms of the extent to which they emphasize one or the other. In the Kagyü tradition, shamatha is primarily taught at the beginning, while in the Dzogchen tradition it is not given that much importance. But all Buddhist traditions teach both shamatha and vipashyana.

STUDENT: In which tradition is it said that perceptions are mind, but the perceived objects are not, and that perceptions happen because of perceived objects?

RINPOCHE: The teaching that perceptions are mind and that the perceived object is not mind, comes from Longchenpa. The question about whether perceptions and perceived objects are mind is possible to answer only after understanding that the mind itself is empty, and therefore that which perceives as well as the perceived are both empty and devoid of any concrete existence. This topic is really complicated; we'll get to it eventually.

STUDENT: You mentioned that we need interest, trust and mindfulness in order to be qualified recipients of Dharma. What should I do when these are not so strong? Should I apply more effort?

RINPOCHE: Yes, definitely apply effort. Also realize that interest is also dependent upon the depth of our understanding. As we understand more, we get more interested. Without already having some understanding, we wouldn't be interested at all. The Buddhist teachings are extremely extensive and profound, as well as being very reasonable and well-founded. They make sense, and as we understand more and more, our interest grows correspondingly. As our interest becomes stronger, our respect, trust and presence of mind will all increase as well. When something is true, the more we study and contemplate it, that much more we will become interested.

STUDENT: Rinpoche, can you describe more about the imprint that you say habitual tendencies leave on our consciousness and how that imprint is passed on to the next life.

RINPOCHE: If you have a really intense argument, an almost physical fight with somebody, and are upset, when you go to sleep and wake up the next morning is there any remnant of that or not? Do you feel some anger still left?

STUDENT: Yes.

RINPOCHE: Do you need to think about it or build it up or is it already there?

STUDENT: It is just there.

RINPOCHE: That is the type of imprint we call habitual tendency. During the state of sleep it is not manifest, but it is latently present. That means that the all-ground, the *alaya*, had received some imprint, and that a tendency was created.

STUDENT: I hear that consciousness is impermanent. Is this what the alaya is, is it an impermanent consciousness?

RINPOCHE: You can say it has continuation but if you want to discuss whether the all-ground is permanent or impermanent you get into a lot of details concerning the all-ground or *alaya*. Because if you say it is permanent then there is something wrong with that. If you say it is impermanent there is also some fault in that.

STUDENT: So the imprints are impermanent?

RINPOCHE: Definitely in themselves they are impermanent. The alaya is actually a continuation, and while continuing you can say it lasts. Yet once the continuation ceases then it is impermanent. For example, take the flow of water; does it last or is it impermanent?

STUDENT: As long as the water is flowing it is permanent.

RINPOCHE: No, because the process of flowing means it is always changing, not lasting. Isn't the surface moving?

STUDENT: Still, there is a continuation.

Rinpoche: What is the word continuation used for? Where do you place the label?

Student: On the flow of water, on the action of flowing — not just on the particles of water. But what you refer to as continuation of an imprint or of *alaya* seems like a permanent phenomenon.

Rinpoche: There is a term for that in Buddhist philosophy: 'continuing resemblance'. Something like the former appears in its place. It resembles the previous phenomenon and has a similar cause, but it is not the same.

Student: What happens to the state of mind of a baby who dies?

Rinpoche: If it is an infant, its concepts of this world have not really developed, so maybe there is not so much anxiety. It has not developed the idea of this and that.

Student: Would you please explain how we can avoid turning away from the Dharma path if everything is impermanent? How can we be sure never to turn away from it?

Rinpoche: By seeing that all the pleasures and luxuries of this world do not last, that they are hollow and futile, attachment naturally decreases. One gains a spontaneous taste for liberation and enlightenment. One can then embark on the path without any turning back. Manjushri said, "If you are attached to this life, you are not a practitioner. If you are attached to samsaric existence, you have no renunciation. If you are attached to selfish aims, you have no bodhichitta. If you have any attachment at all, you don't have the view."

Change

To reiterate: everything conditioned is impermanent, from the whole universe down to the smallest atom. The five aggregates of forms, sensations, conceptions, formations and consciousnesses are also impermanent. On a gross level, the fact that everything changes is called the 'impermanence of interruption'. On a very subtle level, the fact that every single instant everything changes is called 'intrinsic impermanence'. To illustrate this, let's take the example of this vase on my table. For a person who does not really think about it, it seems that the vase is permanent from the moment it was made until it breaks. But someone who really examines this vase will find that it changes every single moment. The vase discolors; it becomes antique — not all of a sudden, but moment by moment. In our case, we change first from being an embryo in our mother's womb to being an infant, a child, a youth, an adult, a middle-aged person, and finally an old one. There is a continual process of change, and each of these stages has a different name. By gaining a really good understanding of the impermanence of all things, we can understand the empty nature of all things. Some people object to this, complaining "We don't really want to hear much about impermanence. It's superficial, it's not very profound, it's not deep enough." As a matter of fact, the moment we start to see how everything is actually impermanent, we immediately connect to the empty nature of all things.

The Buddhist teachings can be verified by different types of correct measures. One of these measures is the intelligence that verifies what is fact — in other words, our own reasoning. We are encouraged to use that. Please clarify any doubt about this first indisputable truth.

The second of the Buddha's four summaries is: Everything defiling is painful. How should we understand the term 'everything defiling'? It means every ego-oriented state involving karma and disturbing emotions. In other words, until we have totally abandoned ego-clinging we are not liberated from the three realms of samsara. Is that true or not? We need to question this thoroughly, because there is no use in believing something false to be true.

There are many different schools of thought, philosophies, and religions in this world, and all of these have a concept of what constitutes correct or positive action. No matter what one's orientation is, it is commonly accepted that one can do good deeds and reap the good results of that. The Buddha, however, taught that unless this good action is embraced with an understanding of egolessness, that deed itself does not result in liberation from the three realms of samsara. We should understand why this is so. As long as we hold the idea "I," there is also "my," "mine," and "me". When there is "me," automatically there is "you" or "that"; this is called duality, dualistic experience. When there is dualistic experience, there is the tendency of holding onto these notions of "me" and "you" and "that," which we call dualistic fixation. And as long as there is the experience of and fixation on duality, attachment and aversion occur spontaneously. Merely holding on to the idea "I am" while no "I" in fact exists is itself delusion. And when in addition to delusion we have attachment and aversion, the three poisons are complete.

In the old scriptures you can find this passage: "Just as a toilet does not have a good smell, the three poisons do not possess any good qualities." Similarly, the statement that all defiling states are painful indicates that as long as we have ego-clinging we create karmic actions. As long as we create karmic actions, we continue taking rebirth within the six realms of samsara. For parents to give birth to a child is a happy event. When the child dies it is painful. In this example, what is the pain based on? It is based on the child being born in the first place. If no child was born, there would be no pain resulting from a child dying. Similarly, as long as we retain ego-clinging, suffering is not transcended.

Enlightenment doesn't mean to go to some other place, some other country. It means to utterly relinquish ego-clinging. The Buddha taught us many ways to give up ego-clinging, but there is something peculiar involved in this process. As long as we have the idea "I must give up ego-clinging," this "I" is still in the way and prevents the ego-clinging from being given up. "I must be liberated. I want to practice Dharma; I am meditating." This "I" involves a tight grip, a sort of conceptual grasping. As long as such intense holding-on is occurring, it is of no benefit to merely say the words "I want to be enlightened" or "I want to be liberated."

Please be intelligent about this: isn't it true that all karmic deeds and disturbing emotions are created by ourselves? When we hear about egolessness, we may first think, "If there is no 'I,' there is no 'me' doing anything. So, if there is no ego, how can there be any experience, any ideas?" It might seem to us as if everything must stop after realizing egolessness. But it doesn't. There is still omniscient wisdom, the awakened state of mind, to run the show.

Everything defiling is painful means that ego-clinging creates negative karmic deeds and disturbing emotions. The result is rebirth in the six realms. It's especially frightening to realize that if predominantly evil deeds are enacted, then one experiences the three lower realms with their tremendous sufferings. If there are fewer evil deeds and more virtuous deeds, then one is reborn in the three higher realms, where one experiences more pleasure than pain. Who experiences the pain mentioned in "everything defiling is painful"? It must be the 'I'. If there is no 'I,' then how can there be the experience of pain? That which creates the negative karmic actions is the disturbing emotions, and disturbing emotions are based on the mistaken idea of an 'I'. Buddhist literature contains extensive details as to how the disturbing emotions create negative karmic actions. These are summarized as the ten unvirtuous actions. To reap the full karma of any of these negative actions, four conditions must be complete. For example, let's take the act of killing, which is the first of the ten negative actions. First we have the idea of an object — that there is somebody else who is not me. Then there is the intent: "I want to kill that person!" Next is the act, to implement that intention by means of a weapon or poison. Finally there is the consummation, which in this case means that the other being dies. Thus there are four aspects. Whether we ourselves personally engage in the act of killing or whether we force somebody else to do it, the karmic result is the same. The karmic result of an act of killing is according to the degree of its severity. It can happen that in following lives we have a short life or bad health; most severely, we can take rebirth in the lower realms. The worst beings to kill are those who are closest to oneself, like our personal teacher, a bodhisattva, an arhat or one's own father and mother. It is also considered extremely grave to murder a practitioner who could have attained liberation if he or she hadn't been killed.

The second negative deed is called taking what is not given. This doesn't only mean stealing; it means taking whatever is not given. This also has four aspects. First is to have the idea that there is some object that belongs to someone else. Second is our desire to take possession of it. Third, we implement that intention by either stealing, robbing or cheating. In doing business, cheating with the scales is another way of taking what is not given. Finally the act is consummated by taking charge of the object; having it come into our possession. Wanting to steal something which belongs to others and trying but not succeeding, we don't reap the complete karma of taking what is not given. The worst objects to steal are valuables belonging to the Three Jewels. Especially harmful is to steal from a meditator, a renunciant, who depends on his belongings for doing practice and attaining liberation. Such theft creates severe obstacles for our spiritual progress.

The third among the traditional ten unvirtuous actions is called sexual misconduct. It means having relations with somebody who is not willing or free or who is under the guardianship of somebody else. As in the above cases, the same four aspects apply: object, intent, action and consummation. One of the worst kinds of sexual misconduct is rape. It is incredibly negative to rape a female practitioner and thereby interrupt her spiritual practice.

The result of taking what is not given is that in future lives we are poor, destitute, and hungry. A thief will sometimes in future lives get some strange sickness, like a growth in the throat, so that he can't enjoy what he has. The result of sexual misconduct is inharmonious family life or the tendency to have very short, unstable relationships.

Something else to point out is that these first three kinds of negative actions are all committed by our body. A thought cannot steal another person's possession; it must be carried out physically.

There are four verbal negative actions. The first is lying. There are different types of lies: severe lies, small lies, white lies. The most severe lie is to pretend to be a guru without having true qualifications; to pretend to have clairvoyance, knowing other people's minds, knowing their future and past lives and so forth. Such deception causes other people who could have followed a true path to follow oneself instead. This can create a severe obstacle for others over many lifetimes.

For a lie to be a real lie, it has to be told to somebody. To sit alone in the mountains and tell lies doesn't really count. First we should have an object, meaning a person who can understand. Then we should have the intention to lie, thinking "I want to fool that person." Some wrong words may just slip out involuntarily, but that doesn't count. A lie isn't restricted to only words. It's a way of communicating that fools others. It could be done by sign language or body language as well. The completion of the act of lying means that the other person is fooled. If one tries to lie but one is not really successful, if the other person is not fooled, one does not gain the karmic result of lying.

It's the small lies, not the severe and ordinary lies, that are very hard to give up, because we love to exaggerate. There is a saying that all conversation turns into exaggeration, because when we praise something that we feel is great, we add a little extra to the truth. When we put somebody down, then we add extra to that also, trying to make it more colorful and interesting. Check yourself during the course of a ten or fifteen minute conversation: how much have you added that wasn't really true, how much have you exaggerated? If we find we are actually lying, we should give it up. Why? Because of the negative effects of lying: already in this lifetime we aren't considered credible by others if we add too much of our own ideas to statements. Other people might say, "He may be a good person but much of what he talks about is not really true." Like everything else, actions create habits. These tendencies will carry on involuntarily, so that next time a situation offers itself, even though we don't especially intend to lie, it happens by itself. It is said that people who frequently lie and speak harshly will have bad breath in future lifetimes. The gravest kind of lie is to cheat or fool practitioners who have given up everything in order to concentrate on practice. If you succeed in fooling such people, the consequences are quite severe.

Another negative action of speech is divisive talk: to say something that separates good friends and causes conflict. This is very evil. There are different ways to accomplish this: directly, indirectly or covertly. An example of direct divisive talk is the following: if you are in a powerful position, other people like your employees are forced to listen to you. You then say to one person while pointing to the other, "You have been saying such-and-such about the other person." Since they are both afraid that they could lose their job, they cannot object to what you say. That is a direct or active way to separate or divide friends. Indirect divisive talk might involve saying something derogatory about a person, not to the person's face, but to somebody else. You might do this knowing perfectly well that it will get back to that individual, and also will influence the mind of the person to whom you told it and make him less friendly towards the second person. The karmic result of divisive talk is that in this very lifetime we become more lonely and have fewer friends. In terms of past karma carried into this lifetime, it might mean that people spontaneously don't like us and we find it difficult to form deep or lasting friendships. Still another effect is that even in this lifetime, if we really fall into the habit of dividing friends, other people will finally think; "How annoying, I don't like this person." We thus become quite alone. The worst case is to disturb a practitioner's peace of mind by divisive talk.

The third example of negative speech is to speak harshly. There are many kinds of harsh words. There is a proverb, "Words may have no sharp points, but they can still pierce your heart." A small cut on your hand can be cured quite easily with some medicine and a bandage, but a really cruel word can hurt for the rest of your life. There are different ways of hurting other people with words: openly, relaying them indirectly through others or even hidden within joking.

Of the fourth type of negative speech — idle gossip — there are many types. The pointless talk we engage in which activates different emotions of anger, attachment or delusion is called major idle gossip. Medium idle gossip is just to chatter away without any real beginning or end. The more subtle form involves unclear words, blabbering or any kind of pointless expression. Idle gossip distracts us from the spiritual pursuits of learning, reflection and meditation.

These four — lying, divisive talk, harsh words and idle gossip — are chiefly carried out by our voice. We can of course with our body language express displeasure and put other people down in different ways, but this is not really called harsh words. We can show a lot of things with our hands, feet, fingers and eyes, like shoving with an elbow or glaring at somebody. We need to check to what extent we are doing that. Sometimes we don't dare to say something out loud, but we still feel we have to show an angry face. At other times we don't even dare show an angry face to the person; we turn around and show it to somebody else.

The last three of the ten unvirtuous actions are mental. They are called craving, ill-will, and holding wrong views. Craving simply means the feeling "I wish that was mine." We see material things, property, luxuries, and fame belonging to somebody else and we want to own them. That kind of attitude is covetousness. The next one is ill-will, to want to hurt somebody else. The third, wrong views, is to disbelieve or refuse to investigate the four noble truths.

The reason I mention these ten unvirtuous actions is that, as I said before, our disturbing emotions do create negative actions. These negative actions then ensure that we roam around in the six realms of samsara collecting painful experiences. To give up the first nine of the ten unvirtuous actions and instead try to do their opposites results in our achieving the highest levels within samsara, and dwelling among gods surrounded by perfect pleasures. However, we never reach liberation. The true cause of liberation and enlightenment is called the 'knowledge that realizes egolessness'. The knowledge that realizes egolessness is the correct view that is uncovered by giving up wrong views. The basic wrong view or incorrect idea is "I am." It involves the tight grip of ego: "I am I." It is extremely important to give up the wrong view of ego-clinging, and to do so we need to engage in the three aspects of learning, reflection and meditation.

Let us discuss what is meant by holding wrong views. The Buddha has taught the Four Noble Truths: suffering, origin, path, and cessation. Regarding the first one, suffering, we know there is pain in life, right? We should simply acknowledge that, as it's not so difficult to understand. The origin or source of this pain is then said to be karma and disturbing emotions. This is also not difficult to understand, although these two are difficult to relinquish. The last two truths involve path and cessation. Cessation of karma and disturbing emotions is achieved by means of the path. There are many ways to abandon disturbing emotions. One is to renounce them; another is to transform them; while still another is to use disturbing emotions as path. That is basically how the three vehicles are defined. It is more difficult to transform them than to give them up, and it is even more difficult to take them as the path. If we can transform something instead of giving it up, however, that is a quicker path. And if we are able to take whatever is at hand and utilize it, that is even quicker than transforming it.

The statement "Everything defiling is painful" means that any action motivated by disturbing emotions results in pain and suffering within the three realms of samsara. This is a fact we need to acknowledge. Let's put aside the other realms right now and focus on the situation of being human. First of all, there are four major sufferings: being born, growing old, falling sick and dying. These four are unavoidable; you cannot get rid of them. Try and think of how it actually is to experience each of these individually. They are distressful, they cause worry. And it's not only other people who go through these processes — we ourselves will. Additionally there is the pain of being separated from our beloved, our parents, close family members and our spouses and the pain of meeting with people we don't get along with, our enemies. In addition, there is the pain of not always achieving our aims, and the pain of meeting unfortunate circumstances. All kinds of misfortune can happen unannounced. Look around and you can definitely understand that human beings experience pain.

The physical body belongs under the 'five aggregates that perpetuate defilement'. It is described as the basis for this truth of suffering because, although our body might be very helpful at times, it is ready to suffer. We might even say it's pre-programmed for suffering. The moments of physical pleasure we experience are actually short and few. Even the tiniest prick of a needle causes discomfort; that is all it takes.

The word defiling in everything defiling is painful implies that disturbing emotions create negative actions. These negative actions result in suffering. There is no point to my repeating this any further: what we need to do now is individually examine whether this is true or not. If it is true, we need to make up our minds and be certain about this point. All the Buddha's teachings can be summarized within these four sentences, and the first one seemed pretty easy to agree on and to understand. The second statement, everything defiling is painful, is something we need to question ourselves about. Is it correct or not? We can discuss this point now.

STUDENT Could you please explain more about what defiling means?

RINPOCHE: Often you find the word defiling, in Tibetan, *zagchey*, used in the context of three types of virtuous activity: defiling, undefiling, and unified. Defiling virtue is any good, wholesome deed which takes place within the structure of the three spheres of concepts: the notions of subject, object and action. Undefiling virtue is embraced by the 'seal' of emptiness, by the absence of conceptualizing these three spheres. Unified virtue means that, within the continuity of the view, one connects or interacts with the conventional level of reality, with physical and verbal actions.

These three types are described in a famous verse: "All virtuous activity — defiling, undefiling, and unified — I dedicate to the state of unexcelled enlightenment." Just as a side-remark, I once had the chance to ask Kunu Rinpoche, Tendzin Gyaltsen, about the meaning of this and some other Buddhist terms. He explained first the meaning of the word 'person,' or *gangzag*, which contains one of the syllables in the word 'defiling'. *Gang* means 'any' or 'whichever' in the sense of any possible world or place of rebirth within the six classes of beings, while *zagpa* means to 'fall' into or 'shift' to one of those places. Thus, the word for 'person' means 'liable to transmigrate'. He also mentioned that there is a traditional discussion about this etymology, since an arhat is also called a *gangzag*, personage.

STUDENT: Won't feeling that we have to give up the ten nonvirtues and avoid creating evil karma just intensify our ego-clinging?

RINPOCHE: It is best if one could immediately drop ego-clinging. However it is not so easy to stop because of what are traditionally called the three obscurations — karma, disturbing emotions and habitual tendencies — which combine to obscure and prevent that. A fourth obscuration, the cognitive obscuration, creates the basis for the continuous return of the other three. Therefore, it is safer to begin by simply giving up negative actions and doing positive actions. At the same time we should try to relinquish the cause of ego-clinging. There is a famous statement dealing with this subject: "When the obscurations are purified, realization takes place spontaneously."

STUDENT: Won't thinking "I must do what is virtuous" become a cause for further ego-clinging?

RINPOCHE: The thought "I must do this; I am doing a virtuous deed" is ego-enforcing. Still, it is good to do so. First of all, the idea "I want to be liberated" is necessary in the beginning, when embarking on the path. Thinking "I don't need liberation" would be a mistake. It would be wrong to think "I don't accept ego-clinging — ego-clinging is bad, so I don't want liberation!" Liberation beyond ego is a result of having thought at one point that the 'I' actually exists. By thinking "I must become liberated," it is possible to arrive at liberation beyond ego. The idea itself is not liberation, but it is the basis for arriving at liberation.

STUDENT: What if you have good intent but the action ends up causing harm? Does it cause good or bad karma?

RINPOCHE: Give me an example.

STUDENT: Say you have two friends and you praise one to the other. By doing that it causes the two friends to have an argument and split apart. To say something good which in fact is taken in the wrong way and causes problems; is that incorrect action?

RINPOCHE: We need to know how to praise and when is the right time. Sometimes it is helpful, while sometimes praise turns into blame. We need to think before speaking. If the two people are really friends, not just superficially, then any praise given to one will only cause the other to rejoice. If they are only superficially friends, praising one might then create jealousy in the other. Usually family members are supposed to be close and get along, but praising one brother sometimes does not please the other one. Likewise, praising the husband might make the wife happy; but it is never sure. You have to check first. The outcome depends on the sense of identity. If two people feel they are united as something, then praising one part of that unity creates more happiness. If they feel they are separate or different in some way, then praising one makes the other jealous. So it depends. What do you think?

STUDENT: I think if the people are really close, then praising one will make them even closer. I guess I was wondering if it was me that caused the problem between them, was it a bad thing that I did, even if I meant to do something good?

RINPOCHE: We should of course have good intention and try to mean well. However, to mean well is not enough: we need to be smart at the same time. We must have the intelligence to see whether something is actually a good thing to do. That is why the Buddha taught us to always unify means and knowledge, *upaya* and *prajna*. We always need these two aspects, even during the course of normal daily life.

STUDENT: Rinpoche, earlier you talked about how habitual tendencies are a reflection of karma. Now you mention that karma, disturbing emotions and habitual tendencies are caused by ego-clinging. Isn't it true that disturbing emotions may be a little easier for us to recognize than habitual tendencies?

RINPOCHE: Disturbing emotions are easier to identify than the tendency for them, which is more subtle. To think, to conceptualize, is spontaneous or instinctive — that is the habitual tendency. Habitual tendency implies a kind of automatic power or energy. Quite often irritation and anger doesn't require much effort on our part. Due to habitual tendency, they seem very spontaneous, and it can blossom into full-fledged anger when the right object presents itself.

Habitual tendencies are difficult to identify and hard to purify. It's like washing a cup — it's easy to clean the visible dirt, but we need to apply more effort to get rid of the smell that still remains. If you had something in the cup that had a bad odor, then it takes a long time to get rid of that. For example, it's very hard to completely clean a perfume bottle: even if you rinse it many times, the fragrance lingers. That is an example for habitual tendencies.

STUDENT: If a child has been a victim of someone's forceful sexual misconduct, how can you help them to understand the perception of impermanence when you know that the pain and misery of this act is with them their whole life?

RINPOCHE: Yes, that is very difficult. That is why it is a very severe negative action, right? Still, the extent to which a negative imprint actually remains depends on the individual. But to be totally free of that hurtful memory is very hard unless one has insight into the nature of emptiness.

STUDENT: Is 'abandoning', 'transforming' and 'taking the disturbing emotions as the path' cited with regard to the practice of the three gradual vehicles?

RINPOCHE: Yes. For the Hinayana practitioner or *shravaka,* the way to deal with disturbing emotions and negative actions is to get rid of them. There is no talk here about transforming them; there is no talk about taking as them as path and utilizing them. A bodhisattva, a Mahayana practitioner, takes a quite different approach. With regard to the ten unvirtuous actions, the three of mind — craving, ill-will, and wrong views — should always be given up; they can never be used. However, the first seven can sometimes, in special situations, be engaged in by a bodhisattva to accomplish the greater welfare of others. This action should always be totally free from any taint of selfishness. That is very difficult. It is easier to simply give up negative actions and emotions. It is easier to give them up than to transform them, and it is easier to transform them than to utilize them, to take them as path.

To take disturbing emotions as path is a special expression used in Vajrayana, which is both risky but also very advantageous. It is risky because such an attempt can easily backfire, causing the practitioner to be merely an ordinary person or even worse. It is very profitable, however, if you know the key points: you can then traverse the path and the bhumis very, very quickly. The Vajrayana teachings state that the disturbing emotions are within you, meaning in your body. The wisdom is in yourself as well. Disturbing emotions need to be transmuted or changed into wisdom. When realizing the vital point then the five poisons are the five wisdoms, the five aggregates are the five male buddhas, the five elements are the five female buddhas, and so forth. Everything is all-encompassing purity. Then phrases like these are used: 'everything is the adornment of pure awareness'; everything is the natural manifestation of the three kayas.

We have the three poisons right now. We also have the three kayas right now. Both of these, the three kayas and the three poisons, are in some way supported by this body. The path of fixating is the path of the three poisons. The path of nonfixation is the path of the three kayas. That which prevents you from meeting the natural face of the three kayas is the three poisons. Not acknowledging how the essence of the mind is empty, we instead conceive of an "I," letting the mind's cognizant nature stray into dualistic fixation. Our basic unconfined capacity strays into the confining pattern of disturbing emotions within dualistic experience.

STUDENT: Is there anything which is not conditioned or impermanent?

RINPOCHE: What do you think?

STUDENT: I think the answer is no, but...

RINPOCHE: What about space? Is space is permanent or impermanent?

STUDENT: Space is not permanent.

RINPOCHE: How is space impermanent?

STUDENT: It changes when something comes into your space. Say there's space over there: when something comes into that space, it's no longer there.

RINPOCHE: When you walk, space changes wherever you go. You make space impermanent because of your movement.. Right? Do you believe that?

STUDENT: Yes. Shouldn't I?

RINPOCHE: Empty, not empty, both are ideas. If we think empty, that's an idea. If we think not empty, that's also our idea. If we think empty, it means that automatically there's the idea of not empty. That limiting quality of conceptual mind is one of the biggest problems. If we think everything is empty it means that usually it's not, because how could there be the idea of not empty without the idea of empty? One is dependent on the other. If there was no idea of non-emptiness, why even talk about the word empty? So that's why ultimate truth is beyond both emptiness and non-emptiness. Regardless of whether space is permanent or not, space in itself — just space — is unchanging, isn't it. From that aspect you can say it's unconditioned and permanent, but when you put up barriers and walls it seems that space is somehow impeded.

STUDENT: How is dissolving anger into unconditioned empty wakefulness different from renouncing it?

RINPOCHE: Abandoning means that one thinks, "I shouldn't feel this way. I must do something to change it." The Hinayana type of practitioner will, when facing an object of attraction, immediately try to have a remedy against the desire. For example, he or she will think, "This object is in fact something impure, it is unclean." A Bodhisattva, instead of trying to see it as unclean or impure, will see that the object of desire itself does not truly exist. Simply thinking "It is unclean," still leaves the subtle idea that there is something which is clean or unclean which we can't get rid of. Once we realize that the object has no real existence, though, there's no problem with the 'it' being pure or impure. Trying to be unattached through training in seeing things as unattractive, sometimes we will be successful, sometimes we will not. On the other hand, when you understand everything is by nature empty, then there is no question of success. It's guaranteed.

STUDENT: Rinpoche, you said that if we really understand impermanence we'd understand emptiness. What's the link?

RINPOCHE: We have the idea of lasting or not lasting, permanent or not permanent, but when we say that something lasts or is permanent, that means there is some continuation. We think that this continuation lasts, right? In fact, it is merely a continuation of resemblance, not the previous thing that still continues to exist. Now we need to examine the three moments — past, present and future or before, now and later — because without these three, there's no idea of continuation. Something that continues implies the need for there to be a past, present and future. Before and after are dependent upon right now. The 'now' thus should be an entity that we can identify as something that exists. Can you find something independently existing, some kind of something, that is the present?

STUDENT: No.

RINPOCHE: So where does this leave us? What can we say now? Right there you've met emptiness, haven't you? That is what is meant by saying that the correct understanding of how all things by nature are impermanent connects you with emptiness. Does this make sense? If not, then it's good to discuss further. Don't leave it without understanding.

STUDENT: I'm thinking about the continuation of the individual person. When we, for instance, believe that it is the same particular person who is born, grows up and gets old —on what do we based this perceived continuation?

RINPOCHE: As long as we don't examine this concept too closely, it does seems that a particular 'somebody' continues as a single entity, because there's a living, breathing body made out of flesh, blood and bones. That entity continues to breathe, and thus there's a material continuation. But this is only true as long as we don't examine or question the matter. Concerning time, we cannot say that time doesn't exist to someone who has not thought about or questioned the matter of its existence. Definitely this person will never believe us. Yet if we say that time does exist; there's something wrong with that. It's really worse to say that time exists than to claim it doesn't. Regarding the continuity of something, it's worse to say that "there is" than to say "there isn't," because there truly isn't any real continuity.

STUDENT: This makes me think of an echo — it's empty but it's resounding. It resembles something that did have substance.

RINPOCHE: Actually, echo and sound are the same.

STUDENT: The echo is empty.

RINPOCHE: Sound also.

STUDENT: The original sound had substance and the echo is a resemblance of the original sound; it is a continuity. If it had enough vibration it would go on and on. Is this a kind of continuity?

RINPOCHE: A traditional example for continual resemblance is the flame of a candle or the flow of water. One moment of such a phenomenon looks the same as the previous moment, but it's not.

STUDENT: So why is there this continuing resemblance?

RINPOCHE: It's only something that looks the same that continues. For example, you are not the same Kathy as the infant Kathy who could not walk but only laid in a cradle. In the same way, we think that the Kathy we see today is the same one we met last year, if we had not seen you in between. Actually, even within that one year, a lot of change has occurred. It's not the same Kathy. If there's no change, there would be no aging. Of course we do change, we do age. And still there's a resemblance to the previous moments, because people will still believe that you are Kathy, not someone else. It's because there's a continuing resemblance. Otherwise, we would mix up Patricia and Kathy. Due to the kindness of continuing resemblance Patricia stays Patricia and Kathy stays Kathy.

STUDENT: Is the capacity to know permanent or impermanent?

RINPOCHE: The normal knower or observer is impermanent, because it is dependent on the object known. There's a moment of cognition of something, then that disappears, and then there's another one. As part of this process, the knower of that object again disappears and becomes something else. We can therefore say the knower is impermanent. But omniscience, the state of enlightenment, is beyond permanence and impermanence. Here's another question for you and everyone else: all sentient beings have Buddha nature, right? So they should be able to attain enlightenment, right? Will they sooner or later?

STUDENT: Yes.

RINPOCHE: Then samsara will be empty at some point, won't it? Does everyone agree on this? Then it's easy; all we have to do is wait. Usually they say samsara is beyond beginning and end, correct? Generally speaking, there is no beginning and no end to samsara, but for the individual, there is an end. There's some debate about this because the general is made out of many individuals. When every individual has attained enlightenment, it's gone. Doesn't this sound really neat?

STUDENT: Is there a view that says that everything both does and does not exist?

RINPOCHE: It's like this. First, we need to classify and establish everything as existing. Then we need to establish that everything does not exist, and finally we need to attain the certainty that is beyond the concept of existence and nonexistence. The Buddha said, "Seeing and hearing are not valid perception." We have eyes so we can see, ears so we can hear. Isn't it undeniable? Next, we start to question and examine; how exactly does the eye see? How does the ear hear? What is an act of perceiving? We will discuss this later.

Emptiness

We have already covered the first and second Seals of the Dharma, regarding how everything conditioned is impermanent and how everything defiling is painful. Now we come to the third statement: All phenomena are empty and devoid of self-entity.

The Buddha, the completely omniscient one, said that all phenomena are empty and devoid of self-entity. Normally, however, we perceive everything to be concrete and possessing individual identity. In short, what we experience and what we believe is the opposite of what the Buddha taught. This is not some minor point; this is immensely important. This conflict is not a little tiny one, it is huge, because what is true and what is false are totally opposite.

To begin our discussion on this matter, first of all understand that a person who has not adopted any kind of philosophy is called an ordinary person. An ordinary person feels, "Whatever I see is really there." For instance, a particular visual form is really there, it exists; it is permanent, it has shape and color, it's red, white or so forth. If something can be taken hold of, it concretely exists. For the ordinary person there's no need to investigate beyond that. In the same way, sounds that are the objects of the sense of hearing are considered to exist. They can be pleasant, unpleasant or neutral, but since I hear them, they exist. What I smell with my nose is called odor or scent; it can be either nasty or pleasant or neutral. I can experience these odors; thus, they do exist. It's the same with all the different kinds of tastes — delicious, unpleasant, salty, astringent and so forth — and with textures, which can be either rough or smooth, heavy or light, hot or cold. Because there are all different things we feel physically, the textures, tangible objects do exist. In the same way, because we mentally recollect what happened previously, we believe the past does exist. Because we plan ahead as to what hasn't yet happened, we think there is a future. Also, because we feel happy or unhappy, we believe in pleasure and pain and so forth. We can experience these; therefore, they must exist. This is how this type of logic works.

This perspective of an ordinary person who has not spent any time questioning or investigating the nature of things is quite similar to the animal way of experiencing: "There's water — I can drink it; there's some grass — I should eat that." Once we start to adopt a philosophy, our perspective becomes refined, which means it's getting closer to what is real — the ultimate truth.

In Buddhism we speak of two types of reality that everything is included within: conventional truth and ultimate truth. Conventional truth is real for a mind that is still under the power of ego-clinging. Ultimate truth is real for the mind free from any delusion. A lot of confusion and problems arise in our mind from not being able to distinguish between these two aspects of reality. In brief, we can say that if there is an objective reference for our bodies, speech, and minds, that set-up is called conventional truth. That which transcends any objective reference of body, speech and mind is called ultimate truth. The ultimate truth lies beyond the domains of ordinary body, speech and mind. What is meant by these three domains of body, speech and mind? The domain of body means anything tangible that we can take hold of; something physical. Domain of speech means anything that can be labeled, expressed or described. The domain of mind is what can be thought of, anything conceivable. Whatever lies within these three domains is by definition conventional truth.

To engage in Buddhist practice means to purify our understanding further and further. Unless we differentiate between conventional and ultimate truth, there's no path to even start on. This does not mean that conventional and ultimate truth are two totally separate entities. It's not like that, because actually the nature of conventional truth itself is ultimate truth.

Let me clarify this further. In the context of everything conditioned being impermanent, when we use a word like 'permanent' as a label, it implies continuity. For instance, this table here seems to exist. We don't even question it. It's a Tibetan table. You can put things on it. It is painted. We might ask: is the table one single entity? No, it's not, because it's made up of many parts assembled together. It's the total assemblage of these many parts we simply call 'it'. If we really think about this, however, we don't find anything whatsoever which is a singular entity. It's the assemblage of these many parts which leads us to use the word 'one'. But when we look very closely at each part, each one is again constituted of many different parts, and so forth and so forth, with no end to be found to the process.

There seems to be some constancy to this table, so we say "the table." It seems like it's the same table as yesterday because of a continual resemblance, doesn't it? Yet the 'thing itself' which appears to us as being that table cannot be found to truly exist. That is what we call ultimate truth, because it is really true.

Let me explain this another way. 'Continuity' should apply to the thing, but if the thing does not exist, what is continued? On the basis of that, we use the words 'it lasts' or 'there's a continuation' of the table. Continuation means it continues through past, present and future. When we start to examine what is past, present and future, we don't even find the present. Moreover, there's nothing that exists in the present, because every entity in our life is an assembly of many parts. The thing itself cannot be found anywhere, and it's that lack of, or absence of, a thingness to be found which is ultimately true. That is the nature of the thing itself that lies beyond the domain of body, speech and mind.

The lower schools of philosophy in Buddhism, called *Vaibhashika* and *Sautrantika,* maintain that there is some basic substance out of which everything is made — an atom, so to speak — and that this tiniest of particles cannot be divided further. They maintain that whatever we see here is made out of something else, something very subtle and very, very tiny, but something that is ultimately there. They are referring to the tiniest part of things, the atom, which cannot be separated further. If there was no such thing as an indivisible tiny particle or atom, they argue, then how could all other objects be or come about? This point of view is quite similar to the old school of Western science, in which the Greek root of the word 'atom' literally means 'indivisible'. Let's investigate if such a singular entity could possibly exist.

As long as there is something material, it must have a front side, back side, top and bottom. When this is so, it becomes impossible to find the smallest singular thing. No matter how subtle or small it may be, still it has parts and sides which can be further divided, doesn't it? The word atom, which means indivisible, is thus a fallacy. When we investigate matters like this, what do we ultimately reach — what's the bottom line? Do we find something that really exists, or don't we? If we don't find some real thing, that's fine, because that's in complete agreement with what the Buddha taught. At the same time, it is undeniable that we can take hold of this table. There's something we can feel with our hands, something solid and concrete. On the conventional level of experience, it seems quite real. Also, we can talk about the table. I can say, "Please remove the cup on my table." The person who hears that will take the cup on the table, not the cup on the chair. It's very practical, really, that we are able to think of the table at the mention of the word. If I am in a different room and I tell my attendant, "Bring the cup on my table," the attendant will understand what I am talking about and will think of the table, go in, take the cup on the table and bring it. Conventional reality possesses an unquestionable or undeniable aspect, which because it is shared, is really very convenient. But ultimately speaking, it's not true.

Based on this fact, the Buddha said, "Everything is like a dream, like a magical illusion." While we dream or while we witness a magical illusion, what we perceive seems real. All sorts of different experiences feel true for the dreamer. But if we start to question where these dream-things come from and where they go, we cannot give any answer.

The dream experience comes about through a combination of causes and conditions. First of all, we have to be asleep to dream, and only then will these different experiences take place. It is the same way with our waking state experience. It seems to us to have a long duration, from the time we are born until we die. However, our waking experiences also come about due to a combination of certain causes and conditions. It is only because they seem to last longer that we think they are more real than the dream experience. Whatever is perceived as belonging within the domain of ordinary body, speech and mind may seem real. Because of seeming real, we assume it is real. Nevertheless, the experience of someone who does not analyze or question anything is deluded as to ultimate truth.

At first we must gain the intellectual understanding that everything is illusory and unreal. To begin to do this, we need the two kinds of knowledge gained from learning and reflection. After obtaining that, we can directly experience the illusory nature of all things through the knowledge resulting from meditation. Even through the knowledge resulting from learning and reflection, we can gain the understanding of this illusory nature. For example, when we start to really examine this table, we progress from thinking it's one 'thing,' a singular entity, to realizing that it's made of many parts. What is the smallest part it's made of — an atom? Does even an atom really exist as one singular entity?

By examining in this fashion, we eventually find that there is no way we can even conceive of a thing called table. In truth, we don't even see a table because 'table' implies the whole thing, the entire object. These two eyes, no matter how clear they are or how smart we are, cannot ever see the whole table, because 'table' means the entirety — the wholeness. Look. Right now you see the front, the front surface. You don't see the two sides and the back, do you? And when you look at the left side over there, you don't see the right side or the front. Is that right? Try it out. Whoever says, "I see the front of the table," please reply!

STUDENT: When you say the whole table, I can see a lot. I can't see all the details but I see the edges of it.

RINPOCHE: To claim that "I see the front of the table" means that we should have a simultaneous, clear, distinct image of the whole front of the table — doesn't it? In short, to claim "I see the front of the table" is extremely pretentious. Is that true?"

STUDENT: Why is it important to see the whole table?

Rinpoche: We didn't say important. We said pretentious. Important, not important, we will know later. Anyone have any doubts? This is no joke; it's a very serious question. I am pointing out the difference between what is seeming and what is real, between conventional truth and ultimate truth. Yet the true nature of the seeming is the ultimate truth. There's no ultimate truth which is somehow separated from the nature of appearance. We have already had the conventional truth pointed out to us by many teachers — our parents, instructors in school, our friends and so forth — who have given us detailed training in the matter. The teachers who show us the ultimate truth are quite few. I am sure that you don't need me to learn more conventional truth. It's probably because you were not really satisfied with the conventional truth that you are studying Buddhism. If that is true, then you must very carefully analyze the difference between what is seeming and what is real.

The dominant among the six consciousnesses for human beings is the visual consciousness — seeing. If we can first understand what is seeming and real about the act of seeing, it's easy to apply that same principle to the other consciousnesses of the five senses and mind consciousness. Now comes the second question: if you don't see the whole front of the table, do you see a part of it — yes or no?

Student: I seem to see it.

Rinpoche: Is this seemingly seeing or really seeing? If it's not seeing, do you see anything at all?

Student: What do you mean by seeing?

Rinpoche: From the time you were a small child until now, you have use the words "I see," or 'seeing' — that's what I'm talking about.

Student: I think that kind of seeing is like being aware of it. I do see a part of the table; I might be looking at the flower in the corner of the table, but I fill in the rest of the details with my mind. I'm not really seeing the whole. I think this 'seeing' means filling in the details but not really actually seeing it at all; my mind is making it. I don't know what this word means anymore!

Rinpoche: The rest of you, what do you say?

Student: Before conception and ideas there is a moment of bright, thought-free consciousness. Is that seeming reality or the true way things are?

Rinpoche: We might not notice it, but in the initial moment of perception, before labeling takes place, there is conception but no discernment. Conception in this case means the feeling "something is there!" That feeling is itself a conceptual state, but it's unrefined. There's no fine discernment as to what is present. We have not yet started to separate the details; we have not yet distinguished one thing from another. It's like a first glance — there's a vague, indistinct presence but the table has not yet been labeled as being a table. To cut this short, with respect to this table here: should we use the words "I see," or not?

Student: It's a useful concept.

Rinpoche: Useful, necessary, without this it's very difficult to communicate — all that we know. Right now, be honest and truthful. We can say, "I see the table if there's a thing to see. But is there really a 'thing' to see? If there is a 'thing' to see then we can use those words, but if there is not, then we cannot honestly use them, can we?

Let me reiterate: As long as we don't question or examine, we can say that we see a table. But if we do question and examine, we don't even see an atom, the smallest thing. Why is this? It is because the thing in itself, in the real condition, has no true existence. It cannot really be found to exist. Because of its inherent lack of true existence, it is by itself beyond the domains of body, speech and mind, as I mentioned before. Anything within the domains of body, speech and mind is conventional truth. And whatever is conventional truth is mistaken or deluded, dualistic fixation.

The different schools of philosophy have come about due to the different degrees of refinement of knowledge or intelligence. The lower Vaibhashika and Sautrantika schools of Buddhist philosophy claim not only the existence of indivisible atoms; they also claim that mind exists as a continuation of experience. That is to say that there's something that continues or connects one instant of experience to the next. It's extremely subtle, we cannot even perceive it, but it's there, they claim. Otherwise, how could there be any experience of anything? If there was not a single atom of matter and no mind as well, everything would fall apart, they say, so it must exist. This is a Buddhist view; they accept that everything is emptiness, but what they understand by emptiness is a little different than the Mahayana schools' view. On the gross level, these Hinayana schools agree that everything is empty. However they claim that the smallest, tiniest atom does ultimately exist, as does the consciousness or the mind that continues from moment to moment. For such people, the statement "All things are beyond arising, dwelling and ceasing" does not fit into their ideas. In truth, it's very difficult to grasp. If, on the other hand, we said, "Everything here is empty and illusory but there's something ultimately real — a subtle basis for creation and the continuation of mind," then the Hinayana follower would agree wholeheartedly.

When we start Buddhist studies it's easier to understand the lower schools of philosophy. That's why one should start studying Hinayana, then Mahayana and finally Vajrayana. Compared to the former, the latter is more refined. For example, the Mind Only school claims that all phenomena are only mind. They use phrases like 'mental perception,' 'magical display of mind,' and 'the mind's creation' to refer to phenomena. To them the mind exists: if it didn't, how could there be any experience? Everything would cease. They mean that only mind exists, that nothing else exists besides mind. The Mind Only school describes mind like a mirror within which everything appears like a reflection. The reflection is a metaphor for experience; and according to their view, mind itself, the mirror, has ultimate existence. When the Mind Only school debates with the Theravada schools in Buddhism, it always wins, because it is a superior path of reasoning.

Higher than Mind Only is the Middle Way school, Madhyamika. It says, "You Mind Only followers claim the existence of an ultimately existing mind. That's wrong. It's a fallacy." The Mind Only follower then asks, "What do you believe in? What do you claim? What do you assert?" The follower of the Middle Way will reply," On the conventional level I will accept whatever you want, whatever people think or say, but on the ultimate level I don't claim anything whatsoever." This is because any claim is faulty; any assertion by itself creates a limitation. If we claim something exists, we're the same as a normal person. If we claim nothing exists, that's falling into that extreme. The Madhyamika follower says, "I don't claim anything, therefore I have no fault."

The statement we are discussing is: All phenomena are empty and without self. I have now described various ways of understanding what is meant by empty. It seems that scientists nowadays have reached the point where even atoms are not possible to identify so easily. This is because scientific research is reaching down to the level of pure space. This fact can be arrived at by anyone who reasons intelligently, and not only through Buddhist analysis. Whatever type of logic you want to use, please go ahead. It's like in classical Greek mathematics, where one starts out with a 'point has no dimension'. To really understand this is the same as connecting with emptiness. One does not have to approach emptiness only through Buddhism. Any real reasoning will eventually arrive at that point. I think that getting the idea of emptiness is not difficult. It's truly experiencing that all things are empty that's difficult.

That was part one — that all things are empty. Next we will discuss the phrase 'devoid of self-entity'. What is meant by a self? Don't use the word 'I' or 'me' to describe it, because it's the same thing. When the word 'I' is used, what is the 'thing' which it describes. What forms the basis for the word? When you really think about it, isn't it foolish to use a word all the time and not know what it applies to? Speak up — what does that word 'I' apply to?

STUDENT: The mind?

RINPOCHE: Is your mind you or is it 'your' mind?

STUDENT: (Pointing at herself) It's me.

RINPOCHE: Is the body you or is it yours?

STUDENT: It's me.

RINPOCHE: And your name?

STUDENT: That's something given.

RINPOCHE: Is it you or yours?

STUDENT: It's mine.

RINPOCHE: What about the body?

STUDENT: That's me.

ANOTHER STUDENT: 'Body' is just a name, a term; it is merely labeled in dependency.

RINPOCHE: It seems that only two opinions have been raised. Does everyone agree with these two? Are there other opinions?

STUDENT: 'I' am the assembly of the five *skandhas*.

RINPOCHE: So, you say it's this combination that is called 'I'. As long as we don't question or examine this notion, it seems all right. But upon questioning and examining, we find that among the five *skandhas*, the physical forms are not the 'I,' and equally sensations, conceptions, formations and cognitions are also not 'I'. If each one of them in itself were the 'I,' then it would be like saying the mind, meaning the cognition, is you, and that the body is also you. Therefore, there are two 'yous'. Is there one 'I' or two 'I's over there?

When we pursue this line of investigation, it rapidly leads to a countless number of 'I's. This is an extremely important point that we've reached. What does the word 'I' really apply to? Is there something there or not? We should spend more time on this, because certainty about this subject is the basis for all practice.

STUDENT: Could the 'I' refer to the continuum of mental activity?

RINPOCHE: Question that, investigate it.

STUDENT: Is the one who doesn't give any answer the 'I'?

RINPOCHE: Usually it's the one who answers the question that is called 'I'. [Laughs]

STUDENT: There is the body, and there is something which is aware in it. Sometimes I say something, but when I don't say anything then there is no 'I'. Body is not me and mind is not me.

RINPOCHE: Then it would seem better to be quiet. Is it better to be a mute in order to realize egolessness?

STUDENT: If ego-clinging stops, then why not?

RINPOCHE: From the simple absence of talk or questioning does it necessarily follow that there's no ego-clinging and no disturbing emotions? Yes or no? I'm just asking you a simple question: does the absence of any question or talk necessarily mean that there's no ego-clinging?

STUDENT: I am aware, I can talk and move, but there is no dualistic fixation. Everything is wide open, like the sky.

RINPOCHE: Well, such an experience is certainly possible; thank you very much for your contribution. As for the rest of you, are there any questions about all things being ultimately empty and devoid of self? Is there a self or not? Is there any fault in claiming "Yes, I exist," or is there nothing wrong with saying "I don't exist"?

STUDENT: If there is nothing whatsoever wrong with the second choice, then it's a bit depressing.

RINPOCHE: There's still the thinker of "There's nothing." And isn't there someone feeling depressed? We haven't really cleared this up completely. If you realize that the 'I' seemingly exists while it truly or in fact does not, then that's fine. To say or think "I don't exist" and then feel depressed about it is not fine, because there's still some kind of tight grip on the 'I'. Whether we feel depressed about it or elated, it's still the 'I' that feels this. If there is someone being happy, then there is also the object of happiness, some 'thing' to be happy about. If there is someone unhappy, there is also the object of depression, some 'thing' to be depressed about. If we feel happy about the absence of a self, the one who feels happy is still hanging around. If we feel depressed about it, there's still somebody who feels the pain. This in itself is the very root of the matter. It's called dualistic fixation. When there's the feeling "I am depressed," or "I enjoy this," that itself is ego-clinging, isn't it?

STUDENT: If there is no one to realize it, then how can it be possible to realize egolessness?

RINPOCHE: Realizing egolessness means facing the fact that there's no ego. That's all: it's really very simple.

STUDENT: In the same way as a point has no dimension, also the 'I' has no dimension; it's merely a name. Actually only the immediate present exists, but whatever we say and think is all dependent upon what has happened in the past. That is delusion.

RINPOCHE: That sounds very good; it's a good way of phrasing it. This is exactly what I meant before, when I said we don't only have to go through Buddhist reasoning.

STUDENT: Could one say that the idea or concept of perception is another mental construct?

RINPOCHE: What do you mean by perception — like I see or hear?

STUDENT: Yes.

RINPOCHE: Yes, that's correct.

STUDENT: If there is nothing whatsoever, then how can it be possible to know anything at all?

RINPOCHE: I have stated repeatedly that all things are empty and devoid of self. I never said there's nothing whatsoever. We'll return to that point later on.

STUDENT: Did you say that the essential nature of seeing is ultimate truth?

RINPOCHE: Yes, I said that. The nature of seeing is ultimate truth.

STUDENT: Seeming or seeing?

RINPOCHE: Seeing. Remember, conventional truth is how it appears. Ultimate truth is how it really is. Conventional truth is superficial, while ultimate truth is authentic or real. Conventional truth lies within the domain of conceptual mind, within the three domains of body, speech, and mind. Whatever is tangible, describable or conceivable is conventionally true or seemingly true, but it's not really so. The real is what is beyond the domain of body, speech and mind. It's not an object of concept. In fact, the very essence of the conventionally true is itself the ultimately true. What we understood before was that which seemingly exists is in reality not a thing. That is how it is by nature or in itself ultimate truth.

STUDENT: Are all mental events, such as reflection on the twelve interdependent links, trust, and compassion, merely aspects of the disturbing emotions?

RINPOCHE: Most emotions are within the grip of ego-clinging. Compassion, for example, which is an emotion, can be either within or beyond ego-clinging. As long as there is the holding-on to the concept of 'I,' the concept of 'that other person,' and of feeling compassion, there's ego-clinging. Pure compassion is beyond that.

STUDENT: There was a reference made earlier to something which I don't know exactly how to follow: the idea of a mental continuum. What does that mean on a conventional level?

RINPOCHE: That's where we come to the point that separates the different schools of Buddhist philosophy. The lower schools claim yes, there is a link between the previous moment and the next; that there is a continuation. Otherwise how could there be past and future? The higher points of view or philosophies don't hold this. We'll return to that.

STUDENT: How to understand the concept of death, when one is still confused and not enlightened?

RINPOCHE: Actually, the feeling "I will die," is based on the idea that 'I' exist, which is really just ego-clinging. As long as there is ego-clinging there is death. There is pleasure and pain, and we do create various kinds of karma, the results of which will be experienced later. But when you realize the nonconceptual wakefulness in which there is no ego, then there is also no death of that ego. Up until that level, there is. To simply accumulate good actions and reap their results will never get one more than a high rebirth within samsara. The only real solution is to realize the original wakefulness that is nonconceptual, meaning not holding the idea of an 'I'.

STUDENT: Some past events are remembered very vividly, while sometimes the memory is very faint or blurred. Why is this?

RINPOCHE: If it's a very clear image or recollection, then it's an imprint of an experience from the past. If it's something not so clear it could just be a poorly remembered image from the past or it could be the product of daydreaming or one's imagination.

STUDENT: Rinpoche, in this state of awareness what words do you use to describe what we normally call experience?

RINPOCHE: What kind of awareness? Do you mean rigpa? Awareness has many meanings. One kind of being aware means simply to listen while someone is talking. If I am not aware, then I can't listen to what you are saying. This is also a kind of awareness.

STUDENT: What I think you are talking about is a higher level of awareness or a deeper level. In this state is there experience or is there another description, another way of talking about it?

RINPOCHE: It's not what I am talking about — what are you talking about? When we feel that things which don't really exist actually do appear, that's called intellectual understanding, because we're describing it mentally as being such-and-such. A direct nonconceptual experience of the 'insubstantial presence' of things is simply and purely like that. That is the view of Mahamudra, Dzogchen, and the Middle Way. At that point you can call that awareness rigpa.

STUDENT: All that we say and do is just like childish play. You just watch that show with awareness.

RINPOCHE: How do you experience it?

STUDENT: In the same way. My experience is in the state of awareness. Awareness is there and so is conceptual mind. Awareness watches the show, while mind thinks things like "Now I am in my house," and so on.

RINPOCHE: So what is the relationship between what you call awareness and what you call mind? Is the mind, the thinking, the expression and all this — is that the creation of awareness? Is it the attendant or servant of awareness? What is the relationship?

STUDENT: The relationship is that from the state of awareness comes confusion, which is like the mind of a child, and one thus behaves like a small child. Both awareness and confusion exist at the same time.

Rinpoche: You need to first of all distinguish between these two things — awareness and what you call mind. They are very different because while awareness is nonconceptual, the thinking mind is conceptual. Awareness is unmistaken, but thinking is mistaken. When there is thinking or fixating, the state of nonfixation is absent. In the moment of no fixation, no thought, then the thinking mind has disappeared, vanished.

Student: They are both there at the same time.

Rinpoche: You should really examine whether or not they coexist.

Student: By just examining you don't gain any experience.

Rinpoche: Of course the act of investigating and examining is conceptual thinking, conceptual mind, but it's necessary in the beginning. Because it's through examining that we can discover the state of no concepts, no thought, a state free from constructs which is not conceptual mind. We'll get more into that in a couple of days.

Experience

To consider again the Four Seals of Dharma: the first statement, that everything conditioned is impermanent, means that if something is changeable, it follows that it is impermanent. This is the logical consequence of any conditioned entity, and this is not just something that's taught by the Buddha. By using our own intelligence we can discover for ourselves that this is true. Then our understanding is in exact agreement with what the Buddha taught.

We have established the validity of the Buddha's first statement. The next one, that everything defiling is painful, means that anything connected to or created by disturbing emotions or karma inevitably results in pain. Here, karma refers either to an action committed right now that is motivated by disturbing emotions or to the painful effect of those karmic actions. The actions can either be painful upon completion or while being performed. In other words, whatever is based on karma and disturbing emotions is by nature painful. Thirdly, although the Buddha taught that all things are empty and devoid of self, what we experience, feel, and believe is exactly the opposite. To us things do exist; they are not empty, and there is a self. We hold that everything that we experience is tangible, solid and real. Just to say everything is empty is incomprehensible; it is in conflict with what we see and hear. As one student told me, "It doesn't feel comfortable." To relate the Buddha's teaching on this to our own personal understanding, we need a bridge. This bridge is the philosophy which clarifies the meaning of the statement "everything is empty and devoid of self."

The reason for the various Buddhist philosophical schools is that the Buddha's followers differ in intellectual capacity. First, we speak of two major types of philosophical schools, Buddhists and non-Buddhists. There are a great number of non-Buddhist schools, and we find mention of them in past Buddhist philosophical debates, but we don't have the time to discuss all of them now. Neither is there that great a need at this point.

Basically, the non-Buddhist philosophies tend towards one of two directions: nihilism or eternalism. The view of eternalism maintains that there is some kind of supreme godhead out of which everything is created. When creatures turn around and please the godhead, their own source, they are then accepted or absorbed back into it. God purifies their karma and disturbing emotions, and they dissolve into God. If they displease the godhead, as punishment they are sent into a state of suffering like the hells. Therefore, it's necessary to act in a correct way in order to return back to God. In this system, everything is considered to last forever, and that's why it's called the view of eternalism.

The other view is nihilism. It literally means the 'view of annihilation' in the sense that it's held that everything right now does exist but the moment this life ceases it is all finished; nothing is left. Nihilism holds no continuation whatsoever; death is like water drying up or a flame being extinguished. It is simply the end. That is why it is called nihilism or 'annihilationism'. Let me state right here that neither of these two views are considered beneficial for liberation.

Within Buddhist philosophy there are four major schools, two Hinayana and two Mahayana. The two Hinayana schools are called Vaibhashika and Sautrantika. The two Mahayana schools are called Chittamatra or 'Mind Only,' and Madhyamika or 'Middle Way'. If you can familiarize yourselves to some extent with these four Buddhist schools it would be highly beneficial.

All four of the Buddhist schools accept the statement 'all things are empty and devoid of self'. They differ with regard to what it means, however. In order to analyze this statement, we need to examine four points: view, meditation, conduct and fruition. The first of the four schools, the Hinayana school of Vaibhashika, holds the view that everything that we see and experience is empty and devoid of self. Everything that we grossly experience and see is empty, and the self, the 'I,' cannot be found as an independently existing entity anywhere. The Vaibhashika school accepts that what we hear, see, smell and so forth is made out of something — that there is some kind of ultimate component or building block to physical manifestations. To follow their logic, for example, the biggest mountain in the world is dependent upon this basic particle or atom, which when grouped together creates a mountain. It is like the flour used to make bread: when enough particles adhere together, then we use the word bread. If we took a handful of flour and scattered it in a large area there would be no trace left; it looks like there is nothing. If there is only a little flour and a strong wind in a steep place, it would look as if it had totally disappeared. But it could disappear only because there was something to disappear in the first place, right? In the same way, the Vaibhashikas maintain that everything in this world — mountains, houses, bodies, anything - is made out of small particles that never really disappear. These small particles can even be divided into smaller pieces, which are called atoms. These indivisible particles are said to truly and ultimately exist. All other phenomena are empty.

This was taught by the Buddha to his Hinayana followers, who are called shravakas. This teaching is very easy to understand; they felt comfortable with a teaching like that. This is not true only for shravakas, but applies to us as well. It seems that this kind of idea, that there are really some particles that things are made of, is very intelligible, very logical. Does it fit in our understanding? What do you think? Do you agree? What sounds best: that everything is made out of small particles or that everything is totally beyond arising, dwelling and ceasing, utterly empty? What do you think? Please speak up.

STUDENT: The first one sounds really good, like standing on the floor. It does make sense, but it is probably better not to investigate it any further.

RINPOCHE: What you're saying is that it's better not to examine further because then what we believe might fall apart, and that would be really scary. It's good to study some philosophy like this, because it helps in our meditation practice — it speeds up the entire process so that we can progress very quickly. Going to one restaurant and sticking to that and eating only one dish there, simply refusing to accept any other place or any other thing to eat — that is called being a stubborn blockhead. Wouldn't it be much better to visit a lot of different restaurants and try a lot of different dishes? Then when we speak with other people we can compare and draw conclusions from our own experience. In the same way, we should study the shravaka view and practice this. To attain some certainty about what the teaching is inevitably involves practice. This kind of certainty or understanding will prepare us for the higher practices, the higher schools.

If we start out by asserting that everything is beyond arising, dwelling and ceasing, it might seem kind of senseless. There is not much room in which to explain it — the matter ends right there. To say everything outside is empty, everything inside is empty, there is complete emptiness, and to discuss the emptiness of being empty and so forth — it all becomes nothing more than words, with no real conviction behind it. What we need to decide now in this respect is: whether there is a basic component or material out of which everything is made? Is there such a thing as an indivisible particle or atom, yes or no? It is a question. If we say yes, we are agreeing with most science. If we say atoms don't exist, we are contradicting most of the older scientific beliefs, at least. We should settle this matter through discussion and our own intelligence.

STUDENT: I believe in emptiness. I have done so since I was a small child. But due to my upbringing, school and so on, I don't have much confidence today.

RINPOCHE: Okay. Somebody else? The question was whether the atom itself exists as something indivisible or not.

STUDENT: Einstein says that the tiniest particle sometimes exists as a material particle with form. Sometimes it exists merely as an energy wave. It depends upon the perceiver.

RINPOCHE: This kind of theory still maintains that there is something concrete. Whether that something is being given one name or another, it is still not higher than the two Hinayana schools. Back to the question about the particle, the atom: if there is something like an atom, is it a material form or not? Does it have matter or not? The idea of an atom is that it is the building-block out of which everything else is formed by various combinations, right? If the basic particle is something that is ultimately formless or not material, can it possibly make up matter?

STUDENT: These days the atom is not thought to be dead matter. Energy makes it appear to be matter.

RINPOCHE: The shravaka schools claim that the atom exists, that it is material. The Mahayana school of the Middle Way objects: there is no existing atom and it is not material — it is emptiness which appears as matter. Due to the seeming substantiality of emptiness, material appearances take place. The Hinayana type of person cannot accept this. Instead, he maintains the existence of an extremely subtle particle which is imperceptible to the eye, but has a concrete form. When the Hinayana and Mahayana schools discuss this matter together — for example, a Vaibhashika follower and a Middle Way follower — then the Madhyamika person will say everything is empty, since no 'thing' can be proven to come into existence, to remain or to cease. All is beyond arising, dwelling and ceasing. The shravaka or Hinayana follower will accuse that statement of being excessive, maintaining that it is totally outside what we actually experience. He would say, "If you assert that everything is empty, doesn't arise, doesn't dwell anywhere, and doesn't cease, then there is no basis for cause and effect and past and future lives. Everything becomes pointless if you talk like that. Also, that means there is no suffering, no origin, no path, and no cessation, and of course there is, isn't there?" The Middle Way follower would then respond, "It is exactly because everything is beyond arising, dwelling and ceasing that the appearance of arising, dwelling and ceasing can take place, just as in a dream. It is because of their basic empty nature that things can manifest." If one's intelligence and scope of mind is only mediocre, then one will not be able to understand these last statements, and instead will perceive and practice in accordance with the lower school. If one can accept the doctrine of the Mahayana, the Middle Way, then one should practice that.

Regarding the existence of the self, the normal person doesn't really question it, but it is the five aggregates taken together which are labeled 'I'. We use the word 'I' to refer to this vague 'something,' whatever it may be. According to Buddhist philosophy, this 'I' is made out of five aggregates: physical form, sensations, conception, formation, and cognition. If each of these in itself were the 'I,' we would experience many egos, many selves — but this is not the impression people have of themselves. Another important point is that there is no 'I' separate from these five aggregates. It is only through the coming together or assembly of these five that we without questioning use the word 'I'. For example, the word 'group' is used to describe an assemblage of many people. When the people walk away one by one, where is that thing for which we used the word 'group'? It is only because there seems to be a basis for the label 'group' that we use it. If we really look, however, there is no such permanent or lasting basis. The individual person is not called the group, right? Do we understand this? It is the assembly of individuals that are described by the word 'group'.

Similarly, in ordinary talk we might say "I see," "I understand," or "I know," but whether this knower is an entity that continues or not is also questioned by the different schools. The two lower schools, Vaibhashika and Sautrantika, say yes, there is something that continues — a very subtle instant of consciousness which continues from one moment to the next. The higher schools of Mahayana maintain that no such thing can be found. The two Hinayana schools say that time exists, that there is past, present and future. The Middle Way, however, holds that because you cannot pinpoint the present, there cannot be any past or future. We might use the word 'now' to try to identify the present, but the moment we say it, it is already gone. We cannot pinpoint a present moment anywhere. It is the same in science: there is no smallest time fraction, right? And isn't continuation based on time? If continuation is defined as lasting time, and if there is no time, how can there be continuation? These different ways of questioning are ways to approach the understanding of everything as being empty and devoid of self.

Through using reasoning and intelligence in the manner we have been doing, we can understand that all phenomena are empty. Truthfully, though, unless we achieve the knowledge resulting from actual meditation practice we do not experience that all things are empty. Far more important than establishing the emptiness of matter is to truly understand and experience egolessness — the fact that a self-entity or personal identity does not really exist. It is because of holding onto this false idea of a truly existing 'I' that we continue within samsaric existence. And it is through realizing egolessness that one goes beyond samsara and attains enlightenment. In fact, the dividing line between buddhas and sentient beings is the realization of egolessness.

Seemingly, or conventionally, the perceived object and the perceiving mind do exist. But really, or ultimately, both subject and object are said to be beyond arising, dwelling and ceasing — totally beyond all such constructs. That is the real condition, the innate state of ultimate truth. Our innate nature that lies beyond arising, dwelling and ceasing is, in general Dharma terms, called 'buddha nature'.

The third vehicle, Vajrayana, brings the understanding of egolessness into actual experience. Vajrayana practice is also described as 'taking fruition as the path'. It is much faster and offers greater advantages than the Sutra teachings, which take causes as the path. This is why these two different approaches are sometimes termed the causal and resultant vehicles. Vajrayana is also more risky, because we aim at a fruition that has not fully ripened yet.

Let's talk briefly about view, meditation and conduct in Vajrayana. What is the view of Vajrayana? The view is the very nature of things, the natural state. Meditation is that which leads us further on the completely perfect path. And conduct is that which cuts the very root of the falsity of illusory phenomena. Finally, the fruition, the result, is to arrive at the stage of exhaustion of deluded phenomena beyond concepts before leaving this very body and life. The Middle Way school calls this 'the innate nature free from limitations,' meaning free from holding any notion about it. The Mahamudra system terms it the 'great seal of the definitive meaning,' which is the ultimate innate state, the true natural condition. 'Seal' means all apparent and existent phenomena included within samsara and nirvana do not transcend the profound seal of indivisible emptiness and cognizance. This view is also called the luminous Great Perfection, Dzogchen, which means that all apparent and existing phenomena — whatever is experienced — do not transcend the sphere or expanse of primordially pure awareness.

These three great views — the Great Middle Way, the Great Seal, and the Great Perfection — are all called 'great' because regardless of which one of them we practice, there is no better method for vanquishing the disturbing emotions, our dualistic thinking, and the conceptual way of fixating on things. An act of fixating cannot cut through fixation; only a state of nonfixation can cut through. Fixation means any kind of conceptual view in which we still have some notion that we hold onto: "This is how it is." That kind of view can, of course, help to diminish our ordinary, rigid fixation on there being a real world with beings, but it can never totally eliminate fixation itself. To cut the very root of or basis for fixation, we must acquire the view of nonfixation. Nonfixation cuts fixated views at their very root.

Taking fruition as the path is based on the fact that there is no difference whatsoever between the buddha-nature present in the mind-stream of all six classes of sentient beings and that of the fully enlightened state realized by all the awakened ones.

These three great views — the Great Middle Way, the Great Seal and the Great Perfection — teach exactly how this ultimate nature is. Having relinquished ego-clinging, what remains is something about which we cannot say it does or it does not exist. It is the essence of experience that lies beyond the reach of concepts.

Sometimes our basic state is called 'primordial purity'. Because this essence is primordially pure, we cannot say it concretely exists.

At the same time, inconceivable qualities of knowledge, compassion and ability are inherently present; this is called 'spontaneous presence'. Because of this spontaneous presence, the basic state also transcends the limitation of nonexistence. Therefore, it is said "because of being primordially pure, it defies the limitation of existence; because of being spontaneously present, it defies the limitation of nonexistence." This is the real condition, the mind of all the buddhas, the final achievement of the path. It is also what we, as practitioners, must implement in practice.

This basic state, our true nature, is something we should realize exactly as it is. As mentioned earlier, there are two ways to approach this — through the analytical style of a scholar or *pandita*, or by means of the 'resting meditation' of a simple practitioner. For the first approach, the analytical style of a pandita, we must have a long life and a lot of free time to be able to study all the scriptures without any bias or prejudice. Through our intellectual understanding, we will eventually come to appreciate all the different scriptures and philosophies as direct instructions about this nature. All the different teachings are then understood to be totally beyond conflict. To have such an opportunity is excellent, because it makes it much easier to gain genuine confidence in the Buddhadharma.

Sometimes scholars come to me and say, "I have studied all these philosophies now, but I really need to receive mind teachings, the direct instructions." That is of course wonderful, but at the same time it shows a fundamental misunderstanding, because all the Buddhist philosophies and teachings are, from the very beginning, instructions about this nature. On the other hand, some practitioners say, "I don't want to have anything to do with studying dry intellectual philosophy. It's all just pointless talk." That is also a fundamental misunderstanding. If one thinks, "I don't like Madhyamika. I don't like philosophy. I only want Mahamudra or Dzogchen, primordial purity, cutting through; I don't need to look at any text," that is a total misunderstanding, because all Buddhist teachings and philosophy are, in themselves, the instructions, the direct teachings, of the compassionate Buddha.

Nevertheless, we as individuals do have different inclinations, different kinds of karmic dispositions. Because of this, we might feel closer to one approach than another. That is perfectly all right: the main point is to reach some understanding, some accomplishment. Regardless of which approach we pursue, it's the outcome that's important.

In terms of gaining understanding of the nature of things, three types of transmission are traditionally explained: mind to mind transmission, symbolic transmission and oral transmission. 'Mind to mind transmission' is when a truly realized master meets a ready and worthy student. Then, by simply resting together in unfabricated meditation, the realization identical to the guru's occurs in the mind of the student. Without using any words, without any symbolic indications, the knowledge realizing egolessness dawns in the student. This is called 'mind transmission'.

'Symbolic transmission' is, for example, when the guru points to the sky and says something like, "Look at space." Or he might simply hold up a crystal or make some gesture or brief indication. Realization can occur in the mind of the disciple simply through these symbolic actions, which is why this is called 'symbolic transmission'. The third type, oral transmission, means the disciple realizes simply through hearing a few important instructions — the key points, not lengthy elaborate explanations. This is the oral transmission through verbal communication.

It is necessary that we meet the ultimate master, the innate truth itself, which lies beyond arising, dwelling and ceasing, beyond all mental constructs. In order to realize or to be introduced to this ultimate teacher of our innate nature, we must depend upon three other teachers, as I mentioned earlier. To reiterate the different types of teachers: the first of these is called the 'personal lineage guru' and is an actual living human being. He or she should possess the knowledge realizing egolessness gained through intellectual understanding, experience and realization. The personal teacher should belong to a lineage of qualified masters who possess the unimpaired continuation of oral instructions. We should connect with such a personal lineage master, and not only in the sense of having an audience or socializing with him. We should genuinely try to assimilate the qualities he possesses. In order to do so, first we must carefully examine the teacher. It is often said that one must first be skilled in examining the master, next in following him correctly, and finally in assimilating his wisdom qualities. We must possess all three of these skills.

To examine a teacher means that we should investigate whether or not he possesses the genuine lineage of oral instructions. Additionally, we should check whether he actually has the personal qualities that result from personal learning, reflection and meditation training.

To follow a teacher doesn't mean only to socialize with him, hanging out and chatting and having food and drink together. That is not what is meant by following a teacher. We need to use the time we have with him in a way which allows us to assimilate his superior qualities. The way to do this is through being intelligent with respect to understanding how to practice, and being diligent in applying the instructions.

The second kind of teacher we must follow is called the 'master who is the scriptures of the enlightened ones'. This refers to Dharma books and texts. It's best if we can study all the extensive scriptures and philosophy, but if we don't have the time then we should at least study the meditation manuals or guidebooks, called *tri* in Tibetan. These texts must be genuine, meaning that we investigate who wrote it before we spend time studying it. Was the person who composed it truly a qualified person? A truly qualified master will write an authentic, valuable text. At best, he should be a fully enlightened master. Next best is a bodhisattva who has achieved one of the bhumis. At minimum he should be a great pandita or scholar who possesses a very high degree of learning in many fields of knowledge. By studying such texts, we can truly actualize some beneficial qualities. In this way, written scriptures also become a teacher whom we can follow. This second way of meeting a teacher, this skillful means, will thus benefit our realization of wisdom.

The third kind of teacher is called the 'symbolic teacher of experiences'. You should investigate all the different kinds of experiences you undergo in this lifetime, whether they appear to be lasting or fleeting, pleasant or painful, worthwhile or totally pointless. The end result of such investigation is that the nature of samsaric experience is understood to be fleeting and illusory, like a dream or a magical apparition. To gain this understanding is to have received teachings from the symbolic teacher of your experiences.

Everything is impermanent. Nothing really lasts, either on a gross level or on a subtle level — nothing is beyond impermanence. Nothing has any core value or real worth. For example, at first glance someone's physical body may seem very attractive and worth getting close to, but if it's really examined, it is just an assembly of skin, flesh, veins, fat, organs, bones, marrow and so forth. If we really examine the matter, there's no real core or essence that can satisfy us.

Take, for example, the vase on this table. It has a nice color and hand-painted flowers on its surface. We think, 'How nice; I'd like to have such a vase'. But the moment it falls on the floor and breaks, there is no thing there that we want to keep. It simply goes into the trash bin. In fact, if we acknowledge the real condition of things, there is no worthwhile core in anything. If we truly take this to heart and understand that all the different things in this world are impermanent and thus futile to pursue, there is no way any samsaric state can fetter us.

Everyone wants happiness and a comfortable life, but no matter who you ask, no one will claim to have perfect circumstances without any problems or worries whatsoever. One will never meet such a person, because such a state of perfect happiness is impossible to achieve. Nothing lasts; nothing has a real, lasting core. Actually, most people live their lives in a state of subtle anxiety. There is always a slight dread that something will go wrong, that one will become sick, that one may die. This anxiety is the basis for hope and fear. We hope things will work out and go well, and we fear that something will go wrong, that things won't work out. The look in a person's eyes reveals his or her anxiety. It's a subtle but persistent undercurrent, until the moment comes when the hope or fear is actualized.

Actually, we are always walking in the narrow defile of hope and fear.

When someone takes to heart the fact that things do not last and are not worthwhile to pursue, that person can truly be called a Dharma practitioner or a spiritual person. Such a person has the attitude that pursuing mundane achievements is not of real value. He or she understands that mundane goals will bring no true satisfaction or happiness. This attitude springs from having gained some insight into the truth that things in this world don't last and lack real worth. Phadampa Sangye said; "You are together for such a short time, like a brief meeting in the marketplace. So, husbands and wives, don't waste time fighting." All family relationships are like that; very brief, just a few years, so don't waste time arguing.

Who should we thank for giving us the understanding that samsara is like this? We should really thank the nature of samsara itself, because things are by nature impermanent and futile. The demonstrator of this, our experience of daily life, is therefore our teacher. The reason for me repeating the first two maxims here — that everything conditioned is impermanent, and that everything defiling is painful — is so that we can truly understand the 'symbolic teacher of experiences'. When we gain confidence and trust in conditioned things being impermanent and defiling states being painful, we meet the symbolic teacher of experiences face to face.

Through the kindness of meeting and connecting with the first three kinds of teachers, we are able to meet and realize the fourth kind of teacher, called 'the ultimate teacher of our innate nature'. This is self-existing wakefulness itself. The whole point of talking so much about how all things are empty and devoid of a self is to make us ready to meet the fourth teacher — the ultimate teacher of our innate nature.

We can have some discussion now.

STUDENT: Regarding the past and future: how can suffering be said to exist since beginningless time, and how can the end of suffering said to be permanent?

RINPOCHE: If there's no time?

STUDENT: Yes.

RINPOCHE: That's the reason for distinguishing between conventional and ultimate truth. In ultimate truth, time does not exist. That means when realizing ultimate truth then time does not exist. Until that realization, though, time seems to exist. We can right now reason, speculate and understand intellectually that time does not exist, but without having practiced a great deal, that doesn't mean that we experience it as such. Compared to a normal person who has not even questioned this, it is of course better for us to speculate, "Does time really exist?" We find out that actually we cannot say if there is time. Our idea of it is merely an intellectual understanding. It is similar to a scientist who uses a lot of instruments, laser beams or particle beams or whatever, to determine that singular atoms do not really exist. He's using physical instruments to determine data which results in an idea of insubstantiality. The whole framework for his life remains concrete and solid, however. That's the difference between conventional and ultimate truth.

STUDENT: The wisdom of the buddhas is absolute truth, correct? What then happens to the relative truth? Does it fall apart or vanish?

RINPOCHE: So-called relative reality is still there, unimpaired and unchanged, but our conceptualizing 'this is this, this is that' is absent. In the beginning, for us, there can occur something like a gap of feeling free and open without concepts. This is what slowly evolves into the omniscient state of enlightenment.

STUDENT: Does inherent wakefulness possess any true or concrete existence?

RINPOCHE: When using terminology like 'self-existing' or 'inherent' wakefulness, it is faulty to assert that our basic sense of being awake, this self-contained wakefulness, either exists or does not exist. It lies beyond any such statements. That is why the phrase 'beyond concepts' is often used.

STUDENT: It seems to me that the image I have of something and what I call it are not the same. Could you explain this?

RINPOCHE: The mental image and the label you attach to it are different; that's true. To clear this up, in philosophy we use the phrase 'thought which holds the object mingled with its name'. This process of thought is the result of our upbringing and education. Conversely, a thought of something might sometime appear without an associated name, because we haven't learned the names for that particular thing yet. That's why mental images and their labels are different or separate things.

STUDENT: How long does it take for perception to occur?

RINPOCHE: It's very hard to pinpoint exactly how long it takes. It seems as though visual impressions occur instantly — you open your eyes and you see something immediately. Actually, though, the visual process is a long sequence of micro-short moments that our minds assemble to create that perception. Exactly how long those moments are is very difficult to define. Long is dependent upon something short, isn't it?

STUDENT: When I walk out on my balcony, the bird in the tree will immediately fly away. He doesn't have to see me coming for a long time before he reacts.

RINPOCHE: If he always flies away immediately, no one could ever shoot him. This is proof right here. We think its action is 'immediate,' but actually it is not immediate. Or maybe it is merely a coincidence. Before you go outside, the bird may have already started to fly away. It doesn't fly away the very instant you appear. You arrive, it notices you, becomes anxious, and flies away — that took time, even if it's not a lot of time.

STUDENT: If a buddha comes to my house and I offer him a cup of tea, will he analyze, "Do I need this tea or not?" Or will relative and ultimate truth arise simultaneously in his mind?

RINPOCHE: If a buddha appears in this world, he does so for the welfare of other people. If you offered him a cup of tea, he would naturally respond, "Yes, please. Thank you," and drink the tea to make you happy. If he were just some kind of magical apparition made of light rays, it would be very hard to feel trust in him. The buddha's experience has two aspects: his or her personal experience and what is experienced by others. His own personal experience is beyond any concept of arising, dwelling and ceasing; yet, at the same time, his discriminating awareness perceives what other people are experiencing. Not only the buddhas, but also accomplished practitioners of the past would say something like this: "On one hand, everything is utterly wide open, to the point where I can move freely through solid rock. On the other hand, everything is distinctly separate." For example, a buddha could talk to a whole crowd of people and without stopping to examine each person, he would know each person individually, whether or not he had met them before. He would also know what he was teaching them at that moment and be aware of all the present circumstances of place and time and so forth. For a buddha, there is no conflict between these two aspects. They are both part of the experience of a realized person. In short, the buddha sees that other beings perceive in a deluded way, but the buddha himself remains free from delusion.

STUDENT: Once we have been introduced to our inherent nature, is that called pure perception?

RINPOCHE: There are two types of pure perception: attempted and actual. In your meditation training you should attempt to see things as pure. This implies that we don't naturally see things as pure, but we try to. The real perfection of pure perception, the experience called the 'all-encompassing purity of what appears and exists,' means directly perceiving that the essence and nature of everything is totally free of constructs and limitations. That experience is also free from the concepts of pure and impure.

According to Vajrayana, which involves the practice of taking pure perception as the path, we should study the Dharma within the framework of the five-fold perfection, sometimes called the five certainties: place, teacher, retinue, teaching, and time. We should regard the teacher's words as the Dharma, his mind as the Buddha, and his physical body as the Sangha. Pure perception is not to be directed only towards the teacher or master who expounds the teachings, but also towards the other participants. We ourselves are the buddhas of the future. Some of us have already progressed far on the path, while some of us have just stepped onto the path and are just beginning to practice. However, we as individuals cannot fully judge or evaluate anyone else's progress and level. It's impossible to know another's experience. Given this, it's much better to apply some sense of respect and appreciation towards one another by thinking that all practitioners of the Vajrayana teachings are dakas and dakinis. With a sense of devotion and respect, we should think, "How nice! How great! How wonderful!" If we have this sense of respect and appreciation for one another as Vajrayana practitioners, then the basis for criticizing, undermining, backbiting, jealousy and competition just totally falls away. It's very important to train in pure perception or sacred outlook, not just towards the teacher, but towards all participants in the teachings. In short, try to embrace the act of studying the Dharma with the fivefold perfection.

STUDENT: Is there a connection between the wisdom that knows everything there is to know and the ability to act in this world?

RINPOCHE: It's because of the wisdom that perceives the ultimate nature as it is that everything in all times and directions can be seen and dealt with clearly. They are definitely integrated.

Pith Instructions

The four schools of philosophy or the four major lineages of Tibetan Buddhism all accept that external phenomena are empty, that the self or ego does not really exist. Now, we have come to the point of examining and explaining this subject through the Third Turning of the Wheel of Dharma, also called the 'third set of teachings on the complete uncovering'. This category includes the views of Mahamudra and Dzogchen.

In the general Dharma teachings, the fourth ultimate teacher of the innate nature, which is self-existing wakefulness or inherent wisdom, is called 'buddha nature' or *tathagatagarbha*. In the style of teaching known as 'guidance texts,' it is called *rigpa*. Guidance texts help destroy the web of delusion. There are, of course, many elaborate, simple and extremely direct methods and approaches used to dismantle this web of delusion. The special quality of Mahamudra and Dzogchen is to focus on the vital points. Usually a master performs three functions: giving empowerments, expounding on the tantras, and explaining the guidance texts. With respect to the latter, who is being guided, where is one being guided to, who is giving the guidance, and what is the guidance?

Who needs guidance? Any deluded sentient being. Where should they be guided to? To the state of liberation and omniscience — complete enlightenment. What is the method of guidance? Giving the oral instructions — the advice or directions. The one who gives that is the spiritual friend, the guide. The purpose of all this is to take the guidance text to heart, so that we can apply the meaning.

The state of mind that is empty in essence and cognizant by nature, but which involves fixation, is called dualistic mind or thinking mind — in Tibetan, *sem*. The state of mind that is empty in essence and cognizant by nature — these two being inseparable in both cases — and free from any fixation whatsoever is called awareness, in Tibetan *rigpa*. Rigpa is defined as awareness free of concepts, free from disturbing emotions and free from dualistic fixation. The opposite of this, *marigpa,* can be translated as unawareness, unknowing or ignorance.

The very basis for all wisdom is *dharmadhatu* wisdom; that in itself is rigpa. The basis for disturbing emotions is ignorance and conceptual thinking, both of which involve clinging, fixation, and delusion. We need to separate or distinguish between the two states of sem and rigpa. In the Dzogchen teachings, it is said, "Ground is what is. Path is to acknowledge what is. Fruition is to arrive in just that." The teachings on how to recognize and sustain rigpa are quite clear. In Dzogchen, there is something called 'pointing out' the nature of mind, which involves an introduction to rigpa, bringing you face to face with basic, thought-free awareness. In the general teaching, this is called seeing the 'innate truth,' or the 'reality of what is,' meaning not merely the superficial or seeming, but what is real or ultimate.

When the master points out awareness, the disciple must first acknowledge or recognize it, then afterwards sustain that recognition. Rigpa is not a 'thing' to be created through meditation, but the nature of awareness *can* be sustained. What is meant by the nature of awareness? Awareness is naturally, of itself, free from disturbing emotions, free from dualistic fixation, and free from conceptual thinking. But it is not at all a state of oblivion or unconsciousness. The word 'sustain' usually means to be involved in the act of holding, guarding or nurturing something from one moment to the next. What is being sustained in this context is the continuity of rigpa, beyond dualistic mind. One simply lets the continuity of awareness last. This is not a deliberate or conceptual act.

In this context, there are three steps: recognizing, training and attaining stability. There are traditional examples for this process: recognizing is like taking hold of the seed of a flower; training is like the act of planting, watering, and applying fertilizer; and attaining stability is the ripening and blossoming of the fully grown plant. Attainment of stability is dependent upon training, while training is dependent upon recognizing. Each depends upon the former. Therefore, the first and most important step is to recognize. Without recognition, there is neither training nor attainment of stability; without planting the seed, there is no nurturing or ripening of the plant.

The approach of a scholar and the approach of a simple meditator can both help us become clear about the ultimate truth. The scholar studies and reflects in order to ascertain the innate nature, the ultimate truth. The meditator receives a few key points of instructions from a qualified master regarding this same subject. Until we realize the ultimate truth, we should not neglect studying and reflecting on the teachings.

First of all, scrutinize the naked and natural state of awareness by means of your master's oral instructions until you see it free from assumptions. That is called 'recognizing your nature'. Remember, the ultimate teacher is self-existing wisdom. The other three teachers we follow are of course exceedingly kind, but they are not ultimate. The first three are transient. The personal teacher can perish; the scriptures can perish; our symbolic teacher of experiences also perishes. It is difficult to say who of these three is most kind; really, they are equal in kindness. Our personal human teacher is extremely kind, but without the symbolic teacher of experience, how could we develop renunciation? When we look at it this way, they are equal in value.

Both our lama and samsaric life are thus kind. We might even say; 'I salute the teacher. I salute samsara'. We could understand it in that way. But there's a difference between saying, "I salute," and saying "Thank you." Maybe to say, "Thank you, samsara!" would sound better.

So, the ultimate teacher is the basic state of awareness. Until we realize this by experiencing it, we have not met our ultimate teacher. We are only connected to perishable teachers. They are kind and benevolent, and can show us some direction, but they are not ultimate. Our innate, intrinsic wakefulness is the true object to be realized. We take the support of an external teacher to realize something that we already possess, something that is within ourselves. Ignorance and basic wakefulness are both within ourselves. We must clear away the ignorance with the innate wisdom. It is not something we borrow from the teacher.

This ultimate teacher, self-existing wakefulness, is exactly what we need to realize. If we have truly realized this ultimate innate state, we don't have to sit for three years in retreat somewhere. If we haven't realized it, then even a hundred years of sitting on our buttocks will not help very much. There is one key point, one vital point, which comes down to this: do we understand it or not? Have we realized it or not? If we haven't realized this innate truth, we continue in samsaric existence. If we have realized it, we attain enlightenment. It's that simple. When we put it this way, we can clearly see that great advantage and great loss are both potentially present within ourselves.

Our disturbed emotional frame of mind, our conceptual thinking, is, in its essence or basic identity, self-existing wakefulness. But please understand this point: disturbing emotions and dualistic fixations are not in themselves the innate state of dharmakaya. The essence of the disturbing emotions and dualistic fixation is dharmakaya, this is true. This is realized by means of our master's oral instructions. The master communicates his experience of the ultimate truth to you, saying "This is what I experience, like this; do you experience it the same?" Then we look for ourselves and say "Yes, sure." Transmission is simply like that.

The problem is that our essential nature, the innate state of dharmakaya, is simply so close to ourselves that we can't see it. It's too easy, so that it's hard to trust. It's so familiar to ourselves that it seems foreign. When something is too familiar it's like a person who we are really close to — we don't have much respect or deep appreciation for him or her. But if someone new comes in, we will stand up and join our palms together in respect. That's why it's said, "The one with whom you are too familiar, too well-acquainted, you disrespect." That which is closest to oneself is one's own buddha-nature, but we lack respect for it in the sense of truly appreciating it. Not appreciating it, we ignore it and foolishly look elsewhere. Therefore, it is said that it is truly foolish to hope for the state of enlightenment to come from some other place.

The buddha-nature is within oneself: self-existing wakefulness is inherent to us. Because of this, when our personal lineage master communicates it to us in a direct, practical way, we are able to acknowledge it, admitting, "Wow! It's actually like that!" This process does not at all involve merely connecting with words about the nature of mind. It means to truly connect with their meaning and recognize the nature of mind.

This meaning is the naked and natural face of your awareness, free from assumptions. Basic awareness is the same as innate wakefulness, buddha-nature. 'Naked' here means authentic. In normal everyday usage, naked means 'without clothes'. Let's discuss the meaning of this term for awhile. To actually walk around without clothes can be quite embarrassing. Clothes are not the real person; they are a false covering. The real, authentic body is naked and unclothed. Cultures differ. In some cultures, one must cover the whole body, while others insist one must cover either the lower portion or the upper portion. In still other cultures you needn't cover either portion or the other; while in some cultures one must cover even the face. Dress codes depend upon the various cultures. Because of our cultural habits, if someone runs around without clothes, other people will say; "That person is crazy." That is our mental creation, a construct made through our thoughts. This is called social convention.

Social conventions are not always in agreement, but they are very powerful. 'Naked awareness' here means awareness free from the garments of conceptual thinking and dualistic fixation. What prevents us from meeting the naked face of awareness? It is our assumptions. There are two levels to that. One is coarse, the kind of thought which arises at first glance: "Ah, there is something there!" This involves the felt presence of an objective reality. The second level is more a subtle labeling, which allows us to discriminate and give names to all the different things in our life. These two mental activities cover up our naked awareness. Until we see this naked essence in actuality, not just as a construct or an imitation, we must scrutinize our minds by involving ourselves in learning, reflecting and training in meditation.

Awareness is also described as openness or unimpededness, meaning it is not blocked by our assumptions. Intellectually studying the qualities of the basic state gives us some intellectual indication of what it's about. Ultimately, though, this is mere conjecture, not the real thing. Without direct experience of the ultimate state, we can only assume or guess what is to be recognized.

Awareness is empty in essence and cognizant by nature. These two qualities, empty and cognizant, are not two separate things; nor are they one concrete 'thing'. The important point is that at the moment of recognizing this basic state of awareness, not even one of the 84,000 types of disturbing emotions has any place to remain. Subtle anxiety, as mentioned earlier, is not present; hope and fear are not present. The *Manjushri Nama Samgirti* says "The true meaning is beyond fear."

It is not enough merely to recognize this state of awareness in a glimpse or two. You must become totally sure of it. You need to resolve or firmly decide upon what your personal teacher introduces to you. In the beginning, it is possible to sometimes glimpse the ultimate state without feeling really sure or totally convinced of it. This results in us becoming a little suspicious or doubtful, wondering, 'Is what I'm experiencing really it or not?' This is due to not having decided or resolved.

The true purpose of following a master is to clear up these three points: recognizing one's nature, deciding on that, and gaining confidence in liberation. First, it's important to recognize one's nature. After recognizing, we need to resolve or gain certainty in it. Having gained certainty, we need to implement that in our experience. The best way to do this is short moments of recognition, repeated many times. This is what is meant by the term 'sustaining' — repeating the recognition briefly, but frequently. It is not enough to have an occasional glimpse of our buddha-nature; we need to decide upon it with certainty. And it's not enough just to decide; we need to train in it until we attain stability. Merely having the seed of a plant is not sufficient; it must be planted and allowed to fully grow. This is a very important point.

As I mentioned before, we must distinguish between two states: dualistic mind and awareness, in Tibetan sem and rigpa. Rigpa, awareness, is cognizance indivisible from emptiness, devoid of mental constructs. Sem is the dualistic frame of mind. Actually, sem and rigpa, dualistic mind and awareness, coexist. When there is dualistic fixation, that is sem. Dualistic fixation, or sem, obscures rigpa. When dualistic fixation falls apart, that is rigpa. In the basic state of buddha-nature, there is no delusion. Failing to acknowledge or recognize that buddha-nature is buddha-nature, that rigpa is self-existing wakefulness, causes us to wander in samsara. This kind of ignorance is called 'coemergent ignorance'. We simply fail to recognize our nature. From this, we stray into grasping at objects as being outside and labeling them, a process which is called 'conceptual ignorance'.

Here is a simple example for this process. You are in a dark place and see a piece of mottled rope lying the ground. Without really knowing what it is, you conclude that it's a snake and become terrified — for no real reason whatsoever. Similarly, our ordinary mind mistakes something false to be true, and labels and holds what is nonexistent to be existent.

We believe our disturbing emotions are pure while they are impure or mistaken, and we believe that deluded experience is reality. This is how pure dharmakaya free from constructs becomes impure. To put it simply, we fail to recognize the awakened mind that is our own basic state. Because of that, we stray into disturbing emotions and create negative karma that results in our continued rebirth in samsaric existence, and in endless suffering. This process is called 'natural awareness unable to keep its seat'. We develop the bad habit of delusion, and this is the basic cause for straying into samsara. When totally free from the delusion of body, speech and mind, it is possible to meet directly and face to face the naked awareness free from assumptions.

Milarepa said, "When training in Mahamudra, do not occupy yourself with virtuous actions of body and speech, because you risk the dissipation of thought-free wakefulness." This means that, at the moment of training in the view of Mahamudra, we should give up normal ego-oriented activities — even conventionally virtuous ones. We should also avoid formulating anything mentally or verbally or reciting things. That is when we are beginners. As we progress further along the path and become more and more familiar with the nature of mind, we can mingle the view of Mahamudra with virtuous activities without any danger of disturbing the state of samadhi. It is then said, "While remaining unmoved from the state of Mahamudra, not only can you engage in virtuous activities; even normal daily life activities cannot possibly fetter you." While remaining in the view of Mahamudra, we may sometimes behave as though we are happy and we can sometimes pretend to be sad. Many great masters possess that level of realization.

Let me go back and clarify a point which may be confusing. Performing virtuous actions, forming mental conceptions and verbally reciting things are all potentially beneficial activities. Beginners should divide their practice into a time of solely engaging in virtuous actions and set aside another time to train only in the view of Mahamudra, which is nonconceptual wakefulness. Compared to anger, compassion is virtuous and very beneficial, but compared to nonconceptual wakefulness, compassion is still clothed in concepts. Whenever there are concepts, there is fixation. Whenever there is fixation, it hampers or obscures nonconceptual wakefulness. A black curtain obscures light, of course, but a fine silk curtain also obscures light.

Of course, in Buddhism there are different stages or level of compassion. Beyond the ordinary compassion directed at other sentient beings is the 'compassion that takes truth as focus'. That is to direct one's attention to all phenomena, all things, and see that nothing is permanent, nothing lasts. Everything is seemingly existent, while having no core in itself. Everything is hollow, empty. Understanding that the deluded mental state is unrealized and is therefore mistaken generates great compassion for the deluded state of mind that does not realize the emptiness and impermanence of all things.

Still, the normal compassion that takes sentient beings as a focus and the compassion that takes the truth as focus are both conceptual. Neither of them are the direct experience of emptiness. The third type of compassion, called 'compassion devoid of focus,' is in itself the direct experience of emptiness.

When explaining the real condition of awareness, a teacher might sometimes say, "At this point, you don't need normal conceptual compassion." Please understand this correctly: it is because of conceptual love and compassion that you we are able to realize emptiness. The state of mind of love and compassion is a very pure state of mind, a very 'clean' concept. Trust and devoted interest are very clean and pure. For that reason, they make very good circumstances for nonconceptual wakefulness to occur. But they are not, in themselves, that state of nonconceptual wakefulness.

The compassion, love and trust of a beginner, of a normal person, are biased and continually fluctuating. Sometimes we feel we can encompass everyone with our compassionate heart. Sometimes its scope narrows down to include only a few sentient beings; and sometimes it completely vanishes. But the love and compassion present in the mind of a yogi or practitioner who has directly realized self-existing wakefulness is unchanging and totally without prejudice. This is a very important point. In the beginning, we do need to develop love and compassion, trust and devotion, because these qualities make it possible to experience nonconceptual wakefulness. However, at the moment of concentrating on the view of Mahamudra, nonconceptual wakefulness, we don't need to engender ordinary love and compassion, because they are conceptual and thus obscure the view.

How do we destroy the delusion of our body, speech and mind? First, leave the body in a relaxed position, and avoid being rigid or tense. The best posture is the seven-fold posture of Vairochana. The voice and breathing should be relaxed and uncontrolled. To prepare the mind, one should have love and compassion for all beings — the attitude of bodhichitta and trust in and devotion to the lineage gurus.

Then the actual practice is to allow nonconceptual wakefulness to unfold. When allowing such awareness, there is initially a short moment totally free from disturbing emotions and normal thought activity. This very clear, fresh and naked state doesn't seem to last very long. It almost immediately vanishes in the jungle of concepts. This is due to the fact that we are not yet accustomed to it; we haven't really trained enough to be familiar with it. We might think, "Ah! Now it's right. I've gotten it! This is the face of awareness; this is the essence that is the uncompounded unity of being empty and cognizant!" Or, we may think, "Oh no! Now I've lost it. This isn't it. This is wrong!" But — and this is very important — whatever thought we have about the natural state, be it positive or negative, immediately obscures it! This is a very tricky issue here. If we 'meditate' conceptually, that's wrong, but if we don't meditate in the sense of training or practicing, that's also wrong. The basic wakefulness is 'self-existing' or 'intrinsic'; that means it is something we already have; our own natural possession. There is no need to create or fabricate it. It is already our basic nature and, as well, it is already the unity of being empty and cognizant. So, simply allow its continuity to be sustained. This is the real thing, not the imitation. Remember, it is not something new or invented for the occasion.

When we receive the pointing-out instructions, the master will, after giving some practical guidance, say, "That's it! This is your buddha-nature. It is indivisible emptiness and cognizance!" Our job is then to recognize, to acknowledge that state. After one or two times of being shown this, we might then feel, "Now I've got it. Now I've recognized buddha-nature." But to simply leave the matter like that is not good enough. It's the same as being given a flower seed and being told, "This is a real, genuine flower seed." If we then ignore it, if we carelessly leave it unplanted, it will never grow.

You may already, through the oral instructions of a vajra master, have directly recognized the face of awareness. But unless you rest repeatedly in that state, again and again, conceptual thinking will always interrupt its continuity. Awareness will not remain naked; it will always get covered up again. In other words, without practice it is difficult to master the experience of the natural state.

First of all, even though the teachings tell us to rest free from thought, it is essential to have one particular thought. We must start with the thought, "I should now sustain the face of awareness." This is called 'mindfulness'. It is both a reminder and a thought. However, it is the most beneficial of all types of thoughts, because this particular thought leads to the nonconceptual awakened state. Without this thought or intention, it is very difficult to sustain the state of awareness. Although we may be distracted, the more often this thought occurs, the more often we will sustain the natural face of awareness. Thus, this thought is something we need to have whether we are sitting in so-called meditation or are engaging in daily activity. When we are distracted, we should always remind ourselves with this thought. First recognize awareness, exactly as it is. Next, when forgetting to recognize, utilize the reminder of mindfulness. Then, no matter where you go or what you do, you will very quickly progress through the paths and bhumis. If we do these two things — recognizing the natural face and being constantly mindful — then even if we stay in the crowded, confusing setting of a big city, we will quickly progress. Without these two essentials, even if we remain on retreat in a solitary mountain cave, we will be no better than tigers and deer.

If we have not recognized the natural face of awareness and we don't have any insight into emptiness, then there can be no genuine practice of that insight to implement. On the other hand, if we glimpse the natural state of mind once and think, "Oh, I've got it. This is enough" — there is nothing worse than that kind of misunderstanding.

Once again, first of all, the vital point is to recognize our nature. Next, we need to train and perfect the strength of that recognition. The only way to train is to be mindful. This 'remindfulness' of thinking "I should rest in awareness" must be repeated again and again, like the constant and steady flow of a river. A river flows continuously; it doesn't vacillate. We need to apply mindfulness in a similar fashion.

Mindfulness is necessary in all three vehicles. Likewise, in ordinary worldly life, we need to be mindful, because if we keep presence of mind, we are gentle and careful. In Hinayana practice, the shravakas consider carefulness and mindfulness to be indispensable. In the context of Mahamudra and Dzogchen, mindfulness may be considered a conceptual frame of mind, a thought. Yet it is because of this conceptual thought that we are led to the state that is nonconceptual.

At this point you might think, why don't we just remain totally free from thoughts and conceptual thinking — why not simply immerse ourselves in a nonconceptual and uninterrupted state of wakefulness. Why doesn't it just happen automatically? Because we are unaccustomed to this state! Because of this, we need the 'trigger' of this thought of mindfulness. Among all the thoughts, the best is, "I must allow natural awareness to be sustained!" This thought leads to the nonconceptual state.

In order to have this presence of mind as a reminder, we need to appreciate that such nonconceptual awareness is both precious and important. By understanding some of the qualities of the natural face of awareness, we will spontaneously feel interest and trust. Feeling this, we will naturally want to put rigpa into practice. One thing is dependent upon the other here: interest and trust are mutually supportive. When we truly recognize this natural state of awareness, interest and confidence become automatic. If we haven't truly or fully recognized, then we stray into laziness and procrastination. When we truly appreciate that there is nothing more important or valuable than the state of nonconceptual awareness, we will not have to force ourselves to be mindful.

When something really important is about to happen in our life — when something captivates our full interest and heart — it stays acutely in our mind. The moment we wake up in the morning, we think about it. It is the same if it is something we dread. Something that is really prized or treasured, and something that is deeply feared — both situations command our full attention.

The whole reason for engaging in any Dharma practice whatsoever, and the key point of all the teachings, is exactly this: how to reach enlightenment. There is absolutely no other purpose than that.

It's in order to approach this that all these pleasant and sweet-sounding teachings, as well as all the various spectacular trappings of religious culture, were created. Therefore, when the teachings tell us that the nature of awareness is the buddha-mind — and when we know this, truly and fully — it becomes impossible not to want to put it into practice. We can't help ourselves. To use a negative example, it becomes addictive, like a drug. Being addicted to heroin is very destructive, but it is because of so deeply appreciating the sensation you get that you are captivated by it.

In the same way, when we personally recognize the state of innate wakefulness, we gain true confidence and true trust. Other kinds of trust involve merely assuming that the teacher is right. Because he sits up on a throne, looks nice and speaks very convincingly, we think that what he says is probably true. Maybe his words make sense logically or sound pleasant. Still, at this point we don't really know this or accept this truth from our heart. In the moment of recognizing mind-essence, we can for the first time give rise to true trust. Confident trust and unshakable trust in one's teacher comes solely from realizing the nature of emptiness.

Sometimes we might disparage ourselves, thinking, "I am unable to remain mindful. Mindfulness always slips away. I can't practice!" But listen to this: by recognizing emptiness, mindfulness becomes much stronger.

While we are beginners, we need to distinguish between two types of thoughts: the thought that serves as a reminder and all other types of thoughts. The thought "I should recognize mind essence" leads to recognizing mind essence; all other thoughts don't. As we train more and more, though, any kind of thought can eventually serve as a reminder. That may sound very strange; it's like saying, "The more thoughts, the more dharmakaya!" If thoughts in themselves were dharmakaya, all sentient beings would be enlightened. But for a yogi, a developed practitioner, any thought leads to dharmakaya. Therefore, he can claim, 'The more thoughts, the more dharmakaya'.

At first, it is difficult to train in a mind essence you haven't recognized. It's also difficult to practice when you have recognized it but have not become accustomed to it. Through training, everything becomes spontaneous and automatic. It is like learning to drive a car: at first it's really difficult because we need to pay attention to all the details. Later, though, we don't have to think about it that much; the feet and hands move automatically, without much conscious thought.

As we become more practiced in recognizing empty, naked awareness free from conceptions, the force of ordinary ignorant thought weakens. Awareness grows stronger, meaning clearer, brighter, and longer-lasting. It's no longer a mere glimpse, but a moment that lasts longer and longer. Awareness also becomes easier to sustain, which means that the moment of awareness increases of its own accord, without having to deliberately try to extend it. Of course this becomes easier during the meditation state, in a formal practice session. But when we leave our cushion behind and engage in daily activities, we should also be mindful, in the sense of remembering the natural face of awareness. Thus, we should be mindful while meditating, and also during post-meditation. When engaging in the activities of daily life, we need to remind ourselves repeatedly: then it will last longer and arise more often. Through such training, it is said that the strength of awareness grows further. In other words, the natural qualities of awareness have the opportunity to develop further.

At this point of your training, when a thought first occurs, you needn't apply a remedy to try to stop it. By simply leaving it to itself, it naturally dissolves. What is important is that, as soon as you start to think of something, you look into the thinker, and at that moment you recognize the emptiness and cognizance which are the natural state. That itself is the remedy. We don't have to apply some other kind of antidote to the thought. When a snake ties itself in a knot, there is no need for anyone else to help the snake untie the knot. It is naturally untied.

STUDENT: What do you need to do to prepare to receive the pointing-out instruction?

RINPOCHE: A lot of preparation is necessary. What is most important, though, is to have sincere interest and a sense of deep trust.

STUDENT: How does one liberate thinking as it arises?

RINPOCHE: When the mind is free from concepts, the empty, luminous essence can be seen. How to be free from fixation is described in many different ways. Although words are inevitably misleading, we still use phrases like 'looking towards the attention,' or 'sustaining the essence'. We start to think, and thinking, of course, is dependent upon our attention holding onto or grasping the object of thought. When this holding on is released, the act of thinking and conceptualizing falls apart. As long as we give it life by continuously holding onto the thought of 'such-and-such,' thinking can never dissolve. This is a very important point: you cannot destroy the thoughts however hard you try, but they can collapse or dissolve.

What method causes thoughts to collapse? On a coarse level, we must let go of the reference points created by labeling things as this and that. On a more subtle level, we must relinquish any kind of concepts of the past, present and future — even the concepts 'it's empty' or 'it's not empty'. In short, when you are free of fixation or of ego-clinging, the thought simply falls apart; it disintegrates. It is not a matter of you actively destroying the thought. Trying to do so really only makes things worse.

STUDENT: Doesn't another thought arise after the first one collapses?

RINPOCHE: Of course it does! That is because we have not trained to the point of becoming fully adept. We don't remain very long in this state because we are not used to it. But still, the moment you completely let go of all fixation, the innate nature, ultimate truth, is immediately met face to face. The reason for this is because all things in themselves are empty and devoid of self-entity. To experience the innate, naked state when one is free from assumptions or concepts is not something that only Buddhists have a claim on.

STUDENT: In the state of stabilized awareness there is no delusion, correct? So, if I don't have the concept of 'my body,' then what does the body do? Will it be difficult for my body or whoever it is that owns my body?

RINPOCHE: Beginners do not experience a pure state of awareness that lasts continuously. Awareness fluctuates, though as you train it becomes longer and longer. At that stage, half the time your normal thinking takes care of your body and the other half of the time pure awareness takes care of your body. When there is nothing but pure awareness, that basic wakefulness takes care of the body. At the attainment of total stability, at the end of this life there can occur what is called 'departure in a rainbow body,' in which the physical body dematerializes or disintegrates into rainbow light.

STUDENT: Right now most of us are continuously under the power of conflicting emotions. Sometimes we might think that we glimpse awareness, but how can we know if this short moment is real or not?

RINPOCHE: There's a big difference between the real and the false version. The false, being false, doesn't possess the qualities of real nondual awareness. The difference is that the real moment of awareness is free from disturbing emotions, free from conceptual thinking, free from anxiety, hope and fear, like and dislike. It's also free from being unconscious, oblivious or dull. If we have a thought-free state which is vacant or absent-minded, that is definitely not the moment of rigpa, pure awareness. Please check it yourself, through your own personal experience. If the state is free from any holding on or fixation, is neither dull nor oblivious, and has a sense of wakefulness, then that is buddha-nature.

STUDENT: What about a state that is free of thought movement?

RINPOCHE: That's the definition of *shamatha* — stillness.

STUDENT: What is the connection between rigpa and the six sense perceptions?

RINPOCHE: Usually, perception takes place because of the meeting between sense object, sense organ and the perceiving mind. When these elements meet, there's a moment called perception, which is then labeled and conceptualized and responded to. But that whole setup is dualistic. When the dualistic fixation is absent, when there is no conceptual link between subject, object and sense organ, this is called rigpa. The usual word for consciousness, in Tibetan *namshey*, means 'making a thought about the object'. That is not rigpa. In other words, mental fabrication is not true nondual awareness. In fact, the absence of mental fabrication is awareness. In the moment of rigpa, there is seeing and hearing, but there is no fixating on that. This awakened state is traditionally described like this: "The five senses wide open; wakefulness free from reference point." Normally our senses are not at all blocked, they are clear and wide open. But if we are involved in labeling and discerning, that is not the state of rigpa.

STUDENT: If there is no attempt to apply any remedy for the arising of a thought, then what is the difference between a samsaric person and a practitioner?

RINPOCHE: At the moment of thinking a thought, a normal person lets the thought remain as it is in the state of thinking and carries on in that state. A practitioner also lets the thought remain just as it is, but he or she also recognizes that its essence is the unity of being empty and cognizant — dharmadhatu wisdom, in short. That's the difference between a samsaric person and a practitioner.

STUDENT When you tell us not to get caught up in conceptual virtuous practice, isn't there the danger of us becoming totally insensitive and careless?

RINPOCHE: You have to make a clear distinction here. Conceptual activity lasts as long as we have not truly realized the nonconceptual state of awareness. Until the state is utterly unceasing, then of course we still stray into concepts, and therefore we commit both negative and positive actions. There are thus results of those actions which we will surely experience. So, we must definitely be careful about how we behave and what we do. We should try our best to engage in virtuous actions and avoid negative actions. However, the one who is totally realized, meaning one who never deviates from the state of nonconceptual awareness, will never engage in a single unvirtuous action and hence does not need to be careful. It's very important to be clear about this.

When I mentioned earlier that one doesn't need conceptual virtuous practice or compassion, I was referring exclusively to the very moment of sustaining the view. This is not a general blanket statement. In the moment of the natural state of awareness, any reference point, any concept or thought is not pure genuine awareness. We must discern the difference. The point is that the natural face of awareness is harmed even by good concepts. Many people think if they merely have a good heart, that will suffice. However, even the thought 'I have a good heart' harms the state of awareness. We already said that love, compassion and trust are extremely precious and vital, and that it is due to these that at the outset we are even able to recognize the state of awareness. But in the moment of the natural state of awareness, conceptual compassion, conceptual love, conceptual trust are all impediments.

The moment of awareness in the case of a developed practitioner does possesses love and compassion, trust and devotion, but these feelings are of a type that is very difficult to comprehend and grasp. They doesn't fit into our normal understanding. They are totally uncontrived and unchanging, and one hundred percent sincere. Our present trust and compassion, in comparison, is usually contrived or fabricated to some extent.

STUDENT: Isn't the love a mother has for her child completely natural and uncontrived

RINPOCHE: It does of course arise spontaneously, but this love is still based on the concept 'my child and me'. Notice that it's 'my child': other people's children are not as important as one's own. This is certainly natural. But tigers and lions also have natural love and compassion for their offspring! It's how they love that is different. We must recognize that the love of a normal person is biased, limited and changeable.

The love a mother has for a child when the child is sweet and well-behaved is different from the love a mother has for her child when it's really naughty. It changes, but never completely disappears, of course. There is also a difference between different mothers' love for their children — it varies from mother to mother. One thing is quite generally true, though. Before a baby is born the mother considers herself the most important person in the world, as is normal for all of us. After the baby is born, though, the child becomes most important and the mother becomes second in importance. That sacrifice of our natural selfishness is why, in Buddhism, we speak of 'our kind mothers'.

When we first train in compassion, we acknowledge and appreciate the love our mother had for us. Actually, all sentient beings have been our own mother in past lives; aside from time, there is no real difference. We then try to expand that feeling of appreciation and gratitude to include all sentient beings and we cultivate the sincere wish to benefit all of them. Since compassion and love should be all-accomplishing and unbiased, this is a method for changing our limited, selective love and compassion into impartial, unbiased love and compassion. If we don't truly recognize that all sentient beings have been our father and mother at one point or another in our countless lives, our love and compassion remains limited. But if we can recognize the universality of our previous connections, it is possible to free our love and compassion from partiality.

STUDENT: One of course feels incredible biased love towards one's own child. How do we break the attachment?

RINPOCHE: This is why I mentioned that all beings — not just all adults — have been our own mothers at one time or another. When we start to acknowledge that, then at best, we will view all beings as equal. At the very least we will not be disdainful towards anyone else, and that includes the children of other parents.

STUDENT: Is there some karmic responsibility involved in being a parent? If you don't do it correctly, do you create worse karma?

RINPOCHE: Certainly. One must be careful when responsible for a child. Being a good mother, a good parent, is important. We should be a good parent to our own children, but that doesn't mean we don't care for other people's children.

STUDENT: Where do discursive thoughts come from, if they are not intrinsic to the mind?

RINPOCHE: They occur through what is called habitual tendencies. A momentary thought arises out of habitual tendency. When you really look into a thought, do you find a place where it arises from, a place where it is right now or a place where it vanishes to? Thought is truly something very strange, because we can't find it anywhere. It's impossible to pinpoint, but still it functions. Moreover, we cannot pinpoint the origin of anything whatsoever in this world, because everything is beyond arising, dwelling and ceasing.

STUDENT: Can thoughts be controlled by other methods?

RINPOCHE: Of course there are many other methods of thought control, but they are more indirect. For example, there is the yogic exercises of controlling breath, essences and channels through utilizing a few key points. Still, one needs to exercise mindfulness, even after these exercises. Without mindfulness, there is no way to master your thinking.

STUDENT: Doesn't the term 'to be aware' mean you must be aware of something?

RINPOCHE: The Tibetan word I use for awareness is 'rigpa,' which can also be used in different contexts. For example, in ordinary Buddhist philosophy rigpa refers to 'knowing,' a conceptual state of mind in which there is subject, object and the act of cognizing. But the same word applied in the context of these teachings refers to a state of mind which is not within this dualistic setup. Here, it is self-existing wakefulness that is called rigpa or awareness. Buddha-nature itself is also called rigpa or awareness. There's no problem with using the word rigpa, the trouble arises when one doesn't know what it is referring to. Here, the definition of rigpa is self-existing wakefulness that is both empty and cognizant, but free from subject and object.

STUDENT: For me, the term 'to be aware' implies a state that is not vacant or blank. How do we avoid straying into dullness if we don't have a conscious focus?

RINPOCHE: The basic capacity for knowing or being aware can either stray into labeling subject and object or it can simply remain as the capacity of knowing. That is the dividing point between ignorance and knowing, delusion and no delusion. At that point, one must be free from the two limitations of eternalism and nihilism, the two extremes of believing "It is something!" or "There is nothing!" If you do so, at this moment you are freed from the belief in awareness being 'something'. After all, this state is described as 'awareness free from reference point,' right? At the same time, the five senses are totally open and there is a definite ability to know, so it is not some kind of 'nothing'. This basic state of mind, free from concepts, should be one of original wakefulness. How does that happen? If we simply space out or sit in an absent-minded state, that's wrong. If we stray into the normal conscious states of "I am here" and "something is there," that's also wrong. What is necessary is that one does not stray into these two extremes. How? We need to experience this original wakefulness. The Tibetan word used for original wakefulness is *yeshe,* which is defined as 'original knowing without any conditions, such as holding anything or conceptualizing anything'. This is an innate natural quality, or energy, if you like.

We should scrutinize until original wakefulness is seen free from all assumptions. In other words, until there are no more assumptions we should scrutinize; but remember the act of scrutinizing is still conceptual. In short, you must use conceptual states to carry you to the nonconceptual. The act of resolving is conceptual, but that which is decided upon is nonconceptual. While sustaining the natural state of awareness, any kind of fixating or thinking is improper. Even normal compassion and trust are a type of fixation, as they are conceptual. This is very simple, but very true. Look at it this way: when a thought arises and you don't fixate on it, it is no longer a normal thought.

STUDENT: How do we relax?

RINPOCHE: It's very easy to relax the voice — simply refrain from talking. Relaxing the mind means to avoid getting involved in subject and object thoughts of past, present and future. There are different analogies for relaxing the body. Sometimes the relaxed body is said to be like a corpse abandoned in a charnel ground. Sometimes it is said that the relaxed body should be placed in the seven-fold posture of Vairochana. This is very difficult in the beginning, but when one grows accustomed to it, it is an extremely good circumstance supporting rapid progress in samadhi.

Rigpa

We have already covered two of the Four Seals of Dharma: how all conditioned things are impermanent, and how everything defiling is painful. We will now continue discussing the third seal, which states that 'all things are empty and devoid of self'.

All three vehicles accept that all phenomena are empty and devoid of self, and we previously discussed the ways in which this idea is interpreted. We are now studying the view of Vajrayana, the pinnacle of which includes *Mahamudra* or *Dzogchen*. As I mentioned earlier, there are two ways to approach the view. One approach is through the analytical meditation of a scholar. We have already touched a bit upon the arguments and logic of this approach. Now we are concentrating on the other approach, the 'resting meditation of a simple meditator,' that utilizes a few words of pith instruction. I will continue in this style, using direct teachings focusing on the vital points and offering the method for sustaining the nature of awareness.

As I previously mentioned, we must distinguish between two terms — sem and rigpa. 'Sem' means thinking; 'rigpa' is translated as awareness. Rigpa here is the same as dharmakaya, while sem is conceptual mind. Once again, whatever is discovered or experienced by the unaware state of mind, the state of mind that does not question or analyze, is called conventional truth. That which is discovered or experienced after correct analysis or examination by the mind free of delusion is called ultimate truth.

Ultimate truth is also defined as that which is experienced by a noble, unmistaken being. On the other hand, conventional truth — a reality which people normally believe to be permanent — is experienced by a mistaken, deluded, non-discerning state of mind. Unfortunately, a misconception is often created through the difference between these two. It is not the case that there is some nasty, evil thing called conventional truth that we should try our best to get rid of or that there is some perfect pure ultimate truth we should try to gain. Actually, the true condition, the very nature of conventional truth is, in itself, the ultimate truth.

For example, in the case of all things being impermanent, 'permanence' implies some continuation, a lasting duration of time. When we examine time itself, though, we find it is only a sequence of present moments. And when we carefully examine the present moment, we find no 'thing' to pinpoint. There is actually nothing that can be called the 'present moment'! In other words, it is empty of a truly existent 'something'. That is its real condition, what is ultimately true. In this way, by carefully examining the conventional truth, we discover the ultimate truth. By fully understanding how all conditioned things are impermanent, we are able to realize emptiness — the ultimate truth.

To reiterate: what is experienced by a mistaken undiscerning state of mind is called conventional truth, while what is experienced by wisdom, the unmistaken state, is called ultimate truth. It is pretty obvious that we should train in experiencing what is truly real — the ultimate truth. This insight is also called the 'knowledge that realizes egolessness,' or self-existing awareness that is nonconceptual and cognizant'. This is a very essential point.

Self-existing awareness that is cognizant and nonconceptual is called rigpa. In Mahamudra, it is called ordinary mind — tamal gyi shepa. Ordinary mind is defined as dharmakaya that is not dependent upon the three conditions of bliss, clarity and nonthought. It is also beyond the four joys — the four types of bliss. This is the real, ultimate Mahamudra. There are other types of Mahamudra, sometimes called the 'Mahamudra of bliss and emptiness or the Mahamudra of clarity and emptiness', but those are stepping stones leading to the real Mahamudra.

Based on or supported by the four types of bliss or the four joys, one can ascend to the real Mahamudra. If one doesn't cling to them, the three conditions or experiences of bliss, clarity and nonthought can be supports for Mahamudra. However, the real Mahamudra, free from mental constructs, is not dependent upon the three conditions, and it transcends or lies beyond the four joys. The innate nature, *dharmata,* which transcends these is called the 'Mahamudra of empty awareness'. This is not different in the slightest from the view of Dzogchen, the Great Perfection. Mahamudra's ordinary mind and Dzogchen's self-existing wisdom that is cognizant and nonconceptual are totally identical.

Of course, there is quite some difference between the ordinary mind that is not dependent upon the three conditions and lies beyond the four joys, and the deluded, ordinary mind that is dependent upon the three conditions or four joys. One type can be shown by a teacher and experienced by the disciple; thus, there is some experience that is dependent. The real Mahamudra, ordinary mind, can neither be demonstrated by the master nor realized by the disciple. It is not a 'thing' to realize or experience. That's why Tilopa said; "I have nothing whatsoever to show you. There is only what you can experience by yourself." What does this mean?

No matter what words we use, they inevitably lie within the domain of concepts. Yet if we don't use words as conceptual pointers, we won't realize the ultimate truth. Paradoxically, holding onto conceptual words and terms impairs the ultimate truth. That is why Mahamudra is described by the words 'mental nondoing'. Any act of doing something mentally is not Mahamudra. Mental nonfabrication is not an object of thought or concept. That's why it cannot be shown or demonstrated. It's also not some 'thing' to be experienced. In the beginning, though, when we start to practice, we must have something that can be shown and experienced. Unless we have that, we will take the wrong track. Yet as we progress in our practice, anything that we can think of, conceptualize or hold as an object of our experience is conditioned and conceptual and is thus not the ultimate state.

As mentioned before, the elaborate leads us to simplicity. For example, the first two of the four schools of Buddhist philosophy teach how all outer things are empty, but hold that on a small scale, atoms and moments of consciousness do exist. In other words, they manage to destroy most ideas we have about things in the world, but some remnant remains. That remnant is destroyed by the Mind Only school, which demonstrates that all things — atoms and moments of consciousness — are empty, but there is still something called self-cognizing mind — some cognizant quality that is considered to ultimately exist. That concept is in turn destroyed by Madhyamika, which realizes that all things are free from the 'four limitations and eight constructs'. When directly and truly realizing the view of Madhyamika free from the four extremes and eight constructs, all ideas are totally destroyed. In this way, by progressing through the four schools our understanding becomes more and more subtle, increasingly refined.

If we believe something exists, that's mistaken. If we hold the idea that it does not exist, that's also mistaken. Any fixation on notions of existence or nonexistence must be abandoned. It is said, 'To hold the idea that things exist is to be the same as an animal. But to hold that they don't exist is even worse' It is also said: "As long as we fail to destroy all fixation on existence and nonexistence, we have not realized the view of the Middle Way." If we believe that things do exist, we stray into the extreme of permanence, while if we believe that things do not exist, we stray into nihilism.

Let me go into more detail about what in the general vehicles is called buddha-nature or *sugata-garbha*. This buddha-nature is naturally present in all sentient beings, without any difference in size or quality. Buddha-nature is also called rigpa or self-existing awareness. Sometimes it is called ordinary mind: that which is not dependent upon the three conditions and which transcends the four joys. It is the innate nature of things, exactly as it is.

This self-existing awareness is cognizant and nonconceptual. 'Self-existing' means it is aware all by itself: it is not made by anyone, nor created in any way. 'Cognizant' and 'nonconceptual' mean it has the capacity to know, perceive and understand without being the normal conceptual state of mind. That's why it is called 'self-existing awareness that is cognizant and nonconceptual'. That is what we mean by the word rigpa.

When sustaining this state of rigpa, we must first recognize what rigpa is — otherwise what is there to continue or maintain? Rigpa possesses the capacity or the potential for the kayas and wisdoms of buddhahood to manifest. It is our innate nature, unspoiled by thinking and concepts, uncontaminated by thought constructs. It is the real condition, innate suchness. Actually, it is very neat to call it 'ordinary mind'. Ordinary mind in this sense does not refer to the mind of an ordinary person. It refers to a state of mind that is totally unspoiled, that is uncorrupted by any kind of disturbing emotions, conceptual thoughts or fixation.

We can call it ordinary mind, self-existing awareness or buddha-nature — whatever we call *it*, that 'it' is always present in ourselves. Unfortunately we usually fail to recognize what is already present as our own basic nature. No one else can recognize this intrinsic self-existing wakefulness for us. The very moment we abandon all conceptual activity such as accepting or rejecting, keeping or sending off, judging or evaluating, ordinary mind, self-existing awareness, is naturally present. If we say we want clear water, not muddy water, but keep stirring it up, will the water ever get clear? In the same way, if you don't muddle self-existing awareness, you will find that it is inherently present all by itself.

On one hand, it's very difficult to talk about this, isn't it? On the other hand, it is so easy that there is almost no need for words. In fact, any dependence on words spoils it. Our true nature is a state which is beyond any statements that can be made about it. And yet even though this is true, we still talk about it. It's incorrect to simply claim, "There's no method!" However, any method or technique we might use is not a hundred percent clean. That's why it is said the true nature 'cannot be demonstrated or shown'. When this becomes real for you, then all these 84,000 types of Dharma teachings may seem pointless, because what you get to at the end is that it cannot be taught. Think about this!

If our basic nature were something that could be directly shown or taught and we could experience it tangibly and concretely, our experience would remain within the concepts of subject, object and action. Therefore, ultimate truth, the real condition or innate state, is, by itself, totally free from and beyond any words, concepts or objects to be experienced. We call it self-existing awareness that is fresh, naked; our innate nature, which lies beyond conception and discernment. Right now, we need to be clear about the difference between sem and rigpa. We have been talking about them and defining their meaning: now we need to discern their meaning.

STUDENT: If the essence of mind is rigpa, why is rigpa veiled by sem?

RINPOCHE: The essence of sem is certainly rigpa. The very identity of that which thinks is awareness. This is what is meant by the famous statement: "The nature of mind is *sugata-garbha*." But you also hear that though buddha-nature is present, it is covered by obscurations — the karmic, emotional, habitual and cognitive obscurations.

STUDENT: Is the essence of the covering itself rigpa?

RINPOCHE: Yes, that's correct. The essence itself is unobscured, but it is covered by concepts. The nature of that which conceptualizes is pure awareness. We have defined ordinary mind, *thamal gyi shepa*, as being independent of the three experiences of bliss, clarity and nonthought and beyond the experience of the four joys or four types of bliss. That kind of ordinary mind is totally identical with *rangjung rigpa*, self-existing awareness. This is a vital point.

That which is experienced by an unmistaken state of mind is ultimate truth. Self-existing awareness is not a concrete thing, an object to experience. Whenever there is a thing to be experienced, that is the product of a mistaken frame of mind. All things, by themselves, are by their nature empty and devoid of self. Thus, the absence of a 'thingness' experienced by an unmistaken mind is called self-existing awareness.

When we say "recognizing the natural face of awareness," is there some 'thing' to recognize? Is there any actual recognizing taking place? If we use the phrase 'recognizing the nature of awareness,' it seems that there should be a nature to recognize, doesn't it. Otherwise, why even talk about it? But if there is a recognizer and a concrete thing being recognized, that is dualistic experience and therefore not self-existing awareness. Understand that without using words we don't understand ultimate truth, but words are never one hundred percent clean; they can never give you the full meaning. That which is discovered or experienced by an unmistaken state of mind is free from any concept of self or 'I'. This is the unmistaken nature of all things exactly as it is. This nature is already empty and devoid of self. When speaking about it, we must use words like 'experiencing,' 'recognizing,' and 'realizing'.

What is actually realized or recognized? To put it simply, it is a gap, an absence of any kind of dualistic fixation, hope or fear or subtle anxiety. What remains in the absence of all those is rigpa. We can call it self-existing wakefulness or, as it is called in the general vehicles, the 'knowledge that realizes egolessness'. Rigpa is described as being primordially pure in essence and spontaneously present in nature — in other words, the unity of emptiness and cognizance. Since the worst two views are eternalism and nihilism, we need something to destroy these two views. Because rigpa is primordially pure in essence, it destroys the view of eternalism or permanence. Because it is spontaneously present, the idea of nonexistence also does not apply. This transcendence of extremes is called equality or the wisdom of equality.

We are already quite accomplished, so to speak, in believing in the existence of a self where no self exists. Up until this point, we have trained in and become used to believing in things as being permanent while they are not. Now we need to change our training. This is not easy at first, because these two viewpoints are in conflict, in contradiction. The moment disturbing emotions, conceptual thinking, hope and fear, accepting and rejecting are absent, that is called self-existing awareness. Although this needs to be sustained, it is not an object of meditation. It is more the act of growing accustomed to something which already exists. If we have already recognized this moment of self-existing awareness, then we simply allow it to be sustained. It doesn't continue perpetually, of course, because it is interrupted again by our normal thinking. Even if we are a practitioner who has recognized awareness and who tries to sustain it, we will still be carried away by thoughts.

As I said before, of the different kinds of thoughts, the most excellent is the thought of mindfulness. The thought of mindfulness will not carry one away into distraction. If there is authentic mindfulness, then no matter how many thoughts occur, each thought will dissolve back into the state of the union of empty cognizance. Here is an example illustrating this: the average person's thinking is like writing on paper, solidified and coarse. For a beginner who tries to sustain awareness, thoughts do occur. We're not free from thoughts. The key point is not to follow the thoughts like a normal person, but to let the thoughts dissolve, like writing on water. When writing on water, the writing disappears while it is being written. As we train in ordinary mind, in self-existing awareness that is fresh and naked, we will still have thoughts, but the thoughts become less strong. Gradually they lose their strength, their grip on us. All the way up through the bhumis or bodhisattva levels, we are not free from thoughts. A practitioner will have thoughts, but at the same time, their impact is reduced: they do not create very much benefit or harm. This is quite an important point to understand, so we will stop here. It's better to say only this much and then have some discussion about it.

STUDENT: If it's impossible to explain the nature of mind in words, why did the Buddha give so many teachings?

RINPOCHE: To show or point out mind essence, a master might say, "What you have within yourself is this. That's it." To some extent it can be taught. Otherwise, if it could not be taught, there is nothing to point out and there's no point whatsoever in giving all the 84,000 Dharma teachings. Milarepa said something like this: "When the Buddha taught the lower vehicles, his clarity and precision were amazing. But when he reached the subtler points of the higher teachings on the Third Turning, the Dharma Wheel of Total Uncovering, and tried to describe exactly how the profound, unelaborate, uncompounded nature really is, even the Buddha's tongue had trouble. The Buddha is very kind and skillful and acts only for the benefit of others; otherwise I might dispute his efforts." Because all things in themselves are totally beyond constructs and concepts, every word we use is basically misleading. A person who has reached the state of complete enlightenment, like Milarepa, is allowed to say these things. If we say it, though, it doesn't sound so convincing. Our viewpoint is hardly ultimate.

STUDENT: It seems like it is easier to dissolve ordinary thoughts, but what should we do with really gross emotions when they arise?

RINPOCHE: When we are really upset or disturbed, everyone knows that it's more difficult. For a practitioner who has recognized the nature of awareness, though, it is better to have an emotion that's really upsetting. For such a practitioner, there is only one remedy to apply — a presence of mind which is even stronger and more forceful than the gross emotion. For a practitioner like this, strong emotions are in fact a better training- ground than a kind of neutral, indifferent, wishy-washy undercurrent of thought which is harder to notice and therefore harder to deal with.

STUDENT: Isn't mindfulness just another thought?

RINPOCHE: Sure, but without the thought to recognize, without 're-mindfulness,' we'll never even think of recognizing the natural state of awareness. We first need that thought, 'I should recognize'. In the moment of having reminded oneself, the reminder should be dropped. The reminder is not itself self-existing awareness. If we just maintain a continuous state of reminding, that is in principle the same as ordinary thinking. For example, when we put an arrow on a bow-string, we first pull back, but next we need to let it go, to release it; otherwise the arrow will never fly. In the same way, we shouldn't keep holding onto the reminder — we should let it go.

STUDENT: Are the three experiences of bliss, clarity and nonthought always harmful or can we utilize them somehow?

RINPOCHE: The arising of any experience which is dependent upon the three experiences of bliss, clarity and nonthought or the four kinds of joy means there is some subtle concept present. Rigpa itself is totally free from the duality of an object of observation and an observer. There are many details to this, which is why in Mahamudra there are twelve aspects of the four yogas. The real, true, ultimate Mahamudra is independent of the three experiences of bliss, clarity and nonthought and beyond the experience of the four types of joy. Still, while practicing on the path, the three conditions and the four joys are aids, and can be used as helpers. Of course, we should know how to *use* them as helpers; otherwise, our involvement with them becomes harmful. If we know how to use the three experiences of bliss, clarity and nonthought, they help to bring about the enhancement of ordinary mind. Otherwise, they become circumstances for going astray.

STUDENT: What is the difference between luminosity and clarity?

RINPOCHE: There is a famous statement in the Prajnaparamita sutras: "Mind is devoid of mind. The nature of mind is luminous cognizance." In this instance, the Tibetan word for 'luminosity,' *ösel,* means that although it is totally empty, there is still the capacity for omniscient qualities to manifest. The Tibetan word for 'clarity' is *salwa*. You can also use it as an abstract noun, *salcha,* which then means 'cognizant quality'. There is a difference between saying, "The lamp is bright" or "The lamp has a strong brightness." 'Brightness' here is more precise, more descriptive.

TRANSLATOR: I would like to add that some of the problems in translating come about because the same Tibetan word is used differently. I'm using two different English words to describe these two different meanings. Here, 'clarity' is used to indicate the temporary, impermanent experience which is among bliss, clarity and nonthought. 'Luminosity,' on the other hand, refers to the cognizant quality which is unchanging. It is the nature of the mind itself.

STUDENT: What is the difference between the experience of nonthought and the state of shamatha? Also, could you explain the differences between the three experiences of bliss, clarity and nonthought?

RINPOCHE: First of all, it is taught that clinging to the three experiences of bliss, clarity and nonthought causes us to get stuck in or stray into the three realms of samsara. When we try to experience emptiness or put emptiness into practice, then these three experiences of bliss, clarity and nonthought are quite likely to occur. These experiences are fleeting and are bound to perish sooner or later, just like a cloud in the sky. It is a grave mistake to equate a temporary meditation experience with realization. That's why it is said, "Experiences are like mist; they fade and vanish. Realization is unchanging, like space."

Here we are mentioning three temporary meditation experiences, but there are not just three; there are many, many different kinds. The best way to deal with them is not to be fascinated by the show. Neither accept nor reject them. Let them arise when they arise, let them disappear when they disappear. When we are not involved in hope and fear, accepting and rejecting, then they are just qualities. But if we think, 'Great! How nice!,' that becomes a fault. In short, the key point is to be free from fixation. We must be free from fixation in regard to the view as well as to temporary experiences.

With respect to your first question, there are different kinds of stillness or *shamatha*. There is something called 'shamatha cessation' that is very similar to nonthought. Then there is nonthought without clarity and nonthought with clarity. If the experience of nonthought is without clarity and is very dense, dull and obscured, this is called 'shamatha cessation' or 'frozen stillness'. If the state of nonthought has a lot of clarity and brightness, a lot of presence of mind, it is very different from the former, and it's described and termed differently. It's very hard to generalize about this. We have to discuss each state of mind in its own context.

STUDENT: Is the moment of cessation of thought the time to be introduced to the nature of mind?

RINPOCHE: The possibility of pointing out the natural state of awareness depends upon both the teacher and the student. We cannot define the exact conditions. For example, the *Madhyamaka Avatara* says "The cessation of mind is the actualization of the dharmakaya." What does the ceasing of mind mean? There should be an absence of conceptualizing and discerning. Nagarjuna gave many pointing-out instructions that are woven into the *Madhyamaka Avatara*. What he means here is that the moment your involvement in thoughts of past, present and future ceases and the intellectual acts of accepting and rejecting, establishing and denying, are absent, then the uncompounded unity of being empty and cognizant — the dharmakaya itself — is vividly present, in actuality.

STUDENT: Does the absence of conceptual thinking happen perpetually or just in that one moment?

RINPOCHE: The thinking mind should cease, but in a skillful way. There are various states of 'no mind': something called the 'state of indifference,' where there is no coarse movement of thought, no involvement, no judging, and no clarity. There is also the state of having fainted or fallen unconscious, at which time there is no thought of 'this' and 'that,' or of good and bad. Then there is deep sleep, when we later have no idea where the time went. The cessation of the thinking mind which Nagarjuna refers to is unlike those ordinary mindless states. It is free from the thoughts of the three times, with cognizance, and without fixation. Dzogchen terminology describes this state with phrases such as 'vividly clear,' 'wide awake,' 'free and easy'. 'Free and easy' means you are almost ready to levitate; you are not at all heavy or weighted down by concepts.

STUDENT: How can conceptual thinking obscure the ultimate nature?

RINPOCHE: The initial confusion, the basic mistakenness, comes from thinking 'I am'. This is called coemergent ignorance or innate ignorance. It is ego-clinging; fixating on something. It means 'I am real'. It then becomes more solidified and almost tangible. That is what obscures. Thinking 'I am' is mistaken, and the act of holding the notion 'I am' is deluded — it's ignorant. If you are the one harming yourself, you are thus the only one who can stop doing so, right? In the same way, the concept 'I am' is what causes us to continue in samsaric existence. It is called innate ego-clinging and it is quite strong right now.

How is it that such conceptual thinking can obscure our vast true nature? Even a small cloud seems to obscure the sky. Likewise, a tiny room effectively manages to block out the whole vast space outside. That's how it is when our obscurations are present and solid and real. That which is obscured may be endless and vast, but it still seems obscured.

STUDENT: Does bringing thought to an end, as described in the term 'cessation of thought,' mean to suppress our thoughts?

RINPOCHE: Blocking one's thinking and bringing the thinking to an end are different. When we try to block off thinking, we cannot. It's impossible. The thinking just gets stronger instead. That's why it is said, "When stopping the mind, one must be skillful."

STUDENT: Is it beneficial to suppress thoughts or experiences by becoming skilled in shamatha?

RINPOCHE: It depends upon which kind of shamatha you are talking about. In the context we are currently discussing, shamatha and vipashyana are a unity. In this specific context, I call 'shamatha' the quality of being uncontaminated by or unengaged in thoughts and emotions. At the same time, there is a natural cognizant awareness which I call 'vipashyana'. This is one of the better types of shamatha, and it is in this context that it is said, "The unity of shamatha and vipashyana is the buddha-mind" — the naked state of empty awareness.

Usually shamatha is practiced to cultivate peacefulness. But no matter how much we try, our minds never remain one hundred percent peaceful, because our thinking and emotions haven't totally ceased. Shamatha practice means that they have only been temporarily suspended. Thus, when we meet with the right circumstances they are ready to pop up again and wreak havoc. What we are talking about here in this context is not necessarily something that lasts for a long while, but at the very moment of the genuine natural state of awareness, there is no thought and no disturbing emotion present at all. It is totally gone, vanished. This is a point of incredible importance.

The View

Up to this point we have covered the first three maxims of the Four Seals of Dharma;

> Everything conditioned is impermanent.
> Everything defiling is painful.
> All phenomena are empty and devoid of self.

Today we will discuss this third point further. All three vehicles accept that all phenomena are empty and devoid of self, but they differ in how they explain the meaning of this statement. The four schools of Buddhist philosophy — Vaibhashika, Sautrantika, Chittamatra and Madhyamika — differ as well in terms of the depth and simplicity of their approach. For instance, the way of explaining through the view of Madhyamika, Mahamudra and Dzogchen while focusing on the key points is known as the tradition of pith instructions.

There are different types of Madhyamika viewpoints, such as the Rangtong and Shentong schools. The correct view in Madhyamika is the wisdom of emptiness indivisible from compassion that is free from the four limits and the eight constructs. That is the ultimate view, and should be applied in one's practice. It's better to call this approach of bringing the true view of Madhyamika into personal experience 'the Great Middle Way of the Definitive Meaning'.

Similarly, Mahamudra can be expounded in great detail — for instance, when discussing Mahamudra of ground, Mahamudra of path, and Mahamudra of fruition. Then there are the twelve aspects of the four yogas of Mahamudra. Another way of explaining Mahamudra is according to the Sutra system, according to the tantras, and according to the essential approach called Essence Mahamudra. In addition, when Mahamudra is explained according to the five paths and ten bhumis, there are an incredible number of details.

In Mahamudra, the phrase *thamal gyi shepa*, ordinary mind, is used to indicate your present fresh wakefulness. To look directly at and rest evenly in your innate state, free from all fixation, is the view of Mahamudra. When you don't try to modify or change this present fresh and naked awareness in any way whatsoever, this is itself the view of Dzogchen, the Great Perfection.

When one begins the practice of the view of the definitive meaning, of present ordinary mind in Mahamudra, there is a method called the yoga of One-Pointedness. 'Yoga' here means that the method is embraced by wakefulness. The yoga of One-Pointedness involves resting continuously in the state of ordinary mind, of non-fabrication. To have cut through conceptions and doubt is called Simplicity. To be free from accepting and rejecting, adopting and avoiding, is called One Taste. To have purified intellectual understanding and experience is called Nonmeditation. In this way, there are many distinctions that can be made.

The eight consciousnesses, or the eight collections of cognition, must be purified. I will now explain how they are purified according to Mahamudra. At the time of One-Pointedness, the aggregate of physical forms and the consciousnesses of the five senses are purified. At the time of Simplicity, the skandhas or aggregates of sensations, conceptions, and consciousnesses are purified. At the time of One Taste, the skandha of formations is abandoned and the defiled ego-consciousness is purified. At the time of Nonmeditation, the aggregate of consciousnesses is abandoned and the all-ground consciousness, *alaya-vijnana* is purified.

In Vajrayana, the term 'empowerment' is often used. This is a very important term which I will go into greater detail about soon. Usually there are four empowerments, the fourth being the 'precious word empowerment'. Everything that appears and exists is primordially pervaded by the empty awareness. When one has recognized, trained and attained stability in this, the five aggregates, the five elements, the consciousnesses, objects and so forth are all purified. Everything becomes part of the continuous state of purity which encompasses the kayas and wisdoms. While training further in the state of Mahamudra and Dzogchen — for instance, through the view of 'cutting through,' *Trekchö* — one perfects the training in the view realized through the fourth empowerment. 'Training' is in the context of recognizing, training and attaining stability. The more we train, the more adept we become, and the closer we are to attaining stability.

The Dzogchen teachings say that ground and fruition are indivisible. On the path, we should, of course, have some degree of comprehension, experience and conviction; but if we retain these at the time of fruition, they are a fault. When we are on the path and begin training, we must have some intellectual understanding of what we're doing. We need to know what emptiness is and have some personal experience of it. Ultimately, though, if we hold onto any kind of conviction about how emptiness is, that is a conceptual frame of mind, a mere habitual tendency. The point where the notions of meditator, the object of meditation, and the act of meditation have been left behind is called 'the dharmakaya throne of nonmeditation'. All habitual tendencies and convictions are obliterated at this point.

For example, if you visit an island where everything is made of pure gold, even if you search for an ordinary stone or pebble, you won't find one anywhere. In the same way, when a Dzogchen practitioner reaches the dharmakaya throne of nonmeditation, everything that appears and exists is the realm of dharmakaya. The world and its beings will all be experienced as the realm of the continuous state of dharmakaya.

At this point, any sense of accepting or rejecting, hope or fear, like or dislike, have been totally cleared away; completely uprooted, eradicated. This is possible because hope and fear, anxiety or any desire to accept or reject are all of a momentary nature. Since ground and fruition are indivisible, these are not present in the ground state. However, at the time of the path, these appear because of mistakenly believing in a self. Habitual tendencies and emotions create karma, and their results are then experienced.

In order to reach the dharmakaya throne of nonmeditation, we should understand and put into practice the ground, path and fruition: the ground as the two truths, the path as the two accumulations, and the fruition as the two kayas. As mentioned before, the two truths are conventional truth and ultimate truth. Conventional truth is whatever is experienced by a mistaken conceptual state of mind that has not questioned or examined anything. Having questioned and examined, the ultimate truth is the discovery of awareness, rigpa, which is totally unconstructed. In another sense, conventional truth is what is seemingly real while perceiving, whereas ultimate truth is what is real while experiencing the essence. Both are real and feel true, but they differ in *how* they are real and true.

In short, we should understand the ground as being the unity of the two truths. After understanding the view of the unity of the two truths, we can then practice the path that is the unity of the two accumulations. The 'two accumulations' are the accumulation of merit with concepts and the accumulation of wisdom free from concepts. The accumulation of merit with concepts is the seed or cause of the form kayas, nirmanakaya and sambhogakaya. The accumulation of wisdom free from concepts, achieved through resting in pure awareness free from any mental constructs, is the seed for realizing dharmakaya. At the time of the path, we should definitely practice the accumulations of merit with concepts, but it must be saturated by the accumulation of wisdom free from concepts.

In particular for Vajrayana practitioners, of both the New or Old Schools, any kind of sadhana or visualization practice always takes place within the framework of the three samadhis. The most important is the 'samadhi of suchness', which is exactly the same as what the general vehicles call buddha-nature. In the terminology of Dzogchen it is called self-existing awareness. Without the samadhi of suchness, any development stage or visualization of deities is by definition imperfect. The other two samadhis, the 'samadhi of illumination' and the 'samadhi of the seed-syllable', should take place within the samadhi of suchness. In short, when we practice the path we must unify the two accumulations. The accumulation of merit with concepts or reference point means there is the notion of an 'I' who is doing that practice. It is not pure in the sense of being free from the three types of concepts. The accumulation of wisdom free from concepts is also called the 'three-fold purity'. The practice of three-fold purity is to relax into the state of nonconceptual wakefulness. In other words, we should not practice the two accumulations as separate or totally different. When we engage in a conceptual Dharma practice, the accumulation of merit, we should embrace that with the accumulation of wisdom free from concepts. Otherwise, the three excellences are never complete.

The three excellences are the excellent preparation of bodhichitta, the excellent main part free from reference point and the excellent conclusion of dedicating the merit. No matter what practice we do, whether we stay in retreat and engage in intensive meditation sessions or whether we chant a single rosary of OM MANI PADME HUNG, we should always embrace our virtuous practice with these three excellences. Even if the spiritual practice we do is very short, when embraced by the three excellences it becomes forceful and profound. Any Dharma practice we engage in without embracing it with the three excellences will be like perishable goods.

The 'excellent preparation of bodhichitta' includes both taking refuge and generating bodhichitta. The 'excellent main part free from reference point' is the particular part within a conceptual practice when we rest simply, either when dissolving the visualization or after receiving the four empowerments in the guru yoga practice. There is always a period like this that should never be abbreviated. The 'excellent conclusion of dedicating' means at the end of our practice, we mentally sum up all its merit and make this wish: "May this be for the benefit of all sentient beings." We should always do this immediately after finishing practice. Any kind of Dharma practice we engage in that is framed by these three excellences becomes genuine and effective. Any practice that is not endowed with these three is not an authentic Dharma practice.

The 'fruition as the two kayas' means that the rupakaya, which includes both the nirmanakaya and sambhogakaya, is pervaded by or embraced by dharmakaya. Dharmakaya is free from constructs, like space. It is the mind of the buddhas. Sometimes, dharmakaya is depicted as Samantabhadra or Vajradhara, but that is of course not the real dharmakaya. Dharmakaya has no form. Sambhogakaya is adorned with the major and minor marks and endowed with the five certainties. There are various types of nirmanakaya: the first, called 'supreme nirmanakaya,' is a rare occurrence, such as the incarnation of Buddha Shakyamuni. Other types include incarnated nirmanakaya, variegated nirmanakaya and created nirmanakaya, all of which act for the welfare of sentient beings.

I have briefly explained ground, path and fruition so that we can understand what is necessary in order to attain stability. This is a topic I will come back to and discuss in greater depth. For now, let me just say that when we grow used to the practice of primordial purity, to recognizing the natural face of awareness, that recognition then continues into the nighttime. It is possible to recognize during the sleeping state so that the state of awareness becomes uninterrupted throughout day and night. In short, it is not enough to only recognize the mind essence. We need to train. Similarly, it is not enough to train just a little bit and develop some slight strength. We need to continue undistractedly like the steady flow of a river until we attain complete stability.

STUDENT: If this state is described as cognizant yet nonconceptual, how does seeing taking place?

RINPOCHE: Perceptions don't disappear, but there is no conceptualizing as to 'this is this' and 'that is that." No reference point is being formulated. In the Dzogchen teachings, this is described as unaltered and unimpaired. Everything, all perceptions, are unaltered and unimpaired. There is no flaw or fault. It is like Tilopa said: "You are not fettered by appearances. You are fettered by clinging. Cut your attachment, Naropa."

STUDENT: Is it all right to only practice nonconceptual wakefulness and nothing else in order to attain stability in it or do we need to do other practices to stabilize our recognition of awareness?

RINPOCHE: First of all, it is difficult to practice only the wisdom free from reference point, even though it is the best. In order to recognize how to practice the accumulation of wisdom free from reference point, we do the accumulation of merit with concepts. Then, conceptual practices of the accumulation of merit are helpful and beneficial in order to enhance and become more stable in that recognition. Remember, the accumulation of merit with concepts is upaya, skillful means, and the accumulation of wisdom free from reference point is *prajna*, discriminating knowledge. The particular definitions of these differ according to the different vehicles. For a Hinayana practitioner, contemplating repulsiveness, impermanence, and dependent origination are skillful means, while that knowledge aspect is shamatha and vipashyana. For a Mahayana practitioner who practices the *six paramitas,* the sixth paramita of transcendent knowledge is the knowledge aspect and the first five are the skillful means. According to Vajrayana, to visualize one's body as the pure form of the deity, to use one's voice to chant the mantra, and to imagine one's environment as the pure buddhafield and celestial palace is skillful means, while resting the mind in the completion stage is the knowledge aspect. Let's have some discussion now.

STUDENT: What is the importance of the guru yoga practice?

RINPOCHE: In Tibetan guru yoga is *lamey naljor*. In the word *naljor,* or 'yoga,' *nal* means the real or genuine and *jor* means to achieve or reach. So what should we reach or achieve through guru yoga? We should receive the four empowerments, purify the four obscurations and attain the four kayas. To put it briefly, we should achieve the genuine, authentic and true natural state realized by the guru — not only achieve it, but assimilate it and realize it. We who practice guru yoga should try to realize the genuine innate nature in exactly the same way as it is present in the mind of the guru, with no difference whatsoever. The metaphor used here is 'like an image made from a mould' — in other words, an identical replica.

Guru yoga is not just thinking of the form of your personal Vajrayana master: it is also a training in devotion and in receiving the blessings. Through visualizing the lama's form, we generate devotion. Through devotion, we receive the blessings. Because of receiving the blessings, realization takes place.

STUDENT: Can a beginner recognize the natural state when a very forceful emotion arises?

RINPOCHE: If our emotion is extremely forceful, then it is certainly difficult to recognize, because we get overpowered and carried away by the emotion. On the other hand, it's also very difficult to deal with a state of mind that is indifferent and unclear, due to an undercurrent of unnoticed thoughts and feelings. It's best to begin training with a state that is somewhere in between these two emotional extremes. In fact, compared to the state of dullness, intense thoughts and emotions are easier to recognize and deal with.

STUDENT: In the Nyingma system, does one practice until recognizing rigpa and then practice rigpa all along the rest of the path to buddhahood? What about the other practices, such as mind-training and visualizing deities, chanting mantras and so forth?

RINPOCHE: Whether it is Nyingma or the other three schools, the practice of the three excellences is exactly the same, beginning with refuge and bodhichitta, then practicing the main part free from reference point, and finally dedicating the merit. Everything is contained within these three points. In the beginning, it is difficult to approach the state of nonconceptual wakefulness itself; so many practices have been developed to act as stepping stones leading to that state. No matter what kind of practice we do, the ultimate outcome of the practice should be enlightenment. The only cause of enlightenment is to realize the mind of the buddhas, and that comes from practicing the samadhi of suchness. The samadhi of suchness is, in itself, the nonconceptual natural state of awareness. If we want to attain complete enlightenment, there is no way we can avoid recognizing and stabilizing the awakened state of rigpa. All other practices are simply helpers that lead to that. The awakened state is a very subtle and difficult point to understand, so we are spending a lot of time on it. It is also the most vital and important point, like the engine of an airplane.

STUDENT: Isn't it because we need to work and engage in daily activities that we are unable to quickly attain stability in awareness?

RINPOCHE: There's no need to blame our inability to become stable in rigpa on our daily activities. Even when we are not engaged in activities, thoughts are being churned out one after the other. We may close our doors and windows and lie down quietly on our bed — but still, although our thoughts have no arms and legs, they do all kinds of things ceaselessly. They will not remain still for even one minute. So don't blame daily life activities for the confused state of our minds — it's not their fault. Really! Right now we have all sorts of different ideas and concepts about this and that: they arise automatically. Whether we engage in daily activities or not, they arise in exactly the same way. There's no difference. There are many conditions which cause thoughts to arise — outer as well as inner. Outer conditions are what we run into when we are out dealing with the world. Inner conditions are what create thoughts even when we are lying quietly in our room.

STUDENT: Are there thoughts in the mind of a fully enlightened Buddha?

RINPOCHE: In the mind of an enlightened Buddha, thoughts have been changed into wisdom. They function as wisdom. When we buy two kilos of potatoes, we understand two kilos of potatoes, right? A buddha will not only understand the exact amount, but he will simultaneously know which particular potatoes of his two kilos have any subtle flaws — which have insects inside and which don't.

STUDENT: I feel there is a contradiction between what most traditional Tibetan masters teach and what you are saying. Can you talk more about the need to practice the traditional path and how it combines with what you are openly teaching here?

RINPOCHE: First of all, you know it's difficult to achieve what is called the precious human body endowed with the eight freedoms and ten riches. It's not easy, right? Among people who have the precious human body, those who have interest in the essential teachings are quite few. Among those who have interest, those who actually put it into practice are even fewer. For those who wish to practice, it is rare that they connect with a truly qualified master. These days, it seems that in many parts of the world there is an increasing interest in the essential teachings, but masters and teachers cannot be in all those places. Therefore, people with genuine interest must often go through a lot of hardships to connect with a qualified teacher.

Things are often difficult from the other end as well. It has often happened that qualified masters have wasted a lot of time in different places because there were no qualified students present. In the past, Smritijnana, a great Indian siddha who was a very accomplished and learned master, through his supernatural powers saw that his dead mother had been reborn in Tibet in unfortunate circumstances. He took a translator with him and went to Tibet to find his mother and liberate her. On the way, the translator died, and the master was left alone in Tibet unable to speak the language. He eventually found work herding sheep on the mountainside, but he was unable to give any teachings, and finally he died. Later on, the great master Atisha heard about what had happened to Smrirtijnana: that he had gone to Tibet, found no students and passed away. Learning of his situation, the masters were extremely saddened, clasping their hands together and shedding many tears. It can happen that way. Recently, a great master named Deshung Rinpoche spent about 25 years in North America. For most of the time he had no students at all, only in the last years did he teach a few. And still he stayed there.

Each master has his own style. Some masters say, "Unless you finish your preliminary practices; I will not teach you about the view." That's perfectly all right for people who have trust in Buddhism, trust in the teacher, and who believe in the cause and consequence of karmic actions, past and future lives. Some people appreciate Buddhism because the view is extremely profound and exceptionally clear. The more we examine, the more we question and the deeper we get, the tastier it becomes. These days, most of the foreigners I meet have a predominant interest in the view. They ask many questions about how to understand emptiness. Some masters, when connecting with a student, will wait a little while before discussing the more profound points of the teachings, thinking, 'I will explain that later'. Other masters will just speak freely and directly. One reason for that might be that nothing is predictable these days, and it is never certain how long a student and master can remain together.

STUDENT: What is the use of all these complicated practices?

RINPOCHE: First of all, can you remain, uninterruptedly, day and night, in unfabricated naturalness? If you cannot, then what's the use of remaining unable to do so? Isn't it better to do something to support the recognition? Conceptual practice is fabrication, and it is artificial, but among the different types of artificial activities it's the most helpful. However, if you go to the marketplace and sit as though you are totally in simplicity, that is also very artificial. When engaging in the preliminaries, to show off how many you are able to do or how diligent you are is likewise wrong. There are many kinds of artifice. Your question is best answered by this statement: It is the contrived that leads to the uncontrived.

STUDENT: Does realization of emptiness depend on intelligence, or can a simple person with diligence in guru yoga attain it?

RINPOCHE: It's certainly possible; in fact, it's not only possible, but has happened innumerable times. You should read the life-stories of practitioners. It might seem as though one needs to study a lot to understand emptiness. However, realization does not depend upon scholarship.

STUDENT: How to combine the practice of prostrations with recognizing mind nature?

RINPOCHE: It depends on the practitioner. If one is not a beginner, but is already quite familiar with the natural state, with the samadhi of suchness, then that can be practiced while doing prostrations. One does not have to leave the state of naturalness in order to do prostrations. Even while circumambulating around sacred objects, one can recognize mind nature. If this is difficult, then practice this way: first generate the motivation. Next, imagine the object to whom one bows down, such as the buddhas and bodhisattvas, and visualize being in the company of all sentient beings. Then everyone bows down together, and at the conclusion rays of light purify oneself and all sentient beings. Afterwards, dissolve what has been imagined and rest in naturalness for a while. That particular duration is called the 'excellent main part free from reference point'.

Conceptual practices are important for a beginner because one cannot just remain in the nonconceptual state for a long time. It doesn't happen that way, so it's better to engage in the conceptual type of spiritual practices called 'gathering the accumulations' and 'purifying obscurations'. It is said that when obscurations are purified, realization occurs automatically.

Indivisibility

The main point of the Four Seals of Dharma is that all things are empty and devoid of self. Not realizing that, we wander in samsaric existence. Realizing this in actuality, we attain enlightenment. This is the Buddhist view that is accepted by all four schools of Buddhist philosophy as well as by the four major schools of Tibetan Buddhism.

According to the Nyingma tradition, when attempting to 'let confusion dawn as wisdom,' one trains in the emptiness and lack of self of all phenomena. The same approach is used in the Kagyü lineage. The Sakya lineage has a teaching called *Parting from the Four Attachments* that states:

> If you cling to this life, you are not a practitioner;
> If you cling to samsaric existence, you lack renunciation;
> If you cling to selfish aims, you lack bodhichitta;
> If you fixate or cling to anything, you lack the correct view.

The fourth line means that as long as one holds the idea that things are not empty and that there is a self, one's view is incorrect. Hence there is no liberation or enlightenment.

According to the Geluk tradition, the accepted view is the unity of emptiness and dependent origination. The great master Tsongkhapa wrote four lines of poetry that state:

> The nature of samsara and nirvana lacks even an atom of existence.
> The dependent origination of cause and effect is unfailing.
> These two are mutually without conflict; in fact, they are a support for one another.
> May we realize the intent of Nagarjuna.

Although both samsara and nirvana seem to truly exist, in actuality they have no real existence. For something to be seemingly existing and ultimately nonexistent is not a contradiction. In other words, everything is devoid of true existence, while at the same time, the dependent origination of the cause and consequence of karma is unfailing. These two aspects are without conflict. That is how the two truths are indivisible and why everything can manifest and appear. That is what is meant by:

> Form is emptiness; emptiness also is form.
> Emptiness is no other than form.
> Form is no other than emptiness

While being empty, everything is experienced; while being experienced, everything is still empty. The indivisibility of these two is called 'the unity of experience and emptiness'. We must realize that all things are empty and devoid of self. The Vajrayana methods of realizing this are extremely clear and direct.

Whichever teaching we practice, whichever of the three or nine vehicles we pursue, the main thing to implement in our own practice is that all things are empty and devoid of self-entity. Traditionally the Buddha gave three turnings of the Wheel of Dharma. The Second Turning emphasizes the empty aspect of things, while the Third Turning describes the unity of being empty and cognizant. Different philosophical viewpoints have emerged from these different turnings: for example, the Mahayana schools of Mind Only and Madhyamika, the Svatantrika and Prasangika, and the Rangtong and Shentong schools.

The term 'Hinayana follower' refers to a person who holds the view that all coarse things are empty, but are composed of something — such as atoms and moments of consciousness — which has true or ultimate existence. A Hinayana follower cannot accept that everything is empty. He believes there must be *something*. That is why this attitude is called 'Hinayana' or 'lesser vehicle'. In opposition to this is the Mind Only school of Mahayana, which holds that nothing really exists and everything is only a mental presence, appearing to and in the mind. In this view, everything is 'mind only'; there is nothing which ultimately exists but the self-cognizant mind.

A higher viewpoint is taken by the Madhyamika school. According to this school, all phenomena are beyond arising, dwelling and ceasing, not existing and not not existing, not both and not neither. Since any statement made about the ultimate state is biased, Madhyamika followers maintain the innate nature is indescribable and inconceivable — in short, that it is utter simplicity. The ultimate Madhyamika point of view is totally free from asserting any claims or value judgments whatsoever. It recognizes the real nature of things as completely beyond any concepts. This is exactly the view realized in the teachings of Mahamudra and Dzogchen, where it is described with phrases such as 'unfabricated awareness' and 'self-existing wakefulness'.

To recognize this self-existing wakefulness that encompasses all samsaric and nirvanic states, also known as the 'unchanging great bliss,' we must receive oral instructions. One approach is to first be introduced to the fact that all experiences are mental perceptions. Then one is shown that these mental perceptions are empty, that this emptiness is unconstructed, and that unconstructed emptiness is self-liberated, naturally free. Finally, one realizes that this self-liberation is dharmakaya and that dharmakaya is primordially all-pervasive.

When we talk about this in the context of Mahamudra, there are three sections: ground Mahamudra, path Mahamudra and fruition Mahamudra. First, the essential nature of things — the mind of the buddhas as well as the mind essence of sentient beings — does not exist in terms of having color or shape, center or edge. Free from limitations and partiality, it knows neither existence nor nonexistence. That is ground Mahamudra. We can also call it 'the great all-pervasive wakefulness encompassing all of samsara and nirvana'. This is the ground.

We cannot say that this great wakefulness that encompasses all of samsara and nirvana is a 'thing' that exists, but neither can we say that there is nothing at all. It does not fall within any limitations or categories such as existing or not existing. Sentient beings are said to be deluded, bewildered and ignorant. However, their very basis, the ground of the great wakefulness, is never deluded, confused or bewildered. The ground is not a 'thing' that can be changed through causes and conditions. We say that the Buddha is extremely skilled and expert, but not even the Buddha can alter this great wakefulness. Although ordinary beings are densely obscured by the veils of karma, disturbing emotions and habitual tendencies, their basic wisdom is not obscured at all.

When realizing this wakefulness, it does not improve in any way whatsoever. In the same way, when this all-encompassing wakefulness is obscured, as in the case of sentient beings, it is not at all impaired or worsened. It is like the sun in the sky: the sun itself is never obscured or veiled, regardless of the clouds which cause it to be invisible. The tantras describe this great wakefulness as '*emptiness endowed with the supreme of all aspects that is indivisible from unchanging great bliss*'. In the *Uttaratantra,* wakefulness is described as transcendent permanence, transcendent bliss, transcendent purity and transcendent identity.

So, the ground is free from delusion. Delusion occurs on the path. What we need to recognize and put into practice is this ground Mahamudra. No matter what name we give to it — rigpa, inherent wakefulness, or ordinary mind — the ground itself is what should be brought into practical experience. The ground itself, and nothing other than that, is what should be sustained in experience. This is called path Mahamudra.

The tradition of pith instructions tells us: "Once you recognize ground Mahamudra, you must sustain it without fixating and without distraction." 'Without fixating' means if we fixate on it being something to understand as 'the view,' this intellectual understanding is not path Mahamudra. 'Without distraction' means the state of ground Mahamudra is sustained when we are undistracted, and dissipates when we are distracted. It is not something we can cultivate mentally. Letting ground Mahamudra continue means to simply sustain the natural state. What is achieved or gained by this? We meet, experience, and realize the innate truth of dharmata.

This is called 'liberation,' and it is nothing other than being naturally free. Unlike a product of a deliberate action, this is not something we *do* in order to get liberated. In short, path Mahamudra is to recognize the ground, your basic state, as unfabricated ordinary mind, and to sustain that without concepts.

Fruition Mahamudra is free from something that liberates, free from hope and fear. That means there is no separate remedy that liberates you. Therefore, the view in Mahamudra is free from hope and fear: free from having to accept one thing and reject something else. When that is sustained, one arrives at what is called the 'exhaustion of concepts and phenomena'. At the time of the path, we usually gain some kind of conviction or certainty; but later on, even that kind of conceptual conviction — 'This is it!' — is dropped. The fruition is thus liberation even from conviction.

At the outset, we must gain some intellectual understanding of what is being communicated. Next, we must have some trust or confidence that, 'I can practice this. I can apply this in my practice'. We must be sure about the difference, the dividing line, between what ordinary mind is and what it is not.

As we gain stability through the training, all thinking will, by itself, become dharmakaya. As I mentioned before, it is like arriving on an island where everything is pure gold; we are unable to find any ordinary stones. At that time, there is no need for conceptual understanding, experience, or convictions, such as, "Now I understand! Now I'm experiencing it! Now, I've got it!" These useless formulations will fall away automatically. It is not that we have to get rid of them. Even if we try to, we can't. There is not much point in that anyway. They fall away by themselves.

So, in this sense, ground and fruition are one, indivisible. It is the space in between, called 'path,' where confusion and the clearing up of confusion takes place. Ultimately, the great wakefulness that encompasses all of existence is the same at the time of the ground as it is at the time of the fruition. Milarepa said, "Practice the Mahamudra of ground, path and fruition as one," meaning that there is actually no difference between ground Mahamudra, path Mahamudra or fruition Mahamudra. The ordinary mind, the unfabricated naturalness that is the ground should be practiced as the path. We do not attain anything other than simply continuing and attaining stability in that. Any questions on this?

STUDENT: Is there a difference between the view of Madhyamika and that of Mahamudra or Dzogchen?

RINPOCHE: That depends upon what you understand by Madhyamika, how it is explained and in what context. Madhyamika is generally connected to the second turning of the Dharma Wheel and focuses more on emptiness than anything else. If it is, however, the type of Madhyamika called 'the Great Middle Way of the Definitive Meaning,' this approach places more emphasis on the cognizant or luminous aspect involving the kayas and wisdoms, which is connected with the Third Turning of the Dharma Wheel. Some learned scholars say that the Rangtong school of Madhyamika is closer to the Second Turning of the Dharma Wheel, while the Shentong school of Madhyamika is closer to the Third Turning. For a scholar in a teaching setting, it is easier to teach the Rangtong view. Those teachers who emphasize practice will lean more towards the Shentong view.

In Tibet, there was an incredibly great scholar, the eighth Karmapa, Mikyö Dorje, who wrote an extremely detailed commentary on Nagarjuna's text called the *Madhyamika Avatara — Entering the Middle Way*. Something strange happened while he was writing it. Most of it is written according to the Rangtong view, but near the end he started to switch over to the Shentong view. When people studied his commentary they became a little baffled and asked him about it. He said; "At an early age, I gained strong confidence and conviction in the Rangtong view through intellectual study and reflection. But as I met many great realized masters, asked questions and practiced further on my own, I came to trust the Shentong view more."

The great, realized and learned master Jamgön Kongtrül Lodrö Thaye wrote a commentary on the *Uttaratantra*. In it he establishes how the two viewpoints of Madhyamika, Rangtong and Shentong, are totally without any conflict or contradiction. It's a very good book to study.

STUDENT: How do you describe the existence of this great wakefulness that encompasses all of samsara and nirvana?

RINPOCHE: When we examine and question things, we discover that things in themselves do not possess any identity whatsoever, that they are not independent entities. It's not too difficult to arrive at this conclusion intellectually. That is the empty aspect. This is why scholars dispute the statement, "There is enlightenment!" because there is a fault in claiming 'is'. Nevertheless, there is a graver fault in alleging, "There *isn't*!" If there is nothing — no knowledge, no omniscient enlightenment — then what is the point in talking about path and fruition? If we were to say there is no great wakefulness that encompasses all of samsara and nirvana, that creates the fault of asserting that there is no enlightenment. The great wakefulness that encompasses all of samsara and nirvana is our innate nature that lies beyond conceptual mind. Because it is beyond concepts, it is not an object to argue about.

STUDENT: What is the difference between Mahamudra and Dzogchen? Is it possible to attain rainbow body through both? Does a great master's attainment of the rainbow body depend on outer circumstances?

RINPOCHE: There are different types of Mahamudra, such as the Mahamudra that is empty bliss, empty clarity and empty awareness. The Mahamudra of empty awareness is the same view as the view of Dzogchen. The other two types of Mahamudra come about through taking as supports the three conditions of bliss, clarity and nonthought or the sixteen types of wisdom resulting from the four joys. They are stepping-stones to reach the Mahamudra of empty awareness, which is the real state of Mahamudra, naked ordinary mind. That is the same as the view in Dzogchen called *Kadag Trekchö* — the 'cutting through of primordial purity'.

The term 'rainbow body' is used about the death of an accomplished practitioner of the Dzogchen practice called *Lhündrub Tögal,* the 'direct crossing of spontaneous presence'. This does not mean a Mahamudra master can't attain rainbow body: an attainment similar to rainbow body can be reached through practicing the Six Yogas of Naropa. Rainbow body is accomplished when a practitioner is well-established in the view of Trekchö and reaches accomplishment in the meditation practice of Tögal. Rainbow body can occur if both outer and inner circumstances are conducive. One of the important factors is whether or not there are any disturbances of samaya. If the person stays alone and has pure samayas, it's easier for him or her to attain rainbow body. Great accomplished masters have said; "No enemies can do me any harm whatsoever. The only thing that can disturb me is violated samayas." This is true whether the broken samayas are between teacher and student or simply through close contact with other people who are samaya-breakers. Broken samayas are the only thing that can taint realization. That's why practitioners who stay in secluded mountain retreats were more likely to attain rainbow body.

There are many stories about great masters, the gurus themselves, who stayed as the heads of monasteries not accomplishing rainbow body while their disciples who stayed in retreat did. Recently though, there was a master named Nyagla Pema Düdül who attained rainbow body witnessed by 500 of his disciples.

STUDENT: What about the mahasiddhas of India?

RINPOCHE: Their life-stories mention that 'they went to the celestial realms of the dakinis without leaving a physical body behind'. That probably means that their physical body changed and became a body of light.

STUDENT: One Zen book I've read describes the practice of simply keeping one's posture. There is nothing to see or meditate upon or to gain or attain: one merely remains beyond thought and description. Is that the same as what is being taught here?

RINPOCHE: I have met several Zen teachers and we have had a few discussions. Their viewpoint is what is expressed in the *Heart Sutra, the Sutra of Transcendent Knowledge*. They are more focused on the empty quality, and they don't talk much about the cognizant or clarity aspect. Otherwise, it is similar.

STUDENT: Is that like the Hashang view which says, "Simply don't think?"

RINPOCHE: The Zen teachers I met didn't say, "Don't think". They said "Remain beyond thinking." That is different from "Don't think!"

STUDENT: Does the phrase 'knows neither delusion nor liberation' mean there is some kind of knowledge?

RINPOCHE: The statement 'Knows neither delusion nor liberation,' doesn't imply anything about knowing — it means 'doesn't have'. It is an English figure of speech, such as 'It knows no boundary'. It doesn't mean it 'knows' but that it 'has' no boundary. Ground and fruition are both beyond confusion and liberation. If you regard them as not being beyond confusion and liberation, there is some fault in that.

STUDENT: How does one actually approach the practice of the Six Yogas of Naropa?

RINPOCHE: Traditionally, the practice of Mahamudra is approached like this: first one engages in the preliminary practices, the ngöndro. Then one engages in *yidam* practice with recitation of mantra. After gaining some stability in that, one is introduced to the Mahamudra practice itself. At that point, one can utilize the path of means, the Six Yogas of Naropa, in order to enhance and progress in Mahamudra practice. So, the Six Yogas are practiced on the basis of Mahamudra, because they cannot really be taught to someone who has no understanding of Mahamudra.

For example, practices such as dream yoga, illusory body, the luminosity of deep sleep and so forth must be trained in while within the state of Mahamudra. There is no recognizing the nature of luminosity of deep sleep separate from the practice of Mahamudra.

In the Six Yogas of Naropa, different key points are utilized. One visualizes the channels, or *nadis,* in the body, and trains in the energies or winds, called *prana.* There are actually two kinds of prana, pure and impure. They are called *klesha-prana* and *jnana-prana,* 'disturbed wind' and 'wisdom wind'. By using certain techniques, one can control the impure aspect and help unfold the pure aspect, the wisdom channels and wisdom winds. That's the basic principle behind the Six Yogas. They are essentially helpers to hasten realization.

STUDENT: I have heard that dullness and agitation are signs of practicing the path. A beginner needs to do something in order to get rid of these, but ultimately one should go beyond accepting and rejecting. How does one know whether or not one should try to change them?

RINPOCHE: First of all, dullness and agitation are, by definition, that which takes over and obscures ordinary mind — the state of Mahamudra — so that one does not recognize it. When there is dullness and agitation, there is no state of Mahamudra. When one becomes naturally established in the authentic, flawless state of Mahamudra, then both dullness and agitation are absent.

Now, for dullness and agitation to cause any harm, there must be some kind of territory belonging to someone which they invade or harm, right? If that somebody or place is not there, then what are they harming? Why use the word 'enemy' or 'thief?' So we ask, "Who are the enemies? Dullness and agitation. Who are they harming? They are harming the stability in ordinary mind." We mentioned before that if the enemy comes from outside, it is easy to deal with because we can do something to be sure the enemy doesn't enter — we can lock the door or keep a bodyguard on duty. However, when it is oneself who is creating the problem — when that which harms is only oneself — nobody else can help this situation. In that case you yourself must be careful and mindful.

STUDENT: Since dullness and agitation come from oneself, why are they so harmful?

RINPOCHE: If you have (a pool of) water which you keep agitating and stirring up while saying, "I want nice clear water," will it ever clear up? If one is always thinking, "Now there's dullness. Now there's agitation," for sure there is! The key point is to simply acknowledge when there is dullness or agitation. You are right when you say these two states are not something other than oneself. However, when dullness is very dense and agitation is very strong then it does harm the state of ordinary mind. It is like the example of water and fire being unable to remain on the same plate. If you feel really dull and sleepy, where is the view of Mahamudra? Moreover, when you're really agitated with a violent thought, the state of Mahamudra has certainly vanished.

STUDENT: Isn't knowing that there *is* agitation the state of Mahamudra?

RINPOCHE: Not at all. Just knowing that there is agitation is not Mahamudra. Noticing what is occurring, what takes place, is called noticing or mindfulness. There are two kinds of awareness.

STUDENT: I didn't know there were two kinds of awareness.

RINPOCHE: The word 'awareness' is used in two different contexts in Buddhism. One is self-existing awareness, the other is to be 'aware of something,' as in being mindful. Self-existing awareness is the state of Mahamudra, which is not a mere act of recollecting or conceptual thinking. Noticing, "Now, I'm deluded, now I'm dull, now there is agitation," these are simply ideas, concepts. The word 'awareness' in this context simply means 'being mindful of something'.

STUDENT: Can one practice shamatha and vipashyana without having done any preliminaries or yidam practice?

RINPOCHE: The traditional system in Tibetan Buddhism is to first complete the preliminaries, then begin the yidam practice. Shamatha and vipashyana practice is taught in conjunction with the yidam practice. Different teachers might emphasize one aspect more than the other, in accordance with their different approaches. Some teachers will tell you to spend a lot of time on shamatha before they will even discuss vipashyana. There are various different approaches, but, in general, it is like this. There's not much mention of practicing shamatha and vipashyana without any preliminaries or yidam practice.

STUDENT: It seems to me as if there are two paths. One begins with the preliminaries, and is followed by meditation and recitation of the yidam deity and finally the main part of Mahamudra. The other seems to involve first shamatha, then vipashyana and in the end the unity of shamatha and vipashyana. Are there such two different paths?

RINPOCHE: In Tibet one would start with the preliminaries and then go on to the yidam practice. Both shamatha and vipashyana are complete within development, recitation and completion of the yidam deity. Different masters would teach shamatha and vipashyana in different ways to their disciples. This may be why you think that these two approaches are two different paths, when in actuality there are not. Some disciples would recognize the thoughtfree wakefulness of vipashyana without having to go through much training in shamatha. Some would have to meditate for years gaining stability in shamatha before vipashyana was introduced. In Tibet the preliminaries were not considered a big deal and they didn't take very long to complete. These days the situation is a little different. The preliminaries seem to be an enormous, overwhelming task!

STUDENT: You mentioned before that the main part of both preliminaries and yidam training is beyond any focus, and that one should rest in this state for a short duration. Is this resting the real path Mahamudra, or is this also some kind of preliminary?

RINPOCHE: That depends on the individual. Even if one is a so-called beginner who has just started the preliminaries, if one has had the view of Mahamudra pointed out and has recognized it, then the training in that is the real practice of Mahamudra. On the other hand, if one is a diligent practitioner who has undergone the preliminaries and has completed a great number of recitations of the yidam's mantra, but who has still not attained any clear certainty about how the view really is, something vital is still lacking.

Traditionally, it is assumed that a beginner has not realized Mahamudra. Therefore, he or she undergoes the preliminary practices in order to remove the obscurations of disturbing emotions and so forth that prevent realization of Mahamudra. As obscurations are purified, the understanding becomes more and more refined. One approaches closer and closer to greater clarity and insight. At some point, through one's practice, what used to be an intellectual version of Mahamudra all of a sudden becomes a direct and actual experience. That doesn't mean that the view of Mahamudra wasn't already taught during the preliminaries. In fact, the Karma Kagyü ngöndro, the text for these preliminary practices, actually gives very clear directions for experiencing Mahamudra.

STUDENT: Do you need a root guru in order to begin the preliminaries?

RINPOCHE: First of all, we must distinguish between a root guru and a Dharma teacher. We don't have to have a root guru in order to begin the preliminaries, but we do need a teacher to instruct us in how to do them. If we have a teacher, and in addition we have interest and devotion to the Buddha, Dharma and Sangha, then we are allowed to start the preliminaries.

Recognition

If somebody asks, "What actually is the view of Buddhism?," we can reply it is 'dependent origination indivisible from emptiness'. We can expand upon that by saying that we accept two truths, two levels of reality. The relative truth is true while perceiving, while the ultimate truth is true while in the innate state.

Relative truth is what appears to be real and true before one begins to question the nature of things. The moment we start to look into what is the nature of this seeming reality, we find that it is mistaken. The nature of this mistaken or deluded experience is emptiness free from constructs — the ultimate truth that is beyond delusion. Ultimate truth is not something separate from or apart from the relative truth; it is its very essence. Words such as 'emptiness,' 'egolessness' and 'simplicity' all refer to ultimate truth. Again, all the apparent and existent phenomena included within samsara and nirvana seems real and true to a deluded state of mind. This is the level of conventional truth, which clings to all the seeming things in the world. The ultimate truth is what is real and unmistaken — the undeluded state of mind which is the very nature of the seeming things in this world. When we gain a degree of clear comprehension about the difference between the two truths, then we are able to understand how things really are.

All things appear in various ways according to the different realms of sentient beings. However, when each of these perceptions or experiences is examined, no thing is found to have any independent identity — everything is empty. That is the ultimate truth. Due to people's diverse intellectual capacities, manifold teachings have developed to explain the single fact that all things are empty and devoid of self. When saying "devoid of self," egolessness itself is not another 'thing' that can be perceived, even by the ultimate state of wisdom. It means 'empty of any self-entity,' or 'no identity'. That is the definition of the Rangtong school of the Middle Way. *Rang* means self and tong means empty. Because a self-entity is not seen, even through wisdom, it is called 'self-empty'. The view of the Prasangika Middle Way, on the other hand, does not claim that this self-nature is either seen or not seen, even by wisdom. It does not claim either of these. The view of the Shentong Middle Way is that all momentary phenomena are empty of self-entity, but that self-existing wakefulness is neither empty nor non-existent. Although all momentary phenomena are empty, self-existing wakefulness is not empty, the Shentong school asserts. This thought-free wakefulness is inexpressible, indescribable. That is the view of the Great Middle Way of the Definitive Meaning. The meditation training is not to separate from the view. The conduct involves not only giving up what harms others, but also trying one's utmost to benefit beings. And the fruition is to realize dharmakaya for the benefit of self, and to manifest as the rupakayas, the form bodies, for the welfare of countless sentient beings.

The Buddha gave the teachings of the Tripitaka, the Three Collections, and the Tantras to enable us to subdue the three poisons. The Buddha gave 21,000 instructions on Vinaya as a remedy to attachment, 21,000 different teachings of Sutra to counteract anger, 21,000 different teachings on Abhidharma to counteract delusion, and 21,000 different teachings on the four sections of Tantra to counteract the combination of the three poisons. All together, he gave 84,000 Dharma teachings. They can all be condensed into the teachings about the nature of mind.

As I have repeatedly stated, this nature is given many names: simplicity, emptiness, buddha nature. Regardless of what names we might give it, it is not something outside that we can achieve. It's present in ourselves. It is the thinker of all your different thoughts; it is intrinsic to your mind. The nature of your mind that is empty and cognizant beyond description is itself dharmakaya. All the different phenomena included within samsara and nirvana are the manifestations of this awareness.

A skillful method used in Vajrayana to directly introduce us to our true nature is the receiving and realizing of the four empowerments. The most vital of these is the fourth, called the precious word empowerment. What is being indicated through the fourth empowerment is exactly this: our unfabricated, innate wakefulness. As long as we continue to regard what is unreal as real, we keep ourselves within samsaric existence. We receive the empowerments in order to acknowledge what really is. In actuality our body is the deity, our voice is mantra, and our mind, although temporarily confused, is, in its basic state, free from any obscuration whatsoever. Original wakefulness is naturally and fully present within us, right now.

Now I will go into detail about these four empowerments. The purpose of the first, the vase empowerment, is to introduce us to the fact that perceptions and emptiness are indivisible. Our body is the unity of being visible and empty. This unity, itself, is called deity. We needn't think that the deity is a god with various faces, many arms and all sorts of different attributes. Our body, our physical existence, is already the unity of visible emptiness, but by regarding the world and ourselves as permanent entities and fixating on them, it looks as though everything is really solid.

The second empowerment, called the secret empowerment, is to introduce the fact that hearing and emptiness are indivisible. What resounds as sound is empty, yet audible. To recognize that is called receiving the secret empowerment.

The third empowerment is called the wisdom-knowledge empowerment. Our bodies have the ability to feel pleasure, pain and many other types of physical sensation. Within our physical body, there are pure and impure aspects of the channels, energies and essences. Based on the impure aspect, we give rise to attachment, aggression, and delusion. The purpose of the Six Yogas of Naropa is to apply the key points of the nadis, pranas and bindus to eliminate the impure aspects and develop the pure ones. By means of this, one can quickly realize the unity of clarity and emptiness, bliss and emptiness, and awareness and emptiness.

We are now within the three realms of samsara, in particular within the human realm, called the Realm of Desire. Beings in this realm have desire and attachment as their predominant characteristic. Of course, individual people differ. Some have all five disturbing emotions in equally strong measure; some have the five to a much lesser degree. Some people have a particular disturbing emotion that is much stronger than any of the others. Still, as a general rule, in the Realm of Desire, desire is the strongest.

The three vehicles in Buddhism deal with this attachment in distinct ways. The shravaka teachings instruct us in abandonment — in renouncing desire and the objects of desire. The bodhisattva path shows us how to transform these attachments. Vajrayana teachings enable the practitioner to take disturbing emotions as the path. By correctly using the special key points of the channels, energies and essences, one can very quickly traverse through the five paths and ten bhumis. But if one engages in these practices without knowing their key points or without having correct understanding, they become an exercise in normal, rigid disturbing emotions and indulgence in desire. One is then simply a normal person who has strayed completely away from the true path. This is one of the reasons why the Vajrayana path, which has tremendously great potential for liberation, is more risky and should be kept secret.

The general Vajrayana teachings — we're not talking about essence Mahamudra or Dzogchen right here — are very much concerned with understanding the nature of the four empowerments, and they explain them in great detail. Furthermore, the practices based on them apply the key points of the channels, energies and essences. The reason is that this physical body is the foundation for both the negative and positive qualities. Based on this body, we can develop to the fullest extent all the causes for the six realms of samsara as the six disturbing emotions. Also based on this body and these practices, we can develop to their fullest extent the different aspects of wisdom and spiritual qualities. That is why the physical body is taken as the basis for the general Vajrayana practices. By applying the key points and the enhancement practices, one can progress very quickly.

Among all possible types of physical bodies, the human body endowed with the freedoms and riches and possessing the six elements is the most eminent support for practice. Through the practice of the four wisdoms with their 16 aspects of bliss, we can arrive at the state of realization called '*emptiness endowed with the supreme of all aspects, indivisible from unchanging great bliss*'. One of the most subtle fixations is attachment. We need to destroy desire from the root. One type of attachment is the fascination between male and female. Only very subtle Vajrayana practice can transcend and relinquish this fixation.

There are a few reasons why I am bringing up this point here about the third empowerment. Buddhism has spread to many countries and has taken on many different flavors, adapting to the respective cultures. For example, in the Buddhist tradition of Sri Lanka, Burma and Thailand, the Buddha is regarded as a single historical individual. The main practice is shamatha and vipashyana. There are no deities depicted with many arms and heads, and there are certainly no male and female buddhas in union. In the Tibetan Vajrayana tradition, of course, there are many different buddhas shown in all different colors and shapes, with multiple arms and heads, and in union. The buddhas are depicted in union in order to point out the wakefulness in which bliss and emptiness are indivisible. To experience such unity of bliss and emptiness is the means of transcending the worldly state of attachment, of utilizing it as the path. The union of buddhas also symbolizes how the basic state of things is — the indivisibility of perception and emptiness. Perception is the male aspect and emptiness the female. There are many different ways of explaining the symbolism. Basically, though, we should understand that the various aspects of Vajrayana are all methods that lead to an understanding of how everything truly is.

The fourth empowerment, the precious word empowerment, introduces the view. It is what is arrived at as the ultimate realization of the previous empowerment, the wakefulness that is the unity of bliss and emptiness. This view of the fourth empowerment is called by different names, such as the view of cutting through of primordial purity, *kadag trekchö*. It is also called 'innate coemergent wakefulness'. We should understand that this view, this innate natural state, is beyond the fleeting experiences of bliss, clarity and nonthought that are only temporary stages on the path. To keep directing our attention toward experiences of bliss or joy is not the ultimate attainment. That is why the primordially pure state of the Great Perfection is defined as the innate nature beyond the three temporary experiences, and transcending the four joys. In short, the innate nature, beyond the three experiences and the four joys, is the cutting through of primordial purity.

This understanding of the innate nature should be free from extreme notions such as permanence or annihilation, eternalism or nihilism. In essence, it is primordially pure and free from the extreme of permanence: that is the empty aspect. By nature, it is spontaneously present; thus, the limitation of nihilism is cleared away. Because our innate nature is totally beyond or already free from these two extremes of being permanent or interrupted, it is empty. While being empty, at the same time, it is cognizant. It is the unity of being empty and cognizant.

When we look very closely at anything, in depth, we find there is no place, no location, to which we can really attach the name of that thing. What do we call that quality of being without an entity that can be pinpointed? We call it 'empty in essence,' or identitylessness. This is in agreement with the fact that the essence of all phenomena is empty. While things are empty in essence, still, all the different displays and perceptions occur. That is called the cognizant aspect.

This cognizant aspect is present simultaneously with emptiness. How do you describe this cognizant aspect? It's like a dream, like a magical illusion. This is why a realized yogi will say that everything, whatever is perceived or experienced, is the expanse of awareness, the display of awareness, the magical illusion of innate awareness. Conversely, a normal person will say, "I see that. This is such and such. It is real to me!" But the moment we look closer, we cannot find such a 'thing'. In other words, most of the time we are just fooling ourselves with our ideas about what we perceive. We need to recognize that everything that appears and exists is, in essence, empty and totally devoid of any mental constructs we can make about it.

The general vehicles first acknowledge that everyone has the potential to reach enlightenment. All beings have mind and therefore possess an enlightened essence, buddha nature. Buddha nature is the basic material for attaining enlightenment; it is the seed of buddhahood. By acknowledging buddha nature and bringing that into practice, one progressively goes through the different stages of the paths and bhumis. Vajrayana teachings go even further by declaring that everything, whatever appears and exists, since the very first, is primordially permeated by buddha-nature. That means everything, whatever appears and exists, is empty in essence, but, at the same time, unobstructedly manifests. In its pure aspect, this is called the three kayas; in its impure aspect, the three realms of samsara. When buddha-nature is recognized and stabilized, what is experienced is the expanse of the three kayas.

How can we apply this to ourselves right now? We do have a mind — we are not mindless — but what is this mind? There is something that notices, that understands and perceives. Check carefully. What is its basis? How is it, really? It is impossible to find a 'thing' that can be truly pinpointed or identified. That it is unidentifiable is called 'empty in essence' — this is dharmakaya. In this way, the essence of our mind is permeated by dharmakaya. It is empty in essence, yet, at the same time, there is a quality that allows anything to be perceived. Anything can be cognized, and this occurs simultaneously with the mind being empty. It is not that mind needs to stop being empty in order to perceive. Nevertheless, at the same time, it operates by cognizing. This is called 'cognizant by nature' — this is the sambhogakaya aspect in our minds. In this way, both the dharmakaya and the sambhogakaya qualities are present in ourselves. Thirdly, it is also a fact that our empty essence and our cognizant nature are indivisible. Mind cognizes while being empty; while being empty, still it cognizes. These are indivisible, and that is called 'undivided capacity' — this is the nirmanakaya aspect of our mind.

To sustain the view of cutting through, of primordial purity, is called 'meditation'. Meditation training in the Mahamudra system is generally said to involve applying the key points of the Six Yogas of Naropa regarding the nadis, pranas and bindus without straying from the continuity of the view. In this context, the conduct is to be totally free from judging, accepting or rejecting, because one experiences everything, whatever appears and exists, as being the display or adornment of the innate nature. This is possible, but not as a way one deliberately tries to be — it's the automatic power of the view.

We must request that this view, the precious word empowerment, be pointed out by a qualified master who has realized it him or herself. When it is pointed out, we gain some understanding that, "This is exactly how it is." We directly experience our basic state of mind as both empty and cognizant, and we realize that these qualities are inseparable, indivisible. Please remember that only gaining the idea that this is how things are, then sitting and contemplating it, is nothing but intellectual understanding, simply theory.

Often a student will ponder like this: "In all the books I've read, and according to what the master has said, the mind is empty in essence while still cognizing. All right! It has these two qualities that shouldn't be separated. They are an indivisible unity; I really believe that. It makes sense, but do I really experience it?" If we simply leave it like that, doubt remains. So when receiving oral instructions from a master, it's very important not to leave the teaching as an idea or a concept. We must assimilate it and apply it in our personal experience, because that is where practice begins. The practice of meditation means getting more and more used to the experience of the view; not just maintaining an idea about it. If we leave it as an intellectual comprehension, there will not be any progress, because there is no practical training. 'Practice' means sustaining the experience of the view.

In the context of Mahamudra and Dzogchen, when we say 'practice meditation,' what is it that we practice or train in growing used to? It is mental nonfabrication. Mental fabrication always holds subject and object, dualistic experience, dualistic perception. That is the basis for attachment and aversion, for hope and fear. The supreme remedy to this is mental nonfabrication, simple nondoing. This state of not creating anything in the mind can be misunderstood in various ways. We can sit in an oblivious state, half-unconscious, as though drunk or absent-minded. This is also mental nonfabrication, but it is not the state of nonfabrication we are discussing right now — definitely not. The former example is an absence of fabrication due to strong dullness. In this, it's true that we can experience a state that is vacant and bare. No gross thoughts of this and that are present, nor emotions nor even a subtle idea — but this is only due to dullness. In contrast, the state of buddha mind, the wakefulness that is the unity of being empty and cognizant, is acutely awake, like the eyes of an incredibly intelligent person.

> Untainted by outer perceived objects,
> Unspoiled by the inner perceiving mind,
> In between, to sustain the naked empty awareness,
> That is the realization of all the buddhas.

These four lines of poetry by the translator Vairochana fully contain the final view of Madhyamika, Mahamudra and Dzogchen. It is by sustaining this naked empty awareness that our obscurations, misdeeds and habitual tendencies can be totally eradicated. The foremost practitioner of this attains complete enlightenment within this very lifetime. The next best type of practitioner will do so at the moment of death. And the third type will recognize, train and gain stability in the bardo of dharmata during the intermediate state after death.

The realization of *'emptiness endowed with the supreme of all aspects, indivisible from unchanging, great bliss'* is the basic state since the very beginning. It is the thought-free wakefulness that pervades all of existence and peace, samsara and nirvana. When realizing this, there is no thing to be meditated upon as an object. It lies totally beyond the dualistic concepts of 'I, the meditator, meditate on that, the object.' It is the primordial state itself — ground and fruition indivisible. Training in this is unlike the normal meditation practice we usually do when we maintain the calm of shamatha with mindfulness or visualize a deity as an object. It is not even like the practice of pursuing further insight, vipashyana. Even though there is not even a hair tip of anything to be cultivated, there should also be no distraction for even an instant. The great master Lingje Repa was told by his master to meditate on the innate nature, practice Mahamudra and do meditation sessions — to sit down and stay in retreat, which he did. Practicing thus, he progressed through the four stages of Mahamudra. Finally, all his concepts of meditation or nonmeditation totally vanished. Then he wrote these lines:

> My teacher told me, "Meditate on the innate nature."
> I meditated and meditated.
> Now meditator and meditation object have vanished.
> My sessions and breaks have fallen apart.
> What should I do now?"

In the beginning, a practitioner needs to have some presence of mind. 'Mindfulness' here means to be attentive. There are actually two traditional words for this state: mindfulness and watchfulness. Watchfulness is a more subtle state of conceptual mind that keeps noticing whether or not the meditation has slipped away. It's a kind of subtle sentry keeping patrol, which is still present at the first two stages of Mahamudra, One-Pointedness and Simplicity. Later on, even that falls away, so one cannot say that there's any act of meditating, any object meditated upon or meditation taking place. That is what is meant when Lingje Repa said that he had gone beyond sessions and breaks.

For a beginner in Dzogchen, the authentic practice of rigpa is likewise free from notions of meditator and meditation object, but such a state does not last very long. It's just a short moment. For an advanced practitioner, this moment is not disrupted; it continues throughout day and night. That level of effortless mindfulness is called 'all-pervasive awareness'. However, the nature of the beginner's short moment and the accomplished practitioner's uninterrupted realization is exactly the same. There is no subject and object of meditation in either. It is not just the idea of a nondual state, but an actual nondual state. 'Awareness resting vividly awake in its natural state' means to simply allow it to be so. Simply let that present wakefulness naked, fresh, vividly awake be as it is. That, by itself, is free from meditator and meditation object. Don't label the clear, empty, present state of mind. Don't think, "Now there's awareness!" or "This is it!" or "I must keep this! I must avoid that!" Don't entertain hope or fear, adopting or avoiding. When not involved in any such kind of conceptual judging, that itself is innate suchness, thought-free wakefulness, genuine ordinary mind. At that point, you don't need to question or doubt whether this is or is not rigpa; it is.

Don't ever hope for improvement or fear degeneration in this nondual state. Drop all kinds of suspicions and doubts. Don't chase transient concepts. Don't be caught up in coarse emotions or subtle concepts. The main practice is to simply rest vividly awake in this nondual awareness. The method is to relax loosely and remain naturally. To totally relax and not check or question; to remain totally free from accepting or rejecting — that is the conducive situation for meeting the natural face of awareness. Apart from this, you don't need anything else to meditate upon.

Although the basic state is not something to practice in the sense of keeping a meditation object in mind, we have to describe it as if it is. Otherwise it will not be right; a grave misconception can slip in. What is to be practiced has nothing to do with thoughts and conceptual mind: it is the innate nature beyond conceptual mind. You don't need to train in anything other than the natural state of the ordinary mind. By repeatedly sustaining the natural state, at some point you will recognize the essence of thought to be dharmakaya. When that happens, realization is baseless and rootless. The consequence of this is the spontaneous liberation of all attachment and the instantaneous relinquishment of all habitual patterns. At that very moment, all obscurations, all habitual tendencies, are totally cleared. Continuing in such a practice, enlightenment is reached very quickly.

STUDENT: I want to practice the uncontrived natural face of awareness. I don't feel very dull when I do this, and I also do not think too much. So am I sustaining the essence of awareness?

RINPOCHE: This state should be cognizant yet nonconceptual. Cognizant means that we are awake, ready to know anything. You are not unconscious, right? At the same time we should not conceptualize or make ideas about it. Awareness but no conceptualizing. When that is the case, and also when we don't dwell on the idea "now it is cognizant and non-conceptual!" — when the mind essence is left just as it is by itself, then that is called rigpa, nondual awareness.

STUDENT: Is it all right to later think "Hey! It happened!"?

RINPOCHE: Afterwards you can feel free to think that. Before practicing as well, it is fine to think, "Now I should rest in natural awareness!" However, when natural awareness is present, if one sits and appreciates "Now this is natural awareness!" then that is incorrect.

STUDENT: To begin with one does not see the essence of thought; isn't that so?

RINPOCHE: This is quite an important point. In the beginning it seems that we alternate between the natural state and thinking. Thinking is different from the natural state because it carries us away. It makes us forget. For a beginner, the natural state does not happen all by itself. Therefore we need the special thought of mindfulness to remind ourselves: "I forgot, I must remember the natural state!" As we train more and more, at some point any kind of thought is immediately liberated. Instantaneously it becomes the natural state without any need for mindfulness and without any lapse into distraction. This progression is an important distinction. In the beginning we need presence of mind, a sense of 'remindfullness'. We need to be alert. It's like having a teacher next to us saying, "Now you are getting carried away, now remember, now remain in the natural state!" or, "Now you are thinking, now you are completely carried away." That kind of teacher, that kind of mindfulness, is very important in the beginning for any practice to take effect. It is like when we learned the alphabet. At first it required a lot of effort. Later as we become proficient in reading, then the meaning of the script comes spontaneously, and we don't have to try very hard at all. It is like that.

STUDENT: Do you mean, for example, the mind is like an ocean and the thoughts are the waves? Could we say that it all is water, and the ocean and the waves are indivisible?

RINPOCHE: There was one student of Milarepa, a female practitioner who compared her mind to an ocean and the thoughts to waves, then asked what should she do when the waves are stormy and in turmoil. Milarepa replied, "True enough, just as waves are the magical display of the ocean, thoughts are the magical display of the mind." When you don't attach any importance to thoughts, when you just leave them without fixating, then they cannot do anything other than dissolve back into the ocean. If we do get fixated on the waves, the turmoil only continues. So the most important point is don't fixate, don't attach importance.

STUDENT: What did it mean when you said that the Buddha clearly sees all three times?

RINPOCHE: Our normal thinking functions sequentially. We can think of one thing at a time, either in the past, present or future. If we think of something that happened in the past, we don't think of something in the future at the same time. We shift at the second moment to the future. It is one thought after another, every moment, but not everything at the same time. The awakened state of a buddha, however, is not confined to one thing at a time. It is knowledge of all aspects simultaneously. The three times are present infinitely in the same moment, in a fashion which is inconceivable to us now.

STUDENT: What does *kadag trekchö* really mean?

RINPOCHE: The very essence of cutting through, Trekchö, is primordially pure. It is pure in essence and by nature free from dualistic fixation. This primordially pure innate nature is empty and, at the same time, cognizant. This is not merely an idea or concept. The knowing of this nature, without concepts, is what cuts through all concepts — it cuts them totally to pieces. You might say it makes piecemeal out of concepts.

STUDENT: How can we sustain the continuity of the view without concepts, without ideas or fixation?

RINPOCHE: The idea, "I should sustain the view!" does not sustain the view. It is an idea. It is actually desire. We think that the view is something desirable which we should achieve. We want it continuously, so we sit and think, "I must keep it! Keep it! Keep it!" That doesn't keep it. To be able to sustain the view we must, first of all, have the view. We must be introduced to the view by a qualified master. That is the causal substance that can be sustained. The contributing factor is our presence of mind, or 'remindfulness,' which is a fixation, a concept. Yet when we combine our personal experience of the view with the reminder "let's sustain it!" that deliberate act can lead to effortlessness. The conceptual leads to the nonconceptual.

Why is it that we are not immediately liberated by recognizing the nature of mind? We are not fully liberated when recognizing the view because recognizing alone does not ensure the ability to sustain it continuously. That's why we need mindfulness. Mindfulness is the best teacher. The person who has the best mindfulness is the best practitioner. The person with wishy-washy mindfulness is a wishy-washy practitioner. The person without mindfulness is not a practitioner at all.

In all three vehicles, the words 'be mindful; be careful; be conscientious;' are always used and are extremely important. The difference between the vehicles lies in what one is mindful of and what it means to be mindful. In this context, if some presence of mind helps one to remember and thereby sustain the natural state of the view, we call that 'mindfulness'.

STUDENT: What is there to do about the danger in merely thinking one is an accomplished practitioner of Dzogchen without having fully actualized the view?

RINPOCHE: There's a famous saying: "At first glance, there is the danger of mistaking a charlatan for a mahasiddha," a realized practitioner. To apply that to ourselves, when we think, "Let me act according to the view. There is nothing to accept, nothing to reject!," that is just an idea that we made up mentally. That does not become genuine absence of judgment or accepting or rejecting. Why? Because it is only a mental fabrication. Deep within, our fixation is still present. When an actor goes on the stage and announces, "I am the king of England," and dresses like a king and behaves like a king, making people believe in him, the actor is still not himself truly convinced that he is the king of England. There is still some doubt in his mind. Just like the actor who never transcends the knowledge that he is simply an imitator, an inflated Dzogchen practitioner is just acting, just pretending to be someone else.

STUDENT: What makes sound so important in the unity of sound and emptiness?

RINPOCHE: There are many details to the unity of sound and emptiness. Basically, sound is a vehicle for meaning. It is by means of sound that understanding can be communicated. In particular, the ultimate state can be understood through words. That is why sound is very important. The reason why sound is more important than the other four sense objects is because it is a medium for expression. The other four sense objects, in this context, are all part of physical form.

STUDENT: How do we view phenomena if all that is experienced is personal perception? On the other hand, isn't there also a common shared perception?

RINPOCHE: There are two major types of ripening of past karmic actions, one of which is called 'shared karmic ripening'. For example, all of us who have ended up as human beings have a shared perception of things. Animals of various species each have their own shared perceptions of phenomena: that is an example of karmic ripening. All different species of beings have their own particular shared experience. At the same time, we also have our 'individual karmic ripening,' our own personal experience or unique way of perceiving. This means that when we go somewhere, for instance, we will each see things differently and think differently about them, though we may be in the same place. This kind of karma is not shared, but individual.

As an example of this, take those of you who are reading this book. I would say that you all have an equal fortune or 'fate' with the other readers. You have a shared interest in understanding a particular topic. Then there is the opposite situation, the equal fate or fortune of those who are not interested in reading this book. Those beings may be reading other books. That's a different kind of karma.

As another example, take the affluent class of the Kathmandu Valley. These are people with equal karma, who feel compelled to attend each other's parties and functions. They meet each other and dress in a certain way. That is their equal fate. No one made any mandatory laws saying that they must conduct themselves this way, but somehow, they are forced into that patterning. Then there are the poor people with equal fate. They dress in rags, have little in their house to eat, and walk around the stupa on special days waiting for someone to come and throw scraps of food or rupees at them. No law forces them to behave this way, but they are still compelled to follow this pattern.

So many different groups who exist at all different levels have their particular *kalnyam* — equal fate. This is the ripening of karma. That is the shared karma. Individual karma, on the other hand, is like this: as each person reads this book, you each will have your own personal understanding of a particular sentence.

STUDENT: How do we maintain the view during all of our experiences, and isn't that also part of practice?

RINPOCHE: Definitely, of course it's part of practice! Unfortunately, distractions and diversions are very strong. Milarepa understood that mind is extremely gullible and easily seduced. He also knew that appearances are very captivating and can very easily draw our attention in a certain direction so that we get caught up in it. Realizing that, Milarepa ran away to mountain caves and stayed there to practice.

Marpa did exactly the opposite. Seen from the outside, he appeared as a normal worldly person, with a wife and children. He would scold and sometimes even beat his followers. When he would talk, he would always use the words 'I' and 'me'. "You're not treating me well. You're not serving me well".

Marpa went to India many times and received many tantras, transmissions and instructions. On his last visit to India, his teacher, Naropa, put his hand on Marpa's head and said, "You're my successor, my emissary for the land of Tibet. Return there, spread the teachings, uphold the lineage, accept many disciples and make the teachings flourish. Many people there will criticize you. They will say you are selfish, simply an ordinary rude person. However, in your own experience, all fixation has totally vanished and you have reached the ultimate state called the 'exhaustion of all concepts and phenomena'. So go back and benefit beings."

We should use ourselves as the measure for how to act. If you are easily distracted and tend to be totally carried away by what we perceive, then you should run away to the mountains and stay at least three years in retreat. If you cannot, then go away at least a few months. If that's totally impossible, at the very least, go and engage in a meditation session privately. Lock your door from the inside, and if someone knocks, get angry. If the phone rings, rip out the cord. A more polite way would be to hang out a sign that says; 'Don't disturb. I am practicing'.

STUDENT: At the actual time of sustaining the view, are perception and thought self-liberated, or is there no arising whatsoever of thought?

Rinpoche: 'Sustaining the view' means sustaining the state of nonthought — the nonconceptual state. The view is the opposite of conceptual thinking. Sustaining the absence of conceptual thinking, means, of course, there is no thought. In the Mahamudra system, it is taught that ordinary mind is the same as buddha-nature, *tathagatagarbha*. It is the absence of holding conceptual notions. What is left at that time is your basic state which is unmade, unconstructed, unfabricated, uncultivated. That is called ordinary mind. The word 'ordinary' refers to what is natural, what is not made up, what simply is. That experience is free from holding any notion. It is also beyond being either confused or unmistaken.

STUDENT: If one has a recollection of the past yet does not grasp and hold onto it, is ordinary mind lost at that moment?

RINPOCHE: The problem lies with how we understand the terminology. How should we define what a memory arising in the mind actually is? In Abhidharma, memories belong to the dhatu of dharmas, the so-called 'constituent of mental objects'. In the duration of ordinary mind, there is no fixating whatsoever, and the dhatus are always connected with fixation. Therefore, there is no fixated memory of the past. On the other hand, in the case of a practitioner who is long accustomed to the state of ordinary mind, then we can talk about the functioning of discriminating wisdom which differs from ordinary memory. But it doesn't help much to say that a beginner's memories are discriminating wisdom. This can easily be mistaken.

STUDENT: At the time of practicing the fruition as the path, how do we bring distraction onto the path?

RINPOCHE: According to the Mahamudra system, one applies one of the Six Yogas called 'illusory body,' the training in magical illusion. One trains in the attitude that everything is just like a dream, like a magical show — in other words, not real. Growing used to that, our normal attraction to or fascination with things weakens and becomes less rigid. Based on that flexibility, the view of Mahamudra can more easily be stabilized.

According to the Dzogchen system, the essence within our conceptual thinking, the essence in each thought, is the nondual, nonconceptual state of wakefulness. For each thought we get involved in, we must rediscover its innate state of wakefulness. The Dzogchen teachings say, "Never be apart from the threefold practice of regarding sights as the deity, sound as mantra and thoughts as wisdom." Having trained like that, the deceptive power of the trickster of conceptual thinking becomes weaker. It cannot deceive us so easily.✦

Key Points

The Vajrayana teachings, the approach of bringing the fruition onto the path, are extremely vast and extensive. There are 6,400,000 sections of tantras within the Dzogchen teachings alone. The heart of all these teachings is included within simply recognizing body, speech and mind to be the three vajras: vajra Body, vajra Speech and vajra Mind. Once we recognize that and grow accustomed to it, we will be observing all the 100 billion samayas simultaneously.

On the superficial level, in the impure aspect there are dualistic experience, disturbing emotions, habitual tendencies and conceptual fixation. It seems as though our body is the aggregate that is the basis for the truth of suffering. It seems that our voice is fragmented, interrupted. It seems that our mind is changeable; that it has the nature of happiness and suffering, pleasure and pain. Yet, in its pure aspect, our body is the unity of perception and emptiness, and is thus the vajra Body; our voice is the unity of being audible yet empty, and thus is vajra Speech; and our mind is the unity of awareness and emptiness, so is vajra Mind. This is how it really is since the very beginning. In order to recognize what is as it really is, we request the oral instructions.

According to the shravaka teachings, we establish the understanding that this body is the conglomeration of 36 impure substances. It is impermanent, impure and the basis for pain. According to the bodhisattva teachings, we gain the understanding that the body is empty. However, by means of Vajrayana teachings we come to understand that the body is the unity of perception and emptiness.

According to the shravaka teachings, we discriminate between good and evil ways of talking. We abandon what is evil and adopt what is virtuous. According to the bodhisattva teachings, we find that all sound is empty in essence and nonexistent. According to the Vajrayana teachings, our voice — sound itself — has the nature of the *nada,* the vajra sound beyond arising, dwelling and ceasing.

Concerning mind, in the shravaka teachings, we try to calm all gross and subtle mental movements into the state of stillness through shamatha. In addition to this, one is introduced to the practice of vipashyana. The Mahayana teachings show us that all gross and subtle mental states are empty in essence. Through the Vajrayana teaching, we realize that all mental states are the display of wakefulness.

There are many types of practices, including the general Mahayana and the specific Vajrayana practices. Within Vajrayana, there are different levels of tantras, called Kriya, Upa, Yoga, Maha, Anu and Ati. Within Ati Yoga, the Great Perfection, there are different divisions or levels of teachings called Mind Section, Space Section and Instruction Section. Within the Instruction Section, there is the view — that is called primordial purity — and the meditation training called spontaneous presence. I will try to explain how to understand the view of primordial purity, and how to implement that in a simple practice.

When we receive instructions in meditation, they are given in the form of directions, practical advice. First, regarding how to sit, the 'sevenfold posture of the Buddha Vairochana' is an excellent posture. It sums up the seven features that we should assume during meditation practice. First, place the legs in a cross-legged position. Then, keep the backbone straight. Bend the neck slightly. Place the hands in the gesture of equanimity or place the thumbs at the root of the ring-fingers and place them on your thighs, straightening the arms. Your gaze should be directed into the space in front of you, parallel with your nose. The shoulders should be stretched out, like the wings of a vulture. The tip of the tongue should gently touch the palate, the roof of the mouth. The purpose of correct posture is that when the body is straight, our subtle channels are also straight, which enables the energy currents to flow freely. This helps the mind to naturally be at peace. If you cannot keep the posture of Vairochana, then sit in the 'posture of ease'. Place the palms of the hands on the kneecaps or folded in the gesture of equanimity in the lap, and loosely cross the legs. There are many ways to sit, but the 'sevenfold posture of Vairochana' is one of the best.

How should we keep our gaze? Some people think it's better to sit with closed eyes, some people think it's better to sit with the eyes open. There are both advantages and disadvantages to sitting with closed eyes. When we close our eyes in any meditation practice we naturally come closer to feeling dull and sleepy. If we don't succumb to that dullness, then it does not harm anything to sit with closed eyes. People sit with closed eyes during shamatha in order to shut down the visual perception of normal sights. When this is shut off, the tendency to fixate on what is seen is absent, and therefore the mind is more prone to simply rest in stillness, in the peaceful state of shamatha. Meditation practice means to 'cultivate'. It shouldn't be sleep that we are cultivating, though! With shamatha, if our meditation is a practice in stillness, not sleep, then it's fine to sit with closed eyes. Now you understand the positive and negative sides of sitting with closed eyes.

Concerning open eyes: according to the Mahamudra system, it is said; "Leave the gaze in the direction of the nose." In particular, in the context of Dzogchen, it is said; "Do not close the eyes, the gates for wisdom to manifest!" Keep the eyes open. There are also some negative aspects to sitting with open eyes. Because of seeing different forms and shapes, we may think about them, feel like or dislike towards them and get involved in that. That's the defect of sitting with open eyes. The function of eyesight is to see. If we shut our eyes, we can temporarily avoid seeing and thinking about what is in front of us. However, at some point, we will have to open our eyes again. Therefore, the key point is to keep the eyes open, but without fixating upon what is seen.

By adjusting the gaze, the defects of dullness and agitation can be remedied. 'Dullness' means we become sleepy, while 'agitation' means we become distracted. When sustaining the awakened state, if we find that we are becoming a little dull and sleepy, raise the gaze upwards. Additionally when feeling dull, it is beneficial to go to a wide-open place with a vast view and mingle awareness and space. For beginners there are extra techniques to combat this. When one feels dull, remove the outer layers of clothes; open the doors and windows. Put water on your head, neck and face. Conversely, we can feel agitated and restless, with thoughts moving about. If this occurs, lower the gaze to about 45 degrees in the direction of the nose. That will calm you down and make the thought activity subside.

The oral instructions of Ati Yoga are often called the 'yoga of simplicity'. They are mainly concerned with the view of primordial purity. This view is self-existing wakefulness, ordinary mind. The meditation of Ati Yoga is simply to sustain that. The conduct is to never separate oneself from the view, and the fruition is to allow the view to continue uninterruptedly. Ati Yoga places no great emphasis on controlling the channels, energies and essences. Other sections of tantra, like Anu Yoga, emphasize the need to control the different aspects of the channels, energies and essences, — especially the energies. For example, it's taught that one accomplishes One-Pointedness by being able to hold the breath below the navel. When the thoughts and movements of prana are controlled at the heart-center, one realizes Simplicity. When they are controlled at the throat, One Taste is realized. When controlled at the crown of the head, the final movement of thought, the prana-mind principle, is totally dissolved, and one reaches the 'dharmakaya throne of Nonmeditation'.

So, to continue with the direct instructions of Ati Yoga: keep the tongue gently at the top of the palate, and leave the lips and teeth slightly parted. Let the breathing flow naturally, without trying to do anything to it. This helps leave awareness in its natural state, and helps one to progress in rigpa. These three points — how to sit, how to gaze, and how to breathe — are very simple, very easy to understand and practice, but we shouldn't underestimate their importance. Remember these key points.

Before one gets to the actual practice of sustaining the natural face of awareness, there is an essential prelude, a preliminary: to motivate oneself by reflecting on impermanence, devotion and compassion, by developing bodhichitta. For the meditation session itself there may be a certain amount of visualization and recitation, depending upon the particular teaching. Finally, the meditation or main part should be to remain free from reference point.

An extremely important point to understand is that the naked state of awareness is not realized without taking the support of a qualified master. For this reason, the root and lineage gurus are extremely important. We will not realize the natural state through merely studying and thinking about the teachings. Both Mahamudra and Dzogchen teachings emphasize the importance of compassion and devotion. When our mind is full of devotion to our root guru and great lineage masters, or when we are filled with nonconceptual compassion for all sentient beings, to the extent that our eyes fill with tears, it is much easier to recognize the naked state of mind. At that time, make the supplication: "May the realization discovered by all the buddhas of the three times of past, present and future, exactly as it is, arise in my being right this very instant."

The occurrence of these blessings depends mainly upon ourselves and our degree of openness. It actually comes down to our own devotion. It is not enough to list all the texts we have recited aloud, the great numbers of mantras we have accumulated, and all the hours we have sat on our meditation cushion. That kind of spiritual pretense is not sufficient to guarantee realization.

From the very core of our hearts we should supplicate. Engender this deep-felt wish: "May the blessings of my root master and of all the realized masters of the lineage dawn within me. Whatever all the buddhas of the three times have realized, exactly as it is, may it dawn nakedly within me now while I sit on this very seat." With complete trust and surrender, make this strong supplication. After that, totally drop everything and rest without any thought of past, present or future. This is the general approach.

Having dissolved the guru into yourself, imagine that your mind mingles indivisibly with his, then sustain the state of intrinsic great bliss free from fixating on clarity or emptiness. 'Great bliss' here refers to a quality of unchangingness. This state is also called '*emptiness endowed with the supreme of all aspects indivisible from unchanging great bliss*'.

When we are actually resting in awareness, we should avoid fixating upon what is seen, heard, smelled, tasted or physically felt. Even though the five senses are wide open, awareness should remain undirected. In other words, we don't fixate on what is perceived as being 'this' or 'that'; we don't attach names to things. This is called the 'absence of reference point' or 'no focus of awareness'. Because self-existing awareness is unimpeded, unobscured in itself, there is no duality, no dualistic fixation at all. While remaining free from fixation, all dualistic notions are absent. The great master Longchen Rabjam said of this:

> Don't analyze! Don't analyze! Don't analyze your mind!
> Don't grasp! Don't grasp! Don't grasp your own mind!
> Don't correct! Don't correct! Trying to correct or modify
> Just makes your state of mind contrived.
> The fabricating mind obscures your essential nature.

That is what is meant by 'don't grasp'. Try to really understand what Longchen Rabjam meant by the words, 'don't fabricate'. When we apply that in our meditation practice, then we discover what is meant by the natural face of awareness, the nature of mind. The great master Chokgyur Lingpa said:

> Resting the watcher in awareness, there is a vivid emptiness
> Free from color, free from material substance.
> Not forming the thought, 'It is empty!'
> That is the moment of seeing the nature of mind.

Do not fixate on the thought, "It is empty." The idea of emptiness is a dualistic notion, as is the idea, "It is not empty." Both are preconceptions. The key point here is to be totally free from holding onto anything. Wide-open awareness, free from any fixation, is unimpeded — that itself is the view of Dzogchen. Unfortunately, it is possible to imitate this state with a false version. This occurs when we don't think of anything — we're not happy, and we're not sad. We are not worried at all. No thought whatsoever arises, but it's a somewhat oblivious, absent-minded, neutral state. In Tibetan, this is called *lung ma ten*, 'indifference'. To a beginner, the state of indifference where one is somewhat absent-minded can be mistaken for the state of wakefulness. But the two are not the same: they are radically different. Not knowing the difference can be the cause of making a big mistake. The reason why they look alike is that in both cases there is an absence of gross fixating thoughts. Yet the state of indifference falls into one of the three poisons, in that it is still tied up in dullness. Dullness and wakefulness are definitely not the same. One is brass; the other is pure gold.

Another danger is falling into the all-ground consciousness or the alaya consciousness, that is actually dualistic mind not thinking, but focusing outwardly with fixation. This state is vivid, conscious and awake. While there are no thoughts, it is not the real awakened state. Additionally, there is an experience of nonthought — being totally spaced out, totally vacant — that likewise is not Dzogchen awareness. And of course our normal thinking, jumping from one thing to another, is definitely not Dzogchen practice. We need to be clear about the authentic state of rigpa.

When a thought moves and disappears, let it be gone without leaving a trace. Don't anticipate the next thought or plan for it. Don't get involved in judgments, evaluations or hope or fear regarding anything at all. In other words, totally let go of any gross or subtle thoughts. Thinking is fixating. Fixation covers up the ultimate wakefulness. When fixation totally vanishes, there is self-existing wakefulness.

We need to recognize this primordially pure view of Trekchö, the natural innate ordinary mind, self-existing wakefulness that is naked and unimpeded. This is the key point of Vajrayana practice. It's what we need to recognize, what we need to train in. It is the fruition, the buddha-mind itself. Consider the first sentence the Buddha spoke after attaining complete enlightenment in Bodhgaya. He said:

> I have found a nectar-like truth,
> Profound, tranquil, unconstructed, luminous, and
>   unconditioned.

That's it. There is something here to realize, something to understand and to recognize, but it is not a 'thing,' not a normal object of our thought or intellect. Whether the context be view, meditation or conduct, this is exactly what should be revealed in its naked state. As a conclusion, dedicate the merit from your training session to the benefit of all sentient beings. We can have some discussion now.

STUDENT: What exactly does the statement mean that thoughts are Dharmakaya?

Rinpoche: As I mentioned before, the *essence* of the thought is dharmakaya, but the thinking itself is not dharmakaya. It's very important not to confuse these two. We cannot say it doesn't matter at all whether I think or don't think. For someone who recognizes the essence in the arising of a thought, the thought dissolves and has no karmic effect. For that type of practitioner, it's true that there is no difference between thinking and not thinking. Through the guru's oral instructions and personal experience, that person comes to the point of recognizing that within any thought the essence is dharmakaya. Such an individual will neither be carried away by the thinking, nor get involved in ordinary disturbing emotions. That is the special quality of a practitioner.

A normal person has gross and subtle thoughts. A practitioner also has gross and subtle thoughts. Without these, there would be no need to practice! The difference between these two types of people is that a practitioner has received the pointing-out instructions, and, through meditation practice, has become aware that the essence of thought is dharmakaya. By virtue of that realization, a meditator has the opportunity not to get caught up in thinking and chase after what is thought of in an ordinary way. Once we recognize dharmakaya, then we will know how to apply that in our own experience. From that point on, whether we do so or not is totally up to ourselves. But we know how to practice. We are free of the problem of not knowing how to deal with a thought.

STUDENT: What is the difference between nonthought and indifference?

RINPOCHE: The state of the 'all-ground consciousness' is to be merely conscious or noticing. That is in itself a subtle fixation, a directedness of attention which is unaware of itself. Although there is no gross duality of subject and object, there is a subtle sense of stillness, of dwelling. It is a very subtle conceptual state in which one is conscious; there is an abiding quality. Of course, meditation practice should not cultivate this state. The Mahamudra teachings state, "One-pointedness of attention is not the real state of Mahamudra." Awareness, rigpa, is free from any sense of dullness. In the *alaya*, the all-ground, some dullness is by nature present. Awareness has brightness and is free from fixating. The dullness in the state of the all-ground is accompanied by fixation.

STUDENT: Isn't visualization inevitably a conceptual state?

RINPOCHE: If 'you are visualizing,' then certainly there is thought. Compared to impure perception, pure perception is good. However, once we fixate or cling to a pure experience, it becomes impure. Conversely, when experiencing something impure without clinging to it, there is no fault at all. Please understand that.

STUDENT: Is there thought occurrence during awareness?

RINPOCHE: If, during the continuity of awareness, there is thought occurrence, that is not the awareness we are discussing. The term 'thought,' in Tibetan *namtog*, refers to our conceptual mind fixating in a dualistic way. Rigpa, awareness, is the opposite of that. It is free from conceptual thought. The term *'nampar mitogpey yeshe'* refers to wakefulness that is without thought — nonconceptual wakefulness. There is a basic difference here between dualistic mind and awareness. Mind depends on subject and object, but rigpa does not depend on dualistic notions. The moment you slip out of the continuity of rigpa, a thought can arise.

STUDENT: What is the real point of the three samadhis?

RINPOCHE: The three samadhis are the samadhi of suchness, the samadhi of illumination, and the samadhi of the seed-syllable. The samadhi of suchness, refers to not moving away from the state of awakened mind which is the realization of all the buddhas. The samadhi of illumination and the samadhi of the seed-syllable are displayed and allowed to vanish within the framework of the first samadhi. If the practitioner is not proficient in the samadhi of suchness, the other two samadhis become conceptual creations.

STUDENT: What is the meditation of rigpa?

RINPOCHE: Whatever we might learn, we must grow familiar or get used to it. Right now, we are really accustomed to dualistic fixation and ignorance. We are not very familiar with the awakened state. At present, it seems so smooth and easy to continue in a dualistic framework. It requires almost no effort at all. Our tendency to fixate is not stopped by anything. In fact, our conceptual mind is almost like Superman in this respect!

Now we need a new habit. The term for 'to meditate' and 'to grow used to' are the same in Tibetan. A famous phrase plays on these words by saying: "There is no meditation, but there is familiarization." 'Growing used to' or 'meditation' in this context is unlike what we are normally accustomed to, which is always a dualistic act that keeps some other object in mind. That is not what is meant by meditation here. All the key points of essential practice are included within these two sentences:

> Not even an atom upon which to meditate.
> Not even an instant in which to be distracted.

Apply these two! What do we understand by remaining undistracted? 'Undistracted' here means not parting from the innate nature in which there is no 'thing' to meditate upon. How will training in that help us right now? When resting in the natural face of awareness, there are of course no gross disturbing emotions present. Moreover, even the most subtle fixation, which is the basis for emotions, is absent. That is why this is called 'taking the fruition as the path'.

At that very moment, the realization of a truly and perfectly enlightened buddha is present in our being. But because it lasts such a short period, it doesn't help us much. Such a brief glimpse of awareness is too short for us to appreciate its qualities. It's like that.

STUDENT: What does 'compassion that holds no focus' mean?

RINPOCHE: Traditionally, Buddhist terminology describes three types of compassion: compassion that takes sentient beings as focus, compassion that takes the truth as focus, and compassion that holds no focus. 'Compassion that takes sentient beings as focus' means that we keep in mind an object, a sentient being, in order to give rise to compassion. Without that object, we would have no feeling of compassion. For a normal person, compassion is easier to feel if it is based on someone you love, such as a close relative or a kind friend. Our compassion towards those who haven't helped us is not very strong, and it is very difficult to feel compassion for an enemy, someone who has really harmed us. If a really dear loved one suffers, our strong sympathy makes us feel almost as agonized as they do. We may feel a little pained when we see some stranger suffering, but our empathy is not so intense. And when their enemy suffers, some people will rejoice and even throw a party to celebrate. So, for a normal person, the compassion that takes sentient beings as an object is always partial and limited.

'Compassion that takes the truth as focus' is based on the understanding that all composite things are impermanent; that the individual self and all other phenomena have no true existence. It is aimed at the mind where such an understanding is not present; towards those who are ignorant.

'Compassion beyond focus' is difficult to comprehend because it is an unfamiliar experience. It is also called 'emptiness suffused with compassion'. In this state, compassion arises as the natural expression of emptiness. The practitioner who realizes emptiness is, at that moment, free from dualistic fixation; and therefore the love, affection and compassion that is present is free from focus, free from reference point. This kind of compassion is neither partial nor limited. It does not hold any expectation of reward, nor does it need anything in return.

Wakefulness

Self-existing wakefulness is our fresh present wakefulness, untainted by the thoughts of the three times. The general teachings call this the 'profound emptiness'. The 'empty' here means that any phenomenon is devoid of true existence. The suffix '-ness' means that while being empty, there is at the same time, the capacity for anything to arise and be perceived; thus it is not exclusively empty.

In the Sanskrit, this state is called *mahashunyata dharmadhatu*. *Maha* is great, *shunyata* is emptiness, *dharmadhatu* is realm of phenomena. This phrase, 'great emptiness realm of phenomena,' is exactly what is pointed out by means of the fourth empowerment, which I described earlier. The fourth empowerment introduces us to the thought-free wakefulness which is the unity of cognizance and emptiness, bliss and emptiness, awareness and emptiness. This wakefulness that encompasses all of samsara and nirvana, which is our indescribable nature, lies beyond the reach of concepts. Anything that is not within the reach of concepts, anything that we cannot find words for, is by its very nature indescribable, isn't it? I will now continue explaining how to recognize and sustain this state of wakefulness.

In the Dzogchen teachings, rigpa is defined as self-existing wakefulness. When we say that our basic state is cognizant, we are talking about the basis for wakefulness, the capacity for perceiving whatever takes place. This cognizance is not made out of anything whatsoever. That is why it's called 'empty cognizance'. While being empty in essence, at the same time, by nature, it can cognize.

If the term 'self-existing' is not used, the description is somehow incomplete. This wakefulness is not made up by our ideas; it is not created by our intellect. Something that we first analyze with concepts, then intellectually fabricate is not self-existing, is it? But our present ordinary mind is self-existing wakefulness that is not dependent upon subject and object. It also transcends the possibilities of being or not being veiled by obscurations and habitual tendencies. 'Self-existing' means there is no maker, no producer. 'Rigpa' thus means our present ordinary mind unspoiled by the thoughts of the three times — the unity of being empty and cognizant, innate self-existing wakefulness.

No matter what we call this self-existing wakefulness, we must first recognize it in an authentic, uncontrivedway. Recognizing this is very precious and vital, but only recognizing is not so amazing. It is necessary to be able to sustain the continuity of that recognition. Apply this to yourself, in your own personal experience. The very moment your mind is free from any act of fabricating, there is immediately a vividly empty and awake state which is free and easy. Trying to find words for it, we fail.

There is a story about a practitioner who went to see a great meditation master and received very detailed instructions on this subject for months and months. After a while, the pupil said, "What you are talking about is something I already knew. Before receiving any of these teachings, my mind would very often just spontaneously be empty, awake, free and easy. It happened many times, even before I heard a single word about it." This is true because buddha-nature is present in everyone without exception.

The very instant our dualistic fixating ceases, that same moment our buddha-nature, our enlightened essence, is vividly present. If that weren't the case, then we wouldn't have any buddha-nature to begin with, which is untrue. The basic substance of mind is buddha nature, but we don't normally encounter it, because our dualistic frame of mind obscures our buddha nature. To be unable to meet buddha nature because of fixating on duality is truly a great loss.

So, the first point is to recognize the enlightened essence the very instant dualistic fixation ceases. Once we recognize, we must decide upon that; we must resolve that "This is it." Otherwise, we won't be able to put this state into practice. If we don't bring it into practical experience by sustaining its continuity, we will not progress through the paths and bhumis.

The view of rigpa should be sustained continuously, not only at the time of meditation practice. It should also be maintained while we are involved in our daily activities. All actions should be embraced by the view. If we lose the continuity of rigpa the moment we stand up from the meditation cushion and walk around, then we don't really have much time for training, do we? Since we spend a very small percentage of our lives actually sitting on a meditation cushion, it's very important to sustain rigpa in our daily activities.

The naked, authentic state of rigpa is not something we arrive at by only speculating and analyzing philosophically. The knowledge arising from learning and reflection is conceptual. The achievements of intellectual assumption can never totally clear away our subtle doubts; we don't feel really sure. But the knowledge resulting from meditation practice is direct experience, totally free from doubts and assumptions. We should recognize a moment that is open, awake, free and easy.

Similarly, the way to sustain the continuity of rigpa is not something we understand from listening to teachings, or by studying or contemplating them. It is something that arises from our own experience, based on our meditation practice. Through this, it is possible to be totally free from doubt.

As we train in sustaining this continuity of the view, confidence and certainty in the practice grow stronger. Our compassion and devotion spontaneously expand, and diligence automatically arises from within ourselves. This diligence is spontaneous because we understood that rigpa is capable of dealing with any situation — that's why it is called the 'single sufficient king'. When we really consider this, it becomes impossible for us to avoid applying the recognition of rigpa. Our delight and enthusiasm in this practice thus naturally grow.

After diligently training, we reach a point where there is a complete absence of fear and hesitation regarding our practice. Even if a thousand buddhas tried to stir up doubt in our mind, we would be totally self-confident. We should definitely try to arrive at such firm realization!

Now let's talk about how to practice this. For a beginner a sense of mindfulness or watchfulness is extremely important. As I have repeatedly explained, mindfulness is the best type of conceptual thought one can have. It is conceptual, it is deliberate, and it is a subtle fixation, but for a beginner it is indispensable. Mindfulness and watchfulness are extremely important in being able to sustain the natural face of rigpa. In the beginning, if we let go too much and become too relaxed, then the state of rigpa blurs and becomes wishy-washy. Therefore it's very important to keep some kind of sharpness or presence of mind. Mindfulness, alertness and watchfulness should first be applied, and then let go of. First, remind yourself 'I should be mindful'; then immediately arrive back in the state that is both empty and cognizant.

In the Mahamudra tradition, there is a technique of holding the breath below the navel as a support for mindfulness. Mindfulness remains to a degree corresponding to the mastery of controlling a part of the breath. When I lived at Rumtek, I received some meditation teachings from the retreat master Dil-yag Drubpön. He never wore a wrist watch, but whenever someone asked him the time, he would rest for a minute and then say exactly what time of day it was. This ability was based on his control of the energy currents.

From one point of view, this ability to know the time without using a watch is something special or extraordinary, but ultimately, so what? It's just as easy to wear a watch! Dil-yag Drubpön was unusual in a different way. He would occasionally take his pee-pot as though it were his thermos, pour the urine into his teacup and drink it. After some time, someone might notice and tell him, "Hey wait! That's your pee-pot you're pouring from." He would say, "Oh, really? It tastes the same." Truly, he was beyond embarrassment and shame. His clairvoyance was almost unimpeded, and when he passed away there were incredible signs.

A long time ago, also at Rumtek, His Holiness the 16th Karmapa was giving the transmission of the *Dam-ngak Dzö,* Jamgön Kongtrül's *Treasury of Oral Instructions*. His Holiness Dilgo Khyentse was there, along with the previous incarnation of Sangye Nyenpa, and many other tulkus as well. The discipline was quite strict. Everyone had to sit in rows, wear their finest robes and brocade vests and so forth. Only Dil-yag Drubpön, the retreat master, didn't have to keep the rules. He was exempted by His Holiness Karmapa. He didn't have to do anything special; he could do whatever he wanted. Sometimes he would arrive without any shirt or shawl, walking in late with his thermos and tsampa in hand. He would walk in all by himself, but never feel ashamed. Occasionally, Karmapa would tell him, "Get up and dance." Then in that big gathering in front of hundreds of people, he would dance around with his skirt fluttering in the air. He was incredible!

A practitioner who is quite proficient in sustaining the continuity of rigpa does not need to depend on rigid mindfulness. For a person who has truly recognized the state of rigpa, repeatedly trained in that and become quite stable, no matter what thought arises, that thought itself becomes rigpa. If this were not the case, then it would be an exaggeration to say that one could attain complete enlightenment in one lifetime. This life would be too short.

'Practitioner' in this context refers to a person who has truly recognized rigpa, the awakened state, and is training in it. Sometimes it seems as though unusually strong disturbing emotions and gross thoughts well up in the practitioner's mind. He or she may think this is really bad, but that's not so. In fact, strong emotions can be a great help. If one is really certain about what is clean, when something dirty appears it is very obvious. You won't be cheated at all. If you really know the color white, when something black appears you immediately recognize the difference. A true practitioner is unlike a normal person who has not recognized innate wakefulness. A common person has not experienced rigpa. Therefore, whenever a thought or emotion moves, immediately that person is carried away by it, caught up in it. In contrast, a practitioner who has been introduced to this moment of rigpa and who has grown familiar with that to some degree will not be carried away. He will use that occurrence as a contrast, to highlight the difference between the grossness of the emotion and rigpa. Therefore, the emotion does not have the same impact as it would have for a normal person.

What does a practitioner do at that time? Because of the contrast, it might seem as though the emotion is even more gross or acute; but it is not. It is exactly the same as any normal emotion.. There is nothing that the practitioner needs to do with the emotion, such as throw it away. He simply lets it pass without either accepting or rejecting it, and he sustains the previously recognized state of rigpa. Through that, the force of the disturbing emotion automatically diminishes.

Another point: when training in the state of samadhi, some temporary meditation experiences can occur. I briefly touched upon these before; they are called bliss, clarity and nonthought. For example, the experience of bliss is when the body feels incredibly blissful and the mind is totally at ease. If we start to get fascinated by this, thinking, "Hey, I like this. This feels good. I'd love to keep feeling it!," that becomes a severe fault. Sometimes we experience clarity, perhaps even accompanied by some level of clairvoyance. We feel we know, either very clearly or in part, what other people are thinking or what is happening some other place. We may be impressed with ourselves, thinking, "Now I'm really an advanced practitioner, maybe a mahasiddha — maybe even enlightened!" If we start to become fascinated with the experience of clarity, that also turns into a flaw. It is the same with the experience of nonthought. If one grasps onto any of these they become a defect. The important point is not to be carried away by them.

Genuine meditation training is not a joke; nor is it deceptive. It's real. There is progress. Experience and realization do take place. When experiences arise in our mind we may feel they are extraordinary, unique, and that we have attained some powers. But please understand that such fascination, or that thinking that oneself is exceptional, can turn into serious obstacles. If you have a vision or a pure experience, or even some temporary experiences and powers, don't think you're special.

Now we come to some techniques to dispel the enemies to practicing and sustaining the state of rigpa. These enemies are called 'dullness' and 'agitation'. Dullness is when we feel obscured and lethargic. When that happens, when there is no real sharpness or brightness of rigpa, then imagine that in the center of your heart is a ball of light or the letter AH. Imagine that it shoots out through the crown of your head and hovers in mid-air. Don't hold the breath in; expel the breath. Having expelled the breath, keep the attention on the ball of light or the letter AH in the space above one's head. That brightens up the state of mind and brings forth clarity.

If you are too agitated, on the other hand, then completely relax your body posture and state of mind from within. Lower the gaze, and imagine that at the tip of the nose there is a ball of light. That will calm down the agitation. For a practitioner, the two main obstacles are dullness and agitation. We should be sure not to fall prey to them, because in the moment of doing so one is no longer a practitioner. To the extent that we are not overpowered by dullness and agitation, there is progress in our practice.

Here is another Dzogchen technique. Seek out a high place in the mountains, above the clouds, with a vast, expansive view and crystal-clear air. It should be a safe haven from robbers, bandits, and wild ferocious animals. If you are afraid to go there by yourself, take a friend who has the same mind-set as yourself. Don't go with someone with different ideas, because then they will occupy your time chatting about this and that. Go there with a friend who is a practitioner and your practice will improve. This is probably the reason why tourists go trekking in Nepal. Trekkers often come to me and say, "We want to go where it is really clear and cloud-free, where the sky is totally blue and there's a great view." Even ordinary tourists' minds are benefited by such a place.

So, in this a high place with a vast view, sit with the sun at your back. It's important to face away from the sun, which can be harmful to the eyes. Gaze into the clear blue sky, and sit relaxed in the posture explained previously, with the breath flowing freely and uncontrolled, and looking straight ahead with open eyes. Rest evenly in the indescribable state of innate awareness, unspoiled by the thoughts of the three times. There is some auspicious link here between the external circumstance and the inner state of mind. A vast and clear open view inwardly supports a state of mind that is bright, sharp and totally free from any fixation whatsoever. This is a special Dzogchen practice called 'the threefold sky practice'.

According to this practice, outer space is wide-open and unimpeded, just as the inner space of rigpa is also wide-open and unimpeded. Remain in the indivisibility of these two. Facing a vast sky that is wide-open and unimpeded helps to brighten and sharpen the state of awareness and to eliminate even the most subtle fixation. In this way, the outer space or the sky is very kind and beneficial. Are there any questions?

STUDENT: What should we do when merging our awareness with the sky?

RINPOCHE: When you sit in a lofty, vast, cloud-free place, the sky is open and wide; it is impossible to pinpoint any middle or edge of it. It's simply expansive. Similarly, our innate awareness is also free from center or edge and is impossible to pinpoint. Just resting in that is the indivisibility. It is not that we have to take our awareness into space and extend outwards or that space has to come into us. It's not like that. It's merely the mingling of the two.

First of all, we have to say that space exists. There is space. How is space? It has no center, no edge, no end. Similarly, if we ask, "Is there something which is rigpa?," we have to answer, "Yes, there is rigpa." Like space, it is something free from center, end or limitation. From this standpoint, the two are similar.

STUDENT: Does a Mahamudra practitioner's ordinary mind and a Dzogchen practitioner's rigpa have the same experience, the same quality?

RINPOCHE: First of all, ordinary mind and rigpa are exactly the same; there is no difference. In the Dzogchen system, rigpa is pointed out immediately, from the very outset. What is it that is pointed out? If we want to compare the two systems, it's the fourth of the four yogas of Mahamudra — the very essence of nonmeditation — that is pointed out from the outset of the Dzogchen system. In the Mahamudra system, there is a gradual shedding of the layers surrounding ordinary mind. As one progresses through the 12 aspects of the four yogas, more and more layers are discarded until finally there are no layers left — only ordinary mind, rigpa. Dzogchen is straightforward and immediate, so it is exceptionally beneficial for the type of person who has a karmic connection to Dzogchen practice. The Mahamudra system of practicing step by step is more appropriate for those without this connection. Mahamudra is more detailed because it proceeds very precisely, step by step, while the Dzogchen system is more direct. In short, the greatest benefit is to practice both systems together.

STUDENT: Ultimately is there a difference between the two systems?

RINPOCHE: There is no ultimate difference, except from the point of practicing the path. From the Mahamudra side, we need to understand the teachings on One-Pointedness, Simplicity, One Taste and Nonmeditation, and how each of these have the aspects of all four. For instance, there is the one-pointed aspect of One-Pointedness, the simplicity aspect of One-Pointedness, the one taste aspect of One-Pointedness and the nonmeditation quality in One-Pointedness. These are steps. The other side is to understand it from the Dzogchen standpoint — what self-existing wakefulness actually is in our own experience. While practicing, any kind of analyzing and checking is of course a fault, but afterwards we can look back and evaluate a little bit, weighing the teaching with our experience and that can be very beneficial.

Someone who truly realizes the state of rigpa according to the Dzogchen teachings will find it perfectly reasonable to proceed step by step according to the gradual teachings such as Mahamudra. It makes perfect sense to understand the different stages very clearly. At the same time, someone who has realized the identity of nonmeditation will also be able to appreciate fully how the Dzogchen teachings enable one to arrive at the state of nonmeditation in a single jump, a single step.

The Dzogchen approach from the very outset distinguishes between the dualistic impure state of mind, with its concepts and disturbing emotions, and rigpa, which is dharmakaya free from disturbing emotions and concepts. Thus, from the very beginning, one is shown what is genuine and what is not. In the Mahamudra system, what is emphasized from the beginning is the power of mind, its capacity. Using that, fixation becomes more and more subtle as one goes along. As one progresses it falls away, until finally there is only rigpa left. These two approaches are like different flavors of oral instructions, but the final destination is exactly the same.

STUDENT: What methods are needed for the student who has not attained stability in awareness?

RINPOCHE: What is needed is what I mentioned before: mindfulness or presence of mind. The possibility of applying this practice is based entirely on an agreement between master and disciple. The master shows that our present state of ordinary mind, wakefulness free from thoughts of the three times — which is open, awake, free, and easy — is itself the state of rigpa. Once we recognize that in our own experience and our personal teacher agrees and confirms it, saying "That's right. That's it!" then that is what should be sustained.

The continuity of rigpa should be sustained as the meditation practice, but that doesn't happen automatically, of course. Because we are so used to not allowing the state of rigpa to continue, as soon as the short moment of rigpa is gone, we start to think about something else. Having forgotten rigpa, how do we get back to it? We need one thought: "I should sustain rigpa!". As soon as that reminder brings us back, we should let go of it, together with all thoughts about past, present and future. After arriving back in rigpa, we are thus free from the thought, "I should sustain rigpa!" If we believe that essential meditation practice involves maintaining the thought of mindfulness, then something is wrong, and further instruction is necessary.

STUDENT: Unless we fully understand devotion, isn't it mere blind faith?

RINPOCHE: If we know the true reason for something, and understand its genuine qualities, that kind of appreciation is not blind faith — in fact, it is faith with open eyes. However, genuine, unshakable devotion does not occur until authentic insight into the nature of mind takes place. The trust and devotion we experience before that is fickle and perishable. When something really makes sense to you deeply and you can establish the validity of it through your own intelligence and experience, then your appreciation for that has an unchanging staying-power. But if it is something you're not really certain about — something that you have been told but you don't really understand — your trust in is not very stable. When we study teachings that talk about everything as impermanent, about emptiness and suffering, we might feel "This is true! It is really so!" That kind of feeling is based on trust. When we hear about emptiness and dependent origination, at some point it really makes sense, so much so that tears come to our eyes. That is an increase in trust.

There are different types of trust. First, hearing about what is true and feeling some degree of admiration for the truth is called clear, admiring trust. Next, there is 'longing trust'. The third type of trust is when we actually gain some personal insight into the nature of things. This is called 'irreversible' or 'unshakable trust'.

STUDENT: When are other times we can recognize awareness?

RINPOCHE: When genuine compassion or naked insight into emptiness arises, that's the moment. This is the whole reason why we should study about 'relative' and 'ultimate' bodhichitta. Relative bodhichitta is always engendered by concepts. It is a clean, beautiful concept, but it is a concept nonetheless.

STUDENT: What are some other methods to deal with dullness?

RINPOCHE: Usually dullness occurs when you sit down, while agitation occurs when you walk around. That's in general. Of course, it's possible to be really dull and obscured while walking around and doing things. At that point, you could apply one of the two techniques mentioned earlier — visualizing either the small sphere of light or the letter AH above your head. Or, go to a place with a vast view.

STUDENT: What if you are at work?

RINPOCHE: Go to the window, open it and look out.

STUDENT: Will making myself physically exhausted help with agitation?

RINPOCHE: In the Dzogchen tradition there is a technique through which one tries to really tire oneself out so that one feels completely exhausted, and then one tries to recognize rigpa.

STUDENT: Could I lie down on my bed?

RINPOCHE: As long as you don't lose presence of mind or fall asleep.

STUDENT: If I'm not sure that I have recognized rigpa, how can I sustain it?

RINPOCHE: If one doesn't know what rigpa is to begin with, then one obviously can't sustain it. That's why one should request the pointing-out instruction from a qualified meditation master. It's just like when you go shopping: if you don't know what you're looking for, what will you buy?

STUDENT: For a practitioner of self-existing wakefulness, who has attained stability in sustaining self-existing wakefulness, what happens to him or her at the moment of death?

RINPOCHE: The best practitioner is already liberated before facing death. The next best-practitioner, someone who has really recognized the state of innate awareness and has trained in it to a certain degree, will be liberated before the last exhalation of breath, meaning at the moment of death. As soon as we have exhaled for the last time, it is no longer the process of dying — we have actually died, and the bardo of dharmata begins. The second-best situation is therefore to attain liberation at the moment of death. The third-best is to attain liberation during the bardo of dharmata or the bardo of becoming.

A normal person doesn't find much to laugh about when he knows he is about to die. Our feelings are dominated by fear and uncertainty, and there is no real sense of confidence at all. As the link to our physical body, which serves as a sort of anchor, grows weaker and weaker, the mental turmoil grows more and more intense. However, a practitioner who has been introduced to rigpa will know the great value in being able to simply rest in the natural state at that point. There is nothing else that can help at that time. No one will save us, no one can really take us out of that experience. It is completely in our own hands at the moment of our death. It is much more difficult to practice then because our confusion and anxiety are much stronger, but if we can practice at that time, liberation is also much easier. It is said that a practitioner who has already acquired great stability will be able to train and be liberated very quickly at the moment of death. Or, if we have recognized the natural state of awareness during the dream state many times, it will be very easy to be liberated at the moment of death. We can say the same for the bardo states.

STUDENT: What happens to the power of our practice, the power of having formed the habit of training in meditation practice. Does it get totally interrupted and disappear at the moment of death?

RINPOCHE: Definitely not! Any positive thing we do has an effect that is carried on to the next life. We can see that even now. The fact that we all are interested in this kind of understanding and practice is clear proof of our link with the teachings in former lives. Either we have studied, or have both studied and reflected, or we have studied, reflected and actually practiced in past lives. Otherwise we wouldn't have the slightest interest in these teachings and in putting them into practice. It's the same with the power of meditation, our ability to sustain the state of rigpa. This isn't somehow cut or lost at the moment of death. It carries on, though it may become weakened or obscured in the next life. There is something called 'the obscuration of a womb birth,' which dims our ability after birth so that it is not as clear as in our previous life.

STUDENT: What is the connection between recognizing nondual awareness and the general Vajrayana practices such as visualization and recitation?

RINPOCHE: There are two kinds of accumulations, as I discussed previously: the 'accumulation of merit' with reference point or focus, and the 'accumulation of wisdom' without focus. The normal practices of visualizing deities and chanting mantras, performing tantric rituals and so forth are all an exercise in making clean thoughts to get rid of unclean thoughts — in other words, get rid of the bad ones and make the nice ones. The training in recognizing innate wakefulness, on the other hand, is the accumulation of wisdom without reference point.

The development stage is the cause for manifesting the two form kayas: sambhogakaya and nirmanakaya. The completion stage of nonconceptual wakefulness, the naked state of awakened mind explained here, is the seed for realizing dharmakaya. In short, it's good if we can practice so that the ground, the basis, is the two truths; the path is the two accumulations; and the fruition is the two kayas.

Nirvana Is Peace

Everything in this world is impermanent. The lives of all sentient beings perish; they do not last. Our experiences of pleasure and pain, happiness and suffering are also transient; they all pass. At this moment, we have obtained that which is difficult to obtain — a precious human existence. We have met that which is difficult to meet — a qualified spiritual teacher. We have received what is difficult to receive — the precious Dharma teachings. In our present situation, we are equipped to practice the Dharma and attain realization. Don't let this chance slip away! Make a firm resolution: "I will engage diligently in study, reflection and meditation!" Truly, we don't know how long we will be in this world. The next time around, there is no guarantee that we will be reborn as a human being with the same opportunities. Therefore, we should resolve with great determination to put these teachings into practice in a genuine and authentic way.

In the practice of Vajrayana one takes fruition as path. We should understand that the vital point of Vajrayana is inherent wakefulness. We should decide, "I will listen to, reflect upon and put these teachings into practice in order to realize inherent wakefulness and to meet face to face the primordial protector, Samantabhadra!"

Earlier I mentioned the four types of teachers whom we should follow. The first teacher is the living lineage master with whom we should connect. The second teacher is the statements of enlightened beings, which we should study, reflect upon and try to understand. The third teacher is the symbolic teacher of our experiences — the fact that everything is fleeting and perishes, that nothing reliable or trustworthy exists to be found anywhere in this world. The teacher of our experiences is someone from whom we receive daily lessons — every day, every hour, every minute. No matter what kind of pleasure or happiness we experience in this world, it never endures. Samsaric situations never last. Therefore, there is always some basic discomfort when we rely on fleeting circumstances. This is a lesson we continuously receive. In this way, the impermanent nature of samsaric existence is our teacher.

Ultimately the sole purpose of meeting and following all these three teachers is so that we can meet face to face with the fourth kind of teacher — the ultimate teacher of our innate nature. Now I will talk a little more on how to do that.

One technique is to rest in a state in which you feel totally free and wide-open. Do not focus on either perceiving or the empty quality, but simply suspend your attention in a vast, open state of mind in which perception and emptiness are indivisible. Do not focus too much on one side of things or the other. We do not need to deliberately unite perception and emptiness. Instead, strip awareness to its naked state — be wide-awake without any fixation, without holding onto anything at all. In such a state, perception and emptiness are automatically indivisible. Whatever originally exists is revealed and present.

When we first try to sustain the continuity of awareness as the main practice, it will not happen continuously. We will think different thoughts about all possible things. At that time, look directly into the thinker and the thinking is thereby self-liberated. Like a wave that arises in the sea, it dissolves back into the water.

We can say that a wave and the ocean's water are the same, but we can also say they are different. The function of a wave differs from the water itself. Although the wave comes from the water its shape and momentum are different. Yet it is also identical, because without the water a wave cannot even manifest. In the same way, we can't say that the state of rigpa and the thought are the same; but also we can't say that they are altogether different. When we are not 100% stable in the state of rigpa, we will inevitably drift into thought activity. It is unavoidable. Thought involvement is itself a straying from rigpa. When our attention get caught in a thought, that is the way of a normal person. A practitioner needs to notice, "Hey, wait a minute. I'm sitting and thinking!" Then, just as a wave is allowed to dissolve back into the water, the practitioner should let the thought-wave dissolve back into awareness. This is called being 'liberated into dharmakaya'.

When that is allowed to happen, it is a sign that genuine practice can begin.

A true practitioner of Mahamudra or Dzogchen needs to differentiate between the genuine, unmistaken state of rigpa and the experience of being involved in either a gross or subtle thought. The main point of teachings on buddha-nature is to recognize the view that enables us to transcend the three realms of samsara. The dualistic state of mind can feel blissful, clear or nonconceptual, but if we cling to those feelings or meditative moods and make them our practice, we do not transcend the three realms of samsara. Instead, we stray into the Realms of Desire, the Realms of Form and the Formless Realms. These higher realms within samsara are actually created through meditation; they are not the state of true liberation.

We need to know the method for stepping out of the entrapment of the three realms of samsara. By merely 'meditating' we do not transcend samsaric existence. Sentient beings have a certain degree of fixation, which is exactly what creates a particular level of existence within samsara. If our fixation and disturbing emotions are very gross and solid, we end up in a material body within the Desire Realms. If our fixation is less solid and our disturbing emotions are less forceful, then we will have a body of light in the Realms of Form. The most subtle states of dualistic mind create the four levels of the Formless Realms. Therefore, it is crucial to recognize our innate nature, which completely liberates us from all the six realms of samsara. This nature is called rigpa in the Dzogchen teachings or ordinary mind in the Mahamudra teachings.

Rigpa is the path of fruition. Rigpa, nondual awareness, is the opposite of marigpa, unknowing or unawareness. Marigpa is usually translated as 'ignorance': 'ma' is 'not' and 'rigpa' is 'knowing'. This unknowing or unawareness is the direct cause for continuing in samsaric existence. To transcend samsaric existence, we need the opposite of unknowing, which is rigpa.

Marigpa, unawareness, is a basis for stupidity, dullness, and disturbing emotions. It connects you with the thoughts of the three times and samsaric existence. Rigpa, on the contrary, is dharmakaya free from the thoughts of the three times. Unspoiled by the thoughts of the three times, it is original wakefulness.

In the state of rigpa there are no such attributes as confusion or liberation, good or evil. When we recognize rigpa and sustain its continuity, there is no basis whatsoever for confusion. Confusion cannot possibly arise within that state. We have already identified marigpa, unawareness or ignorance, as the very opposite of rigpa. Marigpa brings forth dualistic fixation, which creates the basis for disturbing emotions; these in turn lead to positive and negative karmic actions and so on.

Many practitioners in the Kagyü and Nyingma lineages did not study scriptures and teachings very much. However, they had been given the pointing-out instruction to the state of rigpa, which they put into practice. Through their training they then developed the discriminating knowledge that fully discerns phenomena, which is also called the 'spontaneous bursting forth of intelligence arising from meditation'. This is a state of acute intelligence in which whatever one needs to know is understood in a split-second, without even having studied. Through the practice of rigpa, amazing qualities unfold.

Simply relying on the understanding that comes from studying books and contemplating matters intellectually, without depending upon the intelligence that arises from within, is never sufficient. Although one may have studied for seventy years, one can still make mistakes in both words and meaning when expounding the Dharma. But when we hear expressions such as 'the ocean of wisdom overflowed' or 'the power of intelligence burst forth,' where does this come from? From only one place — realizing the view. That is why it is possible for some people, even as young as 15 or 16 years of age, to display incredible wisdom and knowledge. Conversely, other people, who have studied even into their eighties and nineties, may not be that learned when it comes to the point.

Once we truly recognize the view, the state of rigpa, and train in that, we will come to realize that everything, pure or impure, is without exception the expression of rigpa. Through this, it will be very easy to understand everything without error.

In the very moment of sustaining the genuine view of rigpa, there is no dualistic fixation whatsoever, because there is no unawareness present. Therefore, there are no gross or subtle thoughts and no disturbing emotions. In that moment we have transcended the entrapment of the three realms of samsara. In that short instant, we are inseparable from the realization of all buddhas. However, the buddhas' two types of wisdom — the knowledge of seeing the nature as it is, and the knowledge of perceiving whatever exists — have not been fully developed. A short moment of the awakened state does not provide the chance for those two wisdom qualities to fully develop. Still, there is in that short moment not even a hair-tip of ignorance, of ego-clinging, of holding onto things as being real or of disturbing emotions. This is in essence the state of realization, the Middle Way, Mahamudra and Dzogchen. When many masters of the past said, "Buddhahood is not reached through effort, so totally let go and rest in the state of effortlessness," they were describing exactly this view.

To take the approach of fruition as the path is to practice the view, the state of rigpa, no matter which of the five poisons or coarse or subtle thoughts we encounter. Whether we are caught up in a positive state of thought such as devotion or compassion or in negative thought states arising from the five poisons, we must sustain genuine self-existing awareness as the practice. This shouldn't be some version of self-existing awareness that we have personally concocted. The real thing is present in the absence of any artificial attempts to produce something. Trying to create something artificial covers up the genuine. When not creating anything artificial, what is by nature spontaneously present will manifest.

What is meant here by fabrication, making something artificial? It doesn't matter what it is — it could even be our idea of emptiness that we have created through our study of Buddhist philosophy. Perhaps we have read so many books and thought about them so much that it is like this: "Everything is empty! There's no real identity, no real entity, in things. Yet at the same time, the nature of mind is cognizant. These two are not different. They are indivisible. This is how it must be like!" This whole mind-set is an intellectual fabrication. It is still artificial.

Because we have five senses, we perceive the five sense objects. The mental faculty also perceives mental objects, memories and fantasies. These six taken together are called the 'six consciousnesses'. When they are wide-open, we perceive. For example, through our eyes we see visual form, and if the form is beautiful, we spontaneously think, "How nice! I like that." If the form is ugly, we think, "How awful. I don't like it!" If it's something in-between, we don't really care; we feel indifferent. These three attitudes are not yet the full-fledged three poisons, but they are the basis from which the disturbing emotions manifest.

If we are given a beautiful object, because we feel some attraction to it, we will be happy. If we are given a bag of trash, because we feel some aversion to it, we get angry. If we are given a stone that is neither beautiful nor ugly, we will think, "What's this for?" We feel neither irritated not delighted, but remain indifferent, which eventually grows into dullness. This is the normal way the mind continuously functions. We should examine ourselves and see that although our disturbing emotions are not always vividly manifest in a gross way, the seeds for them are always subtly present, and they are thus always ready to return instantly.

Ego-clinging also has two modes — gross and subtle. Gross ego-clinging is quite evident. When someone tells you, "You're bad!" you feel anger. When someone tells you, "You're good!" you feel pleased. This subtle form of ego-clinging is almost continuously present; it props us up, in a way. To keep the notion of a personal identity distinct from other people — 'just me, myself' — that's subtle ego-clinging. When that subtle ego-clinging is reinforced through anger or pride, it can even make the shape of the body change. When it becomes stronger and stronger, the body becomes more stiff and solid. In the meditative state, though, this rigid ego-clinging is loosened, and the body relaxes and feels more peaceful and at ease. At that time, some clarity or brightness may be present as well. On the other hand, this ease can also be produced by drinking alcohol or taking a drug, such as a tranquilizer. One then feels peaceful and quiet. The ego-clinging is more soft or gentle, but the clarity or brightness is lacking. Instead, we feel dull and stupid.

The more uptight the ego-clinging is, the more unhappy and uncomfortable we feel. The more the ego-clinging can be released and relaxed, the more happy and comfortable we feel. In the company of close friends, most people will lean back, relax and talk very freely, feeling at ease. If someone says something that makes us angry, we suddenly become uptight and sit very rigidly. When we are in a group of people and we suddenly feel uptight, the body will react by tensing up as well. That's because the ego-clinging is more acute at that time.

In particular, Westerners are less comfortable with groups of Westerners, while Asians are less comfortable with groups of Asians. Why is that? Westerners know more about Westerners, so they don't want others to know about their education, their feelings and their background. When a Westerner mixes with Asians, though, he is not shy or proud of himself. He focuses his attention on the Asians' lifestyle — what they feel, how they live, how they communicate. Westerners almost seem to believe Asians come from another planet! Similarly, Asians will react the same way with Westerners when they see how they live. They think Westerners are so interesting. They have a lot of funny machines; they live in a god realm.

Logically, when Westerners see Westerners, they should feel happy and at ease in communicating, but often this is not the case. Instead they erect a very subtle wall. For example, when a Westerner is sitting with a group of Nepalese or Tibetans he feels quite at ease with them. If a second Westerner suddenly joins them, the first Westerner will feel a change happening in himself. He will automatically feel uptight because of feeling self-conscious that the other person knows his background. Am I right? This is all based on ego-clinging, which creates pride. Through pride, we feel ill at ease.

The opposite to that is experienced by a yogi, a true practitioner who has trained in this practice for quite some time. Describing such a person, it is said,

Whomever I'm with, I feel free and easy.
Wherever I go, the sun of happiness shines.

A true practitioner doesn't feel uptight no matter who he or she is with. That is because of having left behind ego-clinging. Ego-clinging is based on ignorance, on unawareness, the opposite of awareness, rigpa.

Among the Buddhist vehicles, the shravaka will try to give up and avoid disturbing emotions, while the bodhisattva will try to change their direction. The Vajrayana practitioner, on the other hand, will use the emotion as the path. What does this mean? Being angry, for instance, is of course not wisdom. It is a normal, confused state of mind. However, within the anger, our innate nature remains as self-existing wakefulness. One should recognize just that through the view of Trekchö. Then the opportunity opens up for one to no longer be carried away by the anger. What one needs to recognize and sustain is nothing other than rigpa itself, no matter what happens, nor what emotion arises.

Concerning taking the fruition as path, do not think, "May I attain enlightenment in a future life!" or "May I attain enlightenment at the moment of death!" or "May I attain enlightenment in the intermediate state of the bardo!". This practice is, right at this very moment, to be face to face with the essence of mind in which the three kayas are embodied.

We have two choices: unawareness or awareness. If we continue in unawareness, we will go on creating the three realms of samsaric existence. Nondual awareness, rigpa, which is free from disturbing emotions, is the opposite. The special quality of Mahamudra and Dzogchen practice is that by recognizing the innate wakefulness or ordinary mind, one transcends samsara in this very moment. This is unique, totally different from other practices. It is called 'taking fruition as the path'. Without hoping for or aiming at another state of fruition sometime in the future, one brings it into the path at this very moment.

If we would somehow recognize the awakened state and it would immediately remain unceasingly, non-stop, there would be nothing more to practice. Sorry, it doesn't happen that way for a beginner. Even though one is a practitioner, all different kinds of thoughts and emotions arise. Sometimes we feel very devoted, and sometimes we are totally carried away by anger. Sometimes we feel very diligent, sometimes we feel very jaded, completely fed up. All different things can take place. This is due to the habit of ego-clinging, holding onto things as real and permanent. The only real way to deal with this is by recognizing the very opposite of the basis for clinging and fixation, which is rigpa, innate wakefulness. The very moment we again recognize the innate state of wakefulness, ego-clinging, which is the cause of all problems, vanishes spontaneously and immediately.

Sometimes we are very diligent in our practice, and sometimes we are fed up. Furthermore, when we are sick with physical or mental pain, such as feeling depressed or saddened, these feelings are based on ego-clinging. If we can cut the root of ego-clinging by recognizing original wakefulness, although the sickness doesn't disappear, the pain decreases quite a lot.

As I mentioned before, there are also 'enhancement practices' or techniques we can use to progress. Devotion to one's root teacher, reflecting on impermanence, cultivating compassion and practicing the development and completion stages with and without concepts are all enhancement practices. They are important and necessary.

Concerning devotion to our teacher; the real ultimate supplication is to allow our state of mind to be indivisible from that which the guru has realized. This is the ultimate way of supplicating, also called 'receiving the true blessings'.

How can thinking of impermanence be an enhancement practice? You might think that you already understand that everything is impermanent, so why do you need to think about this again? Everything is of course impermanent, including our physical body. If we compare ourselves with this piece of paper [Rinpoche holds up a napkin], the paper will probably last longer than our body, our life. This paper can easily last for a few hundred years, even 500 years, while this body will definitely not. We may think it is very easy to cut, bend, tear or burn this bit of paper, but really our own body is much more fragile.

Understanding this, we come to comprehend that there is no time to waste; that this life is actually very short. Based on that understanding, we will put much more effort into practice.

There are two traditional examples describing how one feels when really taking the fact of impermanence to heart. One example is of a coward who discovers a snake in his lap; the other is of a beautiful but vain girl who notices her hair on fire. Neither person will waste a single moment. The coward will certainly be terrified by the snake and immediately do whatever is necessary to escape it. The vain girl, seeing her hair in flames, will drop whatever she's doing and focus her attention solely on extinguishing the fire. A truly acute understanding of impermanence makes our mind that one-pointed.

To cultivate compassion means to train in the conduct of a bodhisattva, first by equalizing oneself with others, next by exchanging oneself with others, and finally by regarding others as more important than oneself. If our heart is truly full of compassion, we cannot really get caught up in attachment and anger. Compassion is very beneficial in many ways. It helps us to realize emptiness and to avoid partiality — things like judging others or feeling that one person is close while another person is not. If everyone in this world developed compassion, there would be no war whatsoever. War would be impossible because the basis for fighting and strife would be absent. Any fight would be a game, nothing more than that.

The practices of the development and completion stages with and without concepts, are, in brief, to regard our body as the deity, our voice as mantra and our mind as the state of samadhi. These different practices are simply methods, skillful means to quickly allow us to progress in the training of mind nature.

For example, if we need to get to another country in a hurry, we can jump straight into a waiting car and drive to the airport. We then hop onto a departing plane. Upon landing, we immediately get into another car and go direct to our destination. In this manner, we can arrive very quickly. On the other hand, we could walk outside and the car could not be ready. We might miss our plane and so forth, spoiling all our plans. Of course we'd never arrive at our destination on time. Like our legs, the car and the airplane, these different practices are merely methods used towards the goal of arrival. We can use all these various practices in order to quickly progress.

As beginners we should keep sessions and breaks, training during both the meditation and post-meditation states. When we sit down in a meditation session, we should just sustain the natural face of awareness. When we get up and walk around, we should regard everything as like a dream or magical illusion. This practice brings incredibly great benefit. Even when we go to sleep at night, we should try to practice 'dream yoga'. Failing this, we can also fall asleep with the thought of compassion or devotion, with some altruistic attitude. We should definitely avoid falling asleep while feeling angry, proud or competitive.

Similarly, our state of mind is very important at the moment of death. At this time, it is best to be someone who had interest in or practiced the view of the unity of emptiness and compassion, of Madhyamika, Dzogchen or Mahamudra. Then it will be possible to focus on that practice while we die. We should definitely avoid passing away in a state of anger or with negative thoughts on our mind. Good thoughts at the moment of death bring about a good rebirth, while negative states of mind bring a lot of pain and suffering in the bardo and in the following rebirth.

We may have recognized the view and glimpsed the genuine state of rigpa; however, unless we practice that, sustaining its continuity, it won't help that much. So train in and be diligent in doing that.

The main topic of this book has been the Four Seals of Dharma. The first of these is that everything conditioned is impermanent. I described how all coarse things in the world are impermanent; how oneself, one's body and life span and so forth are impermanent; and how all thoughts and emotions are impermanent. We can understand how all things are impermanent, but that doesn't mean that there's a 'thing' called impermanence. Really, we cannot find that which is impermanent anywhere or impermanence itself. It is unidentifiable. Examining the matter like that, we meet emptiness;

we can understand emptiness. When one takes impermanence to heart, one will have great interest in Dharma; one will apply oneself to Dharma practice and discover trust and devotion. That was the first teaching.

The second axiom states that Everything defiling is painful. In other words, wherever there are the three mind poisons of attachment, anger and delusion there is always the creation of negative karma and the resultant suffering. The word defiling, zagchey, literally means 'involved in falling or shifting'. It has the sense of holding a focus in mind, being associated with a disturbing emotion, with dualistic fixation. For instance, when in an act of giving you maintain concepts of the giver and the gift, the recipient and the handing over, then such a good deed is called 'defiling virtue'. In the context of all defiling states are painful, it means that being associated with karma and disturbing emotion is painful.

The Third Seal says: 'Everything is empty and devoid of self'. In discussing this, I went through the viewpoint of the four philosophical schools of Buddhism, in particular the view of Mahamudra and Dzogchen.

Now we come to the fourth of the Four Seals of the Dharma: Nirvana is peace. The state of nirvana in this context is the buddha mind that is beyond constructs, dharmakaya. Having captured this unchanging stronghold of dharmakaya, one effortlessly masters the two types of form kayas: sambhogakaya and nirmanakaya. Sambhogakaya is a pure form of light, adorned with the thirty-two major and eighty minor marks of excellence. It is visible to bodhisattvas on the ten bhumis, where the sambhogakaya buddhas are perpetually teaching the Dharma.

This 'nondwelling state of nirvana,' the buddhahood of complete omniscience, is totally free from the four obscurations of karma, disturbing emotions, habitual tendencies and the cognitive obscuration. The impulse to accept and reject has been exhausted. At the same time, the two types of supreme knowledge, the knowledge of knowing the nature as it is and the knowledge of perceiving all that possibly exists, are totally perfected. Simultaneously, there are many other inconceivable qualities.

In the state of true and complete enlightenment, the four mara demons are totally conquered. The four maras are of the aggregates, disturbing emotions, death and the divine child. This last means seduction by sense pleasures and procrastination of spiritual practice.

Buddhahood is omniscience, described as the capacity to vividly and clearly see whatever occurs in the three times simultaneously. This complete knowledge is not an act of deduction or inference, but a direct perception in a way that is inconceivable and incomprehensible to conceptual mind. After enlightenment, there is the buddha activity that has the two qualities of being unobstructed and unchanging. For example, there is the activity of emanating guides for other beings, in which one can simultaneously manifest one billion different teachers in one billion different realms to guide billions of sentient beings. That is the second of the form kayas, called nirmanakaya. Usually four types of nirmanakaya are mentioned: supreme nirmanakaya, incarnated nirmanakaya, created nirmanakaya and variegated nirmanakaya. At the time of buddhahood there is only the activity of guiding countless sentient beings onto the path of liberation and complete enlightenment.

The phrase Nirvana is peace can also be applied to your immediate state of mind. The very moment you recognize the essence of mind and allow its continuity to be sustained, no deluded experience is present. Isn't it true that at that very moment there is no longer any clinging to duality, no karma and no disturbing emotions? In other words, the conceptual frame of mind with its judging, accepting and rejecting is not to be found at that instant. There is a moment of true peace, which is the very identity of nirvana. Wouldn't you agree?

Unfortunately, that peace only lasts for a short while; thus, the intrinsic qualities of buddhahood have no chance to fully manifest. With regard to the 'twofold knowledge present in the fully awakened state,' the moment of recognizing the essence of mind is definitely the 'knowledge that sees the nature as it is'. However, the other, the 'knowledge that perceives all possibly existing things,' cannot be said to be present in actuality. You wouldn't claim to be omniscient simply by glimpsing the nature of mind, would you? The statement 'nirvana is peace' can therefore truly be used only when both knowledges — the knowledge of seeing the nature as it is, as well as the knowledge that perceives all possibly existing things — are fully perfected.

To reiterate, generally speaking in Buddhism, to attain nirvana means that disturbing emotions and dualistic fixation, as well as habitual tendencies, have been utterly depleted, have permanently vanished. Vajrayana nonetheless adds that at that same moment the above-mentioned twofold knowledge is 'unimpededly present as a natural possession'. This twofold knowledge is explained as being two aspects of a single identity. The knowledge that perceives all possibly existing things individually and distinctly is utterly unobstructed *within* the state of knowing the nature as it is. In this way, the truly and completely awakened state is described as the 'unconfined spontaneous presence of the twofold knowledge'. It is based on this principle of perfection that Vajrayana talks about realizing dharmakaya for the welfare of oneself and manifesting the form-kayas for the welfare of others.

Nirvana is peace — this can be understood on several levels. One way is the permanent extinction, the final exhaustion, of deluded experience, which ensures complete transcendence of karma and disturbing emotions, accepting and rejecting, and attachment to pleasure and aversion to pain. In this context, the concepts of pleasure and pain we normally operate with are fleeting, mind-made imputations, nothing more than that. Beyond all those normal concepts, there is what in Vajrayana is called the *'emptiness endowed with the supreme of all aspects indivisible from unchanging great bliss'*. That is what in the profound Vajrayana teachings could be understood by the phrase 'nirvana is peace' — that is a deeper description. In the general teachings of Buddhism, nirvana simply means that the stormy waves of disturbing emotions have fully subsided and you mind remains in the state of great peace. That is not so profound a description.

When expanding upon the deeper description, you hear in Vajrayana mention of the kayas and wisdoms, the inconceivable display of wisdom experience. You can find this described in great detail in the *Manjushri Nama Samgirti,* including the profound sceneries of the buddhafields. There is an incredible amount of descriptions and teachings that could be given describing the qualities of this state of complete enlightenment: the virtues of the body, the virtues of speech, the virtues of mind, the virtues of qualities and virtues of the activities. But that would take a long time!

To conclude, I would like to add that my impression from years of teaching is that many, many foreigners are deeply interested in the Dharma. I am really very happy about this. Remember, though: it is not enough to merely be interested and to study teachings. The real purpose of the Dharma is to be a remedy. It needs to be used to counteract disturbing emotions and one's delusion. In other words, it needs to be used in one's training, to be taken to heart. If we do that, if we use the teachings as the medicine which they are meant to be, spiritual practice becomes really meaningful. Therefore, please practice; please use the teachings. I don't mean only my teachings — there are many other great teachers you can learn from. Receive as many teachings as you can and attain some certainty, some clarity about them. Also, study different books. These days many of the instructions given by buddhas and great masters have been translated into English and other languages. Study and reflect on what these books actually are talking about, and if there is something that is unclear, try to clarify it by asking somebody who knows. To practice and think about the teachings is the most effective way to progress very quickly. In a very short time we can cover a lot of material in a real way. Please do that.

Finally, let me add that we have published this book for peace in the world, and the subsiding of disease and warfare and other undesirable things. Everyone please be loving and helpful to one another, in a spirit of friendliness and cooperation. I pray that all sentient beings realize their intrinsic good heart and train in a noble attitude and peacefulness. May you come to eradicate all shortcomings, realize the natural state of emptiness present in yourselves, and genuinely give rise to altruistic bodhichitta, the awakened frame of mind, resulting in your attainment of liberation and the precious state of omniscient enlightenment. May this effort be auspicious!

Acknowledgments

As with all our books this one would not have come about without the kind, talented and generous assistance of our Dharma friends. Special thanks go to the transcribers, Diane Harrington, Robin, and S. Lhamo; to Kerry Moran for her wonderful editing and to Ian Saude and Michael Tweed for their meticulous proofreading. In this volume here, the *Collected Works of Chökyi Rinpoche, Volume II*, sincere appreciation goes to Deidre Goldberg for proofreading both books.

May this work extend the life and activities of Chökyi Nyima Rinpoche and benefit countless sentient beings.

Erik Pema Kunsang & Marcia Binder Schmidt

Present Fresh Wakefulness

A Meditation Manual on Nonconceptual Wisdom

Chökyi Nyima Rinpoche

Preface

These teachings were compiled from two seminars given at Ka-Nying Shedrub Ling Monastery in 1997 and 1998, as well as at retreats at Nagi Gompa in 1997 and Rangjung Yeshe Gomde, USA in 1998. Rinpoche seemed extremely inspired during all these times and offered those of us in attendance the pithy meditation instructions that form the basis for this wonderful manual. In some instances, Rinpoche's teaching style fell into a rhythm that resembles spontaneous poetry. We have set these instances as single lines in the text to highlight their profundity. In other places, we have displayed Rinpoche's teachings in verse form, to capture the rhythm and cadence of his speech. This body of teachings both sprang from and generated a special atmosphere that we felt compelled to share.

Many thanks go to everyone involved in this project, the transcriber, Joanne Larson, our editor, Kerry Moran.

May this work extend the life of the precious master Chökyi Nyima Rinpoche and may it hasten the awakening and training in present fresh wakefulness in countless beings.

Erik Peam Kunsang & Marcia Binder
Rangjung Yeshe Gomdé
Leggett, USA

Introductory Teachings

The great yogi Milarepa said, "This life is mere illusion, a mere dream. Be compassionate towards beings who don't understand this." All our various perceptions, experiences and dreams are simply the magical display of our thoughts. *Until our thoughts are cleared away and dissolve, karma and disturbing emotions will not end.* It is important to understand that *thoughts themselves are karma and disturbing emotions.*

Life is like a magical illusion or a dream. Because we are asleep or unaware, we dream up all types of different episodes, involving various degrees of pleasure and pain. In this sleep, everything feels as if it were real. The moment we wake up, however, it is obvious that all those experiences have no real existence. Yet, within the dream, they felt the same as our daytime experiences. The anxieties, the fear, the worry we entertained in the dream are all completely unreal, but while dreaming, we do not know them to be a dream, to be illusions. Only after we awake do we realize, "Wow, it was a dream – only a dream." We can even laugh at ourselves for being so overtaken! If it was a disturbing dream, we are happy to wake up, while we feel a sense of loss upon awakening from a pleasant dream.

I'm using the example of a dream here as a metaphor for our waking reality. All things, all of our ordinary experiences, are like dreams. They are as essentially insubstantial as the moon in water. Though from time to time we have a hunch that this might be true, only after we have spent some time learning, reflecting and meditating do we fully understand that our life experiences are like a dream.

Three kinds of knowledge are necessary to ascertain the nature of things — the basic situation, you could say. First is the knowledge resulting from learning. We examine, analyze and inspect what we learn. After this, we are able to gain the second type of knowledge, resulting from reflection. Finally, we apply the third type of knowledge: making what we've learned part of our own experience through practice. Through these three types of knowledge, we are able to completely end the cause of confusion.

Everything that we see, everything that we experience, appears due to a combination of factors. Nothing has any independent or true existence. Everything is 'groundless and rootless', yet appears due to dependent origination. While this is definitely true, a buddha does not explain this immediately. Being wise, compassionate and extremely ingenious, a buddha teaches in a manner that is practical for people to understand, which means he teaches in a gradual way. Very few of us are able to grasp the nature of things instantaneously. Therefore, the Buddha turned the wheel of the Dharma in three consecutive ways. The first set of teachings focused on the *Four Noble Truths,* and the second set concentrated on the *Absence of Characteristics* — a synonym for emptiness. His third Dharma wheel fully reveals the nature of things, and is therefore known as the *Total Uncovering.* The first set of teachings is clear, the second very clear and the third extremely clear!

Simply put, the Buddha's message in the first turning of the Wheel of Dharma is that anyone with a dualistic frame of mind suffers. The dualistic mind entertains selfish emotions, creates karma, has worries, hope, fear and pain. Dualistic mind seems to have built-in suffering. There is an immense variety of suffering, but all of these can be included within three types: the suffering of change, the double suffering of unpleasantness piled on unpleasantness, and the all-pervasive suffering of being conditioned. This is not a matter of mere philosophy; it is very real. We can and do experience suffering, discomfort, distress, and worry throughout our lives. Dualistic mind is always ready to be upset. An input from the senses, a memory or anticipation that is either a little pleasant or a little unpleasant always has the power to disturb us. In addition, there is one suffering which we can never ultimately sidestep: death.

Suffering does not mean that life is continuously painful or that everything is unpleasant. It does mean that happiness or pleasure does not last, it is not forever, and it is never perfect. Even when things seem to be wonderful and we have achieved what we want, we still worry, thinking, "Is it going to run out? Is it going to get a dent? Am I going to lose it?" Pleasure mixed with apprehension is rendered imperfect. "Am I going to lose this happy feeling?" "Is there a greater happiness I could get instead?" Worry spoils the pleasure.

The three types of suffering are not difficult to understand. There is the suffering of change. Double suffering is simply the fact that suffering is already unpleasant, and that this unpleasantness can easily become compounded. Things can get worse. The third type is the suffering of being conditioned, which is both more subtle and more all-pervasive than the simple ability to be hurt. For example, if a thorn pierces our skin, we immediately have pain. It does not take much, being in this physical body, to hurt. In fact, it takes very little. Even a bad smell can be enough to upset our sense of equilibrium. If it's a particularly nice smell, our minds also become a little disturbed. It seems that fickleness is a quality that's built into our present state, even more so than the fickleness of a small child.

We can certainly all agree that there is suffering. This is the first point, to acknowledge that there is suffering. The second point is to understand that it is not uncaused; there is a reason. The reason we suffer is due to karmic actions and disturbing emotions. Karma and disturbing emotions have one driving force — the belief in ego. Clearly, there is only one way to solve this dilemma: to realize egolessness. In a nutshell, then, the realization of egolessness is the quintessence of the Buddha's first turning of the Wheel of Dharma.

The notion of "Me" or "I" is held so strongly that it's taken as an absolute given — yet it is mistaken. To reverse this misconception of an existing "I," we need to investigate and come to the conclusion that there is no real ego. After that, we need to train in remaining in the state of equanimity where no notion of self is held in mind, the state of egolessness. This solves the entire problem. It is like cutting a tree at its root: all the branches, twigs and leaves wither at the same time. To have dissolved ego-clinging and to be stable in the knowledge that realizes egolessness is simply another description of freedom, liberation, great peace. This is extremely profound, and it is real.

At the second turning of the Wheel of Dharma, the Buddha went deeper. He taught that not just ego, but all phenomena, are empty and devoid of true existence. The *Prajñaparamita* scripture titled the *Sutra on Transcendent Knowledge in Eight Thousand Verses* teaches that perspective with extreme clarity. The Buddha taught on emptiness in incredible detail, and it may be difficult for one person to fathom all of his sutras and their commentaries. We may not have either the intelligence or the diligence that it takes to study all his words. Based on this, great masters of the past in India composed treatises condensing the vital points of the Buddha's teachings into small scriptures of sometimes only a few pages.

Some of these condensations of the intent of the Buddha's second turning of the Wheel of Dharma are found in Nagarjuna's Middle Way treatises on reasoning. The Middle Way declares that everything from the aggregate of form up until the state of omniscient enlightenment, is empty and unconstructed. The practical application of this settles our mind in a state that is empty and unconstructed, and lets us proceed through the path to enlightenment.

This path is composed of two factors: knowledge and means. The supreme knowledge is the knowledge of profound emptiness, which is the sixth of the six *paramitas* — transcendent knowledge. The most eminent method is described by the first five paramitas, embraced by the profound emptiness of the sixth. This unity of means and knowledge is the very heart or quintessence of the second Dharma wheel, the intermediate set of teachings on the absence of characteristics.

During the third turning of the Wheel of Dharma, the Buddha explained in a way that is even clearer. Not only is everything from aggregate form to omniscient enlightenment unreal, empty and devoid of mental constructs; in addition, everything is *luminosity*.

This third set of teachings is meant for people who are more intelligent and bold. When first hearing a term like luminosity, a student might think, "What the heck does that mean? It sounds secret!" At first glance, it seems the second set of teachings is easier to understand than the third, just as the first is easier than the second. While it's not entirely incomprehensible that all phenomena are empty, from the aggregate of form up until the state of omniscience, the first turning is easier or simpler to understand. Ego is the creator of suffering; the enlightened mind is egoless. This is logical, and understanding this is very beneficial.

The third turning of the Wheel of Dharma, the final set of teachings, is the intent of the tantric teachings. Tantras are described as being of different classes or types: father tantras, mother tantras, and non-dual tantras. Vajrayana is also known as the 'vajra vehicle of secret mantra', the vehicle that uses the fruition as the path. One practices Vajrayana firmly based on the foundation of the two first Dharma wheels, and not as a separate practice.

Vajrayana practice is based first of all on acknowledging suffering. We must be fed up with suffering in order to seek liberation by realizing egolessness. On a deeper level, we experience that everything from the aggregate of form until omniscient enlightenment is empty, unconstructed and insubstantial. Now, in Vajrayana, we additionally realize that everything has a luminous nature. This may be hard to get, especially if one's understanding is merely intellectual, one who only studies the teachings and does not practice. Then it becomes very hard to understand how this can be. During the ages, a lot of debate and dispute has arisen over exactly this point.

The tantric perspective is that of emptiness endowed with the supreme aspect of unchanging great bliss and original wakefulness that encompasses samsaric existence as well as nirvanic peace. This is the intent of the third turning of the Wheel of Dharma. This original wakefulness that encompasses all of samsara and nirvana: where is it right now? Where is this supreme, unchanging great bliss; where is this nature; where is the emptiness endowed with the supreme aspect? All these terms refer to something that is intrinsic to our mind, something that is present right now at this very moment. It is not to be found outside in the earth, in the water, in the wind, in the fire or in physical space. At this very moment, right now, we have some sense of knowing or experiencing, don't we? This is mind. Mind is this knowing. Though there seems to be a knower, when we look, we do not find it. It is unfindable, like empty space. Physical space is described as that which accommodates. The word spacious itself means open and accommodating.

When something is concrete, a physical form, we feel it earns the right to have a name and we attach a name to it. When something is inconcrete, not composed of physical matter in any way whatsoever, just wide open; we also give it a name. In the first example, it is because there is something that we can give it a name. In the second instance, it is because there is no thing, nothing, that we name it as well. This second case involves something that is not and yet functions; something that can both be identified and yet cannot. Exactly how do we identify space? It is not something to see, to hear, smell, or taste; not something touch. It is not earth, water, fire or wind. Yet it does function in that it accommodates everything else. That is the identification of space. Thus, if you want to identify space in a positive sense, in terms of it being such and such, you can do that. And if you want to identify it in a negative sense, in terms of it not being such and such, you can also do that. It's exactly the same with identifying the knower, mind, thinking: it can be identified, if you want, to be such and such. Or it can be totally unidentifiable if that is what you want. It's merely a matter of perspective.

To go back to the tantric perspective: this emptiness endowed with the supreme aspects, this unchanging great bliss, this original wakefulness encompassing all of samsara and nirvana, is contained within the nature of our mind. Because our nature includes such qualities, it is called the buddha nature, literally, the *essence of the sugatas*. We do not have to rely only on assumptions to directly prove to ourselves that we possess a buddha nature. When you see smoke, you can infer there is fire below from which the smoke arises. In the same way, any person, no matter how wicked he or she might be, still has some object of love, of affection. That is a sign that in that person there is love, from time to time. Also, any kind of person, no matter how stupid, still has some wisdom, an ability to discern what is useful, what is harmful, and then to choose. Even if the individual is very selfish, there is still some intelligence. Everyone has an ability to do something. In other words, these qualities are intrinsic to everyone; they are intrinsic to the human mind. They may be very limited, they may be hampered, but we all have these qualities.

Moreover, we have the ability to acknowledge that our mind is insubstantial. The knowledge of emptiness is at hand. When we allow our minds to be undisturbed for a little while, not caught up in likes and dislikes, we experience some sense of well being, an easiness that is carefree. It may not be the unchanging great bliss at this point, but it is present in every one of us. The emptiness in our personal experience may not be the fully-fledged emptiness endowed with the supreme aspect. The original wakefulness encompassing all of samsara and nature is not yet fully perfected. It's as if these qualities are enveloped in something; they are hindered from being manifest. In the Buddhist teachings, that hindrance is called obscuration. Therefore, our nature can be described at this point as obscured suchness.

A sentient being is obscured suchness. A buddha is unobscured suchness. That which obscures the suchness are emotional and cognitive obscurations. That which removes emotional obscuration is the six paramitas, loving kindness, being compassionate. In particular, the true view of emptiness thoroughly removes emotional obscuration. Cognitive obscuration, on the other hand, is much more difficult to dissolve, to be free of and to utterly abandon. Only present, fresh wakefulness — the original wakefulness that does not conceive of anything, that does not hold onto the three spheres of subject, object and action — can totally dissolve cognitive obscuration. Cognitive obscuration means to conceptualize the three factors. That which can dispel it is the original wakefulness that does not conceptualize these three spheres.

When the two obscurations are purified, the twofold knowledges unfold. These twofold knowledges are already present within us. They are the knowledge of knowing the nature as it is — the realization of it as being empty, unconstructed, and insubstantial — and the knowledge of perceiving all possibly existing things. The perfection of the twofold knowledge reveals the two kayas. The two kayas are dharmakaya and rupakaya. Dharmakaya is unconstructed, while rupakaya, the form body, includes both sambhogakaya and nirmanakaya.

When the knowledge that realizes egolessness, the realization of the unconstructed and empty quality of all phenomena, is recognized, trained in and stabilized, one is called a buddha. The word buddha in Tibetan is *sang gye*. *Sang* means purified, and *gye* perfected. A buddha has purified the two obscurations as well as their habitual tendencies and has perfected the twofold knowledges. Such a being has established the natural state and vanquished all delusion. All confusion, disturbing emotions and karmas are obliterated. Unless the intent of the third turning of the Wheel of Dharma, the luminous nature, emptiness or original wakefulness is fully realized, that accomplishment is not considered true and complete enlightenment. Without that, the complete qualities of the awakened state are not manifest. These complete qualities include the twofold knowledges.

To reiterate, the twofold knowledges are the knowledge of knowing the nature of reality as it is — the realization of it as being empty, unconstructed, and insubstantial — and the knowledge of perceiving all possibly existing things. A buddha can, in a single instant, simultaneously perceive the manner in which all seemingly appearing phenomena appear through dependent origination. A buddha simultaneously sees how phenomena are perceived by sentient beings as being real, how this mistakenness occurs, when it occurs, when it occurred, when it will be dissolved in the future, and what the causes and consequences of everything are. All of that can be perceived in a single instant. That is called the knowledge of perceiving all possibly existing things.

The basis of delusion is to hold onto the idea of I, to cling to ego-clinging. Delusion is grounded in a lack of understanding of how the nature of all things is empty and insubstantial. The basis of delusion is also to fail to recognize the luminous nature of things. By realizing the nonexistence of a self and releasing the tight grip of ego, we will naturally and automatically understand that all other things are empty and devoid of self. In this way, the intermediate set of teachings are more profound than the first. It is not just the mind that is insubstantial; everything else as well is naturally empty. Not knowing that everything is naturally empty is ignorance and confusion. Similarly, compared to the second set of teachings, the perspective of the third set is more profound. Not only is everything empty and unconstructed: it is all a state of purity totally endowed with immense qualities.

When hearing what the Buddha says about how things are, we as individuals can understand something. We do get a feeling that, "Oh yes, it is like this." We have some confidence. The Dharma and especially the pith instructions address exactly what is wrong and how to change it. They hit home.

You may study Buddhism. You may think about it and reflect. But, most essentially, we need to practice, to train in the great meditation of nonmeditation, as soon as possible. Do not think, "I will practice later." That attitude makes it never: our time simply runs out. Time will not wait for us. The ultimate practice is undistracted nonmeditation, which obliterates the root of confusion. It totally and permanently obliterates all karma, disturbing emotions and habitual tendencies.

To begin with, we need some method, some techniques to lead us to the ultimate. The best method is of course effortlessness, but effortlessness cannot be taught, or striven after. Even if we try – especially if we try — we can't become automatically effortless. Effortlessness just does not seem to spontaneously take place. Still, it is a fact that confused experience falls apart the moment we simply let be in a nondualistic state. Right now, for most of us, every moment of ordinary experience is governed by conditioning. Our present habit is dominated by a deliberate effort. We have therefore no choice but to use our present habit of deliberate effort to arrive at effortlessness. Once we are accustomed to effortful meditation, we can be led to the effortless.

In this book, I will unfold the various ways to arrive at nonconceptual, present, fresh wakefulness, beginning with conceptual practices. I'll cover many topics quite quickly, so it is best if you gain familiarity with my other books, if you have not read them. *The Union of Mahamudra and Dzogchen* and *Indisputable Truth* contain many detailed teachings. For that reason, I do not feel the need to repeat here in this book what I have previously said.

A Spiritual Person

In our life, the greatest good we can do is to act for the welfare of infinite sentient beings. Therefore, generate this noble attitude: "I will study the Dharma and apply it in practice to establish all the infinite number of sentient beings in the state of supreme and irreversible, unsurpassable enlightenment. To do so, I will learn, reflect and practice meditation."

Beings are countless, and they all suffer in innumerable ways. All their anguish is created by their negative karma and disturbing emotions. As long as beings continue to make negative karma and act out of disturbing emotions, permanent happiness is unattainable. Permanent happiness is only possible once dualistic fixation and the habitual tendencies for that are brought to an end. The only way to completely end dualistic fixation and habitual tendencies is by the practice of the sacred Dharma.

It's as if we are suffering from a disease for which the Dharma teachings are the remedy, with the teacher serving as the doctor. By applying the teachings in practice, we are following the cure which will allow us to get well. Every one of us in the six classes of beings undergoes a tremendous amount of pain and misery in terms of the deluded experience created by our own disturbing emotions and negative karma. We need to clear this up; we need to recover from this disease. Otherwise, samsara will go on endlessly. Out of ignorance, we wallow in selfish emotions that cause us to hurt and harm others, over and over again. This is our sickness. Rather than continuing being infectious, we need to find an antidote.

The medicine for this sickness of self is the sacred Dharma, which is true and unfailing, undeceiving. On a coarse level, you could say that any knowledge is Dharma. But Dharma in this context is the knowledge that acts as a remedy towards selfish emotions. Dharma is the perfect information, if you will, that counteracts clinging to the idea of a self and all of its accompanying disturbing emotions.

Honestly, the sacred Dharma is simply how things are — the

reality of what actually is, when unconfused and unmistaken. The very definition of Dharma is 'the unmistaken', that which is not confused. The way to be unmistaken is by first learning, next reflecting and then training in being unconfused. Through this training, we can completely and totally clear up deluded experience.

The teacher of the sacred Dharma, among the thousand buddhas who will appear in this aeon, is the fourth one, Buddha Shakyamuni. Other buddhas in the past have taught the sacred Dharma, and in the future, countless other buddhas will teach. From their undeluded state, buddhas give teachings that are in exact accordance with how things are.

The Buddha is described as being like a loving relative of you and all sentient beings; a relative that we may not even know. For a buddha it makes no difference whether other beings like him or not or are respectful or not. Within the awakened state is a love that encompasses all other beings without any prejudice whatsoever. The qualities a buddha is endowed with are inconceivable, and cannot be fathomed by ordinary thought. His activity is the representation of the awakened state, the buddha's mind. His speech is the teachings, endowed with the supreme qualities of abandonment and realization. Among the different miracles that a buddha can perform, the greatest miracle is that of the teachings, which have the ability to dissolve deluded experience and bring karma and disturbing emotions to a complete end. The sacred Dharma can grow in us and manifest the eminent qualities of loving kindness, compassion and insight. Equally amazing, also a miracle, we have the ability to receive these teachings still, to this very day.

To sum up, it is through the teachings of an enlightened buddha that all faults can be eradicated and all good qualities can be made manifest. There is actually nothing superior to that which we need; nothing better that we could possibly achieve. The greatest miracle the sacred Dharma can perform is to bring selfish emotions to a complete and permanent halt, and to make deluded experience dissolve or subside. That is the capacity of the sacred Dharma.

I mentioned earlier that until our thoughts dissolve and are cleared up, karma and disturbing emotions will not end. Being angry, attached or dull are negative thoughts that create a great deal of suffering and trouble for us. We make the bad habits of being aggressive, attached, stupid or close-minded into our 'second nature,' so to speak. When these tendencies have become ingrown, they perpetuate themselves in life after life. It is these intensified thought states that create the fuel for future rebirths. They produce the very states of sentient beings who inhabit the hells, as well as the hungry ghost and animal realms. Therefore, in order to benefit both our immediate situation and our lasting welfare, we should do something about changing our states of mind from being angry, attached or close-minded.

You might be laughing now, because maybe you are the type of person who doesn't believe that there is a life after this. Simply look at how human beings are right now. Some people make being aggressive, selfish and unpleasant towards others a strong habit. They are not nice to be with – in fact, they are not even that happy to be with themselves! Other individuals are very kind, unselfish and helpful towards others. They are nice to be with. In this way, we can see that whoever has the habit of being involved in selfish emotions is unpleasant for themselves as well as others. Isn't that obvious?

Isn't it also possible that someone starts out being a kind-hearted and loving person, but then gets into bad company? Through the influence of others, they develop nasty traits. They become evil, and do things that are hurtful and harmful towards others. Haven't you seen that happen?

Conversely, we also find people who start out being selfish and uptight about their own welfare, conceited, attached and very unpleasant. They hurt others through their words and actions. But they also can be influenced by the knowledge gained through study, reflection and meditation. They can change their ways and become relaxed and peaceful when they speak. They become gentle, kind and helpful to others.

Either way, the point is that we can grow used to being in a certain way. And it is definitely easier to be selfish than to be kind.

We do not really have to study to be selfish! To be nice, to be gentle, helpful and kind, is something that a person must learn and train in. Someone who gives in to common thought patterns of attachment, aggression and dullness is called an ordinary person. But someone who gains understanding through learning, through reflection and through meditation starts to change their way of being. He or she speaks and acts in a way that becomes more relaxed, softer, more considerate. Such a person is called a practitioner, a spiritual person.

On a more advanced level, someone for whom all selfish emotions have totally subsided and dissolved is called a buddha. But being a buddha is not just a matter of being purified of these selfish emotions. Accompanying this absence of self absorption is a wonderful presence that is the sublime knowledge of knowing the nature of things as it is, as well as the knowledge that perceives all possibly existing things. Thus, the definition of a buddha is to be both purified and perfected. As human beings, we set aims and goals for our life and we try to pursue them. A businessman tries to earn profits and make money. A soldier tries to win battles. A scientist tries to unravel the mysteries of the universe or the uniqueness of a particular field of knowledge. In Buddhism, the aim that we try to achieve is to be a purified and perfected person, a buddha. The attainment, in short, is buddhahood. But this attainment is not reached through our own striving alone. It does not happen by pushing, by being smart and trying to figure out everything that is possibly knowable. *Buddhahood is the state free from the web of conceptual thought.* All other kinds of understanding or discoveries, all other kinds of intelligence, are within the web of conceptual thought. The innate nature that is beyond conceptual thought, beyond the web of thinking, is not understood through thinking. In short, *the state of enlightenment is thought-free wakefulness.*

Thought-free wakefulness is not discovered or realized through thought. The understanding we gain through study and reflection is not enough to realize the ultimate state. We need different methods. We need to realize the twofold wisdom free from the two obscurations, which is called buddhahood. This buddhahood is realized through the combination of learning, reflection and meditation. We do not realize enlightenment only through use of sharp intelligence. It is not enough to only have understanding through learning and reflection. However, based on that understanding we can acquire the knowledge resulting from meditation. That is the way to enlightenment.

The state of enlightenment that is free from the two obscurations and endowed with the twofold knowledge is, on one hand, difficult and far away. For example, it does not seem likely that an animal can easily get enlightened. According to the Buddha, there are also hell beings, hungry ghosts, jealous gods and gods. We do not see those beings, so therefore we may decide that they do not exist.

Some human beings suffer tremendously in their life. They may be as dull as animals or as aggressive as hell beings. It is very difficult for such people to pay attention to being free from the two obscurations. They simply don't seem to have the opportunity to do so. Even among more fortunate human beings, very few are interested in being free from the two obscurations and realizing the twofold knowledge. Compared to other sentient beings, a human being has the likeliest possibility of becoming a buddha. Human beings are in fact the closest to being a buddha, because they are suited to learning, reflection, and meditation. They are fundamentally capable — yet very few are interested.

For those few who want to apply themselves, to understand, reflect and practice meditation, there are still many hindrances. There are so many reasons for why we believe we have no time! Our biggest preoccupations are known as distraction, discouragement and laziness. We do not say that; we do not admit this to ourselves, of course. Instead, we say "I have work to do. That is why I have no time. I have family, I have parents and children I need to take care of. That is why I am busy!" It is true that our responsibilities make us busy, but not that busy! The reason we are really busy is that we constantly occupy our attention, with what we see, hear, smell and taste and so forth - with what we think of. That makes us busy. Or perhaps we are just lazy, or telling ourselves that we cannot.

Being a buddha seems very far away for most beings. As humans, our preoccupation with being busy creates immense hardship for ourselves. Honestly, though, it is not that difficult to become enlightened if we really apply ourselves to practice.

Right now, have that precious opportunity of being a human. We already have an enlightened essence, a buddha nature. We can meet or maybe even have met already with spiritual teachers; we can receive the instructions. The only thing that is left is to apply them. When we apply the instructions and practice, it is not that difficult — the only thing that is left is to be a buddha!

It is like cooking. Cooking is difficult. You need to arrange many things. Especially if you want to eat good dishes, like French food, you need to have many special and valuable ingredients. The actual cooking process also takes a long time. Even the skilled cook needs to apply effort; it is not easy. But finally, when the food is cooked and served, there is only one thing left — to eat. If you do not eat the food, your effort is useless. The food is not for show; it is for eating. When we eat, the effort of having cooked becomes useful. Similarly, when we hear teachings, when we know about practice, all we really need to do is practice. Having learned and reflected, our real job is to apply the teachings in practice. To learn, to reflect, to practice meditation, to become enlightened is not that difficult. We merely need to apply ourselves.

I would like to mention one more troublesome point here. We humans are very busy, so we tend to think that spiritual practice is sort of a side job. It is not a main pursuit; it is more like a hobby, but not even a true hobby. I know some Westerners whose hobby is not a small thing. They take their hobbies very seriously. Take the example of playing golf! Some play golf for money and fame; some play golf for fun. They play golf from morning to night. This is not a hobby; that is like work. In the morning they wake up, eat breakfast and play golf. After lunch, they play golf. All they do is sleep, eat and golf. They put so much effort into this. If we practitioners were to put that much effort into practice each year, we would become liberated very quickly. Unfortunately for practice, not many people apply as much diligence as dedicated golfers.

The point is, it is best if from the time you wake up in the morning until you fall asleep at night you could apply yourself at every moment with great care, with great mindfulness. Make sure that every time there is the impetus to be selfish or carried away by disturbing emotions, that you instead do something to change that. Apply some method, no matter what that method is. Just do whatever helps. If it helps to intellectually study the teachings and think about them, then do that. If it helps to bow down or make offerings and be formally nice in different ways, do that. If it helps to do the practices that purify obscurations and gather the accumulations, then do that. Do development stage, recitation and completion stage and so forth. Whatever the level of training that we've learned that we use in order to reduce our selfishness, our disturbing emotions, our stupidity, we should use those practices all the time, from morning to evening. Someone who does that is called a practitioner and for such a person it is not that difficult to progress to enlightenment.

To the same degree that our selfish emotions diminish, the qualities of realization spontaneously grow. It is similar to the sunlight increasing as the dark clouds vanish. The brilliance of the sun is unchanging; it doesn't increase or decrease. It only seems to decrease or increase due to the presence or absence of clouds. In the same way, the nature of mind — the very identity of that which thinks and feels all these thoughts and emotions — is unchanging, just like the sun. In our essence, our basic nature, the qualities are primordially and perfectly existent. But at the same time, although our nature is originally perfect, the cloud covers of the two obscurations prevent these qualities from being manifest. In our case, the two obscurations have not yet been purified, but they *can* be purified. Like the clouds, the obscurations, are temporary; they can disappear. If the clouds were inseparable from the sun, it would be impossible to ever have a clear sky. But the clouds are not an intrinsic component of sunshine. Because they are temporary, they can vanish.

We should apply this example of the sky with clouds to our own situation. This is one of the special qualities of the Buddhist perspective. In essence, *every sentient being is actually a buddha. Every sentient being has the potential for being a buddha. Every sentient being has a basic nature that is completely enlightened. That is because the identity of that which thinks is already a state of thought-free wakefulness.* The thinking, the clinging to duality, is like a layer of clouds, covering the thought-free wakefulness, which is like the shining sun. To experience the pure sunshine of our true nature, we need to be free of all the diffferent kinds of karma, disturbing emotions, habitual tendencies and obscurations that cover it. The heart of the matter is simply this: *we need to be free of our thinking.*

It is our thinking that obscures our nature. Our thinking makes all the disturbing emotions. In fact, all of samsara, all disturbing emotions and karma, unfolds from our thinking. Do you remember the definition of a buddha as one who is both purified and perfected? 'Purified' means our thoughts are purified or dissolved. 'Perfected' means that the knowledge of knowing the nature as it is, perceiving all possibly existing things, is perfected.

In order to achieve this state, we need an understanding of how to train in meditation that is based on learning and reflection. *Meditation is simply a technique against our selfish emotions and thoughts, this constantly busy, restless attitude. All the different meditative methods can be condensed into three types: stillness, insight and loving compassion.* These three types of practice can be applied to overcome any kind of selfish emotion. *The most eminent way to overcome this nasty frame of mind, the selfish attitude of being attached, angry, dull, conceited, and jealous, is the knowledge of emptiness.* The preparation to facilitate the realization of the state of emptiness is the practice of stillness, or shamatha.

Shamatha practice is an easy method to apply to reduce the unpleasant manifestations of our nasty mind. Shamatha practice, training in being quiet, reduces this selfish attitude. When our mind is quiet, the selfish attitude is not evident, not visible. However, that is not enough. Merely being quiet does not uproot selfishness, it does not cut it from the very root. What else is necessary? It is clear insight, *vipashyana*. If insight is indeed an essential element, you might wonder why the Buddha didn't teach that from the very beginning? "Why not teach the best from the beginning," you might think – "Why wait?" The simple reason is that our mind has a very strong habit of getting involved in thoughts and feelings towards or against different things. To immediately teach the opposite of that, clear insight, is not so easy to either understand or to adopt. For this reason, the Buddha first taught us how to relax, how to calm down our minds.

In order to solve an intense argument with someone else, isn't it better to first calm down and then talk it over? Westerners say, "Leave me alone!" Isn't this one way of calming your mind? When your mind becomes calm, you can negotiate much more easily. When you are hot-tempered, it is difficult to negotiate. In a sense, then, we could say that saying 'Leave me alone!' is a form of shamatha practice!

When we allow ourselves to simply be at peace as in shamatha practice, our strong emotions calm down until eventually they are not visible and may seem to not be present at all. When training in being at calm and at peace, many different methods are traditionally taught. Some involve holding an object in mind, while others involve holding nothing at all in mind. Of course, it would be better to remain calm without directing your attention towards something in particular – to be able to rest in a totally undirected state of attention. But if that is not easy, it helps to first begin with directing your attention towards a particular focus and to grow used to that. Eventually you can practice suspending this point of attention altogether.

Focusing your attention is a way of remaining undistracted. You use the focus as a support; you keep your attention on something in order to not drift off and think of all sorts of different things. The object of meditation does not need to be particularly fancy or ornate. It could be a pebble or stone. Or you can use the movement of breath, the inhalation and exhalation. When you direct your mind, your attention, to something, at some point you will discover that you've wandered off and are thinking about something else. Once you notice that, immediately direct your attention back to the object. That is the training.

People are different: different individuals have different kinds of natures. For some it is more practical to focus on a solid stone or pebble, while for others it's better to use the movement of the breath, to simply follow the breathing. Traditionally, most people benefit from using the breathing as an object of meditation. The reason is that we always breathe; we have to, naturally. The notion 'breathing' is something neutral; it is a neutral concept. You do not have to rejoice that you are breathing. You do not have to be depressed about it. The only thing that is necessary to do here is to pay attention, because the breathing happens by itself. You do not have to breathe deliberately. You simply notice that the breath is being inhaled. You can feel it coming in through the nose. You do not hold the breath in continuously or forever — you have to breathe out again, you need to exhale. Again, you notice that also. It is not something you have to do or regulate in any fashion; you simply pay attention to it. When you can keep your attention on the movement of breath for a long time without starting to think about all sorts of other things, there is some sense of calm that accompanies that. This is called the attainment of shamatha.

When someone grows increasingly accustomed to this and becomes trained in this practice, the real character of that person changes. You can say that he or she has calmed down. The effect of this practice shows itself in all the other moments in life. You can see that the person has calmed down and has become gentler and more relaxed. Shamatha practice has a lot of benefit. By calming down, you become much less involved in selfish emotions.

When you have trained like this for a while and are relaxed and peaceful, your mind is still directed towards something – it's still focused on the object of attention. The next step is to let go of that and rest in undirected attention; to move from focused shamatha to shamatha free of support.

Again, you start here by directing your attention to the movement of your breath. Chant refuge and bodhichitta — that is the excellent preparation for any practice, regardless of which one we are doing. Now we come to the main part, which is shamatha. Shamatha practice means simply being at ease, very physically and mentally relaxed. Don't get involved in thoughts of past or future. Simply pay attention to the movement of breath, and nothing else, with a sense of thought-free wakefulness.

These two words, shamatha and vipashyana, are used in all three vehicles. The same words refer to slightly different meanings. The type of vipashyana taught in the general teachings in Buddhism is, from the perspective of the higher vehicles, actually considered a subtle form of shamatha. For example, in terms of the four applications of mindfulnes, the inspection or inquiry is actually subtle shamatha. This kind of situation is called 'similar word with exalted meaning.'

Another method that speeds up the realization of emptiness is loving compassion. There are two types of bodhichitta: relative and ultimate. Loving compassion is the relative bodhichitta. The more we apply being loving and compassionate, and the more we train at the same time in stillness, the more opportunity we have to realize or actualize ultimate bodhichitta, which is the realization of emptiness suffused with compassion. Through the practice of relative bodhichitta, compassionate emptiness is realized increasingly, and this realization is both effortless and spontaneous.

Student: Could you explain a little more about shamatha with support?

Rinpoche: As I just said, shamatha practice is to be quiet and calm. This is very unlike the usual state of our mind, which is continually disturbed by waves of emotions and thoughts. These waves need to subside. Shamatha practice allows these emotional waves to calm down. There are many types of shamatha, but they can all be included within two types: shamatha with focus, and shamatha without focus.

To train in shamatha with a focus or support, you might start by placing a small stone or stick in front of you, at a comfortable angle for viewing. Simply look at it, without forming a lot of thoughts about the object or investigating what it is. Just keep your attention focused on it, as a support for not thinking of anything else. Simply do that. Do not try to discover something special about the stone or pebble. Another support I mentioned is paying attention to the movement of the breath in the natural process of exhaling and inhaling. This type of practice is also something neutral; it is a way to calm down our attention, to settle our focus.

The more calm and quiet our attention can be made through this training, the easier it is to be introduced to vipashyana, the clear seeing which is thought-free wakefulness. That is why shamatha is important. In the New School lineages of Tibetan Buddhism, it is taught that one should ideally train in practicing shamatha for one year, to begin with. Next best is to practice it for six months, or at least for three months. This is how it is written in the guidance manuals for meditation. It is also taught like this: first be skilled in remaining calm, remaining in shamatha. Next, be skilled in destroying the calm, because it is not good enough to be stuck there.

Student: What does the statement that every sentient being has the potential for being enlightened mean?

Rinpoche: The very heart of Vajrayana practice is the view of Mahamudra and Dzogchen. We train in this view until we attain stability in the view, which is the nature of mind, the natural state. According to the general teachings of the Buddha, everyone has the capacity to be enlightened. Buddha nature is present in each one of us, as a seed, as a potential. That is why it is logical or reasonable that anyone who practices will eventually be enlightened. When you take the seed of flower and you place it in a situation which is conducive for its growth — good soil, plenty of fertilizer, the right amount of warmth, space, and water, and the right amount of time — then whenever these factors are present, every single instant the seed will grow. On the other hand, perhaps you have all the conducive factors — the fertile soil, the fertilizer, water and warmth, the space for something to grow — but what you plant is not the seed of a flower. Maybe you've unfortunately mistaken a pebble for a seed. If you have planted a pebble, then no matter how long you wait, nothing will grow.

If it wasn't for the fact that all sentient beings already had the seed potential, the substance of enlightenment within them, then no matter how much effort we put into practice, nothing would happen, we wouldn't be enlightened. If you churn water, you never get butter, right? Only if you churn milk do you get butter. That is what is meant by potential. Because all of us have the potential for being enlightened, whoever truly perseveres can be enlightened.

Of course, when an individual is densely obscured by the two obscurations, by intense negative emotions, it is not very easy. You could say that for such a person buddhahood is far away. Conversely, for someone in whom the layer of disturbing emotions is thinner, the intelligence is brighter, and such a person would have an easier time progressing towards enlightenment. It's an easier process.

No Samsara Apart from Thoughts

Up until this point, our main meditation practice has been to rest our mind in a calm way, in stillness. Now, let us take it a step further and move into vipashyana, or clear seeing. While in the relaxed state of shamatha, we train in seeing the mind's nature very clearly. These two practices of stillness and insight, shamatha and vipashyana, are the very heart of Buddhist meditation training. Our minds have two sides, positive and negative. Because there is a negative aspect to our minds, our nature at present is called obscured suchness. We need to change this, and remove the obscurations covering the suchness or essential nature. The way to do so is by means of vipashyana, which in this context can be considered *thought-free wakefulness.*

While thought-free wakefulness is an excellent starting point for training, it is not so easy to simply start here. The preparation or prelude that makes it easier to recognize the state of thought-free wakefulness and train in it is shamatha practice. Training in simply being at peace allows our busy minds to calm down and remain quietly. Through training in shamatha, we will become much more able to recognize the state of thought-free wakefulness.

In the previous chapter I talked about shamatha. Here, I would like to introduce the training of vipashyana. First of all, what is the difference between shamatha and vipashyana — how do we distinguish between these two? When training in shamatha there is some sense of resting, of being quiet and tasting a feeling of quiet peace. There is a sense of being fond of that feeling, of being attached to it. When remaining in a very calm and quiet way, we are primarily undisturbed by sense impressions. None of the six kinds of sense impressions move us. If we really become absorbed into this state of stillness in a steady, stable way, it doesn't matter if the weather is too cold or too hot or if an insect bites us. Discomforts like these won't bother us; in fact, we may not even feel them. There is a taste of tranquility, a taste of serenity in shamatha practice that we could become too addicted to, to such an extent that we don't want to get involved in anything else. We enjoy remaining uninvolved.

True stability in shamatha is accompanied by many powers, even if one has not yet attained stability in vipashyana. In stable shamatha, some miraculous powers such as clairvoyance may occur, as well as many other qualities. But shamatha itself is not liberation. One does not become free through shamatha, and definitely not enlightened. There is no freedom here because of that fondness, the clinging to the taste of shamatha. It's because we are so interested in that feeling of quietness that we are hindered from moving further. While shamatha is not the ultimate practice, it is important because it is the support or basis for vipashyana. When the surface of a body of water is calm, it can reflect your face. Similarly, when your mind, your attention, is calm, it is possible to see clearly the nature of mind. This is vipashyana.

The sole difference between enlightened and unenlightened beings is the presence or absence of obscuration. It may be a cloudless, clear, sunny sky, or a sky obscured by clouds. In either situation, the sun always rises in the morning, moves up and across the sky, and sets at night. The only difference is whether or not clouds are present in the sky, and how dense the layers of clouds are.

The *Uttara Tantra* as well as other texts describe three stages of mind: impure, half-pure and totally pure. It is like the example I just mentioned of the different kinds of weather. The sun can be completely obscured; it can be covered by a thin haze; or perhaps there are no clouds at all, and the sun is totally unobscured. The example of thick clouds points at our emotional obscuration, our preoccupation with selfish emotions. Aren't we sometimes totally caught up in love or hate? Just like water boiling, we find we cannot control ourselves. This situation is called disturbing emotion, and it is definitely an obscuration. At that very moment of loving or hating, our innate suchness is densely obscured. Similarly, we may also have more docile or mild thoughts of attraction or aversion, which run like this: "I like this. I don't like that." These ordinary likes and dislikes are not such strong involvement in emotion, and yet they do obscure the basic suchness of our minds.

The most subtle type of obscuration is to simply conceive of something — like simply thinking, "It is." *Holding a notion of something is still a way of conceptualizing the three spheres: subject, object and action.* Whenever there is a thought which conceives the three spheres, karma is created. People ask, "What is karma? I don't get it! Where is karma?" Actually, karma is our mind conceiving something. Karma is conceptual mind. This subtle forming of a notion of anything is like a web, a haze that obscures our innate suchness just as mist obscures the sun from being vividly seen.

The great master Nagarjuna said, "*There is no samsara apart from your own thoughts.*" Samsara is based on thought; samsara is made by thought. A thought includes all attachment and all aversion. A thought by its very nature involves an attitude of selecting and excluding. Every thought is hope and fear. Hope and fear are inevitably painful and brings suffering. Implicit in hope is the idea that "I have not yet achieved." That is painful, isn't it? Likewise, fear is accompanied by the thought, "It may happen and I don't want it." That is also painful; that is also suffering. Whenever there is involvement in thought; whenever a thought is formed, there is disturbing emotion. There is hope and fear, and therefore there is suffering.

Generally speaking, from a Dharma perspective, freedom or liberation means *free of samsara*. Samsara is commonly associated with the six classes of sentient beings in the three realms — desire realms, form realms and formless realms. We may think, "To be liberated is to be free from the six classes of sentient beings in the three realms." We may even think we have to go to some other place in order to be liberated. But honestly, connecting this directly to our own experience, *freedom means free from any type of thought* — bad thought, good thought, neutral thought. After hearing this we may think, "Certainly we should be free of evil thoughts, but not good thoughts — we should keep good thoughts. If we need to go beyond good thoughts, who will do good? All good actions are done by a good attitude, a good thought. If a good thought is thrown away, who will do good?" However, we need to understand that there are different kinds of good. There is conditioned goodness and unconditioned goodness, the goodness of the state of unity. Conditioned goodness is any good action, words or attitude formed out of a good, wholesome thought. That is definitely merit; that is virtue. But unconditioned goodness means being free of thought and acting while in the state of the innate nature, out of dharmata. Unconditioned goodness is nonconceptual; it is beyond thought.

We need to gain the taste of freedom or liberation through experiencing the awakened state, and then proceed to enlightenment. *In actuality, freedom means freedom from dualistic mind. Freedom from self,* holding the idea of "I", freedom from holding the notion of other, "of that". Free of any type of conceptual attitude that something is, something isn't. Without that, there is no freedom. To hold the notion "It is" is still a way of holding. To hold the notion "That isn't" is also a way of holding. When we have the notion, "All this inside and outside of me; all this exists," it is a conceptual attitude. Likewise, when we form the notion, "All this inside and outside of me does not exist," it is also a conceptual attitude.

Shamatha practice involves allowing our state of mind to be calm, to be at ease. Vipashyana is simply letting the mind be in equanimity, free of forming concepts, in thought-free wakefulness. For this vipashyana, the insight of clear seeing, to take birth in us, it is important to gather the accumulations, to purify the obscurations, and to train in shamatha.

Merely being calm is not true liberation. It is closer to liberation, because it is free from waves of emotions. If somebody asks, "Are you now free of emotions in the state of shamatha?" you could answer, "Almost!" But the root cause for further emotions is still being held onto in this state. When the root is kept, the plant will grow back. The root of further emotions needs to be destroyed. There is only one way to do that, and that is through training in vipashyana, the clear seeing which is thought-free wakefulness. Nothing else can do that job totally; nothing else can completely cut through the root of all thoughts. On a more general level, the root cause of samsaric existence is ego-clinging, the attitude of holding onto a self. In a more subtle way, it is conceptual attitude, the mental doing, the forming of a thought. So to be free of samsara we need to train in the direct opposite of its root cause; we need to train in the thought-free wakefulness which is the absence of any conceptual attitude. This entails also being free of ego. But it is not only being free of ego — it is the *knowing* of the state that is free of ego. In other words, it is *the knowledge that realizes egolessness,* also called the knowledge of the threefold purity, the wakefulness that does not conceptualize the three spheres.

According to the Tibetan tradition, *true vipashyana is to see the natural state while being free of dualistic fixation.* Traditionally, this natural state is introduced after the practitioner has undergone the *ngöndro,* the preliminary practices of the four or five times hundred thousand, as well as the yidam practice with its detailed recitations. After completing these, the student is given the pointing-out instruction according to the tradition of Dzogchen or Mahamudra or one of the other traditions of ultimate wisdom. That is the general way, but times have changed somewhat in the sense that people these days are from the beginning truly drawn to the essential teachings. My late father, Tulku Urgyen Rinpoche, used to give the pointing-out instruction to whoever was sincerely interested, whether that person was a long-term practitioner or a beginner. He also gave me the mandate to do so. With this perspective in mind, I feel that it would be a good idea to go into more detail about vipashyana.

All of my root gurus were great masters who had realized the natural state. I am not someone who has complete or perfect realization. But I do have one thing, deep respect and trust from the core of my heart. Based on this respect and trust, I have the courage to feel that I probably have received blessings from the masters of the lineage. What I am going to explain are instructions my own root gurus gave me. I will simply repeat a few things.

Confusion is made by our minds. Karma, disturbing emotions, and all the different modes of experience are all mind-made. Mind is the main creator of everything. If we allow our mind to continue forming dualistic fixation, samsara will continue endlessly. If you want to leave samsara behind, if you want to be free from samsara, you need to dissolve dualistic fixation. In order to let it dissolve, you need to train in the opposite of dualistic fixation. Thinking itself involves dualistic fixation. The opposite of this dualistic fixated thinking is nondual wakefulness. You arrive at nondual wakefulness the moment that thought vanishes — the moment that dualistic thinking falls apart or collapses. The moment dualistic thought vanishes, nondual wakefulness is clearly present.

Samsara is simply our thinking. Likewise, disturbing emotions and karma are merely our thinking. When we know the opposite of thinking, the essence of thought, we are free of samsara. In order to be free, we need to recognize this. Generally speaking, we need to be free of disturbing emotion. In a more subtle way, we need to free from forming notions, free from conceptualizing that something is or that something isn't. This includes metaphysical conceptualizing such as, "I am mistaken, I am deluded," or that "All things are like a dream — it is all an illusion." This kind of thinking is also a way of fixating.

Unless we allow every single kind of conceptualization, of forming a notion of something, whether it is a coarse way or a subtle way, shallow or profound — unless we allow all of that to dissolve, to simply evaporate, we do not clearly see our innate nature. Thinking "Because this is, that isn't. This should be selected, that should be excluded," is all mind-made. To think 'is' excludes 'isn't,' so it is actually included. Whenever something is denied, something is affirmed at the same time. Whenever something is rejected, another thing is automatically accepted. This dualism is the very nature of conceptual judgment. What we need is to be in a way in which there is no involvement in making any conceptual reference point of any kind, regardless of how subtle or philosophically astute this might be.

How do we experience or see this freedom? Instead of using the phrase "*to see the nature of mind,*" maybe it is better to say the way to freedom is "*to sustain the continuity of mind essence.*" 'Mind' here means simply thinking. 'Mind essence' is buddha nature, also known as innate suchness. Innate suchness transcends all philosophical positions. A philosophical position is something we arrive at after having given detailed thought to what is. We thoroughly inquire, investigate, analyze, reject and accept, prove and disprove, until we reach a position that we feel we have verified, and can thus establish the conviction "This is how it is." We then hold onto that position, thinking "This is the ultimate, absolute formulation of how reality is. I've got it!"

The natural state of mind, innate suchness, transcends all philosophical positions because it is not a philosophy; it is not an idea. Any rational viewpoint, no matter how deep or profound, is still conceptual. It is based on concept, and thus within the domain of conceptual mind. Innate suchness is naturally beyond the bounds of conceptual mind, rather than within the domain of conceptual mind. We need to distinguish between mind and mind essence, thinking, and thought-free wakefulness. We need to differentiate the conceptual mind from the basic state.

How dualistic mind or conceptual mind operates is described in the Buddhist metaphysical scriptures called the *Treasury of Abhidharma* as well as in other texts. The Abhidharma describes conceptual mind's different ways of operating in great detail, in terms of primary mind and the subsidiary fifty-one mental events. The latter explain all the various ways in which dualistic mind becomes involved in experience. Primary mind simply means the consciousness that is conceptual. Sense impressions themselves are not conceptual. When hearing, seeing, smelling, tasting, or noticing texture, we are not engaging in conceptual thought. It is only when the primary mind, consciousness, directs its attention to one of these sense impressions and starts to evaluate and judge that it becomes conceptual.

The Tibetan word *sem*, which we translate as the English word mind, actually has an explicit connotation of thinking of and holding something in mind. The Tibetan word for thought is *namtog*, which means conceptualizing an object, thinking of something. Whenever we see something nice we start to form thoughts about it, don't we? If we hear a nice sound, we want to investigate it further, create thoughts about it. We think, "Oh, what lovely music — I like that." This process is namtog. When thinking of any object, we generally react in one of three basic ways: either we like it, we don't like it, or we don't care about it that much. To like is subtle attachment. To dislike is subtle anger. When we feel neutral or indifferent, it is subtle dullness. Any object that we involve our attention in through any of our five senses in this way creates karma, because we are forming the attitude of either like, dislike or indifference. This creates an habitual pattern of being fond of or against something. Through forming the habits of liking this and disliking that, over and over again and again, our minds are structured to automatically attach a solid reality to whatever we think of.

It's the same when we dream or daydream. When we think of a beautiful flower, mentally we experience a bit of enjoyment. Conversely, when we think of the disgusting, filthy garbage lying around the streets in Boudha, we have an opposite reaction. We understand these different reactions and connect them to some attitude we've formed in the past; in other words, we plug these concepts into pre-existing attitudes. These words hold power in a way which is called habit, or habitual tendency. So, instead of saying, "I like such and such," we might just as well say, "It is my habitual tendency to be fond of that."

To summarize, dualistic mind has many defects and shortcomings, because it likes, dislikes and feels indifferent. It hopes and fears, accepts and rejects, and thus it suffers. Whenever there is thought, there is hope and fear; we've already discussed this point. Hope and fear itself is suffering. If we want to go beyond suffering, we need to be free of thought. If you want to be free of disturbing emotion, you need to be free of thought. If you want to be free of all the myriad of deluded experiences of samsara, you need to be free of thought. To want to continue thinking and still be free of samsara is impossible. (Rinpoche laughs). To remain attached to conceptual thinking and still arrive at liberation is impossible. To want to stop being hungry and yet refuse to eat creates an impossible situation, doesn't it?

Next, we need to look at where and what is buddha, the awakened state. The Buddha said, "Buddha is present in everyone." How is this nature or quality present? Is our dualistic mind the buddha?

If we say that dualistic mind is the buddha, then all sentient beings would already be buddhas and there would be a lot of buddhas who don't happen to manifest any enlightened qualities! If the dualistic mind is not the buddha, then what exactly is it in us that is the buddha? This term must refer to something. Mind essence is the buddha. Mind is that which knows pleasure and pain. *It is the very essence or identity of this knowing that is the buddha.*

Where exactly is this mind that knows pleasure and pain? If we were to ask each of us, we would all have to say "It is in me." What we refer to when saying 'me' is this body of flesh and blood, this voice that speaks, and this mind that experiences, that feels pleasure and pain. But again, we need to ask: what exactly is it that feels pleasure and pain?

One of the characteristics of mind is that it is empty, in the sense that it has not come into being as anything; it does not assume any particular form. At the same time, it is aware. It has a nature that knows, *unobstructedly*.

Mind's *nonarising* essence is empty and its nature is cognizant, unobstructedly aware. We speak about mind's two qualities, essence and nature. These two words describe the same identity. These qualities are an indivisible unity, just as you cannot separate water from its inherent wetness.

Now we need to ask: does this empty nature of mind exist, or not? Is there such a thing or not? If we say that it is, does it exist in the same way as something concrete, like earth, water, fire or wind? We have to agree that mind is not material. The nature of mind does not exist in a material way like earth, water, fire and wind. Yet if you say it does not exist, you have to deal with the fact that it is not a total nothingness, because mind is capable of knowing in all different ways. We cannot deny our own basic intelligence; the fact that there is something in us that knows, that experiences in countless ways.

Thus, we cannot say that mind is non-existent, that there is no mind. At the same time, we cannot say it exists in material form like the elements. We cannot say that mind is something we can see, hear, smell, taste or touch. If mind was a visible thing, we should be able to describe its shape: either square, round, spherical, or oval, whether it is long or short. Similarly, if mind were to have a physical form, it should also have a color and a smell. It is impossible for anything to have form and not have a color, isn't it? If you say that mind has form, it must have a color — so which color does your mind have? Likewise, anything that has form and color also has a smell of some sort. Does mind have a nice smell? Does its smell change over time, perhaps according to how hard we think? We are talking about mind, that which experiences. Does this mind have a physical form, a shape, a color? If mind had physical form, we should be able to touch it, to catch hold of it, keep it, and put it in a nice place.

Mind, however, is called immaterial mind, inconcrete mind, because it is intangible, formless. Being formless, it has no color, no smell, no tangible characteristics whatsoever. Still, if it exists, we have to be able to describe it. We can start by saying that mind is empty. Empty mind is similar to space. It is important to note here that it is not the same as space; that this is only an example, not the literal meaning. If the example was the thing itself, there would be no need to use an example! People might say that your face is beautiful like a flower. If your face really was a flower, how would you look, with your head being an actual flower? You can't judge poetry too much; it's enough that it sounds nice. It's the same with examples. But if they are totally dissimilar, you could not use that as an example either. What if we said, "Your face is beautiful like a withered flower" — how would that sound? Both are flowers; the only difference being one of time, in that one of the flowers is older. Just because of that, one example is nice, the other is not that nice.

Our mind, the knower, is like space because it has no form, color, or shape. In short, mind is empty cognizance. Space is merely empty. The empty quality of mind and the empty quality of space are similar. But mind can cognize; it can know, while space cannot. Because of this cognizant quality, its intrinsic ability to know, mind is called empty cognizance, while space is called empty void, empty nothingness. Mind is naturally empty *and* naturally cognizant. It is empty in essence and cognizant by nature — and these qualities are an indivisible unity, primordially, from the very beginning. No one made the self-existing, innate nature, the way it naturally is. It is not made by either a divine or devilish power, nor did any human being create it. Nobody made mind the way it is; it is just naturally so.

It is because of mind's cognizant quality that we experience. And it is because of experiencing that we become confused. It is not through the empty quality that confusion arises — only through cognizing. This cognizant quality, when directed towards experiencing, fixates on things like "It is," and all thoughts of "I and mine, you and yours." In this process, there is attachment to the notion of me, and a subtle aversion to what is you and yours. This subtle attachment and aversion is mistaken, though, because really, ultimately, there is no basis for these concepts of I and you! It is precisely our failure to know this that constitutes ignorance. This unknowing is the basis, the very root, of confusion. If this is where confusion starts, this is also where it should end, through becoming free. The originally empty cognizance fixates; it creates confusion. To be free, we need to experience the empty cognizance that does not fixate.

The unity of being empty and cognizant is how our mind essence naturally is. We can also describe this through the three kayas. The aspect that is empty in essence, totally unconstructed, is the dharmakaya. Cognizant by nature, unobstructed, is the sambhogakaya. And the capacity of this unity of emptiness and cognizance, which is ever-present and manifesting in manifold ways, is the nirmanakaya. To employ Mahamudra terminology, the nonarising essence and the unobstructed nature have the capacity to manifest in myriad ways.

To apply this in terms of practice, we need to not be caught up in thinking. *The very moment of being free of thought is dharmakaya.* It is not a matter of thinking any particular thought which makes us thought-free — it is not through thinking that we become thought-free. While a thought cannot remove thought, the presence of a thought can prevent thought-free wakefulness from manifesting. In thought-free wakefulness, there is no thought. In thinking, there is no thought-free wakefulness. Presence and absence do not happen at the same moment; they are mutually exclusive. A conceptual attitude cannot dissolve a conceptual attitude. That which dissolves conceptual attitude is *the absence of holding anything in mind*. A fixated thought does not dissolve the presence of fixated thoughts. *The absence of fixation dissolves fixation*. We need to clearly understand what the remedy is. The remedy to ego-clinging is the knowledge that realizes egolessness. The remedy to thought is non-thought. When we know the remedy well, we can overcome what needs to be overcome. It is when we're not aware of or familiar with how to use the remedy that we fail to do that which needs to be done.

Let's practice for a few minutes right now. Remain wide open. Don't hold any reference point. If we focus on something, on anything in particular, we are not wide open. When you are free of reference point, free of focus, you are wide open. It is actually very comfortable to be wide open.

STUDENT: Rinpoche, you talked about the process of conceptualizing. How is this different from discernment?

RINPOCHE: Mind is that which observes everything; that which notices or experiences whatever takes place. Mind, in this context, is the mental cognition that works through the five senses. Unless the mind pays attention, we do not see, hear, smell, taste or feel any texture. Mind is thus the basis for all pain and pleasure. Whether we are deluded or not depends upon mind. Whenever we are caught up in the duality of perceiver and perceived, we experience delusion. When we are able to cut through this chain, this bind of perceiver and perceived, we are free.

The *perceived* is easy to understand: it is simply the objects we experience; whatever we see, hear, taste, smell or feel as a tactile sense. But there is also the perceiver, the mind within, which connects through the five senses and then takes hold of these objects and forms thoughts, concepts. For instance, when the eye consciousness connects with the visual form and takes hold of it, it will form a thought about what is seen. When we simply look with our eyes towards something while our mind is strongly occupied by some other topic, we do not really see what is in front of us. Whenever our attention is directed towards what is seen, however – when we are interested in what we are viewing — we actually see it.

What happens is that the object seen through our eyes is connected with mind through the act of seeing, and then thoughts are formed. The process of the forming of thoughts in this way has two aspects to it, two degrees. One is more coarse, the next more subtle. For example, let's say we notice the outline of a human being. This is called conception. In other words, we form the concept, "There is a human being." But it is not clear to us yet who this person is, or whether we know that person or not. As we move closer in our minds, paying more attention, then we distinguish the details, "That is someone who looks such and such, I know whether it is such and such person." Maybe it is an acquaintance, maybe not. That is a more detailed form of thought which we call discernment. Thus, there are two levels: conception and discernment. At the first level of conception, our emotions of liking, disliking or remaining indifferent cannot really gain any foothold. But when we start to discern, they can occur very strongly.

Take this example. The moment we discern that what we are looking at is beautiful, we experience some sense of being attracted, of having the notion, "I like that." Or, if the feeling of attraction becomes very strong, it's "I love it!" Our attention is attached to that notion of liking and attraction. If we are discerning something that is ugly, then in a subtle way we feel ourselves to be opposed to it; we feel some aversion. In a more strongly developed way, we absolutely hate the sight of it, we detest it.

Now, if the object we are looking at evokes neither of these reactions – say that it's something that is not really interesting, something that doesn't fascinate us in any way, something we don't want to investigate any further - then we shut off our mind to it; we simply close off. This is in a subtle way a kind of indifference. In a more strongly developed way, it can be outright dullness. So these three possible reactions of liking, disliking or being indifferent, which when experienced to a stronger degree manifest as attachment, hatred or dullness are all involvements of our mind towards the object we perceive. This process happens again and again in the course of our daily lives, our ordinary perceptions.

As for the coarser or more strongly felt expressions of these three basic reactions, we do not have to be particularly religious to understand that they are no good. But you might ask: is there anything wrong with just feeling liking or dislike, or feeling indifference, towards the objects we see and hear, towards the sounds, the smells, the tastes, and the textures we perceive? Is there anything wrong with liking something we hear, see, smell, taste or feel? What about when we feel mild aversion or dislike — is there anything wrong with that? And what's wrong with closing off our mind and remaining indifferent?

How about a noble attitude, a good heart? Is it something we should keep? It's supposed to be good, isn't it? So why should we destroy that? The best feeling we can have is to wish to help others and to directly act from that virtuous attitude. Is it good enough to always train in that? Or is there something wrong with that? If there is some shortcoming in that, then what exactly is this shortcoming? We need to know this very clearly. If there is an imperfection in simply being good, we need to understand what that is. If there is something superior to being good, we need to know what it is and how to train in it.

My point here is that we need to be really clear. Let's say we think there is something better to simply being good, though we don't quite know what it is. Therefore, we conclude that being good, having a good heart, a virtuous state of mind is something that should be given up. We then throw away the good heart, and because we are not clear on what is superior to this, we fail to attain it! That would be a huge mistake. We need to be very clear about this point.

Let's take a step back and look at the situation. All these good thoughts, the nasty thoughts, the neutral thoughts — why do these thoughts come about? They are all due to a subtle formation of a conceptual attitude. This attitude is as insidious and dangerous as a nasty disease, like a cancerous growth that starts out in one tiny little place in the body. If it is allowed to grow, this disease can spread all over the entire body, making the chances for a cure extremely difficult. In the same way, the Buddhist metaphysical studies outlined in the *Abhidharma* discuss something called *subtle developers*. Unless we can get rid of these cancer-like subtle developers, there is no way for us to be free of full-fledged negative emotions.

In Buddhist teachings it is said that there is a root cause for all kinds of deluded states of mind, for all deluded experience. There is a root cause for all kinds of karma, all types of emotions, all kinds of thoughts and conceptual thoughts. The root cause for all these is the very subtle formation of a conceptual attitude. Unless this subtle conceptual attitude, this mental doing, is released and dissolved, there is no way in the world that one can be free from delusion; there is no way to be free from thoughts, from emotions, and from karma. In the same way as the example of a spreading cancer, one needs to be free of the very subtle root cause. Once we are free of that, all the rest can disappear quite naturally. *The root of karma, the root of emotions and the root of delusion is a subtle conceptual attitude.* To identify that root cause and the means of eradicating it is an extremely important point in Buddhist study.

Divorce

We are trying our best to attain liberation and enlightenment; that is what we are setting out to do. The reason we study, reflect and practice meditation is to attain liberation and enlightenment. Anything that helps this process is good and should be adopted. Likewise, anything which obstructs and prevents enlightenment should be avoided and abandoned. Some circumstances are adverse, meaning they prevent liberation and enlightenment. Those include stinginess, in other words, the emotional obscurations. They obstruct the attainment of freedom and omniscient enlightenment and are always to be avoided. Other circumstances are conducive to being free and awakened. These are *the six paramitas,* the five first of which are means, and the sixth which is knowledge – in particular, *the knowledge of realizing egolessness.*

As the paramitas indicate, we need both means and knowledge. These two aspects should always be combined. Means without knowledge does not help much. Similarly, knowledge without means does not help much. Means and knowledge are like our feet and our eyes: if we can walk and we can see, we can get to our destination. If we have legs but cannot see, we will not know where to go. Likewise, if we can see but have no legs, we cannot arrive. We need both. The first five of the paramitas, the means, are like legs to walk on, while the sixth, transcendent knowledge, is like the ability to see clearly. When we can both walk and see, we won't waste our effort because we will be moving in the right direction. If we unify means and knowledge, no effort that we put into proceeding towards freedom and enlightenment is wasted.

Every thought is always an involvement in hope and fear. Because this is an important point, I will reiterate it once more. We need to know exactly what freedom means from a Buddhist perspective. Generally speaking, freedom means being free of rebirth among the six classes of beings within the three realms — free in the sense that we do not need to involuntarily take rebirth in a state of suffering against our own wishes. That is freedom. The driving force that spins us through samsara, among the six classes of beings in the three realms, is nothing other than our own thinking. Whatever one does in the state of being caught up in deluded ordinary thoughts only increases the cause for further samsaric existence. When our disturbing emotions and our grasping is not so intense, we end up in the realms of humans and gods. When our emotions, our clinging, are very intense, the experience we have is that of hell realms, of hungry ghosts and of animals. Even though we may look like a human being, if our emotions and selfishness are incredibly rigid and uptight – if we are very aggressive, angry, hateful and attached, jealous, and so on — our experience is like that of being in hell.

It is also possible that in the first part of our life that we are totally caught up in selfish emotions and hold on very rigidly to a solid permanent reality. Eventually, though, we may begin to learn, to question and find out how things are. Through this process we may loosen our mental grip on things and become more relaxed, more content, and more at ease with ourself. That is also possible. To sum up everything I've just said, we could say that the maker of all pleasure and pain is mind. The joys and sorrows experienced by all sentient beings of the six realms are made by mind. Even the happiness and suffering experienced during the course of one single day is all experienced by mind.

Although mind is inconcrete or insubstantial, it cannot be fulfilled. Its craving is inexhaustible. The problem with normal mind is that it never gets enough. If mind could somehow become satisfied, then there would be an end, a limit. But even when we get what we think we want, it is never enough. It seems that we always want what we do not yet have. We want whatever is most difficult to get, and that is hard. If we do happen to achieve what we aimed at for so long, that which was so hard to get, that again is not enough. We set a new aim in mind. It turns out that the achievement was not that great after all, despite our enormous desire for it.

In other words, *every thought is always an involvement in hope and fear.* The hope and fear may be subtle, of medium strength or quite intense, but there is no thought that does not have in it some degree or some sense of hope and fear. Hope and fear is by definition an uptight, narrow-minded mental state, and that is painful. Intense, strong hope and fear is intense suffering. When we are occupied by intense hope and fear, food does not taste good, and it's even hard to sleep. The objects of the five senses are no longer beautiful. As hope and fear quiets down to a medium level, we can start to enjoy what we see, hear and taste, at least a little bit. When we are only slightly annoyed with a subtle level of hope and fear, we say, "I am happy — how nice! What a nice day!"

If we look back upon that fine, nice day, however, we will notice that even then there were repeated moments of subtle hope and fear. They are always lurking in the background as latent or potential; just waiting to pop up in full bloom. We probably don't notice them in the course of our everyday experience, but they are still there. We try to convince ourselves that we are not anxious or annoyed about anything, and we call that happiness. It seems that we need to fool ourselves in this way, because acknowledging reality is simply too painful. So really, there is never any moment in which we are truly happy, right? Honestly, those moments of being happy, unafraid, at east and totally fearless are very rare. For this we have conceptual thinking to blame: truthfully, it does not have that many great qualities.

We need to be free of selfish emotions. Selfish emotions are merely thoughts. Thought states are given different names: emotional thoughts, neutral thoughts, virtuous thoughts, hostile thought, selfish attitude, emotional attitude. Compared to selfishness, a neutral frame of mind is better. For example, thinking "Water is water; the sky is the sky" is a neutral thought. To think water is water is not necessarily good nor evil. Compared to a neutral thought, a wholesome or virtuous frame of mind is better — for instance, thinking "I want to help others." Any kind of noble-hearted attitude is a good thought. Therefore, at any time and in any situation a good thought, a good attitude, is something we should try to adopt. An aggressive, hostile attitude based on selfishness is always to be abandoned, because ill will and a hostile, aggressive frame of mind is upsetting. It makes both ourselves and others uneasy. As well, it makes us carry out actions that create negative karma.

This is exactly what I meant when mentioning conducive and adverse circumstances. To be deeply upset physically and mentally in the ways that we label jealousy, anger, attachment, dullness, conceit — all these make it more difficult to experience thought-free wakefulness, and therefore they are called adverse circumstances. That is also called negative karma. The opposite of that — when we have a benevolent, loving, helpful attitude and we carry it into our words and actions — is called conducive, virtuous, wholesome karma, good karma. Those are helpful circumstances. The person who wants to progress in shamatha and vipashyana, stillness and insight, should adopt whatever is helpful, whatever is a conducive circumstance. That is truly intelligent. To understand that whatever interrupts that progress and whatever works against it is not good, and to also actually avoid whatever prevents or hinders, that is also intelligent. Intelligence doesn't only involve creating situations of temporary comfort until we die. That is not necessarily complete intelligence. True intelligence means to look a little further and see what facilitates that which is of ultimate benefit — liberation and enlightenment. That is real intelligence.

Here, true freedom or liberation means freedom from selfish or disturbing emotions. All emotional states are basically thoughts. We understand now that thoughts can be of three types: evil, neutral and good. Evil thoughts or negative states of mind are always to be abandoned. They create negative karma and suffering. Neutral thoughts do not help, they do not harm; they are indifferent. They are also to be abandoned. Good thoughts, however, should be adopted. Good thoughts create conditioned virtue, conditioned goodness, the result of which is rebirth within the higher states of samsara. Experiencing a lovely environment and a pleasant situation is called rebirth among gods and humans. Conditioned virtue brings pleasant results. That is not liberation, however; one is still within a samsaric state. One has not transcended the basis of thought, which is dualistic fixation, the dualistic frame of mind. In order to go beyond that, we need to train in its opposite: we need to first recognize the state of thought-free wakefulness. Recognize that and develop its strength through training, and finally attain stability in thought-free wakefulness. That is how to be free of samsaric existence.

Why does the training in thought-free wakefulness make us free from samsaric states? *Because it undermines, eliminates, completely dissolves the very root cause for further samsara, which is fixation on duality. It destroys the conceptual frame of mind that holds on to self and other.* Since training in it destroys the cause of samsara, thought-free wakefulness is a primary cause for freedom and liberation. It is the essential training in Buddhism.

To adopt a virtuous frame of mind, a wholesome attitude is good; it is regarded as a method. Similarly, avoiding a negative attitude or an unwholesome frame of mind is good; it is also regarded as a method. But neither of these are enough to be free from samsara.

Imagine that an individual could somehow sponsor all human beings and animals and insects, and give them whatever they needed so that everyone could take a holiday for the rest of their lives and not have to work. That one single person would be the benefactor of all beings. Would the enormous amount of goodness created by this action be enough for that individual to be liberated from samsara? No, it would not. Undoubtedly it is a great kindness, it is very powerful action, and it would be an immensely good thing to do. Still, something is lacking, and that is the knowledge. There is a lack of insight into the root cause of confusion.

You may be familiar with the ten non-virtuous actions and their opposites, the ten virtuous actions. Imagine that we carry out the first nine of these for an incredible long time in an amazingly vast way. For example, instead of taking the lives of others, we save lives. Instead of taking what is not given or stealing, we are generous in a spectacularly lavish way. Instead of being frivolous, we practice pure ethics in relationships, according to whatever religion we follow or whatever civilization we are in. Those are the three ways of virtuous actions through one's body.

Similarly, instead of slandering, we reconcile all disagreements. Instead of speaking harshly, we speak gently. Instead of idle gossip and pointless talk, we speak meaningfully and with purpose. In terms of mental virtues, we should give up ill will. The opposite of craving is to rejoice in the happiness of others. To give up ill will, to be loving and kind in all different ways, again and again — all these are good. But the most important of all is the last one, the tenth virtuous action. Without this, something is missing.

Unless we can embrace our activities with the tenth virtuous action, which is olding the true correct view – the opposite of harboring wrong views — we may perform the first nine virtuous actions over and over again for a very long time, carrying them out in immense ways. Yet still, the result of that will be nothing other than in a future life we will be beautiful, wealthy, and have long life, good health, and many agreeable companions. We will experience all sorts of perfections in an astounding way, but we will still never be truly free, because the nine virtues are still only conditioned goodness. Conditioned goodness is good, it is beneficial, and it brings pleasant results. Still, it is not ultimate.

In this world, there are plenty of people who are not religious in any way. Still, if you ask them, "Is a good heart good, or not?" They will say, "It is." "Is it good to help others through one's words, through one's physical actions?" They will answer, "Yes it is, it is good." Basically, most everyone in this world agrees about what is good and what is evil. No matter where, people always say it is bad to kill your fellow citizen; it is bad to beat up your neighbor; it is bad to deceive a friend with lies; it is better to be nice. The tenth virtue, the true view, is both the most difficult to have and the most beneficial. If you have that, it in itself is enough; it is sufficient. Similarly, when you lack this one thing, nothing else ultimately helps. This one thing is to recognize our intrinsic wakefulness, our innate nature. This may seem difficult, because our basic nature is not an object of thought. But it can also be very easy, because it requires no effort.

Most of our trouble is troublesome precisely because it requires effort. Something is hard because you need to apply physical effort:

you have to say something, or you have to make a mental effort. When something requires an effort for a long time, we say that it is difficult to do. When something requires only minor effort, we call it easy. When someone says, "Take the day off — today you don't have to do a thing," that means we are not required to make any physical, verbal or mental effort. Then we think, "How wonderful! It's going to be a holiday!"

The difficulty in recognizing our innate nature is the ingrained habit of always trying to do something. When we are finally told, "Don't do anything," it is not easy! From the moment we wake up, we think that we need to occupy our minds with something. We need to think of something. It is a habit. When we do not think, it feels uncomfortable; it is like something is not right. We need to think of something, hold on to something, get something, pursue something — either good or bad, it doesn't really matter. We need to have an attitude about something, and if we do not, we feel uneasy. It makes us feel like, "I lost myself; there is something wrong." It may feel scary.

We occupy ourselves in numerous ways. We can hold on to things through our eyes, through our ears, through our nose, whatever. All this is merely mind making itself busy, occupying itself through various ways. The moment this mind occupies itself through the eyes, it thinks about what it is going to see. A sound is heard, so we pay attention to it and make thoughts about that. And so on, and so on, chasing and chasing, running and running. In the course of this constant process there is no stability, no steadiness; *there is no being in itself.*

These impressions are seductive, while the experiencer itself is fickle. It is so easy to get carried away after this and that. Mind seems to be powerless, as it is continuously overtaken by objects. No matter how much mind tries to occupy itself with nice sense impressions, beautiful sights and melodious sounds, these are very difficult to experience continuously. Even when we achieve pleasurable sensations for a while, it is still not good enough. We chase after sense pleasures for months and years, regardless of how difficult it is to do so or how much suffering it causes us. That kind of attitude seems to have a lot of perseverance. The fickle, restless frame of mind shows immense fortitude in relentlessly chasing after sense pleasures. That is how it is.

Right now, sights, sounds, smells, tastes and textures appear to be concrete and real to us. But the mind that chases after them is inconcrete and has a hard time catching them — a very hard time! Maybe it's better that there is a divorce! If the concrete and the inconcrete could somehow have a harmonious relationship, well, all right — let them live together. But the concrete seems to haunt the inconcrete mind; it seems to torture it. Of course, we cannot have a permanent split between mind and concrete reality, a real divorce. However, wouldn't it be a good idea to separate and occasionally have some space? That means the practice of shamatha and vipashyana. When one is resting in stillness, calm mind, the conceptual attitude that grasps is not blatantly present; it has subsided somewhat. And when one practices thought-free wakefulness, even the subtlest attempt to grasp is totally absent, totally dissolved.

In this world, we regard intelligence as something important and precious, don't we? And not only for human beings – we also say admiringly "What a smart animal!" Intelligence is certainly good. *The highest degree of intelligence is the knowledge that realizes egolessness. True intelligence is the intelligence that sees the absence of self.*

We also speak of being good, being a gentleman, a nice person, a gentle lady. *The best goodness, the highest goodness, is to be compassionate.* Whether it's experienced within or expressed outwardly, compassion is always good. Whenever somebody asks you what Buddhism is about, and you want to make it simple, just say these two words: intelligence and compassion. Of course, there is a lot to say about compassion, which is a very vast topic in Buddhism. Briefly, there are two types of compassion: with and without focus, or directed and undirected compassion.

To summarize, freedom means to be free of disturbing selfish emotions. It means to be free of all of samsara. To be free of all of samsaric states is to be free of any conceptual state of mind: free of all thoughts, whether they be good thoughts, neutral thoughts or evil thoughts. It is also to be free of any conceptual attitude that holds onto anything as being or not being permanent, solid, or real. To be totally free of all this is true freedom. *The moment any type of conceptual attitude dissolves that is the true view.*

The true view is not a philosophical position. When we are free from any type of conceptual attitude, we are not taking a mental stance of holding something that it is or is not. When we are free of all that, the innate nature at that moment is no other than what it simply is. We are resting in the true nature of mind. At that moment, you can say that the obscurations have dissolved; they are purified, cleared away. That is called unobscured suchness. To change from experiencing obscured suchness to actually being unobscured suchness, it is necessary to train. In the beginning, the training is deliberate; it involves effort. The kind of deliberate effort we need — deliberate training — eventually leads to effortlessness. The real training is effortlessness. To be free of any trying or effort, to be effortless, is also called training. It's rather paradoxical, because actually there is no *thing* being trained in, and there is no act of doing anything either. Yet it's still called training! It can also be called meditation, but there is no meditating on something. To make this effortless training an actuality for ourselves, we need to first apply some effort. Here is how.

Right now, do not follow any memory of the past. Do not plan anything for the future. Whatever appears to you in this present moment through your senses or in your mind, do not conceptualize or judge or evaluate it. Remain totally disengaged. Leave your eyes open. In the practices of Mahamudra and Dzogchen, the eyes are called the gates of wisdom; do not close them. In the general teachings and specifically in shamatha practice, one closes the eyes in order to avoid being occupied by what is seen, and thus being disturbed from the state of calmness. But from a Vajrayana, Mahayana or Dzogchen perspective, this logic is flawed. If it helps to close the eyes, why only the eyes? You would have to close your ears, nose, skin, and everything else too, in order to be totally shut off.

The instruction is this:

Leave the five senses wide open.
Let awareness be undirected.
Remain totally open.
Do not get involved in perceived objects.
Do not form thoughts about them.
Be composed in that way.
Wide open.
Awake.
Empty, awake, wide open.

That is how it is described. Madhyamaka teachings emphasize the utterly empty quality of this state, while the Anu Yoga and the new tantras use the description sheer bliss, very blissful. More elaborately, this state is described as "the emptiness endowed with the supreme aspect indivisible from unchanging great bliss." The Dzogchen teachings on the primoridal purity aspect of *Trekchö* describe it as total nakedness. These words and their meaning are extremely profound, but also quite appealing, quite delightful.

Utterly empty emphasizes the view of emptiness. *Sheer bliss* emphasizes the training in the unity of bliss and luminous clarity. The key point is phrased as "Blissful, yet unattached; clear, yet not fixating." That is very important. It is all right to be blissful, but not to cling to the bliss. Similarly, clarity is how wakefulness actually is. But to fixate on that, to cling to that, is a defect. The Dzogchen teachings on nondual awareness use the word *total nakedness*. That means that rigpa or self-existing wakefulness, once it is distinguished from dualistic mind, is free of duality and totally laid bare, all by itself.

At the beginning it is a good idea to train in being awake and wide open in our meditation sessions. Otherwise the training is likely to be interrupted by distractions. The whole purpose of having monasteries and retreat centers or hermitages is because our attention is so easily carried away. These diversions can be outer distractions, the company of the people we are with, or simple laziness.

There are so many things to do in the city at all times, and good and bad company actually does influence us. Therefore, compose yourself during during formal meditation periods and practice remaining undistracted.

> *The view is not a thing to be viewed.*
> *Meditation is not an object to be cultivated.*
> *Train in being unpolluted by conceptual attitude.*
> *Utterly empty,*
> *Wide open,*
> *Sheer bliss,*
> *Total nakedness,*
> *Vividly awake,*
> *Alive,*
> *Vibrant,*
> *Vast and spacious.*

In this context, 'meditation' means training in being this way, in a state in which dualistic fixation has been suspended. At that moment, there is no samsara. Samsara has dissolved. There is no practice superior to this one, to having dissolved samsara. In this moment, there is no karma or selfish emotion being formed. There is nothing to affirm, nothing to deny, no hope, no fear.

You do not need to hold onto the concept that *this state is*. You do not need to hold onto the concept that *something is not*. Basically and fundamentally, our mind is utterly empty, sheer bliss, totally naked. We do not need to make it like this; we do not need to cultivate it by meditating, to create this state by meditating. The mind is primordially free, free of karma and disturbing emotion, free of samsaric deluded experience, free from the conceptual attitude of holding onto is and is not, free of the need to be accepted, the need to be rejected, free of all hope and fear.

We need to persevere; we need to apply a lot of effort in being effortless. We need to meditate in a way of not meditating. Nothing to do — that is a big job! Not doing anything at all is something we really have to apply ourselves to. It is okay to not move. That is effortless. To move is effort. To speak is also effort. We do not need to speak at all. Similarly, to hold something in mind, to form thoughts about this, that and the other, is also mental effort. Totally drop, completely let go of, every mental effort, Give up thinking of anything at all, about the past, the future or the present. Remain thought-free, like an infant.

Not fixating means not forming the thought "This is it." Remain unpolluted by any notion of holding anything in mind. Let totally go, recognizing it is like space. Can you see space? Can you experience space? When you see or experience space, do you see it as a presence or an absence? Do you somehow see that absence?

Space is not a thing to see. To see that there is no thing to see is called 'seeing that there is space.' If we were somehow seeing it as a thing, it would not be space, it would be an entity like earth, rock or water, some elemental substance like that. Space, however, is not composed of physical form; it is openness. We give a name, we apply a label to that which has no form and is wide open: we call it space. Space is utterly unlike concrete things. It is exactly because it is inconcrete that we call it space. When seeing concrete things, we see the presence of something that is. When seeing the inconcrete. we actually see its presence as an absence. Seeing that there is something to see is usually called seeing. Seeing that there is nothing to see is also seeing; it is okay to call it seeing. It is just a different manner of seeing. In the same way, when seeing or experiencing emptiness, empty means that there is no physical form, shape, color and so on to notice — just like space. The -ness in emptiness means cognizance, knowingness. All wisdom experience unfolds out of this cognizance. All the experiences of the kayas and wisdoms come out of this cognizance.

The empty quality, the quality of basic space beyond all constructs, is dharmakaya. This empty cognizance is already present as our minds. When anyone asks you to define mind, the answer "empty cognizance" is quite alright. If someone says define fire, and we say "hot and burning,' that is okay. To define water as "wet and liquid" is also fine. We can define wind as "light and moving." And we can define space as "vast, open, accommodating, impartial, with no center and no edge, intangible." That is space. It is nonexistent, because it does not exist as a solid, concrete thing. It is rather an all-pervasive absence. In the same way, defining mind as "empty cognizance" is a good definition. The general definition of mind in Buddhism is cognizant and conscious. Samsara evolves from this empty cognizance that is mind when the cognizant quality fixates and gets involves in clinging. When the cognizant quality remains free of fixation, the immensity of the wisdom experiences of kayas and wisdoms unfolds.

STUDENT: I'm confused!

RINPOCHE: *Confusion can be understood as the mistaken or deluded way that ordinary beings experience reality.* Confusion means to be mistaken about what is; thinking that things are real and permanent while they are not. Actually, it is impossible for anything to really or truly exist; existence is only something that one believes. This belief happens because we are unaware of, ignorant of, the true nature of all things. First there is ignorance; then the act of holding onto an 'I,' a self, where no such self actually exists, and of believing there is an 'other' where no such 'other' exists. This ignorance is the very basis for the notion of self and other: it is the failure to know that these concepts have no reality to them whatsoever.

The basic ignorance of attachment to 'self' and aversion to 'other' has been perpetuated in our mind stream for a very long time, in a vast, immense way. We need to dissolve this strong habitual ignorance, but this is not something that happens from one moment to the next. While dreaming, the dreamer only believes that what is dreamt is real. He is not likely to think, "This is all illusory illusion." Even if he were to think it, it would be very hard to simultaneously experience the dream as unreal. In exactly the same way, all that we experience right now is illusory. But it is very difficult to have that confidence and to actually experience everything as being insubstantial and unreal.

We need to allow our confusion to dawn as wisdom; we need to let our deluded way of experiencing dawn as original wakefulness. How does this happen? It is only possible through recognizing and realizing the nature of mind.

Innate suchness is unobscured the moment you are not caught up in thinking. The very moment we acknowledge the real, how reality truly is, any delusory notion about how things are is gone. How do we remain unspoiled by mistakenness? By not being caught up in duality.

According to the tradition of pith instructions, that which obscures is our conceptual attitude. The clinging to things as being real, as being me, as being permanent, concrete, existing, and so forth — all the different varieties of conceptual fixation — are in short, our present thinking. In this present thinking, a nasty thought certainly obscures, but even a noble thought obscures the innate suchness. An unwholesome thought is a way of holding something in mind. A noble thought is equally a way of holding something in mind. They are equal in the sense that there is still the holding of an attitude; it is that holding which obscures, not the particular content of the thought. You remain bound, fettered, whether it be by an ugly iron chain or a beautiful golden chain studded with diamonds.

Being caught up in present thinking obscures innate suchness. Innate suchness is unobscured when you are not caught up in present thinking. How can we be not caught up? During a meditation session, sit relaxed, with a straight back. The guidance texts say, "Place your body like a bundle of straw where the string tying it together has been cut." You are upright but sitting loosely, not in a rigid, forced way. The more relaxed, the better. "Your voice should be left like a sitar where the strings have been cut." Do not speak. Breath in a gentle and unforced way.

"Your mind should be left like a water mill where the water has been diverted." In the past, in some places in the world, mills were driven by the flow of water. When the water was routed in another direction, the mill stopped spinning, because the mechanism was disengaged. Leave your mind like that. Disengage from following after what has happened in the past. Disengage from thinking of what is going to happen in the future. Do not evaluate or judge anything in the present moment. Remain without the need to react, correct, improve, accept or reject. *Simply leave whatever is exactly as it is.* Whenever there is a thought, let it come. When there is no thought, let there be no thought. In this way, the buddha mind can be revealed.

To paraphrase what Padmasambhava says in one of the verses among the *Supplications in Seven Chapters,* it is okay to perceive, but do not cling: Whatever moves in the realm of sight, allow it to happen, but hold onto nothing. This involves not only what we see, but also what we hear, smell, taste, touch and experience in the realm of mind: let it all happen, but don't fixate on it.

In other words, what we need is the opposite of conceptual thinking. Leave behind fixating, which is duality. Abandon the normal way of thinking, which is full of disturbing emotions. We need thought-free wakefulness in order to come face to face with our innate nature. Acknowledge the mind of the buddhas of the three times, the view of the Great Perfection, of Mahamudra, of the Middle Way. To recognize this and sustain it, we need to perfect the accumulations and remove the obscurations.

The Lamp that Dispels Ignorance

To realize the original coemergent wisdom, the natural state of wakefulness, we need to purify the obscurations, gather the accumulations and take the support of the blessings of an authentic lineage of masters expressed through a qualified teacher. Understand that any effort besides these is merely a cause for tiredness.

Actually, all these points are embodied in the ngöndro practices. The idea of tiredness here in this context means that any other thing that we may try to do or believe that somebody else can do for us, any intellectual information or effort to figure out the situation through reflection, is not going to be enough. Going on and on in those conceptual ways will only cause exhaustion. What we need to do is purify the obscurations, gather the accumulations, receive the blessings of a qualified master and obtain the pith instructions on how to realize the original state of wakefulness.

There are many stories of how this realization took place in the past — realization in Mahamudra being the original coemergent wisdom, while in Dzogchen it's described as cutting through to a state of primordial purity. Realization happened when accomplished masters met with worthy, receptive disciples — disciples who were totally ready, who had undergone prior training in this or former lifetimes and who had purified their obscurations and perfected the accumulations. When such a disciple connected with a master, it was sometimes not necessary to even speak a single word or to show a single gesture. Their merely being together was enough for the state of realization to be transmitted. That is called "the mind-to-mind transmission of the buddha of the awakened state."

There is also the symbolic transmission of the knowledge holders, of the vidyadharas. Here, again without words, an accomplished master would merely show a gesture to the ready disciple, someone who has already undergone purification. For example, the master would point into space without saying anything, or hold up a natural rock crystal and point to it. Through this gesture the disciple would realize the original state of wakefulness and attain a state in which the realization of the guru was identical with his or her own. There are also many examples of the master speaking only a few words, perhaps a single sentence or four verses of teachings. He would whisper these through a copper tube, so that no one else could hear. These few words would be sufficient for the disciple to attain the same state of realization of that of the master. There are many examples like that in the past.

Nowadays, however, it seems that unless there is a foundation of study and reflection and the understanding gained through these, the knowledge that is the result of meditation training does not begin to happen. This understanding that is the result of meditation training requires study and reflection. Thus, study and reflection are exceedingly important. We may want to start meditating without first studying, and that is okay. However, it is quite possible that we do not know how or what to practice. It is a very good idea and extremely beneficial to learn something first and afterwards practice meditation. *On the other hand, if we only study and reflect and do not get true understanding through practice, we only have theory, intellectual understanding. Intellectual understanding is not enough to cut through selfish emotions.* First we need to have some basis in study and reflection, and then apply that to gain the understanding through meditation training.

Now for the essential, mind. Mind is that which thinks all different things, one after the other, restlessly. That which accepts and rejects, judges. Who is anxious, who is restless, who is happy, who is sad? Isn't there something that does this, something that knows? That is mind. And when we investigate what is it that knows, we do not find a thing. Isn't that true? Do we all agree that there is something in us that knows? And also that we don't know where it is? It seems that it is wherever we are, right? If we believe it is in the brain, it is in the brain. If we believe it is in the arms and legs, it could be in the arms and legs. It is not non-existent. Because if we claim that there is no mind, we do not know anything, there is no experience. There is some knowing in us, so we have to say, "Yes, there is mind."

Can we take hold of this mind? Can we pin-point it? This knowing, is intangible, yet is.

The other day we analyzed to some extent that mind has no physical form? And that which has no physical form is not an object you can look at. It is not something you can listen to or hear. You cannot smell it, taste it or take hold of it. It seems like there is no mind. Doesn't it? On the other hand, mind is not totally non-existent like space. You cannot say it is like space. Mind is similar to space, but not identical with it. Having no physical form and no sound, smell, taste, texture is why space is called empty. Mind is empty. Mind is 'empty in essence', meaning devoid of a concrete identity.

Mind is naturally empty, originally empty. No one made mind empty, no one can. Yet, mind is not exactly like space, void and nothing else. Mind is empty, *yet it can know*. Mind is cognizant. Cognizance means conscious, able to know, able to feel, able to experience, able to perceive. This ability to know, to experience, to perceive, is in the empty mind. That is why we describe mind as being empty cognizance — because mind is both empty and cognizant. While cognizing, mind is still empty. This being empty and being cognizant are primordially a unity. It is an original, natural unity, not a fusion created by anyone. No one had to unite empty cognizance; no one is able to do that. We call this a union, but honestly, it means indivisibility. There are two kinds of unity: a unity that can again be separated and an indivisible unity. An example for indivisible unity is like water being wet or a flame being hot. These cannot be separated. The empty and cognizant quality of mind is indivisible, like water and wetness. That is the meaning of unity.

This unity of being both empty and cognizant — is that something that was formed, or is it unformed? Intellectual philosophers in particular like to question in this way. A unity implies that there must have been two aspects, one empty, and the other cognizant, and that they became a unity at some point. Otherwise, why call it a unity, right? Being a unity of two aspects, it must have been formed from two separate entities. Anything that is formed is impermanent; anything that is formed perishes. That is how a philosopher might think. If one were to believe that the unity of empty cognizance is something that was formed, that is conditioned; it eventually should also perish, vanish, disappear. Is that clear?

However, this unity of empty cognizance is not formed, because it is empty and at the same time cognizant; while cognizing, it is empty. The term unity is a mere name attached to it because of these two qualities being indivisible. Actually, it is not something formed; it is unformed. Therefore, it does not perish; nor does it come into being. This unity is beyond birth and death.

In short, our mind in essence is empty; by nature it is cognizant. This unity is unformed, and therefore does not arise, nor does it cease: it is beyond death and birth. This being empty in essence is a natural emptiness; this being cognizant by nature is a natural cognizance; and these being a unity is a *natural* unity. The unformed nature of this unity is *naturally* unformed. This word 'natural' is very important. To repeat this important point: in essence our mind is empty; by nature, our mind is cognizant; and this empty cognizance is our basic state. At any moment that this natural empty cognizance does not fixate on anything, then it is just like that, as it *naturally* is.

How does knowing that our mind is empty in essence help us? It helps us eliminate any idea that mind is a permanent, concrete thing that solidly exists. All such concepts are naturally eliminated by the simple understanding that the essence of this mind is empty. Do you understand this? This is the effect, the direct result, of understanding 'empty in essence.' Next, while being empty, our mind cognizes. Understanding the basic cognizance automatically eliminates any idea we may have that mind is nothingness — the nihilistic view. Again, our mind is naturally an empty cognizance. In the very moment that we become aware of this fact, that we recognize it, *in that same moment,* any kind of incorrect belief is automatically eliminated. Any kind of belief in eternalism or in nihilism is automatically released, discarded. All other kinds of wrong views are automatically eliminated by the mere fact of recognizing how our nature is.

Ordinary kinds of philosophy emphasize one of these two aspects. Either they assume that, based on the cognizant quality, there is something — there is a maker, a creator, something permanent — or, emphasizing the empty quality, they maintain that there is nothing at all, that existence or being is actually nothing. These are the two extremes of eternalism and nihilism.

You have heard that the Buddhist view is beyond these two extremes, right? If you simply allow yourself, your own mind, to just be for a moment, without fixating on any concept whatsoever, that in itself eliminates any extreme view. To hold the idea 'it is' is clinging. To hold the idea 'it is not' is also clinging. If you have to choose one of these, it is actually better to hold onto the idea 'it is,' because it is taught that if one clings to this eternalist perspective, one can still take rebirth in the higher realms. But if one holds onto the nihilistic idea 'it is not,' it is very hard to get a high rebirth – and thus it is very easy to take a low one. We need to go beyond both extreme views.

When we let be in equanimity, how do we compose ourselves? First, we let our body be straight — upright, yet relaxed. Sit upright, but in a very relaxed, very free way. If the body is straight and relaxed, all the channels are straight and free, unconstrained, and thus it is much easier for the mind to be at ease. When beginning the actual training in Mahamudra or Dzogchen, one gives up chanting during the meditation state. Mentally, we give up any kind of doing, even the virtuous kinds of visualization like giving and taking, *tonglen* practice. Give up all kinds of mental involvement. Leave your mind freely and evenly, as an unconstructed and unconfined empty cognizance. Cognizance can be experienced in two different ways. It can be aiming at something and holding that in mind, or it can be undirected, holding nothing. When holding something, that is called dualistic mind. When holding nothing at all, it is free: that is mind essence itself.

Leave the five senses wide open.
We have eyes,
we have ears, nose, tongue, body,
leave all these venues wide open, unoccupied.

Let your awareness be undirected.
This empty cognizance is mind.
Do not aim it at anything,
do not hold a reference point;
leave it wide open.
It is also said like this:
do not focus outwardly,
do not concentrate inwardly
do not place the attention in between, either.
Totally unimpeded.
Rigpa is totally free, unimpeded.
Self-existing awareness is unimpeded.
Not obscured, not blocked,
not obstructed by anything.
Compose yourself like this.

(After a while, Rinpoche takes questions)

STUDENT: What is the benefit of training in samadhi?

RINPOCHE: Goodness. Among all types of goodness, the strongest and the most profound is to remain evenly composed in samadhi. Nothing is more effective than remaining in the samadhi of stillness and insight, shamatha and vipashyana. When it comes to accumulating merit, when it comes to pacifying disturbing emotions and selfishness, nothing is better than this. The Buddha often taught that, compared to making lavish offerings to all buddhas in the ten directions, or to giving alms to needy for aeons and aeons, it is much more effective to remain in the composure of recognizing the natural state of mind, even for a very short time. This superior method eradicates personal faults and perfects the accumulations of merit and wisdom.

In the actual recognition of mind essence or self-existing awareness, all selfish emotions have dissolved and there is no forming of karma and disturbing emotions. Deluded perception is absent at that moment. Even if one has not recognized the natural state of mind and simply *pretends* to be in the natural state, it still brings incredible benefit, because it is closer to knowing how it really is. Similarly, the mere thought "All things are empty and devoid of identity," while conceptual, is also true. All things are empty and devoid of identity, and thinking this brings us closer to realizing how this is in actuality.

Where does the thought that all things are empty and devoid of self come from? It comes from understanding, which is the result of study and reflection. The conviction that, "All things are empty and devoid of self" comes about through learning and studying, which is what we are doing right now. We are learning. This is what these teachings are about; that is what this book is about. Learning is extremely important to gaining understanding. Thinking things through with our own power of reflection enables us to gain true understanding through meditation training. That is why it is said that "learning and reflection are lamps to dispel ignorance."

The teachings of Buddha Shakyamuni are very detailed and very extensive. There are many different topics, each with a lot of material. Regardless of how much perseverance and how much intelligence we may have, there is always more to study; the subject will not run out. We can inquire, analyze and question as much as we want, and that is perfectly all right. However, please understand this: *It is vital is to take the teachings personally, to apply them to our own situation. Understand that all the different details are actually personal instructions, and that all the teachings are without conflict, without contradiction.* This is essential, because if we do not take the teachings personally, if we do not take them to heart, we may think they are simply information. With that attitude, we keep on gathering information, lining up one point of view or philosophy against another. We end up sharpening our discriminating intellect and becoming increasingly judgmental, trying to defeat other positions. We think we are promoting the true Dharma, but actually we are promoting anger and attachment. Whatever we learn, we should use it to reduce our own selfishness. Learning is actually the remedy against disturbing emotions — that is what it is meant for. It's just like the way that medicine is meant for curing disease. Any medicine that can cure disease is authentic medicine; it is useful; it can be effective. But any medicine that does not work, no matter how expensive it might be, is no good; it is to be avoided.

In short, whatever we learn and whatever we understand, we should put to use to improve our mind, our attitude. Otherwise, we are merely learning something by rote. We listen, we hear it, we understand it, and we are able to repeat it in the same way — so what! The whole reason the Buddha taught was so that the teachings could cure our disturbing selfish emotions, our rigid minds. Learning Buddhism should change our way of being, in thought, word and deed. In body, in speech and in mind we should be more loosened up, more relaxed and flexible.

In the Bodhisattva teachings, like Shantideva's "*The Way of a Bodhisattva*," there is an instruction: "When you look upon another being, do so gently, with loving eyes and a smiling face. Appreciate other beings with this attitude: "With the help of these beings, I can develop the precious enlightened attitude, bodhichitta. With the help of these beings, I can progress towards Buddhahood. The fact that it is possible for me to train in the six paramitas, in the four means of magnetizing and so forth, and in the vast activities of a bodhisattva, is only possible because of other beings – so, thank you very much!" The teaching of the way of a bodhisattva continues, "Speak gently; speak softly; speak meaningfully. In your heart be free of conceit, be free of hypocrisy, be free of deceit and competitiveness, rivalry and aggression. Always keep a loving, compassionate frame of mind, in a very sincere way."

When we study the words of the Buddha and understand their meaning, something should change in us. A person who learns and reflects about Buddhism should simultaneously diminish his or her involvement in selfish emotions. Compassion and understanding should grow further and further. If that is the case, you can say that learning and understanding are progressing correctly.

On the other hand, as we continue studying more and more Dharma, if our character becomes increasingly rigid, if we become increasingly rude and unkind, something is wrong. There is the risk that one can become insensitive, numb, unless one takes the teachings personally. A great sinner, someone who has been extremely evil, can still be changed by the Dharma. But someone who has learned a lot yet who has not taken it to heart, someone who has become very insensitive, is very hard to change through the Dharma. Do not keep your understanding of the Dharma as merely intellectual information. Bring it into your experience, assimilate and train in it. Otherwise, we can end up gathering more and more information, yet using the teachings to inflate ourselves with egotistical aims, while increasing our attachment and aversion.

If you take a stone from the river and split it in half, it is still dry in the middle, even though it has spent years in the water. Shouldn't it be wet or saturated somehow? In the same way, we can spend years and years in Dharma circles, but unless we make the teachings our experience through practice, it is like being that riverbed stone, still dry at the core. There is a Tibetan saying: "The Dharma-numb person cannot be helped by the Dharma, just like the butter skin is not softened by the butter." Usually a piece of hide or skin is softened by applying oil or butter and kneading it so that it becomes really pliant, flexible. In Tibet, butter is kept in skins. That skin spends all its time with the butter — it becomes saturated with the butter — yet it grows totally stiff and rigid because it hasn't been properly kneaded or worked. It's the same with the need to apply Dharma teachings; we need to work them, knead them into our being.

While there are so many things we could study within Buddhist teachings, the essential point at any time is to be certain about what you learn, and then to use it, to apply it. In particular, we need to become clear about the nature of mind by means of the 'perfect measure' of the Buddha's words. 'Measure' here refers to the perfect way of becoming certain. There is the perfect measure of the Buddha's words, the perfect measure of your own intelligent reasoning and the perfect measure of the pith instructions of your personal teacher. Combine these three and gain confidence about the natural state of mind.

All of samsara and all of nirvana is simply the magic of your own mind. All joys, all sorrows, and everything to be affirmed or denied at the path stage — all this is made by our minds. It is the mind's doing: all is dependent upon mind, experienced by mind, and made by mind. Mind is the doer of all, the maker of all. The purpose of all philosophy and practice is to soften this mind. The essence of our mind is the Buddha, the awakened state. It is through not recognizing it that all problems arise. It is like a poor man who does not know that a stone set in the floor of his own house is actually made of pure gold, and thus continues to starve. The wish-fulfilling jewel is our mind essence, which has always been present, primordially, as our own nature. Not knowing this, our troubles continue. In short, all the suffering we have undergone is because of not recognizing the nature of our mind.

We spin through samsara because of ignorance. Ignorance means not knowing — not knowing the natural state. Sentient beings are confused through not knowing the natural state. What we need now, instead of not knowing, is to know. This knowing is called 'seeing the nature of mind.' Knowing the natural state is called Buddha. Not knowing the natural state is called sentient being. When knowing the natural state, it is free, liberated. When not knowing the natural state it is called deluded, confused.

The natural state in itself is unmistaken and unconfused. The natural state, our basic being, is not created by the Buddha; it is not an invention. In fact, even the Buddha is unable to make it. Even a buddha cannot construct it, so how can we? If the Buddha had somehow created it, it would not be that great. What is made is not natural. Our basic state is not made up in any way whatsoever; it is not created by anyone. Whether or not the Buddha appears in this world, and whether or not the Buddha describes it through teachings, our basic state, the natural state, still remains exactly the same. The cleverest buddha cannot improve it. The stupidest, most dense sentient being cannot worsen it. Knowing the natural state, how the basic condition actually is, is called seeing the innate nature — seeing *dharmata*. This 'seeing' does not mean to see a concrete thing. It is also not to see an inconcrete thing. It is the seeing which is totally free of any kind of formulation. Thoughts like 'it is,' 'it is not,' 'it's concrete,' 'it's inconcrete' — it is utterly free of all that. Concrete is defined as the opposite of inconcrete, and thus it is dependent upon formulation.

How much do we need to learn? We need to continue learning until we have complete confidence about the natural state; then it is enough. We can use any kind of method to do so. Whatever helps is fine — use it. Whatever does not help — give that up. Use whatever is beneficial; give up whatever is a hindrance. Continue until you reach what you set out to do; that is the purpose of learning.

To realize the innate nature is to know it through direct experience, not just intellectually. The moment of direct knowing in actual experience is not something we learn about or have heard of. That moment you feel sure and decide, "This is the natural state, the innate nature" — that is the proof that your understanding is no longer intellectual. You are not an intellectual anymore.

Any other questions?

QUESTION: You said that when we are certain we've experienced the natural state of mind, we can study or do whatever we like. At the moment when we are experiencing that, there is nothing to do. The comment of, "Oh, that is it" — that feels like a thought that comes later. That, "Oh, a moment ago that must have been the natural state. Oh yeah, that's what we've been talking about."

RINPOCHE: That is fine. There is a difference between the meditation state and postmeditation. During the meditation state, when we remain composed in the unconfined unity of empty cognizance, there should not be any thought of, "Now I see it, now I experience it." Afterwards, however, we may reflect on how the experience was. We are able to appreciate that it was an experience in which there was no concrete thing being dwelled on as the experience. That would be called postmeditation.

There are different ways to define meditation and postmeditation, but basically, whenever there is thinking, it is postmeditation. By recognizing the nature of the thinker, the thinking dissolves. When the thinking dissolves, that is the meditation state. When thinking reoccurs, it is postmeditation. Generally speaking, when you sit the body down with a straight back and keep sitting, you call it meditation. When you stand up, it is postmeditation. The practitioner who trains in the natural state, in mind essence, initially trains while sitting down, but then at some point he or she trains while involved in other activities. So really, no one but yourself knows whether you are in meditation or postmeditation.

The essence of all teachings is called rigpa, or in Mahamudra, ordinary mind. It is our natural state, unpolluted by any conceptual attitude. That means we recognize in actuality, not as an idea. It needs to be the natural state laid totally bare, stripped of any conceptual frame of mind. Otherwise, our training is merely a training in the *idea* of it. We may tell ourselves that our present experience corresponds to what we read in a book or what we heard. "Yes, mind is empty:" that is one thought. "It is also cognizant" — that is a second thought. "They are a unity," is a third thought. "Oh, this is emptiness, this is simplicity. Yeah, this is an absence of constructs, this is mental non-doing." Forming those thoughts is simply mental doing! Any such way in which we try to sit and formulate the natural state is nothing other than a resemblance or a fascimile, not the real thing. It cannot be anything other than that.

On the other hand, words like rigpa or ordinary mind point at the natural state by describing how our nature already is. It is not something we make, not something we construct or something that we do. It is how our basic state is when not doing anything to it whatsoever. When we do not try to contrive or form it into anything at all, it is *already* rigpa, ordinary mind. That is why Milarepa said, "The Buddha's tongue is eloquent when describing the general vehicles, but gets stuck when teaching the definitive meaning."

In other words, the ultimate state is ineffable, indescribable. At the same time, it is very hard to realize the meaning without some description. But we need to remember that *the descriptions are only methods*. Any description, no matter how exceptional, is never one hundred percent accurate. It cannot be, by its very nature. When you hear that all phenomena are beyond constructs, that essentially all phenomena neither exist nor do not exist, both or neither, you try to understand it and think, "OK, that is how it is." Yet that is still only a formulation. The moment you think "Beyond constructs," that itself is a construct! That is the trouble with words: they are innately conceptual. Still, if we never say that all things are beyond constructs, we are in bigger trouble.

If we grasp the thought and cling to the words, the actuality of the meaning escapes us. "Everything is emptiness beyond constructs" — to hold that thought is still clinging. When we cling to an I, it is clinging. To fixate on egolessness is also clinging. To say "There is no ego" is still fixation. You can fixate on something as being, or as not being, but both are fixation. The knowledge that realizes egolessness is not just knowledge; it is transcendent knowledge beyond holding any notion of the three spheres.

STUDENT: How do we turn away thoughts?

RINPOCHE: The method to dispel thinking is thought-free wakefulness. The training instructions in the primordially pure state of Trekcho or the "Thorough Cut" say, "Do not block or suppress thoughts." Since you cannot block thoughts anyway, do not even try. Allow whatever happens to happen: if a thought forms, let it form. Then the instruction is, "When a thought moves, be carefree; don't attach too much importance to it." When we don't attach any importance to what is thought of, that thought cannot do much damage. It cannot get a foothold; it cannot be 'solidly' formed. But if one is unable to be carefree and attaches importance to a thought, the thought is fully formed. The more importance generated towards a thought, the stronger the thought becomes. Take the example of an old man watching children play. The kids build houses in a sandbox, saying, "This is my castle," and thinking that what they made is very important. They say, "I am the owner and you are not." They build up all kinds of seriousness around the play. But the old man who is watching does not attach that much validity to it at all. He knows this is children's play, this making sandcastles — no big deal!

In a similar way, whenever a thought moves, the more carefree and relaxed we can be about it and the less importance we attach to it, the easier it is to arrive back into the natural state of rigpa. On the other hand, the more importance we attach to what is being thought of, the more it obscures the awakened state of rigpa. There is another example often used of a small child in a temple. He looks around and he sees all the bright colors and images, but he attaches no value to what is seen. It is not that the small child is not seeing, not that he is blind, but rather that he has not formed any rigid ideas about he sees. It is not that we don't have ideas or thoughts; rather, it's that we don't cling to them, solidify them and make them rigid.

Release

Generally speaking, it is the tradition to first introduce the meditator to shamatha practice, the training in stillness. Having attained stability in that, he or she then proceeds to being pointed out the state of vipashyana — to practicing vipashyana based on shamatha. This is the sequence particularly in the Vajrayana schools called Sarma, the New Schools of Kagyü, Sakya and Geluk. According to these traditions, shamatha is emphasized as a vital starting practice before practicing vipashyana. Without a calm mind, it's difficult to see one's own nature clearly, just as it's difficult to see one's own face clearly in the surface of a lake that is disturbed by waves.

According to the Old or Nyingma School of the early translations, shamatha practice is necessary, but not *that* necessary. All schools make the distinction between dualistic mind and buddha nature, rigpa. Shamatha practice is to reduce the force of dualistic mind, and as dualistic mind lessens and becomes weaker, buddha nature becomes increasingly evident, obvious and manifest.

Often in the Nyingma tradition, rigpa and dualistic mind are separated from the very beginning and one focuses on training in rigpa. For some students, it is very convenient to immediately separate dualistic mind and rigpa, and to begin by training in nondual awareness. If they are able to do so, they can progress in that way. For other students it is not so convenient, it does not seem so easy to differentiate between dualistic mind and rigpa. For this type of student, it is more realistic to follow the Sarma tradition. For this and many other reasons, it is good to have both traditions, Sarma and Nyingma. Different types of students require different types of practice.

Within the Sarma tradition, Mahamudra, as followed by the Kagyü schools, is described in terms of the twelve aspects of the four yogas of Mahamudra. It is known as the path of liberation. This Mahamudra path is a gradual path, moving through progressive stages, beginning with one-pointedness and proceeding into simplicity, one taste, and finally to nonmeditation. I will explain these in more detail later in the book. Right now I'd just like to note that at the final level of nonmeditation, the two obscurations and their habitual tendencies are totally finished, dissolved. The two aspects of sublime knowledge have been perfected from within. This is complete buddhahood, true and complete enlightenment, the great realization of Vajradhara. If the student is intelligent and has very strong perseverance, it is possible to reach this level within this very lifetime, or, if not, then at the moment of death, or in the bardo. At the very least, one will reach it within three or six lifetimes, by reconnecting with the teachings and a qualified master. When one has not damaged one's samayas (another subject I will discuss later), then liberation is definitely possible.

Now let's briefly discuss death and the bardo. It is easier to be liberated at the moment of death and in the bardo, because we are not tied down to the body. Unfortunately, it is also easier to be confused at this time, because anxiety, hope and fear are more intense. In the bardo state, consciousness experiences fear a hundred times more intensely than the same fear experienced while alive. Likewise, the hope and the yearning are a hundred times more intense during the bardo.

Right now, our minds are encased within a physical body, which you could say weighs down or anchors the spirit. The moment that mind and matter separate, the moment the spirit leaves the body, mind is much lighter. Because it is unfettered by the physical chains of a body, it may also be much more paranoid, much more susceptible to being influenced by any thought that arises. Sometimes it's described as being like a feather blown in a strong wind. When the mind is liberated from the body, one has only to think of a place, and simultaneously one arrives at it.

Therefore, it is definitely helpful and extremely important that we train right now, in this very lifetime, so that we can help ourselves when we come to the moment of dying or being in the bardo. Dharma practice definitely does help at death. We should fully understand the meaning of this; why and how it helps. Liberation at the moment of death does not only mean you've done virtuous deeds, so you bring along the good karma when you die. It's not like you carry your good and bad karma into the bardo, like the black and white contents of a bag. If we die deluded, we bring along that delusion. We need to be free of a deluded state of mind.

The vital point in being able to be liberated at the moment of death and in the bardo is *how to be free*. We need to train in being liberated right now, while we are still alive. The meditation manuals describe a measure, a test through which we can assess the degree of stability we've reached. During the dream state, first become aware that you are in the dream state. If you are then able to recognize the nature of mind and sustain it for as long as it takes to flap a long Tibetan sleeve seven times, you will also be able to be liberated in the bardo state. The most important point here is to train while we are still alive and are awake, then check your progress in the dream state. Compared to the waking state, we have less control over dreams.; however, compared to dreaming, we have even less control than in the bardo states.

Of course, it is best if we can train in a way that we make progress, receive teachings, practice them, and check the degree of progress during our dreams, so that when we die, we will be liberated at that time or in the bardo. Otherwise, it is not very sure whether we actually will be free. Wouldn't it be much better to be a hundred percent sure right now? How wonderful to be totally fearless in the face of death, because of having reached stability in practice right now!

Generally speaking, it is not that easy to recognize the state of emptiness, the nature of mind. But compared to recognising, it is much more difficult to attain stability. It is not easy to sustain a noble or excellent quality continuously. It is much easier to be selfish or negative all the time. This is not only true for states of mind: it is the same with material things or animals. Special good animals are very rare and difficult to keep, but unpleasant insects are very abundant, very common! Similarly, an object that is very beautiful and very rare is hard to obtain and hard to keep, while lousy things are easy to get.

The nature of mind is like a wish-fulfilling jewel: it is the Buddha, the awakened state. To recognize it in actuality and then to sustain the continuity of that is very important. It is not anybody other than ourselves who prevents us from recognizing our natural face, the real Buddha. We can label that which prevents us with religious terms like bad karma or disturbing emotions — we can pass the blame with those words. But actions and emotions are merely names, labels made by our thoughts. *That which prevents us from being face to face with the real Buddha, the natural state of mind, is our own thinking, which seems to block the natural state.* This thinking can be of many types. There are the bad types, which are the selfish emotions and thoughts and so forth. Then there are the good types, the virtuous emotions and thoughts. There are the neutral thoughts. The bottom line is that all three of these are thoughts. When it comes to obscuring our innate nature, it is not only evil thoughts that obscure our true nature: good and neutral thoughts obscure it just as well.

No matter what way one clings or is attached, it is still clinging, it is still attachment. When a wealthy person is attached to his treasure chest of money, that is attachment. When a poor person is attached to his walking stick and begging bowl, it is still attachment. Clinging and attachment does not depend on the price of the object, nor on its beauty. *Attachment or clinging is an attitude, a mental attitude.*

We need to understand very precisely that it is not only evil or neutral thoughts that obscure innate suchness, our buddha nature, but that good, wholesome thoughts obscure it as well. Innate suchness is obscured by holding *any* type of concept — basically, by having a conceptual attitude towards something. The great bodhisattva Manjushri said, "The one who cling lacks the true view." If there is any clinging in one's mind, the true view is not present, because any conceptual stance seems to cover the innate suchness. Here's another way of saying the same thing: "Mahamudra is mental nondoing." When nothing is done in the mind, when no conceptual attitude is kept or retained, that is Mahamudra.

Whether you use the teachings from the sutras or the tantras, the three vehicles or the nine vehicles, all agree on one point: the clinging to personal identity, a conceptual attitude, needs to be dissolved, left behind. The moment you are free from mental doing, at that same moment, the nature of mind which is the unity of empty cognizance is present, right there. The Dzogchen teachings describe the view as *kadag trekchö*. 'Kadag' means primordial purity, 'trekchö' means thoroughly cut through. The meditation is lhündrub tögal. 'Lhündrub' is spontaneous presence, 'tögal' is direct crossing.

The *trek* in trekchö means thoroughly, while *chö* means cut through. It is not cut through a little bit, with some conceptual attitude still remaining. It means having thoroughly and completely cut through deluded experience altogether. This is the essence of Dzogchen practice: having thoroughly cut through karma and disturbing emotions, deluded experience and concepts. It is the recognition of the moment in which the stream of thinking has been severed — when the past thought has ceased, the future one has not arrived and the thoughts of the present are not being formed. We cannot say exactly how long this moment lasts for the practitioner; that is an individual matter that depends on the power of training. But in that moment of having cut through, samsaric experience is interrupted. All attachment to joy and sorrow, accepting and rejecting, hope and fear have dissolved, vanished, are no more. For that duration they are cleared away. This moment of innate suchness is endowed with tremendous qualities.

There is perhaps a philosophical problem at this point, in that it is hard to grasp suchness intellectually. For an ordinary person, it is very easy to claim there is something. For instance, there is earth, there is water, there are stones, there are trees, fire – it seems very straightforward to make such a statement. For an intellectual used to making philosophical arguments, it is very easy to claim that there is nothing and to establish that logically. For a practitioner, however, the situation is different. The practitioner's experience is not the same as the solid, concrete reality that an ordinary person experiences, which has color and form and all sorts of other attributes.

Mind is not a solid thing, but neither is it a complete nothingness like some intellectuals claim. The reality of our minds is not a matter for philosophical denial. Mind is not merely an empty space. Many intellectual philosophers claim that everything from the aggregate of form up to and including the state of omniscience is empty and devoid of true existence. However, according to Buddhism, "Though everything is empty, to not be empty of the kayas and wisdom is the way of the Buddha's teachings". For a philosopher, such a statement may sound as if things are not empty. This formulation is risky. Trouble begins, and things get very complicated. People have been arguing for thousands of years about the right way of articulating ultimate reality, and they do so even today.

The reason for the problem is mental habits are so strong. Whenever we hear that something is, we nail it to being just that way. When something *is not,* it is just that. We may feel that these are irreconcilable differences. However, in the statement 'there are kayas and wisdoms' their way of existing cannot be understood as being the same as the usual existence of things perceived by deluded mind. The kayas and wisdoms do not exist in the same way as we do, or as things apparently do from the perspective of the conceptual 'I'.

When we hear the statement that there is nothing, it seems like this doesn't ring true either, because things do exist in our experience. We use our habitual experience as the basic measure for what is and what is not. This is entirely understandable. But how can we do that, really, when our experience is mistaken, deluded? What really decides everything? "Me. It is my mind which is important." But how can mind, which is caught up in karma and disturbing emotions, decide what is real?

Instead, again and again compose your mind in the view of Mahamudra or Dzogchen, and train in that. By repeating the recognition of innate suchness, totally free of mental constructs, we lay the basis for accomplishing the mind of the buddhas. Free from delusion, karma and emotions, this practice is the training in realizing dharmakaya. The development stage practices, including visualizations and recitations, are training in accomplishing sambhogakaya. When we make pure aspirations to benefit others in a boundless way, whether it's in our home, in a holy place, or in front of a sacred representation, we are training in actualizing nirmanakaya, at this very moment. We make the strong wish that "At some point may I be able to emanate, through the force of my body, as many replicas of bodhisattvas as there are atoms in the universe, each of which accomplishes the benefit of beings." In the future, out of great compassion, this sincere wish to benefit others will form the basis for the ability to manifest the nirmanakayas.

Let us train in realizing dharmakaya, the mind of the buddhas. Please compose your minds in the state free from involvement in past, present and future. There is no duality to be kept here, no split between meditator and meditation object. Still, since we have five senses, we are in the habit of making thoughts about what we perceive. When practicing, we try to be in a way that is not like usual samsara; we try to turn away from that. The samsaric way is to immediately become involved in what we think of, and to hold that very firmly and solidly in mind. We try not to be in that way, to not hold onto what is perceived.

My father, Kyabje Tulku Urgyen Rinpoche, gave one simple instruction known as the pointing-out instruction. He showed how to disconnect from clinging to what is perceived. What usually happens is that our six senses, particularly sight, follow after perceived objects. The mind, our attention, looks and makes a thought of what is seen, and we are stuck in that thought, and are unable to be free. That is the samsaric way. The pith instruction is a way in how to release that, how to be free, how to not cling. Leave the five sense wide open but not engaged, not involved in holding the sense objects. Recognizing mind nature is called taking your natural seat, the natural seat of nondual awareness. The moment attention is caught up in what is perceived, the natural seat is lost. Your awareness loses its natural seat, its innate stability when attention get caught through the five senses and apprehends a sense object. We need to let be in the way that is utterly empty, utterly naked and wide open.

> *Release your awareness undirected*
> *into wide openness.*
> *Such ordinary mind, such original wakefulness is always in us.*

It is our basic state.
We have never been apart from it for even an instant.
Though our innate nature is never apart from us
for even an instant,
our conceptual thinking obscures it.
Understand that dualistic thought obscures.
Now we must use a method to remove this obscuring.
We must clear it up.
Since original wakefulness is never apart from us,
And has never been so, for even a single instant,
the moment dualistic thinking dissolves,
the Buddha is discovered from within.
This is why we can be enlightened.
This is why we have the readiness to awaken.
This is why our natural state,
our original mind,
can be discovered from within
the moment the clinging dissolves.
This is what we call buddha nature.

There are many types of philosophy, truth-seeking positions about what is. Buddhist philosophy has one special quality: that the awakened state is within, and we are in a state of readiness; it is ready to be discovered. That is the special quality in Buddhism. It is said in a scripture, "All sentient beings are buddhas, but they are covered by temporary obscurations." Every sentient being has as their nature original wakefulness — what in the general teachings is called buddha nature. Because of possessing this original mind, the buddha potential, everyone can be enlightened. Everyone is allowed to be a buddha; everyone has that ability, that readiness.

If you squeeze sand, you will never get oil, because sand does not have an oily nature. But sesame seeds have an oily nature, and you can squeeze oil out of them. Even if someone says it should not happen, it still does. It is allowed to happen; it is all right. You cannot make a prohibition against sesame seeds having an oily quality;

you cannot deny it or dispute that fact — it is just like that. But it does take some effort, just a little bit of effort, a little squeeze, to releasethe oil.

One could say that we as well have an oily, buttery nature rich in enlightened qualities, which can be brought forth. We have what the scriptures describe as original wakefulness, ordinary mind, the natural state. We need to provide the right circumstance for it to be experienced as an actuality. These circumstances are, in general, to perfect the accumulations and to purify obscurations. More particularly, after learning about how our natural state is and understanding it, we need to apply some method to recognize it and sustain the recognition. Spiritual practice is necessary.

All of you readers, please practice well to absorb this meaning within your personal experience. One can go on endlessly talking or reading about reality, especially about how our innate nature really is. But intellectualizing it is as futile as trying to measure the sky with the span of one's arms. Ultimate reality is so much bigger than the grasp of our conceptual minds.

Means and Knowledge

We should remember three extremely important principles, called the *three-fold excellence*, or three noble principles. The excellent preparation is beginning with refuge and bodhichitta. Refuge is the nine-fold object of refuge. Bodhichitta is the wish "May I attain realization of the dharmakaya nature to bring benefit and welfare to infinite sentient beings, as infinite in number as the sky is vast."

Next comes the excellent main part. We need to know that our natural state, the basic nature of our minds, is the buddha mind, the awakened state. It is because of failing to recognize this that we get caught up in deluded experience, create karma and disturbing emotions, and undergo the myriad types of experiences of the six classes of beings. The third part is the excellent conclusion, in which we dedicate the merit to benefit all sentient beings.

To return to the excellent preparation, the practice of refuge and bodhichitta can be very delightful. It's possible to take refuge with a lot of appreciation, a lot of joy. It is a very sincere attitude, a very delightful attitude. In the same way, the compassionate wish to help all sentient beings without exception is also very wonderful and sincere. Refuge and bodhichitta are basically devotion and compassion. Among all states of dualistic mind, there are no cleaner, purer, or more sincere states of dualistic mind than devotion and compassion.

Devotion in this context means a trust that comes through understanding the meaning, the ultimate purpose. Compassion is a benevolent state of mind that is impartial, free from any prejudice or limitation. Our compassion can embrace all sentient beings spinning in samsaric states, from the deepest pit of hell to the highest god realm. Among the six classes of beings who takes rebirth in the four different ways, no single sentient being in the three realms is beyond karma and disturbing emotions. When the causes of karma and disturbing emotions are present, their result, which is suffering, will ripen. Unless and until we are free ourselves, we are not able to help and liberate others.

The devotion we feel through knowing the meaning is an understanding of the qualities of the Three Jewels: the precious Buddha, the precious Dharma, the precious Sangha. In particular, it refers to understanding the qualities of the awakened state of buddhahood, omniscient enlightenment. These qualities and virtues of enlightenment include loving compassion, wisdom knowledge, enlightened activity, and the ability to protect and help others. These qualities are only fully available in the state of buddhahood. If we want to achieve these, we need to awaken to true and complete enlightenment. There is no instruction that shows us how to fully awaken to those qualities other than the sacred Dharma. Therefore, there is no way around taking support from the sublime teachings and instructions.

Where do we receive these? We may try reading books on our own, but this alone does not really work. We need to receive the living word from spiritual guides; spiritual friends who are endowed with these teachings. Reflecting like this, there is no way around taking refuge in Buddha, Dharma and Sangha. Temporarily we take refuge in the Sangha and the Dharma teachings. The ultimate object of refuge, however, is the omniscient state of buddhahood endowed with the qualities of wisdom, love and abilities. Knowing this is called 'trust through understanding the reason.'

There are different levels of devotion. There is devotion that is admiration, devotion that is a longing or yearning, devotion that is deep trust, and devotion that is irreversible, unshakable. We progress through these different levels as our understanding and experience deepen. The understanding we have that is a result of study and reflection, intellectual understanding, will never be more than admiration and longing. As we gain direct personal experience, we can develop the devotion that is trust, real trust and confidence. The final stage, unshakable or irreversible devotion, is only possible when we are totally free of doubt.

As we understand more through our studies and reflection, the teachings are understood to have authentic value, and our interest grows in a way that is sincere and without pretense. This is devotion that is admiration and longing — we yearn to be this way. The understanding that comes through our personal experience unfolds as we gain more and more of a taste within our minds. We start to notice that the teachings, when applied personally, actually do work. We notice that we are able to realize what needs to be realized. We are able to manifest in ourselves qualities of love and compassion, of sharp intelligence and renunciation. At this point, we have some confidence in the teachings based on our own experience. It is no longer intellectual information that sounds good — we know from within ourselves. That is a different type of devotion: it is a devotion that displays real trust and confidence. *As we grow increasingly familiar with and experience the natural state of mind, our basic nature, then this trust, this devotion can become unshakable.*

We especially appreciate those who we received the teachings from. We received them from our own teachers and masters, who are the holders of a living lineage. Therefore, there is a lot of appreciation of and trust in the source of the teachings — not just our personal teacher, but all the masters of the lineage. In particular, the source of all the teachings is the Buddha Shakyamuni, the fourth guide in this aeon. It is from him that all the different lines of transmission stem. We begin to have a trust and confidence from the very core of our being in the Buddha of this time.

The activity of the Buddha is beyond the reach of normal thought: it is unfathomable. The representative of the Buddha's activity is present today in a way that we can connect with, in the form of This sacred Dharma is the Buddha's modern-day representative. It instructs us on how to rid ourselves of all shortcomings and faults and how to make the enlightened qualities blossom. The Buddha was able to perform great miracles through his body, speech, and mind. His clairvoyant powers manifested in many different ways. But the greatest miracle the Buddha performed was that of teaching the Dharma. The words of the Buddha are in harmony with the nature of things, without any conflict with how things actually are. It is perfectly all right for us to have a critical attitude towards the Dharma, to examine and analyze whether or not these teachings are true. It is perfectly all right for us to test out the teachings within ourselves to see whether they actually work. We should try to see whether we can prove the Buddha's teachings; whether we can endeavor to become freer of shortcomings and gain greater good qualities. In this way, we discover that the words of the Buddha are totally free of fault and are endowed with all good qualities.

All the teachings of the Buddha can be condensed into just two points: means and knowledge. You can say that means are relative goodness. Knowledge is the view of emptiness. Until we allow our conceptual attitude to fully dissolve, there is good as well as negative karma, and there are past and future lives. If we do good, there is a good result; if we do evil, there is an unpleasant result. As long as this conceptual attitude has not been released, time does not vanish; there is a yesterday; there will be a tomorrow. Therefore time does seem to exist — there is moment after moment, like right now, an apparent moment arises after a moment. In a more general way, one day follows after another — yesterday, today and tomorrow. Expanding the picture still further, there is lifetime after lifetime.

In reality, however, time is just a construct: it cannot be found to exist. No matter how much we examine, we cannot pinpoint it. The fact we are unable to identity or nail down time does not mean that we are incapable. It means that time is intangible, insubstantial. Time is not a concrete thing that can be found anywhere. Time never had a real existence. Time comes about only because of the thought that thinks that there is time; it is a creation of thought. It is the same way with solid matter, with material substance. Substance only seems substantial because one *thinks* it is. Both time and matter from the very first do not possess any real existence. The basis for all the world's strife, all these problems, all these arguments, does not really exist! But believing that it does, one sincerely and whole-heartedly gets involved in them.

Unless our present conceptual attitude dissolves, samsara does not vanish. Unless our present conceptual attitude dissolves, selfish emotions do not vanish. Unless our present conceptual attitude dissolves, ego-oriented clinging does not vanish. The moment the present conceptual attitude dissolves, there is no karma and there are no disturbing emotions. When the present conceptual attitude vanishes, there is no maker of karma. In the recognition of the true view, there is no karma — it is beyond karma. Another way of putting this is to say that in the absence of the conceptual state of mind, there is no further creation of karma. The moment that mind fixates or holds onto a conceptual attitude, karma and disturbing emotions are formed right there and then. On the other hand, the very moment that the conceptual frame of mind dissolves, there is no making of karma — there is no forming of disturbing emotions or selfish attitudes. The hair of concept cannot remain in the flame of original wakefulness.

Among means and knowledge in the general Buddhist teachings, means is to avoid evil and do good. Goodness with concept, with focus, is called conditioned or relative goodness, and it accumulates merit. From the moment we wake up until the moment we fall asleep, we should try to notice what attitude we have. At any given moment during the day, we should try to be more aware and mindful of how we actually are. Whenever we notice we are being negative, unkind, or outright mean, we should try to change that as much as we can, as often as possible. We should try to change even the slightest negative attitude. Similarly, when we notice that we have a good heart, a noble and pure attitude, a loving and compassionate way of being, we should try to expand it to embrace an even larger amount of beings, until it becomes very, very vast. Train in this as often as possible, even in the smallest way. This is the practice of conditioned goodness, and it is always to be adopted and trained in.

People think, "I have no time to practice." This is not true — we do have time to practice. In every situation we can try to be kinder or better in our actions, words and attitude. That training is Dharma practice. The opposite of that is to be selfishly involved in the negative emotions that seem to happen spontaneously, but that actually arises out of habit. It is necessary to be on guard. We should not confuse what should be accepted with what should be rejected.

This thinking mind of ours is something hidden; it is not always so evident how it is. It is sometimes downright nasty. It can be very naughty, in that it does not listen. We may think we are nice, and are not. We may try to be good, and we cannot. This nasty mind needs to be changed into being gentle. The nastier one is in one's actions, the stronger or more intense the karma being created. The more noble-minded we can become, the stronger the noble-mindedness or the goodness we experience, the stronger the good karma being created.

At all times and in all situations, be on guard; notice how your state of mind is. This mind, our attitude, is the most vital, the most crucial point. What we say and how we behave physically is secondary to this. Body and speech are the servants of mind. We need to train this mind, this attitude, and the way to do so is to begin with refuge and bodhichitta, to bring these two attitudes to mind: taking refuge and forming the bodhisattva resolve. That is the conditioned goodness which accumulates merit.

To review again, the main part of the practice free of reference point means allowing ourselves to be totally free of conceptual attitude. To be very empty and vividly awake — that is the accumulation of wisdom.

The final goodness is to conclude the session with dedicating the merit to all sentient beings, which is again the accumulation of merit. In this way, all our practice will be carried out within the framework of the two accumulations. Through this practice, we perfect the two accumulations. It is often said: "As the ground, understand the unity of the two truths. As the path, carry out the unity of the two liberations. As the fruition, realize the unity of the two kayas."

"As the ground, recognize the unity of the two truths." The two truths are that everything experienced, everything perceived, is devoid of true existence. Yet, you cannot deny that that experience unfolds. It does so unobstructedly. At the same time it possesses no concrete existence whatsoever. Experience appears, while being empty. This indivisibility of experience and emptiness is the unity of the two truths.

"The path is the unity of the two accumulations": the accumulation of merit and wisdom, with and without conceptual focus or reference point. "The fruition is the unity of the kayas": dharmakaya and rupakaya. The more we understand ground as being the unity of the two truths, the easier it is to train in the path, which is the unity of the two accumulations. The more we train in the path as the unity of the two accumulations, the closer we are to realizing the fruition, the unity of the two kayas.

In another way, we can say that means is compassion while knowledge is emptiness. Through compassion we automatically embrace what is good and avoid evil. The compassionate frame of mind spontaneously refrains from causing harm to others; we do what is beneficial and helpful. Compassion is the source of all goodness. Its opposite, selfishness, is deluded and the real meaning of evil. The most eminent of all types of knowledge is the knowledge that cuts the very root of samsaric existence, that completely ends samsara. This is the knowledge that realizes egolessness, also known as the profound view of emptiness. In short, *emptiness suffused with compassion is the very heart of Buddhist practice*. And it is through the unity of these two, the unity of emptiness and compassion, that we can cut through the very root of all disturbing emotions. In terms of the two accumulations, the accumulation of merit is with focus, the accumulation of wisdom is beyond focus. In terms of the path, our training in compassion and the view of emptiness naturally perfects the two accumulations. To condense this teaching even further, *in the moment of recognizing the nature of our minds as the unformed unity of empty cognizance, the view of emptiness and impartial compassion are naturally present*.

As we train further and further in recognizing the empty and cognizant nature of our minds, the compassionate means and the knowledge of emptiness becomes clearer, stronger and further and further developed. This is the knowledge that is free of holding concepts and the compassion that is beyond partiality. It is often said that in the moment of having a deep-felt sense of compassion arising from the core of your heart, you are much closer to knowing emptiness. To quote the third Karmapa: "In the moment of love, the empty essence dawns nakedly."

To truly manifest what is good and to avoid evil, we need to be compassionate — there is no way around this. If we want to lead all beings towards enlightenment, we need to be compassionate. In fact, all buddha qualities spring out of compassion. The knowledge of emptiness ensures that we go beyond samsaric existence, but compassion guarantees that we do not remain passively in the state of nirvana. Compassion makes us engage in infinite enlightened activities for the sake of all sentient beings. There is a famous statement: "Not straying into samsara, not abiding in nirvana: that is done through knowledge and compassion."

When it comes to personally practicing this, we need some reminder. This reminder is called mindfulness or presence of mind. At the beginning stage it might be the thought: "Now I'd better recognize the nature of mind." Yes, this is conceptual, it is a thought — but it is a necessary reminder. Someone who does not usually recognize nature of mind and is not in the habit of doing so needs to be mindful, needs a deliberate reminder. We need to deliberately remind ourselves to recognize the nature of mind, or else it will not just happen.

It is difficult for a beginner to mingle the practice with the activities of daily life. This is because one is not in the habit of reminding oneself to recognize the nature of mind. And that is why it is necessary to do a practice session, to make a time where one does just that — like a short retreat. Sessions and retreat are very important in a session one trains. In a meditation session, our involvement in distraction, busyness, being carried away, is much less.

On a more practical level, we still become distracted during sessions, of course. This distraction can take the form of either agitation or dullness. Dullness is a form of laziness, when we do not bother to realize that we are half-asleep. When we are distracted, whether agitated or dull, we have gone away from the practice; we have left the training. Agitation and dullness are two enemies of meditation practice. When agitated or dull, we are unable to recognize the natural face of samadhi, of stillness and insight, shamatha and vipashyana. It is through the reminder or remindfulness that we are again able to sustain the essence of unified empty cognizance. The *non-clinging* unity of empty cognizance is the real training. The moment the mind starts to cling, this training is left behind. Mindfulness is simply a reminder to practice. If one just stays mindful in a dualistic sense, one has still not arrived at the real practice.

When we first began to write the alphabet, we had to pay close attention and put all our energy into forming each letter. Now we do not have to think much about it at all, do we? In the beginning, though, if you were not careful about the shape and size of the letters, the position of your hand, then the writing became awful — unclear, mistaken. As we became trained in writing, we could write the right shape, with the right alignment. Our writing became unmistaken. Each character on a line can now bring forth its power and meaning, clearly and distinctly. Where did this ability to write in such a way come from? Without training, it could not possibly have happened. Our writing potential has manifested because of our training. We are now accomplished in writing.

It's important to acknowledge that in the beginning, we needed effort. We applied effort, put our hand to work, trained repeatedly, and now we do not need so much effort. Our writing is now practically effortless. It's the same when we learned to read. At first, we distinguished each character in order not to confuse it. In the beginning, when you looked at the letter and tried to read, you could not pronounce it. Even when you pronounced it, you still could not read. Now that you are fully trained in reading, you do not have to think about which character is A and which is B — you simply read, like the flow of a river. This is a good example for the need to train in order to transcend deliberate effort.

First, we need a deliberate reminder. With a certain degree of mindful energy, we can do what we are doing well. As we continue training, we do not need to use so much force. Effort is necessary when we are not proficient. Right now, we are not fully trained in being the nonclinging unity of empty cognizance. To begin this training we need to remind ourselves deliberately. As we apply this deliberate reminding again and again in order to recognize our basic state, we become increasingly trained, and the need for the deliberate reminding becomes less and less. At some point, we are so used to it that there is no more need to apply deliberate reminding. This is not a new chapter or a new state; it comes totally naturally. It is not like we say, "In the past I was practicing deliberate mindfulness, and now I am shifting over to effortless mindfulness. I have opened a new chapter in my practice!" It doesn't happen like this at all. If you could do this, fine! But does it really happen by just intending? It is more a natural process that arises spontaneously as the need for deliberately reminding ourselves becomes less and less and less. The need simply falls away.

The Mahamudra instructions have many short phrases that sum up the essence of meditation advice. These are very precious instructions. One is: "The better the reminding, the better the meditating." This means that the more often you deliberately remind yourself to recognize your nature, the better the practice becomes. Another one says "The more thoughts, the more dharmakaya." This means not giving into ordinary thought involvement, but rather recognizing the state of thought-free wakefulness for each thought. This type of practice – "the more thoughts, the more dharmakaya" – also implies "the more disturbing emotions the more wisdom." Do you understand this?

What is it that brings us face to face with the natural state? At the beginning, it is a deliberate reminding. Later, it is effortless reminding. Later still, after having trained further and further and become stable, any thought movement becomes the embellishment of nondual awareness. Any movement of thought automatically becomes that which introduces us again to the natural state. When each movement of thought, by itself, does not trigger any involvement in ordinary thinking, but instead becomes the state of thought-free wakefulness, then you have reached quite a high level of practice. You are beyond one-pointedness, beyond simplicity, and beyond the lesser and medium stage of one-taste. You can almost say it is the higher stage of one-taste in Mahamudra. Then only non-meditation is left, the dharmakaya throne of non-meditation.

It is like this with everything we learn: in the beginning it is difficult, and later it becomes easier and easier, until it is completely easy. Please understand this point very well: in our present situation it is the training in deliberate reminding that allows us to sustain the continuity of buddha mind.

This reminding in general Buddhism is called mindfulness. The same word is used. It is considered very important because mindfulness is very important. But its function in Dzogchen and Mahamudra is different. The general role of mindfulness is to remember to avoid misdeeds and to remind oneself to do what is wholesome. In terms of shamatha practice, to be mindful means to remember to apply the method of stillness, to compose your attention in a calm way. It is said, "From moment to moment don't lose mindfulness." Haven't you heard that phrase often? That kind of mindfulness is conceptual. In other words, keep noticing. The watcher is needed to keep watch, to keep asking, "What is happening?" This is also good for another type of practice. The mindfulness I am talking about here means there is one moment of reminding. In the next moment, the watcher, the noticing, is dropped and allowed to dissolve.

Otherwise, if the act of noticing is held onto, it becomes conceptual. It becomes a way of formulating what is. Unless this notion of 'keeping mindful' is dissolved, there is no real seeing of emptiness. Without dissolving the notion, you do not realize egolessness. Without dissolving the notion, the concept, you do not see the unity of empty cognizance, the nature of mind. The nature of mind is the nonclinging unity of empty cognizance. When this notion is held in mind, it becomes an empty cognizance that clings. To summarize, the very moment any type of conceptual attitude, any type of notion is allowed to dissolve so that you are free of it — at that same moment you have arrived at the innate nature of buddha mind.

Small Freedom

As soon as our teacher, the incomparable Buddha Shakyamuni, had awakened to true and complete enlightenment at the vajra throne in Bodhgaya, he uttered four lines:

I have discovered a nectar-like truth,
A profound and tranquil simplicity, an unformed, luminous wakefulness.
No one to whom I describe this will understand.
So I will remain silent in the jungle.

With these few words, the Buddha expressed that not only had he recognized and trained in this recognition, he had attained complete stability in the realization of the nature of mind. There is nothing more profound than this. The realization of the nature of mind is totally unperturbed by any movement of disturbing emotions, like the surface of a huge ocean which is absolutely tranquil, unruffled by any movement of waves. In the same way, this state refers to the perfection of shamatha, or complete stillness. But also, it is simplicity, free from any mental constructs, totally unconstructed. That is another word for the view of emptiness, emptiness beyond constructs, which is exactly the intent of the second turning of the Wheel of Dharma on the absence of characteristics.

The nature of mind is not merely empty. The Buddha used the term luminous wakefulness, or luminosity, to describe it. The nature of mind is endowed with the capacity to know. There is an innate wisdom or wakefulness within this state, a perfect knowledge. It is profound, tranquil, unconstructed, luminous wakefulness that is unformed. Everything that is formed arises and then ceases; it takes birth and vanishes again. This profound, tranquil, unconstructed, luminous wakefulness, however, does not arise and does not cease. It is beyond birth and death.

The Buddha recognized the original state, trained in it and attained stability. This is how he awakened to true and complete enlightenment. We ourselves need to realize and achieve this. While caught up in the dualistic habit of fixating, our basic identity still has the nature of non-fixating non-duality. The very moment the fixating on duality dissolves, the non-dual, non-fixating essence is right there. Based on this small freedom, this moment of small liberation, the vast liberation can be attained. Without having tasted and experienced the small freedom, we will not all of a sudden somehow reach the vast liberation. The small freedom is the very identity of the fixating, dualistic mind, which is a non-fixating, non-dualistic state. Recognizing that basic state is itself small freedom — freedom from karma and disturbing emotion.

The root cause of samsara, that which creates samsara, is nothing other than our disturbing emotions and thoughts. In a moment of non-dual wakefulness, no thought can be formed and no thought can remain. Therefore, that moment is totally free of karma and disturbing emotions, hope and fear, accepting and rejecting. In that moment of freedom, no conceptualization is formed and none can remain.

> *Allow your mind to be in the natural state,*
> *the unity of being empty and cognizant.*
> *Not fixating on anything,*
> *not forming any conceptual attitude,*
> *you arrive at the innate nature.*
> *At that moment, no negative or positive attitude is present.*
> *There is no creation of either good karma or bad karma,*
> *there is nothing to be accepted or rejected in that moment.*
> *This is the natural state itself.*
> *For a short while*
> *there is total freedom from samsara,*
> *because of being totally free from karma and disturbing*
>   *emotions.*
> *Even though it is so short,*

It is an amazing quality!
For a brief moment we have awakened
from the sleep of delusion.

There is still something wrong here, though. Because we are not used to composing ourselves in that natural state, the continuity of our innate nature, the ongoingness of that basic space gets lost again. What is it that kicks us out or makes us stray from the basic state? It is karma, which in this case is our ingrained habit of thinking. We are very used to forming and getting involved in thoughts. Due to this habit, we start to think again, automatically. We don't even have an idea of where that thought came from, or what happened. Therefore, you can say that that which obscures the innate nature is every kind of thought, any kind of thinking. It is by the force of habit of thinking that a thought is formed, whether it be of past, present or future. A past thought involves memory: what happened, what we did, what took place. A future thoughts plan what to do, what will happen. And present thoughts form a notion of what is taking place through any of our five senses or in the field of mind. Because this mind's attention is so childish and the sense impressions, memories and so forth are so seductive, we are very ready to be distracted, ready to be carried away. We become distracted through any of the five senses, or by inwardly becoming agitated or drowsy. All this prevents the natural state from being experienced.

The question is: when exactly can we recognize our buddha nature, the nature of mind? The answer is: when we are uninvolved in thoughts of the three times. When polluted by the thoughts of the three times, the state is contrived. That which contrives, modifies, or obscures the natural state is our thinking. On a coarse, general level it is the disturbing emotions; in a more subtle way, it is any thought that conceptualizes the three spheres. We are shrouded by the emotional and cognitive obscurations. Being entangled in thoughts of the three times, being caught up in conceptualizing the three spheres, seems to prevent a recognition of the basic state — the reality of what actually is. This is called the cognitive obscuration.

A buddha is someone for whom the two obscurations, as well as the habitual tendency towards them, are completely purified.

> *We try to recognize the natural state,*
> *And for a moment or two we recognize*
> *being free from subject and object.*
> *In fact, our recognition is identical in nature*
> *with the realization of a fully awakened buddha.*
> *It is a small version of total freedom.*
> *The same moment, no matter how short,*
> *Our dualistic experience has dissolved,*
> *It is identical with the nature of complete enlightenment.*
> *Yet, it is merely a small gap in dualistic fixation,*
> *that gives no chance for the wisdom qualities to fully*
>   *manifest.*
> *It is like a glimmer of light in the middle of a dark night.*
> *The light is light; it illuminates.*
> *But being so brief,*
> *It does not dispel the entire night's darkness.*

The vajra vehicle of Secret Mantra takes fruition as the path. Vajrayana is a very swift path, and to make it real, to actualize it, we need to use all sorts of different methods and apply ourselves. The Vajrayana approach has great advantages, but it is very risky. The great advantage is that through it, we can awaken to true enlightenment, either within this lifetime, at the moment of death, or in the bardo. We do so by truly recognizing the unconstructed basic nature and persevering in this training, rather than undergoing a path that takes three incalculable aeons. The risk lies in failing to genuinely recognize the unconstructed basic nature and instead training in a mistaken version.

At the very heart of Vajrayana practice is the true, correct view: we need to train in this. When the view is correct and pure, the training in that can be correct and pure, and the conduct can be correct and pure. Finally, the fruition, the result, will automatically be correct and pure. The correct view is not realized by being smart or stubbornly pushing oneself through practice. Intelligence and perseverance alone are not sufficient. It is necessary to purify one's obscurations, to perfect the accumulations and to receive the blessings of a qualified master with the transmission of the lineage. That is how to first recognize mind essence and then progress to deeper and deeper levels. This is the entire reason why a Vajrayana practitioner must undertake the general and extraordinary preliminaries, and go through the practices of development stage, recitation and completion stage. These practices purify our obscurations and perfect the accumulations.

Once again, as I have mentioned before, please motivate yourself with this thought: "I will realize self-existing wakefulness, the natural mind, to bring benefit to all sentient beings, as many as the sky is vast." After engendering the proper attitude, make the request to all enlightened masters of the lineage, "Please grant your blessings that I may be able to do so." Then, compose yourself in the state that is unpolluted by any thought involvement with the three times. Rest in present, fresh wakefulness untainted by thoughts of past, present or future. Leave your body like a bundle of straw where the rope has been cut. Leave your voice like a sitar where the strings have been cut, and your mind like a water wheel where the inflow of water has been cut.

Seeing the true view takes place without something seen, without a seer, and without the act of seeing. There are different traditional ways of describing the view in the sense of viewing conditioned things, viewing the unconditioned nature, or viewing which is self-knowing. 'Viewing conditioned things' means observing the seeming situation, the relative truth. 'Viewing the unconditioned' means looking into the nature of things. And the 'view of self-knowing' is the view of the state of non-duality, which is the unity of the two truths, the unity of appearance and emptiness. In any case, the true view here should be without a viewer, something viewed and act of viewing. Remain free of the three spheres. Dualistic attention and dualistic thinking are characterized as being narrowed-in, confined, limited, focused on a reference point. That is not the meditation practice according to Mahamudra and Dzogchen. We do not need to train in duality any longer — we have already done so our entire lives without even trying. We know how that feels! I'm talking about something else here: a way of being that is vast, open, free of reference point, free of conceptual attitude. When we set about being in a vast, open way that is free of conceptual attitude, free of reference point, keep your five senses wide open and your awareness undirected. Do not focus outwardly, over there. Do not concentrate in here, inwardly. And do not place your attention anywhere in between, either.

First, we generate the intention, "Now I will recognize my natural state, the unformed unity of being empty and cognizant." In the second moment, we see *how it is*. At that time, dualistic thinking has dissolved. In the moment of recognizing, we see — *we see that there is no thing to see*. In the moment of seeing, it is free; free of dualistic fixation.

Mahamudra means mental non-doing, no thing to do. In mentally doing, what is being made is samsara: one sits and makes samsara. If you want to continually create samsara, fine! Just sit and continually create more samsara; keep on doing it. As long as we continue mental doing, samsara does not cease. But the very moment that mental doing is released, samsara has been left behind, without us having gone to some other place to be free.

In order to engage in the real practice, we must leave behind mental doing. In the very moment of being totally free of mental doing, the real state of Mahamudra is seen. We can check and see by ourselves whether or not we are recognizing the natural state. It all depends if we are still involved in mental doing, conceptual fabrication, to even a subtle degree. When all mental doing has been released, dissolved, there is nothing further to do.

It is all about our attitude. This attitude, this mind, is the creator of everything. When this mind does not judge, does not discriminate, does not accept or reject, does not form any dualistic notion; when it remains free, is allowed to be free, all by itself, it is this nature: the identity of that which thinks is dharmakaya, self-existing empty cognizance. This is the innate nature. That is the moment of being unmistaken.

This is also *the reality of what is,* the basic nature known as the primordial buddha. The primordial Samantabhadra is the self-existing wakefulness that is empty and cognizant. The symbolic Samantabhadra we can see painted on a *thangka* or a wall in the temple, or the buddha that we can have a vision of in a dream, in meditative experience, or even in actuality. When self-existing wakefulness is recognized and the continuity of that recognition is ongoing, that is called meeting the real Buddha Samantabhadra. To meet the Buddha in person means to meet the Buddha's mind, the awakened state. Simply seeing the physical form and hearing the sounds of his voice is not meeting the real Buddha. We need to meet and experience the Buddha's mind, which is unfabricated naturalness. *Unfabricated naturalness is the awakened state.* When totally free of mental doing, that itself is the awakened state. The thinner the layer of our involvement in mental doing, the closer we are to the Buddha's mind. When this layer is totally absent, totally free of dualistic fixation, that itself is the real awakened state, the real buddha mind.

In order to be able to do this, certain factors must be present. Right now, we are in a situation in which all these factors are present. First of all, we are human beings: we are capable, we are educated, and we can understand what is being said. Second, we are interested: we have the intelligence to discern the meaning of the words, and we want to apply this meaning. To have all these factors combined is extremely fortunate, so please rejoice in that.

Please compose yourself in a way that is totally free of mental doing. Saraha and many other great masters spoke like this:

> *In this there is nothing to be discarded,*
> *Nor is there anything to be added.*
> *When looking naturally into the natural,*
> *You see the natural and are free.*

The third Karmapa, Rangjung Dorje, said:

When regarding objects, there are no objects; they are empty.
When regarding mind, there is no mind.

When regarding objects, there are no objects; it is all mind. When regarding mind, there is no mind; it is empty of essence. He continues:

When regarding both, there is no duality: it is liberated in itself.
May we recognize the luminously wakeful nature of mind.

If your state of mind is wide-open, free of hope and fear, free of conceptual attitude, that is a good way to practice. When what you train in feels more constricted, more narrow and aimed towards a particular focus, you need to refine the view further. A good sign that we have recognised is when the recognition of the nature of mind becomes easier the more we train.

In short, what we need is a way of training in which the natural state is easy to see and easy to sustain. Whenever it is easy to see and easy to sustain, that is the proof — the indication that we are putting to use the essential instructions of the great lineage masters. When it is difficult to see, difficult to sustain, that is an indication that we need to learn more, need to understand more, resolve matters further. Together with an authentic teacher, we need to clear up our uncertainty. We do not need to be afraid of an authentic master; we do not need to be ashamed about this. This is important. It is not enough to only have an assumption about the awakened state, to leave it as intellectual understanding. We need to have a genuine experience. And that is why a meditation master is important, because it is together with such a person that we can clear up our misunderstanding, our uncertainty. It is not enough to merely read about the natural state in books.

Wide open, laid totally bare, utterly empty. Leave your eyes open. Do not form any thought about what is seen through the eyes. Among our five senses, we get most involved in making thoughts about what we see. These eyeballs are very funny — we can cover them with a single fingertip, but when the finger is removed. we can see a vast panorama. It seems like these eyes can accommodate so much. Everything can fit in there, including that which should not.

Remain composed in a way that is utterly empty, wide open, free from any kind of reference point. When training in this way, sometimes we feel drowsy and dull, while sometimes we are unsettled and agitated. When dull, the remedy is to raise your gaze and look upward. When agitated, lower your gaze and look down, at something like a forty-five degree angle. It is alright to keep your eyes open, but don't start to form a lot of thoughts about what is seen. That is what is meant by *undirected awareness*. Tilopa gave Naropa instruction in how to train in this:

> *My son, you are not bound by the perceived, but by the clinging,*
> *So cut your clinging, Naropa.*

The perceived includes objects in our field of vision. To merely see is not binding; it is the clinging to what is seen. It is the same with hearing. It is all right to hear, but clinging to the sounds is what binds.

Once you have the received the pointing-out instruction, then it is true that the nature of mind can be seen the moment you look. In the moment of seeing, dualistic fixation has dissolved and is free. That is a small liberation. It is liberation from all types of disturbing emotions and thoughts. Being confused or being free rests on simply one thing: knowing or not knowing. *Knowing the innate nature is to be free. Not knowing the innate nature is to be confused.*

In this context, the word 'looking' does not imply that there is something to look at. It is a looking that is free from both subject and object. That is very important. The word meditation does not mean that there is a meditation object. It is a meditating free from subject and object — without even an atom of meditation object, yet without even an instant of distraction. When training in that way, without meditating on as much as an atom, yet without being distracted for even as much as an instant, we will very swiftly progress through the paths and bhumis.

Nondistraction is essential. Usually nondistraction means to not wander off from whatever you have been told. In this context, however, it means not being distracted from holding nothing whatsoever in mind. Not meditating on even as much as an atom, yet not wandering off for even an instant. Our inner teacher is this presence of mind, this nondistraction. The Mahamudra teachings say, "When undistracted, your meditation practice is good. Nondistraction is the highway of all buddhas." Nondistraction is the king of all kinds of mindfulness.

STUDENT: What do you mean by 'the key point of mind'?

RINPOCHE: The secret of mind, the key point of mind, is so easy that it is hard to believe. It is so close that it is hard to see. The natural state is not an act of meditating. You cannot cultivate the innate nature. Any act of cultivating innate suchness in meditation practice is nothing more than a fabrication of thought. It would be mind-made innate nature, because in such a case it is the thoughts that meditate. Rigpa is not cultivated in meditation. The awakened state is not an object of the intellect. Rigpa is beyond intellect, and concepts. It is *innate suchness*. We cannot really describe it very well, because it is not a thing that truly can be described. Although it is not something to be cultivated, we still need to grow used to it. That is why if we understand how to not meditate even as much as an atom, while, at the same time, also being totally undistracted, we very quickly become enlightened.

Were you to hear a thousand teachings, the essence is still within these two points: *undistracted while not meditating*. It is easy to say but hard to apply. It may feel extremely difficult to truly experience being free of both something cultivated in meditation and someone who cultivates it. It is difficult because it is so simple. Nothing needs to be done there, and that is not our habit. We are used to doing, and doing requires effort. To simply be without doing anything ought to be easier. But because that is not our habit, to practice non-doing seems difficult.

It is so close that it is hard to see. The buddha mind, which is ordinary mind unspoiled by thoughts of the three times, is always with us. We have never been apart from it for even an instant, and yet our thinking causes it to be unnoticed. Because of being too easy, we do not trust. Because of being too close, we do not see. The view of Mahamudra, the view of Dzogchen, the view of the Middle Way, can be explained for months upon months in great detail. But when condensing these to the very essence, it is like this: not meditating or cultivating on as much as an atom, while at the same time not being distracted for even an instant.

Renunciation

To review a bit, the teachings of the Buddha that enable us to proceed towards liberation and enlightenment are, generally speaking, first the shamatha practice of being calm, being quiet, and next the vipashyana training of seeing clearly, which is thought-free wakefulness. In the context of this book, the latter means to recognize that our basic nature is essence, nature and capacity: an essence that is nonarising, a nature that is unobstructed, and a capacity that is ever-present, all-pervasive. These qualities are, in fact, the three kayas of the buddha mind, and they are present in everyone already. This is our basic nature.

What normally happens, in philosophical terms, is that this nature becomes obscured by the two veils, the two obscurations. In terms of simple practice, this means that the moment the meditator thinks about something, there is no longer the knowing of how this essence, nature and capacity actually *is*. In other words, *the present thought obscures the knowing of the innate nature.* Our thinking is the obscuration that fools us. We then fall under the power of negative emotions and karma.

> *To deal thoroughly with this tendency,*
> *it does not help to continue as before,*
> *allowing our attention to be caught up again and again*
> *in thoughts about the objects of the five senses,*
> *in new plans and old memories.*
> *Instead, recognize the identity of thought*
> *and allow present wakefulness*
> *to be totally fresh, bare and naked.*
> *Leave awareness in its naked state*
> *Do not correct or modify anything whatsoever.*
> *Maintain a slight presence of mind,*
> *As a small reminder.*
> *Once you are carried away*

and start to think of other things,
this reminder immediately brings you back.
We are brought back to the state
that is not an act of meditating,
yet it is not being distracted.
It is simply the naked state of mind.
To allow that to be as it naturally is
without altering or correcting it in any way,
that training is itself the very heart
of all the Buddha's teachings.

Samsara does not exist apart from our own thinking. Our thinking *is* samsara. Our thinking *is* karma; it *is* disturbing emotions. When thinking is allowed to take the upper hand — if we give in to what is being thought of — the stream of samsara remains unbroken; deluded samsaric experience goes on. To turn away from samsara means to turn away from deluded experience, to turn away from this thinking. Even a moment of thinking anything, whether in a negative way or a positive way, still creates a habitual tendency, a habit. Until the point where this thinking falls apart, karma is still being formed and disturbing emotions are still being created. It is like the shadow of the hand being there. As long as karma and habits are formed, we risk being overcome by them. We need to stop this flow.

In a very detailed sense, you can say there are eighty-four thousand different types of disturbing emotions. But, more briefly, we can identify six primary and twenty subsidiary disturbing emotions. There are also so many, many types of karma: there is virtuous karma, there is unvirtuous karma and neutral karma — but the bottom line is that there is no karma that is separate from mind clinging.

In short, we need to clear up karma and disturbing emotions. Our ability to clear up the formation of karma and disturbing emotions depends entirely upon our conceptual attitude. When our mind clings, disturbing emotions arise and karma is made. The mind clings when there is a conceptual attitude that causes all the deluded experiences of samsara to unfold. In other words, as long as mind clings or holds a conceptual attitude, there is no recognizing of our natural face, our innate nature. The moment this clinging is absent — the moment it dissolves, the moment it vanishes — the innate nature is just simply *there*, present and fully endowed with all perfect qualities, free of all thoughts. You can call it whatever you want, but it is the original ground, your mind essence.

That which covers up innate nature or mind essence is the conceptual attitude of our thinking. This thinking, whether it be of 'Nice!' or 'Not nice!', whether it be virtuous, unvirtuous, or neutral, is our habit. We have grown fond of thinking of this and that. The situation right now is that we do not really want to give up conceptual thinking, which is the root cause of samsara, yet at the same time we want to be free. Even when you truly want to give up conceptualizing and actually try to do it, you may not be totally sure of how to go about it. Another thought cannot free us of thinking. One more thought cannot make us free of thought. A new kind of clinging, a new conceptual attitude, cannot obliterate the previous conceptual state. Only the state of non-clinging, the wakefulness that does not conceptualize, can totally put an end to thinking. Thought-free wakefulness can cut through the very root of conceptual mind for good.

As I mentioned earlier, in Dzogchen, *the main practice is to separate dualistic mind and rigpa.* Dualistic mind means the state of being involved in the three spheres of concept: subject, object, and action. Dualistic mind continually judges and analyzes. This act of judging has two phases. The first one is *conception*, a vague impression, like "There is a house." The second, *discernment*, is to look closely and to evaluate exactly what type of house it is, investigating the conception in detail. All thought activity has these two stages. Rigpa, on the other hand, is not caught up in judging. It is wide open. The identity of rigpa, the moment of rigpa, is free from both coarse and subtle judging. That is why the tradition of pith instruction describes the awakened state of rigpa as utterly naked.

Rigpa is vividly present,
wide awake.

A moment of no thought,
not being caught up in judging.
Rigpa is empty, and at the same time cognizant.
Cognizant and at the same time empty,
utterly naked awareness.
Do not focus outwardly
do not concentrate inwardly
do not place the attention in between.
Let be without even as much as a hair-tip of mental doing.

If something has to be done mentally, no matter how subtle, you are not experiencing the innate nature as it is. The mental doing pollutes your uncontrived, original natural mind. We need to recognize the uncontrived and original. This is not done by contriving or fabricating something new — the usual work of dualistic mind. Honestly, it is nothing other than our moment to moment thinking that corrupts, that covers up this original uncontrived natural face that is our basic state. There is nothing other to disturb that: there is no god, there is no devil who can cover it up apart from our own thinking. The forming of karma and disturbing emotions can only take place based on this conceptual thinking; there is no other source, no other foothold. No matter where we search we only find one basis — our own thinking. Pleasure and pain, hope and fear are all our own thinking. They have no existence apart from our own thinking. The myriad types of deluded experiences that are so immense and so long-lasting have no existence apart from our own thinking.

To practice and to train means to not give in to ordinary thinking, not to be caught up in ordinary thinking. It is the nature of things that the very identity of what thinks is the thought-free wakefulness itself. This is how it always was; it is the original way. At any moment that we recognize the identity of what thinks, the thinking dissolves, the clinging dissolves. The identity of what thinks is thought-free wakefulness, in actuality. In the very moment of recognizing it, you are free of karma and disturbing emotions. At that moment the stream of karma has been cut, interrupted. At that moment, the continuity of disturbing emotion has ceased. At that moment, deluded experience has ended, because delusion is nothing other than our thinking – good thoughts, bad thoughts, neutral thoughts, all of them. These thoughts that seem to have their own subject and object, when investigated, are found to not really exist. Intelligent reasoning can figure that out, but this alone is not enough. While knowing that thoughts are deluded, we still are caught up in delusion. Even when we try not to become carried away, it seems impossible to simply let be without again being caught up in deluded thought. That is due to karma, which is habit. Habit is like an addiction. We know that something is overpowering and we still cannot help it.

We need to be clear about this point: delusion is our thinking. *There is no deluded state separate from thinking.* Apart from thoughts, there is no good karma or bad karma. Besides our thoughts, there are no eighty-four thousand types of disturbing emotions. When our thinking dissolves, there are no extra disturbing emotion or karma to be cleared up. Karma and emotions are like a magical display of our thinking. When the thinking dissolves, they vanish automatically.

This thinking mind, the maker of all, has different aspects. There are the five sense cognitions, which are conceived of, conceptualized and judged by the sixth consciousness. The sixth consciousness thinks all thoughts, then gets caught up in like and dislike. This is the thinking and it can be any type of thought. For instance, the thought to help, to assist, is called a good thought; it creates good karma. The thought to harm, to hurt, is called an evil thought; it creates negative karma. The wish to hurt is an attitude, but it is because of this attitude that it can be expressed — that the words or physical action that actually hurts others are carried out. If you think, "I'd like to punch that guy," and you keep that in mind, eventually you may hit him. If you think, "I should tell him some nasty words about how he really is," eventually those nasty words may come from your mouth. That is the creation of karma, whether it be good karma or bad karma. It is the same with disturbing emotions.

To like, that is attachment. To dislike is anger. To not want to investigate something is dullness. Through the five senses, through plans and memories, our mind becomes involved in attachment, anger and dullness. It happens countless times in just one day.

We try our best to heal these tendencies by many different methods. We may jog, do yoga, get a massage, sit in a sauna, eat pills, swim and climb mountains. No matter how much we try, nothing seems to totally work. All those methods entail a lot of effort. On the other hand, if we use the method of effortlessness, all this busyness automatically quiets down.

What the Buddha really taught was *as long as you cling, you do not have the view*. Do not do a thing. Give up the thought of non-doing as well; give up thinking, "I do not want to think." We may have a problem, in that we think "I do not want to do" and then cling to this "I do not want to do." When totally free of all types of mental doing, you are automatically also free of karma, disturbing emotions, and deluded experience. We need to know one thing, only one thing: is *how not to do*. This is the real Buddhadharma, not to do a thing. Not to think of anything. It is said, "Having totally abandoned thinker and what is thought of, remain as a thought-free child." Thinking is delusion. We need to understand that our thinking is karma and disturbing emotions. Once you understand that this thinking is deluded, you are ready to apply a remedy.

We need to know the difference between being deluded and being free. When caught up in thinking, we are deluded. To be free of thinking is to be free. *Confusion and liberation both depend on thought*. Karma is like information saved on a computer. Thought is saved on the hard drive — the hard drive of the all-ground, the alaya. It is a strange type of hard drive; you cannot erase it so easily. To erase it, to be free, you need to be free of thinking. Not just nasty thinking, but even good virtuous thinking; you need to be free of that as well. Since even good thoughts create karma, we need to be free of good thoughts as well. That every thought creates karma implies that a focus is held in mind: there is holding of subject, object and action.

We can justifiably throw all the blame on the thinking. Up until now, we have had countless thoughts. We have been caught up in incessantly thinking of one thing after another, and all the while we have been thinking that this is fine and dandy, nothing wrong with that. Studying the way of the Buddha is a way of developing our personal intelligence in order to see clearly. We are developing what is called "the intelligence that reveals the nature of all things" — an insight that distinguishes between all phenomena. This intelligence that is within ourselves makes us see increasingly clearly, and allows us to identify exactly what is to blame for any trouble. Developing this type of insight is very different from someone who has no idea of what Buddhism is about being told out of the blue that "Your thinking is bad. Your thoughts are bad because they create all this bad karma, they make all sorts of negative emotions. All the trouble is in your thinking." When one is told like that, one gets annoyed, because it feels the same as being told, "You are bad." One takes it too personally.

The Buddhist perspective is actually very, very subtle. In Buddhism, we speak so magnificently about freedom from samsara, freedom from karma and freedom from disturbing emotions. That freedom consists in how to be free from our thinking.

RINPOCHE: Do we agree that the thinking means to like, to dislike or to be indifferent? Yes or no?

STUDENT: Yes.

RINPOCHE: Do we agree that liking, disliking or indifference, which are attachment, anger and dullness, is the creator of karma, the former of karma?

STUDENT: Yes.

RINPOCHE: So we agree that thinking is karma and disturbing emotions?

STUDENT: Yes.

RINPOCHE: Is there is any karma, any disturbing emotions that are not from thinking?

STUDENT: No.

STUDENT: Don't you only mean the clinging to the thinking? We do need a thought in order to experience emptiness, don't we?

RINPOCHE: If there is something being experienced, then that is not emptiness. Emptiness is an experience that is free of something being experienced and an experiencer, an experience free of subject and object. The Buddha once said, "People use the phrase 'to see space,' but please examine what that really means." How do you see space? People use the words "I see" when a concrete thing is observed and then registered. However, space itself is not a concrete thing. It is the absence of concrete atoms. It is simply openness, totally bare; the absence of concreteness. Yet, when looking at that, people still say, "I see space." In the same way, to see the emptiness of mind essence is an experience that is free of something seen and someone seeing.

Whenever there is thinking, it necessarily follows that karma and disturbing emotions are formed. Whenever there is freedom from thinking, as in the moment of thought-free wakefulness, it necessarily follows that there is no forming of karma and disturbing emotions. Whenever there is thinking it follows that conditioned karma is formed, either conditioned goodness or conditioned evil. Virtuous thinking creates good karma, and as a consequence of that there is rebirth in and the experiences of the three higher realms. Unvirtuous thinking creates evil karma, and as a consequence there is rebirth in and the experiences of the three lower realms. As long as the web of thinking has not dissolved, there will repeatedly be rebirth in and the experiences of the six realms. This continual circling around in the cycle of birth and death is named samsara. The higher realms of gods, demigods and human beings result from the creation of good karma out of positive virtuous thinking. But that is not freedom. It is simply the creation of good karma while not knowing how to be free.

If you want to be free of the whole of samsara, you need to know how to dissolve thinking. The whole truth is right there. If you want to dissolve the web of samsara's deluded experiences, you need to know this key point. Thinking cannot be dissolved by replacing it with another thought. Thinking cannot dissolve thinking; it does not work. You can replace negative thinking with positive thinking; that is possible and helpful. But if you want to be totally free of conceptual thinking there is only one way: through training in thought-free wakefulness. Only thought-free wakefulness dissolves thinking. Only nonclinging dissolves clinging.

Strip awareness to its naked state. There are many practices in the Dzogchen tradition to lay awareness bare, totally naked. One such practice is called 'separating samsara and nirvana'. Another technique is shouting the syllable PHAT in a way that interrupts the flow of thought and strips awareness to its naked state.

To enhance the recognition of mind essence, there is a very special technique that is also perfect when we want to overcome obstacles and avoid pitfalls and sidetracks on the path. That technique is called devotion and compassion. Among all kinds of thoughts, these are the most pure, the cleanest, the most noble. Devotion here refers to a trust that is the result of understanding the meaning of the natural state. It is an intelligent type of devotion that understands the value of being unconfused. It also involves the understanding that being caught up in thought and thinking necessarily also means being caught up in karma and disturbing emotions.

No one who is caught up in forming new karma and disturbing emotions can be beyond the three types of suffering. This understanding brings about overwhelming compassion, the compassion that understands how beings suffer through not realising the truth of their own nature. Devotion towards the unconfused state is intelligent devotion through understanding the meaning, through understanding why. Similarly, intelligent compassion understands the causes of suffering. Among all thoughts, devotion and compassion are the purest and the most helpful in facilitating the realization of the natural state.

To summarize, we need to have renunciation towards all kinds of thinking and devotion towards the state free of thought, thought-free wakefulness. Any further involvement in thinking only creates more karma and disturbing emotions, nothing else.

> *Now, compose yourself in thought-free wakefulness.*
> *Be awake without clinging.*
> *Five senses wide open. Awareness undirected.*
> *You are wide awake now, aren't you?*
> *Undirected awareness means not directing your awareness*
> *and not focusing on anything.*
> *Not fixating on that,*
> *not clinging to what is experienced.*
> *Utterly naked,*
> *totally empty*
> *very comfortable.*
> *Don't cling to the comfort.*
> *This clinging is a new disturbing emotion.*
> *Clinging to this awakeness is also disturbing emotion.*
> *Compose yourself in a state in which you are awake,*
> *comfortable, blissful, without attachment.*
> *Do not cling, do not attach values, thinking this is good! this*
> *   is no good!*
> *Be without reference point,*
> *without conceptual attitude,*
> *totally unspoiled.*
> *Distinguish between dualistic mind and awareness.*
> *Rigpa has its own brightness.*
> *This bright awareness, free of fixating on anything,*
> *is the source of all kayas and wisdoms, all the enlightened*
> *   qualities.*

It is no good to sit and be dull. Instead, be utterly awake. Have a totally naked mind. Be bright, clear, lucid. It is said that the purest part of the body is the organ of the eyes. Through the eyes, we have the clearest experience of all our senses. That is why when training in Mahamudra and Dzogchen we definitely have to keep the eyes open. The eyes are the gates of wisdom. Having open eyes, we see visible forms. But, do not judge the forms. It is very good to have open eyes, yet not to judge what is seen. That is how in our practice we have more clarity, more brightness and less dullness.

QUESTION: What about subtle, almost unnoticed thoughts? Are they still present in rigpa?

RINPOCHE: Stripping awareness to its naked state means that your awareness has to be laid totally and completely bare, to be rigpa. Then there is no subtle clinging. In general, blatant thoughts and emotions like attachment, anger and dullness of course are a disturbance. In the context of shamatha and vipashyana, Mahamudra and Dzogchen, there is another obstacle for meditators, called the undercurrent of thought. This subtle undercurrent is often hard to notice. It makes the shamatha a little restless, slightly uneasy, while it makes the vipashyana a little unclear, a little hazy. You can say that this undercurrent of thought is not like a straightforward bandit of meditation; rather, it is a thief, a sneaky thief. Usually thieves need to be sneaky, but this is a very sneaky one.

QUESTION: It seems to me that when I practice, I can sometimes cut through my conceptual thoughts, but at some point I become aware of something cooking, this churning going on. Maybe it's not conceptual or really thoughts, but there is still something churning or bubbling. Would this be the undercurrent of thought?

RINPOCHE: No need to call it an undercurrent. There really is cooking happening over there (*points to the kitchen*). Whatever this experience, is it happening in cooking time, or does it have nothing to do with cooking, and it's just coming in your mind?

QUESTIONER: I am talking more about something that goes on in my head

RINPOCHE: During meditation time?

QUESTIONER: Yes.

RINPOCHE: I see. The undercurrent of thought involves movement in the mind, but it is not noticed, you are not clear about it. There is thought activity going on, but you are unaware of what you are thinking about. You cannot remember it afterwards. It's like being absent-minded and still thinking. The traditional example is that straw has been laid out to dry on the ground, but water is seeping in beneath. You cannot see the water, but it causes the straw to rot. This doesn't happen to every farmer. Experienced farmers know that moist fields sometimes carry water that you cannot see because the straw is lying on top. So they will build something of wood or stone, and they will put the straw to dry on top of it. They will take care from the beginning that all their straw does not rot.

In the same way, a skilled meditator will take care not to sit and spend all of the sessions in that state. The undercurrent in meditation is not like when you are blatantly involved in being attached, angry or dull. It is more something that looks like meditation but is really an act of thinking. When one suddenly regains one's senses, one does not remember anything that was thought of. That is an experience of this undercurrent. We can find out by checking each other, by examining the other practitioners' faces. Sometimes their look is relaxed, a little laughing; maybe some subtle good daydreams are going on. Other times their look is very uptight; maybe some not-so-good fantasies are going on.

QUESTION: I don't see how rigpa could ever be sustained.

RINPOCHE: Are you saying that the opportunity to recognize rigpa could never happen, or that, having recognized, sustaining the continuity of rigpa could never happen? Those two are different.

QUESTIONER: I'm saying the latter.

RINPOCHE: Recognizing once, that is sustaining one continuity. Repeat that again and again.

QUESTIONER: And then get frustrated!

RINPOCHE: If it helps to be frustrated, please go ahead!

QUESTIONER: In Dzogchen there is not much talk about merit, correct?

RINPOCHE: First of all, we need to know that Dzogchen practice covers the basis of Mahayana and Theravada. This principle of the higher level containing the precepts of the vehicles below is called 'upwardly contained'. This is why anyone who practices Vajrayana authentically also possesses the precepts of all three vehicles without conflict. Someone who is practicing only one of the vehicles below may not comprehend that. Vajrayana is primarily mental practice. Especially in Mahamudra and Dzogchen, the training is not to stray from the empty awareness that is the awakened state of the buddhas. This empty, aware state of all buddhas, the awakened state, is also compassionate. At the shravaka level, the precepts are primarily concerned with physical and verbal behavior. Vajrayana precepts are mainly about one's frame of mind. By not straying from the empty and aware awakened state, one automatically never breaks the precepts of the lower vehicles.

In terms of the accumulation of merit and wisdom, the accumulation of wisdom has much deeper impact. Among all ways of accumulating wisdom, the most eminent is to not stray from the empty and aware awakened state. There is nothing higher than that. It is also the most effective way of purifying obscurations. The empty and aware awakened state is the most eminent way to both perfect the accumulations and to purify the obscurations. But in order to initially recognize this empty and aware awakened state, one needs to accumulate merit and purify obscurations.

Please investigate this point with reasoning. Isn't it true that the two obscurations obscure our basic nature? It is obviously hard to be in samadhi and be stingy at the same time. Whenever you are frivolous, impatient, short-tempered, lazy, and lacking concentration, it is very difficult to be in samadhi, isn't it? The opposites of the six paramitas are obviously not the state of samadhi. And conceptualizing subject, object and action obviously obscures being in the view, doesn't it? In Dzogchen it is necessary to distinguish between dualistic mind and rigpa, because dualistic mind conceptualizes the three spheres; it obscures the view. Dualistic mind is itself a cognitive obscuration, as I explained earlier. That which needs to be really recognized, the natural state, is not being known while one is conceptualizing the three spheres. It is actually hindered.

QUESTION: It is one thing to think "I should not think! I should not cling!" But actual experience is another thing.

RINPOCHE: The training I mention here is not only the thought "I should not cling" — it is simply *not clinging*. That is enough. To think, "I am confused about this" is also an obscuration. "Everything is illusion" — to think that is also not okay. Nor is the thought, "All phenomena are emptiness." Or "All things are simplicity, beyond the eight constructs and the four limits. It is like this." We cannot actually realize the nature of things only through studying books, because no matter how profound the books are, they are still words kept in mind.

"Things are beyond constructs." Just the first two words, "things are," is already wrong! But of course it is even worse to say that things do possess mental constructs. Compared to thinking "All things are real," it is much harder to get rid of the idea "Everything is emptiness," because the latter is definitely true. It is much easier to get rid of something that is untrue, because you can argue the point and get rid of the idea. Everything is emptiness, it is actually like that. However, to hold onto that idea makes it hard to get rid of.

Right now it is twelve o'clock: time exists. Relative truth is undeniable. It is true. Relative truth is real for the deluded mind. Relative truth is the domain of conceptual mind. It can be grasped. But ultimate truth is not the domain of conceptual mind; it cannot be grasped by conceptual mind. The seeming way is the domain of concepts. But the real way is beyond concepts.

Devotion and Pure Perception

Ego-clinging is simply a thought. Clinging to the notion of self is a thought. Clinging to the notion of other is also a thought. Clinging to duality is a thought. The concept of good is a thought, and the concept of evil is a thought. A neutral concept is also a thought. Whenever there is thought, it follows that there is clinging. The attitude of clinging follows the tracks of the three poisons. Since the formation of thought involves the three poisons, that means that thinking causes samsara. Whenever there is involvement in thought, our experience will be samsaric. *Deluded thinking is the root of samsara.*

Deluded thinking forms karma and disturbing emotions. When there is thinking, there are the acts of accepting and rejecting, of pleasure and of pain. The circumstances maybe external, but the thinker is this mind within. Beauty and ugliness appear to belong to external objects. However, that which creates the beauty or the ugliness is actually the forming of a concept in this mind, here. Also, the liking and the disliking of what is considered beautiful or ugly are actions taken by this mind. The circumstance is the sense object, but the main factor is our mind.

Most people identify the main factor as being over there, inherent within objects. For example, a single dish of food, given to twenty or thirty people will elicit different experiences. Some will say, "I like this food," some will say, "It's okay," and some will say, "It is very bad." Who is correct? Who is right? It is based on the perceiver; it is in the eyes of the beholder.

Similarly, with any opinion of what is perceived, understand that the main factor is this mind, the perceiver. Everything is based on mind. Certain people are not at ease with themselves, not happy. They are not fulfilled. Whatever craving or desire they have experienced has not happened, so they are unhappy. But desires and ambitions are like ripples on water. *As long as one is not content, one cannot be happy.* Whenever there is a short moment of contentment, we call that happiness. Whenever we are satisfied, that is pleasant. Something is wrong with us: the tendency to not be happy with what we already have, but to want what is over there, what somebody else has.

On a very simple level, people are happier when they can be content and crave less. The more craving, the more dissatisfaction, the more pain they experience. In order for all six classes of beings to be totally free of the entirety of samsara, we need to solve the problem of the thinking that forms the causes that propel us around through the various realms. We understand now that thinking is delusion. However, to want to be free and at the same time to want to hang on to conceptual thinking – to not want to give up conceptual thinking — is a contradiction in terms. It is something that will not happen. It is an impossible task.

If you want to attain liberation and omniscient enlightenment, you need to be free of conceptual thinking. Meditation training, in the sense of sustaining the nature of mind, is a way of being free from clinging and the conceptual attitude of forming thoughts, and therefore free from the causes of samsara: karma and disturbing emotions. Please do not believe that liberation and samsara is somewhere over there: it is *here,* in oneself. Thought is samsara. Being free of thought is liberation. When we are free of thinking, we are free of thought. The problem is that the causes for further samsara are being created continuously. We spin through the six realms and undergo a lot of suffering.

Compared to the other life forms in samsara, we human beings do not suffer that much. We don't experience the unbearable, overwhelming suffering that countless other beings do. And even for some humans, the mental or physical pain may be unbearable. If we continue to allow our ordinary thinking to run wild, we cannot predict what is lined up for us in the future, where we will end up, in what shape or form.

The bottom line is this: *we need to know how to dissolve thoughts.* Without knowing this, we cannot eliminate karma and disturbing emotions. And therefore, the karmic phenomena do not vanish; deluded experience does not end. We understand also that one thought cannot undo another thought. The only thing that can do this is thought-free wakefulness. This is not some state that is far away from us: thought-free wakefulness actually exists together with every thought, inseparable from it — but the thinking obscures or hides this innate actuality. Thought-free wakefulness is immediately present the very moment the thinking dissolves, the very moment it vanishes, fades away, falls apart. Isn't this true?

When described in detail, we can say there are eighty-four thousand different types of thoughts. In a condensed way, there are six root emotions and twenty subsidiary ones. An even shorter categorisation of thoughts is that of the three poisons. Whatever the number of types of thoughts, the Buddha taught how to eliminate all of these by giving the eighty-four thousand sections of the Dharma.

Perhaps you do not have the time to study and learn all these teachings, or maybe you don't have the desire, the ability or the intelligence to do so. In this case, the buddhas and bodhisattvas very skillfully condensed the teachings into a very concise form. This is called the tradition of pith instructions that deals with overcoming all the disturbing emotions simultaneously. The basic instruction here is to understand that all of these disturbing emotions are merely thoughts. Even ego-clinging and dualistic fixation is simply a thought. *The pointing-out instruction shows how to dissolve the thought, how to recognize the nature of the thinker, our innate thought-free wakefulness. That is the intent of the fourth empowerment, and that is the training in Mahamudra and Dzogchen.* It is a very skillful way, an instruction through experience, *nyong-tri*, a few words with a clear and profound meaning.

The root of confusion is thinking, but the essence of the thinking is thought-free wakefulness. As often as possible, please compose yourselves in the equanimity of thought-free wakefulness. It is said: "Samsara is merely thought, so freedom of thought is liberation." Great masters explain this in more detail, because simply being thoughtless is not necessarily liberation. To be in a state of unconscious, to faint, to be oblivious, is not liberation. If those states were liberation, attainment would be swift since it is very easy to be mindless. That would be a cheap liberation!

Simply suspend your thinking within the nonclinging state of wakefulness: that is the correct view. One important point about the teachings on mind essence is that they need to be simple and easy to train in. There are different types of view discussed in Buddhism. There is view directed towards the conditioned, the view directed to the unconditioned, and the view of self-knowing. To study these in detail is not a simple subject; it takes months, even years. *But if you simply suspend your thinking within the nonclinging state of wakefulness, that is the correct view.* Particularly in Mahamudra and Dzogchen practice, the view is said to be open and carefree. The less you cling and grasp, the more open and free it is. It is the nature of things. The less rigid our conceptual attitude is, the freer the view.

Empty, cognizant, a unity, unformed. Please make the meanings of these words something that points at your own experience. You can also say "the unformed unity of empty cognizance." These are very precious and profound words. Empty means that essentially this mind is something that is empty. This is easy to agree on; we cannot find it as a thing. It is not made empty by anyone, including by us — it is just naturally empty, originally so. At the same time, we also have the ability to know, to cognize, which is also something natural and unmade. These two qualities, being empty and cognizant, are not separate entities. They are an indivisible unity. This unity itself is also not something that is made by anyone. It is not a unity of empty cognizance that at some point arose, remains for a while and later will perish. It does not arise, does not dwell, and does not cease. It is not made in time. It is not a material substance. Anything that exists in time or substance is an object of thought. This empty unity of empty cognizance is not made of thought; it is not an object of thought.

Whenever there is a thought of time or substance, its upkeep becomes very complex; it takes a lot to sustain or maintain that kind of thought. This unformed basic nature, however, is very simple, not complicated at all. So many complications are created based on concepts of time and substance — so much hope and fear. Honestly, substance and time never did exist; they never do exist, nor will they ever exist in the future, either. The conceptualization of time and substance is the habit of the thinking mind. Although right now time and substance do not exist, it seems to the thinking mind as if they do.

Concerning substance, if you look around, it seems like everything is solidly and precisely there. In the experience of a real yogi, of course, time and substance do not exist. Even a scholar can, through intelligent reasoning, feel convinced about this fact. When we think that which is not, is, then, it seems to be. As perceived by a buddha, however, all the experiences that samsaric beings have are no more substantial than dreams. It all looks like dreaming.

Something of vital importance must be repeated. There is a saying in my country that something of vital importance must be repeated. I feel this strongly, and this is why I am repeating these essential points over and over again. Because it's acutely on my mind, it always comes out. If you can understand something right here, then it can be applied whenever and wherever you are afterwards, even on the toilet.

At the very foundation of Vajrayana practice lie two principles: devotion and pure perception. We should have devotion towards the unmistaken natural state, in the sense of sincerely appreciating that which is truly unmistaken, unconfused, never deluded. In reality, the nature of all things is totally pure. Impurity occurs only due to temporary concepts. That is the reason why one should train in pure perception.

In this context, there are three levels of experience: the deluded experience of sentient beings, the meditative experience of yogis, and the pure experience of buddhas. Whenever there is dualistic mind, there is deluded experience. The deluded experience of sentient beings is impure because it is involved with karma and disturbing emotions. Karma and disturbing emotions are called impure. In deluded experience, there is the attempt to accept and reject; there is hope and fear. Hope and fear are painful: that is suffering. Whenever there is thinking, there is hope and fear. Whenever there is hope and fear, there is suffering.

The meditative experience of a yogi is free of giving in to ordinary thought. It is something other than being involved in normal thinking. We can call it the state of shamatha or vipashyana or other names, but basically it is unlike ordinary thinking. The meditative experiences of yogis are good experiences. These meditative states or moods become evident because of letting mind settle in equanimity. The most famous of these meditative moods are called *bliss, clarity and nonthought*. They occur during vipashyana, but they can arise even during shamatha practice. Through meditation training, the mind becomes more clarified, more lucid. But if we are not connected with a qualified master and if we do not know the right methods of dealing with these meditative states, we may believe that we are somehow incredibly realized beings. That becomes a hindrance; it can even turn into a severe obstacle.

For instance, in the experience of voidness, we may feel that the entire universe is one vast expanse of emptiness, utterly insubstantial. Through the experience of clarity we might feel so clear that clairvoyant powers arise, and we sense what people far, far away are thinking and even what they are talking about far. The experience of bliss may be a type of delight and well-being that is unprecedented. We have never felt so deeply blissful in both body and mind. These experiences are okay if we do not cling to them; if we do not fix our attention on them fondly and hold onto them. They are explained as enhancements of the practice. But clinging to these states is itself a great error, a great fault. Clinging to these feelings is exactly the root cause of the three realms of samsara. Since we are now meditators practicing shamatha and vipashyana, we should understand this point: no matter what kinds of experience occurs, if we do not cling to them, they become an enhancement in the training. The clinging creates an obstacle, a hindrance.

Other meditative experiences, like those in Tögal practice, come about by applying certain key points of body and mind. These meditative experiences unfold without parting from the view of Trekchö. This is the way of inner signs occurring outwardly. It is a practice in which one can progress very quickly, attaining enlightenment in a single lifetime. Those are some of the meditative experiences of yogis.

The Mahamudra path is presented as the twelve aspects of the four yogas. As I mentioned before, these four yogas of Mahamudra constitute the path of liberation. The first of these, one-pointedness, essentially means that you can remain calmly undisturbed for as long as you want. The next yoga is simplicity, and means to recognize your natural face as being ordinary mind, free from basis and free from root. "Simplicity is rootless and baseless ordinary mind." We need to develop the strength of this recognition; otherwise, we are as helpless as a small child on a battlefield. We train by means of mindfulness, first effortful, then effortless. We train in simplicity at lesser, medium and higher levels, and then arrive at one taste, the third of the four yogas of Mahamudra. One taste means that the duality of experience dissolves, that all dualistic notions such as samsara and nirvana dissolve into the state of non-dual awareness. It is the ongoingness of rigpa, one taste, one nature.

Having perfected one taste through the levels of the lesser, medium and higher stages, the fourth yoga is non-meditation. This is the point at which every type of conviction and the fixing of the attention on something completely dissolves. All convictions and habitual tendencies have dissolved, are left behind. One has captured the dharmakaya throne of non-meditation.

In the beginning one needs to be convinced about how reality is: one needs to have confidence in the view. Ultimately, however, any form of conviction is still a subtle obscuration, still a hindrance. At the final stage of non-meditation, and all types of habitual tendencies and convictions need to be dissolved, left behind. There is nothing more to cultivate, nothing more to reach. One has arrived at the end of the path. All that needs to be purified has been left behind, has been purified. Karma, disturbing emotions and the habitual tendencies have all been cleared up, so that nothing is left. The path is necessary as long as we have not arrived. The moment we arrive, however, the need for the road to get there has fallen away. As long as we are not at our destination, then it is also necessary to have the concept of path in order to get there. But once the destination has been reached, once whatever needs to be cultivated has been cultivated and whatever needs to be abandoned has been left behind, the whole need for path is over. That is what is meant by non-meditation, literally non-cultivation. This is the dharmakaya throne of non-meditation; the exhaustion of all concepts and phenomena that is the ultimate level of experience in Dzogchen. This is the state of complete enlightenment. Both these levels of realization are equal to that of all buddhas.

At this point, for oneself, there is exclusively pure experience. At the same time, other beings are still perceived as having impure experience, as being deluded. Take the example of the six classes of beings. When their experiences are compared with each other, each being will feel that their way of experiencing is more profound than the realm below. In general, everyone thinks that what they experience is real. The difference in the experiencing of the different realms is the difference in the density of their karma and obscurations. The less dense the karma, the closer to real experience. Compared to the ordinary samsaric sentient being, the meditative experience of a yogi is more real, more pure. But compared to that, the pure experience of a buddha is more real and more pure still.

Ignorance clears when knowing the natural state. We need to dissolve impure deluded experience. Deluded experience comes from not knowing the nature of mind; it comes from unknowing, in being ignorant of the natural state. When not knowing our nature, we are sentient beings. Ignorance clears when knowing the natural state, the state of a buddha. While not knowing, there is the forming of karma and disturbing emotions. While knowing, karma and disturbing emotions are not formed. If, in the very moment of knowing innate nature and sustaining the continuity of that, you never stray again, you are a buddha.

Buddhist philosophy has many splendid words to describe what happens. The *Chittamatra*, the Mind-Only school, presents a threefold classification of reality as the imaginary, the dependent and the absolute. In the Dzogchen teachings, ignorance is described as three aspects, conceptual ignorance, coemergent ignorance and the single-nature ignorance. These are all very nice words. Basically, it is in the state of not knowing that confusion can take place. Not knowing our own essence is confusion. The essence of what thinks is dharmakaya. The thinking itself is not dharmakaya, but the *identity* of that which thinks is dharmakaya. Thinking is thought. Thinking is not the thought-free state. It is the identity of that which thinks that is thought-free.

Whether we use the words mind-essence, Trekchö, the primordially pure state of cutting through, original coemergent wisdom, or the Great Middle Way of definitive meaning, Madhyamaka, one point is true: the moment of not being involved in thought, you spontaneously have arrived at the true view, automatically.

There are two ways to approach the view. One is through scriptural statements and reasoning, and the other is through experience. The first way is called "establishing the view through statement and reasoning." Although we want to train in Mahamudra or Dzogchen, still, without some feeling of certainty about the view obtained through studying and our own reasoning, it is not that easy to be sure and certain.

It is sometimes possible to transmit or communicate the view without using any scriptural statements, but this requires that a totally qualified master possessing the nectar of learning, reflection and meditation meets with a qualified disciple who is receptive. As I said previously, there are three types of transmission. The first two, the mind transmission of buddhas and the symbolic transmission of the knowledge holders, are like that. Mind transmission uses not even a single word or gesture, no sign. Yet, something is communicated — the wisdom of realization is communicated and realized; it is fully recognized. Symbolic transmission uses no more than a word or sentence — no explanations, just a gesture — to point out the wisdom of realization and have it recognized. The third type is the hearing lineage, which uses a very brief spoken teaching.

In these times we are in, most people would have a hard time if we were only to use mind transmission, symbolic transmission and hearing transmission with nothing else, no explanation. Explanation is generally necessary in order to point out the natural state. There are two ways to do so. One of these is the *analytical approach of a scholar*. The other is the *resting meditation of a simple meditator*. There are some people who can trust a master and be introduced to the natural state without using any lengthy explanations. They do not need to establish the meaning through reasoning or through quotes from scriptures. Maybe they are not interested, or maybe they just do not need it. It is possible for them to understand the nature of mind simply and directly. For other people, this is not enough. Then it is necessary to use scriptural references and intelligent reasoning in order to establish certainty in the view.

The analytical meditation of a *pandita* or a scholar means that we examine everything. We use our intelligence to repeatedly analyze and understand. The scholar closely looks to find out what is valid, what can be verified. He uses a variety of methods to verify the words of the Enlightened One, the statements of great masters, and the authenticity of his or her own intelligence. By combining these factors, everything is analyzed until there is nothing more to analyze. Analysis has run its course. That is the point of arriving at the intellectual understanding of the true view. At that point, the scholar still needs to receive the blessings of a qualified master and to receive the pointing-out instruction from such a master.

Do you have doubts about anything? Does anything need to be cleared up?

STUDENT: Could you give a few more details about pure perception?

RINPOCHE: To refrain from hurting others and to abandon the basis for harm is the main precept of the Hinayana teachings. To help others and to create the basis for benefit is the main precept for Mahayana. Vajrayana is called the path of pure perception, taking sacred outlook as the path. This is done on the foundation of the two previous precepts: the attitude of wanting to avoid harming others, and of wanting to help them. In addition to this, we train in pure perception — not only in a spiritual context, but also in any normal life situation in human society.

The Vajrayana statement to regard everything as pure could at first sound strange, maybe even awkward. But examine very carefully and you will discover that the very nature of everything is one of purity. Therefore, to regard everything as pure is very reasonable. Pure perception is very close to the ultimate reality of how things actually are. All sentient beings have an enlightened essence, buddha nature. It is said that all beings are buddhas, yet they are covered by temporary obscurations. Even though all beings are veiled by obscuration, they are still in reality buddhas, and therefore, it is perfectly all right to see all beings as perfectly pure. In addition, there is an immediate benefit in trying to perceive others as pure: among one another, among our Dharma brothers and sisters, our tendency to be competitive and conceited becomes less and less. Disturbing emotions diminish through the training in pure perception.

The shravaka precepts of refraining from hurting others are vital. The Mahayana precept of the will to assist other beings is extremely important. In addition to that, the Vajrayana training in pure perception is tremendously profound. It is a training in recognizing and acknowledging the natural purity of everything. Therefore, the Tibetan approach to Buddhism is one in which the three vehicles are not separated, but are practiced in combination.

We need to very carefully examine this principle of pure perception, because seemingly things are not pure. On the seeming level, we can have notions of something being pure or impure, but on the level of what really is, everything is pure. The Vajrayana perspective of pure perception is that everything, since the very beginning, is the three kayas in reality. All movement of thought is the play of original wakefulness. We discriminate and judge because of not knowing this.

To have the opinion that something which is pure is actually impure is a mistake. But to regard that which is pure as being pure is correct. Compared to the attitude of regarding things as being permanent and concrete, the attitude of regarding everything as being impermanent and insubstantial is correct. To regard everything, all phenomena, as not only being insubstantial and impermanent but as being completely pure is an even higher view.

QUESTION: With regard to pure perception, it seems easier to see oneself as pure, doesn't it?

RINPOCHE: Without pure perception, Vajrayana is very difficult. Vajrayana is the swift path because through the power of trust and devotion it becomes much easier to realize the nature of things.

Generally speaking, pure perception means appreciating that everyone has the capacity to be enlightened, everyone has a nature that can be totally revealed and perfected. Moreover, the five elements, the five aggregates, the five poisons — all the different aspects of experience — are by nature already pure. It is only because we see these in a confused way that they appear as impure. In the pure experience of not forming concepts of clean or unclean, pure or impure, everything is seen as it actually is, as manifestations of original wakefulness.

When someone understands the value of devotion and pure perception and is willing to train in this way, he or she is a suitable recipient for Vajrayana teachings. This suitability for Vajrayana entails being both broadminded and sharp. Everything is total purity, all-encompassing purity. Unless someone is very open-minded and has a sharp intelligence, he or she just does not understand that this is how reality is.

Moreover, we should also train in perceiving the teacher and our fellow practitioners as pure. Appreciating one's vajra brothers and vajra sisters means thinking like this: "They are all practicing Vajrayana; they are all probably more experienced and realized than I am; they are all great — how wonderful." One person cannot truly judge another. Therefore, we should have appreciation for each other. As for the teacher who expounds the Vajrayana, we shouldn't have the attitude: "He is just another guy, another human being, probably a little special, but what do I know." Not like that! Have a pure appreciation of the teacher as well. There is great power in such pure perception.

According to the Vajrayana tradition, it is through devotion and trust that realization dawns in our stream of being. Devotion springs from pure perception of everyone. All sentient beings are potentially buddhas. They are temporarily obscured, but in essence they are buddhas. Obscured suchness may become unobscured suchness, which is buddha. The obscuration can be purified; it will be purified; it is able to be purified. So pure perception is very profound and precious. It is through pure perception that we can have true devotion. And through this devotion, realization dawns.

Milarepa said to Gampopa, "Unlike now, there will be a time in the future, my son, when you will see me as the Buddha in person. At that point, the true view will have dawned within your stream of being."

Vajrayana is not like the general teachings of the Buddha. A Vajrayana saying goes: "Regard whatever the teacher says as excellent, whatever he or she does as pure, and mingle your minds as one." Unless a person is very open-minded and sharp as well, it is just not easy to be that way. When seeing somebody as pure, it does not mean being blind. That is not what we are talking about here. That would be stupid admiration, false admiration. Real trust has more to do with acknowledging the basic purity of all things.

Devotion or trust and pure perception are the basis for Vajrayana practice. And that holds true whether we are listening to a Dharma talk, whether we are applying those teachings or whether we are interacting during daily activities: in any situation pure perception is vital.

Vajrayana cannot be understood unless someone is very open-minded, because every attribute, such as clean and unclean, is only a thought construct. Unless one is very open-minded, one will not understand this point. For instance, it is said that the five nectars, the five meats — excrement, urine, semen, blood and flesh — are to be accepted. That is difficult to understand, isn't it? What it actually means is that someone who really understands the nature of mind can suspend the concept of clean and unclean.

On the other hand, when someone is able to scrutinize and understand the view of Vajrayana with certainty, it is possible to have complete confidence, total certainty. The yogi realizes that in the true view, in the experience of the nature of mind, concepts such as clean and unclean are thought-made. Anything, therefore, which needs to be accepted or rejected is a mental construct. This happens by virtue of sharp intelligence and complete open-mindedness. Vajrayana teachings on view and conduct are given only to people of the sharpest faculties. But it comes down to one thing: the true view. 'View' in this context means beyond something viewed, beyond the act of viewing and beyond any viewer — beyond those three.

Earlier, I covered the fact that the root cause of samsara on the coarse level is attachment, anger and closed-mindedness. On a more subtle level, it is good thoughts, negative thoughts and neutral thoughts. In an even more subtle way, it is any thoughts of disliking, liking or feeling neutral. But on the very subtlest level, it is any moment of a conceptual attitude, any thought that fixates. Out of this very subtlest cause, all kinds of emotions can arise and create further karma.

QUESTION: Is there is a difference between the actual experience of purity and the training in seeing things as pure?

RINPOCHE: Sure. When dualistic mind is caught up in thinking and emotions, making karma, that is called 'the deluded experience of a sentient being.' When practitioners train in a state of mind which is calm and insightful — shamatha and vipashyana — then other types of experience unfold, depending upon the degree of progress in subtlety. These can be experiences such as bliss, clarity, and non-thought. They are described as the meditative experience of yogis and practitioners. Third, there is the pure vision of a buddha.

When various experiences arise in our meditation training, we should regard them as a way to progress, not as something to cling to: this is very important. All the great masters of the past agree on this one point: that whatever experiences or unusual things happen in our field of experience through practice are a further embellishment of our understanding. They should be regarded as an adornment, but not as something special in themselves. If one feels unusually at ease, blissful, clear-minded or totally free of concepts, this is not to be regarded as an end in itself. These states don't need to be either affirmed nor denied. Instead, remain totally open; let whatever unfolds unfold.

The basic nature of our minds is one is that is both cognizant and empty. I have discussed this in detail. This is how our nature already is. This is how it *naturally* is; this is how it *primordially* is. When we start to practice meditation, by for example remaining at ease in shamatha, this basic situation is further clarified. It becomes even more obvious when we train in vipashyana. When these aspects of our nature are further revealed, this corresponds to one of the experiences of a yogi.

To repeat what I said earlier about these experiences: the experience of emptiness is where one feels, "I have disappeared, I am gone." Yet there is still the knowing of that. Because it feels totally wide open, one may think this is extremely special, something totally new, and be quite impressed with oneself because of that. It is also possible to have the experience of clarity, to have some kind of glimpse of extrasensory perceptions — some splendid way of perceiving different from how we ordinarily perceive. Perhaps we are able to see what happens in far-away places. We have a glimpse of this and that, or the impression that we clearly know what other people are thinking or what their moods are. At this point one may mistakenly think, "Now I have reached accomplishment: this is enlightenment."

The bliss experience is when the ordinary disturbing way that the attention moves into thoughts and emotions is quieted down through the practice of shamatha and vipashyana. This bliss feels like an unprecedented way of being that is so smooth, so at ease. We feel, "This is amazing! This is something really special; I never felt like this before. I want to continue feeling this way." Then when it fades away and one is again crowded with thoughts, one may feel downcast and depressed. In short, all these experiences are simply signs of practice; they are positive if we do not cling to them. Conversely, they become obstacles if we do cling. Be careful to make that differentiation.

Not Meditation but Familiarization

Mundane people do not have to be taught or forced to be caught up in the eight worldly concerns. Day and night it occurs spontaneously, automatically. The eight worldly concerns are when we seek material gain, pleasure, praise, and good name. These make us happy; we like them. When their four opposites happen, it is irritating, frustrating; we get angry. In other words, these eight are basically like and dislike. When it comes to achieving something for me, either getting what I want or pushing away what I do not like, there is often an unhealthy tendency not to not shy away from negative action. Not being aware of the consequences of one's actions is stupidity. Thus, at the basis of the eight worldly concerns lie attachment, aversion and stupidity.

For the sake of material gain, pleasure, praise and good name, people do not shrink back from hurting others. There is a lack of concern for the well-being of others. One does not think, "If I do such-and-such for me, will it hurt this other being?" One does not even consider that. That coldness is a lack of empathy. Also, one has no concern for the consequence of the creation of karma. It is more a preoccupation with selfish aims: "I want whatever is good for me!" That self-interest is the root of the eight worldly concerns. But no matter how great the material gain, pleasure, praise and good name one gets, one is never really satisfied. When you have one of something, you want ten. When you have ten, you want a hundred. When you have a hundred, you want a thousand, and so on and so on, endlessly. Do we ever feel "this is enough" in terms of material gain? Do we ever feel, "I do not need more than this"? When there is some enjoyment, some pleasure, do we think, "How nice, that is good enough"? When we are praised once, hear flattering words or get a good reputation, do we think "This is good enough"? Be honest: it's never like that.

To whatever extent that our ambition is not preoccupied with the eight worldly concerns, to that same extent we are a good practitioner. When totally free of the eight worldly concerns, one is a noble being. A son or daughter of noble family is someone in whom the eight worldly concerns have been cleared up. Whether we are a worldly person or a practitioner, the eight worldly concerns cause trouble.

Concern with material gain in this context is not only a craving for wealth. It is also the yearning for the possession of beautiful sights, sounds, smells, tastes and textures. To be concerned with pleasure means wanting pleasant physical sensations or pleasant states of mind. For the sake of fame, good name and renown, people undertake a lot of trouble, a great deal of hardship in order to become famous. Some people want to be known in a nice way. Some people merely want to be known, even if it is as a scoundrel. The concern with praise involves both words and facial expressions: basically, we want feedback that we are appreciated. Isn't it true that when we get that we like it, we are pleased? Just a few words and an indication that we are appreciated, just a small little thing, it creates some pleasure, doesn't it? Then there is, of course, also the opposite — we get irritated if someone does not appreciate us with even a few words. *A practitioner should try not to be swayed by the eight worldly concerns.* Of course we need a dwelling place, we need clothes to wear, food and a bed to sleep in. That is a given. But to only be occupied with getting piles of possessions is useless. We also need pleasure, this is true. But to enslave ourselves by chasing after each little pleasant sensation is useless. Praise and fame are not that necessary. The Kadampa practitioners of the past deeply detested fame and praise. To be praised and appreciated can severely disturb one's practice. Being praised or not, appreciated or not, can create so much conceit, so much rivalry. Conceit is a direct hindrance for samadhi.

The more our mind is preoccupied with the eight worldly concerns, the more we are distracted from meditation practice. Due to the eight worldly concerns we get involved in many disturbing emotions. When we make that a habit, we may well realize at some point that it is useless to be so preoccupied with the eight worldly concerns, yet it feels like we cannot help it. We do not have control over ourselves.

The heart of the matter is this: it is very helpful to go a place of solitude and practice there. Milarepa said, "When I practice in an unpeopled valley, my body is at ease and my mind is happy. There is no circumstance to promote anger or attachment, so my experience and realization progress." The outer circumstance is a pure natural place, an undisturbed place where the company is that of wild animals. In such surroundings we can quickly progress in practice. Solitude has very good qualities. In the West, I often hear business people or busy city people say, "We have a vacation place, a summer house, a weekend house, a very quiet place." When the external circumstance is quiet, there is a relationship with how we feel when being there, and also with how we are in our innermost heart. There is a relationship between outer, inner and innermost solitude.

It is taught that the best place to practice is in solitude, in mountains or caves. Second best is in a monastery. Third best is to be a lay person in the city. In terms of practice, the easiest is to be in a mountain retreat, to live in a cave. The most difficult is to be a householder and at the same time progress to a high level of realization. Why is that? You are in an environment with so much to catch your attention, so much *demanding* your attention, that if you are able to progress in this situation, you must have a high level of diligence and also be very intelligent. Then you are the best type of practitioner. In Vajrayana practice it makes no difference whether you are young or old, whether you are educated or not, whether you are male or female. Whoever receives instruction and uses it is a practitioner.

No matter what practice you do, before practicing, you should repeatedly form the attitude of renunciation towards attachment, anger and dullness. Anger, attachment and dullness create the three realms of samsara, and nowhere in these three realms of samsara is one not permeated by the three types of suffering. Understand deeply from your heart that the creators of all suffering are karma and disturbing emotions. If karma and disturbing emotions could not possibly be cleared away, there would be nothing we could do. Karma and disturbing emotions are the nasty roots of suffering and deluded experience, but they can be abandoned. They have one good quality: they are momentary; they can be cleared up.

There are two ways to clear up karma and disturbing emotions: the mundane, regular way and the spiritual way. The mundane way is when we tell one another, "Don't worry, relax, take it easy." Understand those words, because they are in fact very powerful. Often the one who says, "Relax, take it easy, don't worry," may not be aware of what those words hold. Regardless, they are extremely beneficial to say to one another. And not only to say them to human beings but to our pets as well. We pat them and say, "There, there, relax, take it easy." It does help. "Don't worry" means don't think so much; don't think so much about whatever you're thinking of. It can also mean don't think so much at all. "Take it easy" means be carefree. "Relax" means don't fixate on anything, release your conceptual attitude. These three phrases actually do have a very powerful meaning. "Relax, don't worry, take it easy." Without particularly knowing how to be relaxed and not worry, just to be told may not ultimately help so much. But listen to their opposites: "Be uptight! Worry, please! Be jumpy! Be nervous! Be speedy!"

> *In short, disturbing emotions come about because of thinking.*
> *Thoughts produce emotions,*
> *thoughts create karma.*
> *Therefore, don't follow past thought,*
> *don't invite the future thought.*
> *In the present moment, do not correct,*
> *do not modify,*
> *do not accept or reject.*
> *Don't try to rearrange your present wakefulness.*
> *Instead, leave it as it naturally is*
> *without any attempt to alter it in any way.*
> *That is called sustaining the natural face.*

The moment you let be in uncontrived naturalness,
the essence of your mind is empty
and at the same time cognizant.
Cognizing while being empty,
This is the natural state.

Letting be in naturalness does not mean being absent-minded or dull; it is conscious and cognizant. But this clear and cognizant sense of being awake does not necessarily hold onto anything. The Dzogchen teachings call this the primordially pure state of cutting through, the intent of the fourth empowerment, the non-dual great bliss, which is present throughout all states, samsaric or nirvanic. When we apply this to ourselves, it is the sense of being empty and uninvolved, utterly naked, wide awake, and vividly clear. When involved in thoughts of the three spheres, naked awareness is not seen. When not conceptualizing the three spheres, original mind is empty and wide-awake, free from fixation. This is also called awareness wisdom, the knowing wakefulness. On a coarse general level, there are no disturbing emotions present at that moment, and on a more subtle level, the conceptual attitude that fixates is absent.

Like mercury is unmixed with dust, this empty and cognizant original mind is untainted by karma and disturbing emotions. In the same way, empty and cognizant wakefulness is forever untainted by the dust of conceptual attitudes. For a short moment, our body may be human, but our mind is a buddha. Because it lasts for such a brief moment, the qualities of abandonment and realization have no chance to become fully manifest. However, there is one special, unique quality already manifest which is unlike any ordinary state of mind. At that moment of recognition, there is no karma or disturbing emotion. The stream of karma and disturbing emotion has been interrupted; it is not present. This is the experience of emptiness, but we have not yet mastered it, we have not trained fully in it. This original, ordinary mind, the primordially state of cutting through, is real, but because of not being completely used to it, the continuity is not sustained. We may momentarily recognize the empty, aware state of Mahamudra, the natural state, which is the Great Perfection, Dzogchen. But unless we grow used to it and have some stability, it will not help that much. Imagine a small child on a battlefield. The child is in a hopeless position, utterly unable to fight, to defend itself. In the same way, the recognition of mind essence may be genuine, but it has not really "grown up" enough to be able to cope with all situations.

Mahamudra training and training in Dzogchen is not an act of meditating, because any act of meditation is by definition conceptual. Whatever is a training in being conceptual is not a training in the natural state. Mahamudra and Dzogchen training means not fabricating anything, just allowing the continuity of our natural state. This is not our habit. We must train in developing a new habit, but this practice is not *meditation*, but *familiarization*. When we finally arrive at the dharmakaya throne of non-meditation there is nothing more to cultivate: there is not even an atom to meditate forth, and yet we are not distracted for even an instant. We need to train in this. It is also phrased as mental non-doing. Nothing is to be done or made in the realm of mind. Mental non-doing is Mahamudra, but do not just sit with the idea: "I should not do." To make something in one's mind is conceptual, and to think, "I should do nothing in my mind," is also conceptual.

In the guidance manuals for meditation, it is often phrased like this: do not alter your present fresh wakefulness. Do not rearrange even as much as a hair tip. Just leave it exactly as it is. This is very profound, and there is a lot to understand here. When people hear about the awakened state, buddha mind, they think it must be something fantastic, something flabbergasting, totally out of this world. Everything must have disappeared, fallen apart, dissolved. It must be totally unique, unlike anything that they have experienced. With all these enormous preconceptions, one easily ignores the actual reality of buddha mind.

> *Try to compose your mind*
> *Empty and awake, alive and vibrant,*

Allowing it to be as it naturally is.
Leave it without the need to modify.
Do not alter this present ordinary mind.
Be free of accepting and rejecting,
Correcting or rearranging,
Your present fresh wakefulness.

That itself is the empty, awake awareness of recognition. When this awareness is not focused towards something, then it is naturally wide open, undirected. That is exactly what is meant in the statement "the five senses wide open, awareness undirected." Be like that. Rest in the equanimity of that.

There is a sense of awakeness in our present ordinary mind that is not fixated on anything whatsoever. It is unpolluted. When leaving this fresh ordinary mind as it is, without correcting or modifying it, without altering it in any way, without accepting and rejecting, there is no fixating on anything. When one does not direct the mind towards anything, the normal conceptual attitudes that hold things to be permanent, to be real, that "this is me and that is other" — they are all absent. There is total freedom from karma and disturbing emotion.

The key point of the training is this: short moments many times. Trying to keep awareness too long produces dullness or agitation. Rather that worrying about the length of experience, place the emphasis on that which is genuinely the naturally empty, awake and non-fixated state. Even though it may not last very long, that's okay; it's better to be genuine. Any other state we try to prolong is a made-up "natural state". We may be able to keep that for a long while, but even though it lasts a long time, it is not going to be helpful for true progress.

How do we identify that our natural state is genuine, real, authentic? It must be unmixed with concept. The moment a conceptual attitude is formed, rigpa is polluted, corrupted. *Short moments many times* acknowledges that the length of our recognition at this stage probably is only short moments. When we try to stretch out its duration, what we nurture becomes conceptual; it becomes artificial.

But if due to our training the innate nature continues naturally for a relatively long while, it doesn't mean that we have to cut it short. That likewise would be conceptual. The point is that we do not have to do anything to it: we do not have to make it short, nor do we have to make it last long.

The Dzogchen teaching tell us to strip awareness to its naked state; to separate dualistic mind and rigpa. This means be free of fixation, be free of conceptual attitude. If we hold any conceptual attitude or fix the attention on something, rigpa is not naked; it is covered. The moment no conceptual attitude is formed, the moment attention is not fixed on something, present fresh ordinary mind, present fresh wakefulness, is by itself naked and awake. Just sustain it like that. Ordinary mind or self-existing awareness is characterized as being wide open, while dualistic mind is confined.

Therefore, in our practice, when we notice the state that is wide open, vast, free of reference point, that is ordinary mind, self-existing awareness. When we notice that our state is confined, focused on something, with a reference point, that is dualistic mind. We should know how to make this distinction. Believing that we are sustaining the natural state of mind while we are caught up with ordinary thinking is not much use. We need to identify the genuine, the authentic — this is important. We need to identify that which is utterly empty, utterly naked, not confined to anything, totally clear and cognizant yet not fixated on anything.

Do you have any doubts, any uncertainty?

QUESTION: Why are only the five senses wide open and not the sixth sense?

RINPOCHE: The sixth is connected to the other five. To just have open eyes does not mean there is clear seeing, unless that is connected with mind consciousness; isn't that so?

QUESTION: Is it possible to be in a state of emptiness and still be involved in fixation?

RINPOCHE: When composing ourselves in equanimity, we notice if there is physical discomfort. It catches our attention again and again. It is not like our minds are half empty and at the same time half distracted. It is more a back and forth movement between the two states. Our attention is caught by something, then it is released again.

QUESTION: Rinpoche, you were saying there is an awareness without concepts. Is that true?

RINPOCHE: Awareness, Dzogchen awareness, is unmixed with concept.

QUESTIONER: Wow!

RINPOCHE: Good reply.

QUESTION: In rigpa, I sometimes recognize the quality of emptiness, clarity and bliss, but I do not get the vastness very often at all. Does that come with more familiarization? Is that a sign that I am somehow fixated, spatially?

RINPOCHE: When you totally release every single type of focus and reference point, totally let go, it is impossible not to have that openness and vastness.

QUESTION: I must be sticking somewhere then.

RINPOCHE: Yes. A sign of some subtle clinging lingering on.

QUESTION: What is the most skillful way to deal with dullness?

RINPOCHE: There are outer ways and inner ways. The outer way is you go up to a higher location with a vast view, a greater vista; you wear less clothing so that you're not so warm; and you raise your gaze upward. You can also expel your breath forcefully, all of a sudden. There is a specific oral instruction in exclaiming the sound PHAT, abruptly and forcefully.

The inner way is to apply mindfulness; either the deliberate or effortless type of reminding, both of which remind you to just be empty, awake, and totally clear again. What that means is that the feeling of being dull or drowsy is just another thought. Abandon that thought.

QUESTION: Practice is one thing, but as soon as I stand up, I solidify my experience again. There is immediately an "I" when I get up. Whenever I try to apply the method while not formally practicing, while walking around or doing anything, it is nothing but fabricating. It drives me crazy because I realize how distracted I am, all the time. The method does not seem to work unless I am really sitting down practicing.

RINPOCHE: This is where you see the importance of keeping sessions. We have our waking time; we divide that up into sessions and breaks. That is important. During the sessions, there is the meditative state and the post-meditation. When you put your body in a certain balanced posture with the back straight and the breathing is natural and unforced, there are certain factors that are aligned. These factors coming together have a certain influence on our state of mind. It is said, "When the right coincidence is formed through the physical body, realization occurs in the mind." Isn't it true that when you put yourself in this posture your state of mind feels different, more relaxed and open? The posture forms a coincidence for the state of realization.

Now we are training in the meditative state, right? As we train, we become more and more used to being this way. When one is really trained, to the extent of being stable, it becomes possible and easier to be that way during the post-meditation. You can mingle the meditation state with everyday situations of eating, sitting, speaking, and lying down. The most difficult is when lying down, when sleeping, when dreaming. We need to train during all these situations. Lingje Repa, one of the great masters of the Drukpa Kagyü lineage, said,

The guru said, train in the original nature,
Which I did, again and again.
But now my meditation of sessions and breaks have vanished,
What should I do now?

What you have said is true. But some people get more thoughts when they sit. They find that if they move, the situation is a little better, especially if they travel in a bus or taxi, not driving themselves.

QUESTION: I am a little fearful to give up everything, even though I do experience emptiness and clarity. I have this Western tendency to feel there must be something material there. There cannot be just nothing.

RINPOCHE: That must be the blessing of science.

QUESTION: Will this eventually dissolve through practice?

RINPOCHE: Intellectually you can convince yourself that this empty cognizance is immaterial, in the sense of being inconcrete. And through your own practice, you can prove that experientially. During the authentic meditation state you understand that it is not solid matter. Therefore, when you train repeatedly in letting go of thoughts and preconceived ideas, again and again they will increasingly vanish. It will get better and easier.

QUESTION: Other than trying to practice during the day, is there a particular practice when falling asleep that can help create the circumstances for recognizing mind nature?

RINPOCHE: That practice is one of the Six Doctrines of Naropa. The training in the luminosity of deep sleep is a combination of development and completion stages in which you use a visualization combined with recognizing the nature of mind. Deep sleep is a small version of death, so it is very important to practice in this state. Whenever you feel drowsy, sleepy, and you are about to doze off, those stages need to be embraced with some presence of mind that recognizes mind essence. The best way is to fall asleep while sustaining mind essence. This is not easy; in fact, it is very difficult. because the absentmindedness, the tendency to become oblivious, is so strong. Also, when you try too keenly to have presence of mind, you do not fall asleep; you stay awake. Therefore, take a good thought, a positive thought to heart, and fall asleep with that. That is very important for Dharma practitioners. When you fall asleep with a good attitude, that thought state continues throughout the sleep, and you gain merit. It is virtuous sleep! Sleep in a state of goodness. You could also fall asleep really angry, with the thought "I want to hurt that person, I want to harm him, I want to take revenge." The whole sleep then becomes unvirtuous.

QUESTION: Is there any value to remembering and writing down our dreams?

RINPOCHE: When someone talks nonsense, we say they're speaking as if they're in a dream. In other words, dreams are not something to attach a lot of importance to. In general, dreams are not to be given any importance. Sometimes what we dream could come true, it could have significance, but mostly it is just nonsense. That is why the dream state is used as one of the eight analogies of illusion: *like a dream.*

Since we are practicing in order to not to remain in a confused state while awake, in order to go beyond delusion we should also try to train in not being deluded while dreaming and while in deep sleep. The first step in dream practice, practicing while dreaming, is to become aware of the fact that the dream is a dream. This is called *recognizing dream as dream*. After that are other steps called transforming, multiplying, and so forth. Recognizing here means not just once in a rare while. To recognize once or twice that the dream state is a dream is quite easy. But recognizing during the state of deep sleep that this is the state of deep sleep is much more difficult. A good practitioner is someone who can practice while dreaming, and who can practice while being in the state of deep sleep. Those situations as well must be embraced with the training.

STUDENT: How do we prolong the recognition of mind essence?

RINPOCHE: Meditation in this context is the duration of sustaining the essence. Essence here refers to what we really are, the awake and empty state that is not made out of any material thing whatsoever — utterly open, yet wide awake. We need to sustain this, or, in other words, to keep this as an ongoing presence. For that to happen a method is necessary. It is indispensable to remind ourselves to recognise our essence, to use the method of "remindfulness". There is no way around this as long as we are beginners. At first, this remindfulness is an intentional reminding called deliberate mindfulness; later it becomes effortless mindfulness. Mindfulness of whichever type is definitely necessary; otherwise, we never recognize. After forgetting the natural state, apply the reminding repeatedly. Do so not only when sitting down in a session, but at any given moment.

It is as I just said, *short moments many times.* When we sit down to meditate, it may seem as if we have to get into a particular state: "Now I am meditating, and it lasts for a long while." This is possible for the very rare person, but mostly when one thinks, "I am in the natural state for quite a while," either it is just make-believe, like pretending to oneself, or it is a complete fabrication. We really need to question whether it is the genuine natural state if it lasts for quite a while. It would be better if we were just very honest about this, since we do not really need to pretend to ourselves that we are in a superb ongoing natural state. It is much better when we just allow it to be as long as it lasts, without trying to create something artificial. First, we remind ourselves to recognize our essence; next, we allow that to last. If it lasts only a short time, let it be short; if it lasts a long time, let it be long. We do not have to cut it short, because that would be artificial. We do not have to sit and hold it for a long time, which is also artificial. Be totally without artifice! That is how to train.

As soon as you forget the natural state, use the reminding again, either deliberately or effortlessly. This is how we can progress:

through short moments many times, through recognizing repeatedly. To reiterate this point, recognize not only during the meditation session, but at all possible times. Honestly, if we are lucky we set aside twenty minutes a day, and we call that the meditation practice. But real practitioners do not limit their practice to the meditation session. They practice while walking around, reminding themselves to recognize the essence. By practicing while talking, while eating, while doing any kind of activity, they have all their time to practice, instead of only short periods. If we only practice for short periods and nothing much happens after many years, we may blame the Dharma or the teachings: "Those instructions were supposed to be so high and profound, but look what happened — not much!" Really, though, we only have ourselves to blame.

Instead, train all the time in sustaining the essence. When we do so, real and swift progress is possible. It is like medicine: it only helps if you eat it. Medicine is meant to cure disease. In the same way, our practice is meant to cure the basic disease that causes all of our karmic doing, emotions and deluded states. That root cause is the very subtle conceptual attitude. And the only thing that can really cut through that, at the very root, is to recognize the nature of mind and simply allow it to be that way, as it naturally is, without any contriving or modifying. Do not try to correct or improve upon it by accepting, rejecting, or replacing our mind in a certain state. Rather, train in being totally uncontrived and natural; this is how the root cause of samsara is cut through. At the very moment of recognizing mind essence, there is no karmic doing, there are no emotions, there is no delusion. All these have been cleared up totally, at that moment. We need to train in it; that is the training. We need to grow used to it. Growing used to it does not mean that it is an act of meditating, like visualizing a deity or concentrating on a sense of quietness, as in shamatha. This training in the vipashyana that is thought-free wakefulness is not an act of meditating, because there is no thing being cultivated by meditating. Being totally free of meditating, being totally free of holding something in mind — that is the ultimate training.

The Heart of the Practice

Up to this point I've given quite a lot of material. Now now I'll summarize the essential points. In general, we need to understand that the entirety of samsara is futile and pointless to pursue. In particular, we need to understand that karma and selfish emotions are like poison. Selfish emotions make us create an enormous amount of negative karma and negative actions that only create suffering. In this way, selfish emotions are the basis for deluded experience. If you are weary of samsara and want to renounce everything, you should abandon karma and disturbing emotions.

The objects of our compassion, from the core of our hearts, should be all sentient beings who repeatedly undergo self-created suffering. The Mahayana scriptures repeatedly mention that each and every sentient being has been our own fathers and mothers, our own brothers and sisters, our children, our intimates, in various lifetimes. We are connected to everyone, without a single exception. By practicing the true view and pure compassion, we can truly help others and bring them to a permanent state of liberation and enlightenment. Do so with this kind of motivation: "By training in the true view and pure compassion, I will bring all sentient beings to enlightenment!" At all times, keep this very precious bodhichitta attitude. Do not let it be mere lip service, but endeavor to make it deep-felt, from the core of your heart. Keep disenchantment with and renunciation of samsara as the very foundation of your practice, as well as loving kindness and compassion. In addition to that, train in the true view, the pure view of recognizing mind essence.

At all levels of Buddhist practice we combine two aspects, means and knowledge. In the general level of Buddhism, the means is the pure ethics, the discipline, as well as meditative concentration. The result of that is the knowledge, the insight of realizing there is no ego, there is no self. Through this way, we can attain freedom. In the Mahayana teachings, the means are the first five of the six paramitas, while the knowledge is the sixth, prajnaparamita or transcendent knowledge. Through these two, we realize the true view of compassionate emptiness. Profound emptiness is indivisible from great compassion. In this way, we can progress through the paths and bhumis, all the way through the tenth bhumi to the eleventh bhumi of true and complete enlightenment.

When it comes to the vajra vehicle of secret mantra, the special quality of Vajrayana is pure perception. Because everything to begin with is already pure, whatever appears and exists is all-encompassing purity. To train in seeing everything as pure is a very profound method that is part of the means. The knowledge aspect in Vajrayana is non-dual original wakefulness, the recognition of the very nature of our minds. It is only due to temporary confusion, moment-to-moment mistakenness, that we apprehend the existence of an 'I' where no such personal identity exists, and of a 'that' and a 'you', where no such entities truly exist. Through such temporary mistakenness, all the different experiences come about. Both the shared and individual types of experience are due to this moment–to-moment confusion.

To clear away this mistakenness, this impure perception, we not only train in pure perception but also in recognizing the true view of thought-free wakefulness. There are a variety of means to facilitate this in Vajrayana. They include the reflections called the four mind changings; the ngöndro of the four or five times hundred thousand, as well as the development stage, recitation and completion stage. Vajrayana methods are very easy, there are plenty of them, and they do not require much hardship. However, they are tremendously effective to purify momentary confusion.

Let us take the example of the connection between firewood and fire. A lot of firewood makes a huge fire that can burn for a long time. You could say that the fire's size and its ability to burn for a long duration is thanks to the firewood. Nevertheless, when the firewood is used up, the fire is finished. Fire does not burn without wood. In the same way, the accumulation of merit is necessary and beneficial. When, in addition, this merit is combined with the accumulation of wisdom — with the view of profound emptiness — then that merit fuels the wisdom that enables us to transcend samsara. Therefore, means and knowledge, merit and wisdom, are extremely important. Knowledge can make us free of samsara. Perfect knowledge comes through the accumulation of merit, the means.

The training in goodness with a conceptual focus means to avoid what harms others, as well as the causes that harm others. It follows that as we avoid inflicting harm, we are also able to do what is helpful for others. We are then able to create the circumstances that are beneficial for understanding; we are able to connect with teachings, to arrive in places where there are spiritual teachers. It becomes increasingly easy, naturally.

You may at present be unable to practice meditation; you may lack the opportunity to embrace the practices of development stage and completion stage; but you can still sincerely take refuge in the Three Jewels, the three precious ones, the Buddha, Dharma and Sangha. Accept these three objects as your help and support. By forming this virtuous frame of mind, at some future point, you will be able to reconnect with the teachings. You will be able to come into circumstances where you can learn, understand and practice. Being able to practice the Dharma comes about through the combined power of the blessings of the Three Jewels and our own trust and devotion. It is said that although the blessings of the Three Jewels are like a hook that is always present, unless the ring of our openness or faith or trust is also present, the hook cannot take hold of the ring.

The bodhisattva vow is the sincere wish to help others. We think, "as much as I am able to do so, I will help other beings directly and indirectly; I will do whatever it takes." The bodhisattva precept is to form the resolve to bring all sentient beings to enlightenment. This is not just during the ceremony of taking the bodhisattva vow, but also on a daily basis — whenever we do some practice, it is part of the chant. Whenever we sit down to do a meditation session, we take the bodhisattva vow: it is like a prelude to meditation practice. It may seem that it doesn't help that much, that it is just a nice way of thinking. This is not true. From the initial bodhisattva vow comes the ability to truly help others, which enables a bodhisattva to be courageous and brave, to embrace the vast activities that accomplish the benefit of all other beings in actuality. This actual ability springs directly out of intention. A bodhisattva first forms a strong resolve, the very deep-felt and strong wish to be of help to others. The bodhisattva vow we take is the seed of the activity. From this seed, the ability will come in the future to actually put it to use for the benefit of others. Taking the bodhisattva vow has tremendous benefit.

The Vajrayana precepts are called samayas. They are obtained through receiving empowerment. Through receiving the four empowerments of Vajrayana practice, we are introduced to the real condition of things — how things really are.

Through the first of the fourth empowerments, the vase empowerment, we are introduced to the fact that whatever we see, all sights, are visible emptiness — not just the celestial palaces, buddhafields and deities that we visualise, but everything we see. The second empowerment introduces us to the fact that all sounds, not only mantra, are audible emptiness. To recognize this is to realize the voice of the victorious ones. Through the third empowerment, we are brought to the understanding that all sense impressions, especially blissful ones, are indivisible from emptiness. That is very important for us as humans, because the world system we are in is called the Desire Realm. For beings in this type of realm, attachment to pleasant sensations and the feeling of desire are very strong; they run very deep. Through the third empowerment, we are introduced to the state of wakefulness in which bliss and emptiness are indivisible, in order to be free of that habitual attachment to pleasure. The fourth empowerment, the precious word empowerment, points out our innate nature of mind, intrinsic wakefulness, as being indivisible emptiness and awareness.

The best situation, of course, is to receive the four empowerments and simultaneously realize what is intended and pointed out in our own experience. In that particular way, being empowered and being realized go hand in hand. If this does not occur, the empowerments at the very least still bestow blessings. This makes one receptive to realizing the intended meaning of the empowerment at some point in the future.

Honestly, empowerment is the mind transmission of the buddhas. Empowerment is also the symbolic transmission of the knowledge holders, the vidyadharas. And the oral transmission of masters, the teachings we receive, is a way of being empowered as well. Up until this point, in every chapter here I have taught about the nature of mind, about the value of recognizing it, and how to train in that. These teachings are also connected to the meaning of empowerment. Actually, there is no empowerment without teaching and there is no teaching without empowerment. Still, there is still a difference between the two. During these teachings, I have not made use of the formal mandala and the various ritual implements of empowerment.

The path of Vajrayana is means and knowledge — means as the development stage and knowledge as the completion stage. Without understanding the purpose, the development stage can become as irrelevant as a child playing in a sandbox. Development stage has both temporary and ultimate benefit. These benefits are logical, profound, and can be proven through the instructions and through our own experience. The practice of development stage gradually reduces our attachment, our clinging to the solid reality of our body and dwelling place. As a matter of fact, everything is already the unity of experience and emptiness, or appearance and emptiness, so visualizing things as being in such a way is in harmony with how things actually are; there is no conflict. All sounds are audible emptiness; the voice of all buddhas is audible emptiness. All sensations, if we really look closely into how they feel, are nothing other than blissful emptiness. This is especially true when we apply the key points of the vajra body with the three channels and five chakras to ignite the tummo fire and to experience the blissful heat. Through experiencing the example wisdom, we are enabled to realize the true wisdom, the real wisdom, which is the naked state of empty awareness.

There is a reason to for this. In general, all phenomena originates dependently, based on causes and conditions. Mind is very powerful. When the mind directs itself towards what is good, we can do tremendous good things. When it is directed in a negative way, we can do immense evil.

Isn't it true that someone who forms the deep-felt wish, "May I benefit innumerable beings! May I attain that ability to truly help others in vast, vast numbers!" can do great good things out of that attitude? The converse is true for one who forms the strong wish, "May I gain power over a great number of people and destroy my enemies." Out of such a distorted wish, one can do tremendous evil. Motivation itself has no physical form. A person who forms such a wish looks like an ordinary person, and yet the forming of that type of wish could be extraordinary. This is the power of great aspiration, but it could also be the power of a negative desire.

Some people say, "Buddhism may be good, but its followers do not really do anything for others. Buddhists merely sit and make good wishes for other beings, they do not really do it. In other religions, people reach out: they establish hospitals, they build schools, and they actually do something for others." In terms of immediate benefit, it is accurate to say that. If we think about what is of real benefit, however, what is of ultimate benefit, there is a lot more to say. Certainly it is one type of benefit to help others while their body is still alive, by curing them, educating them and so forth; by giving them food, clothes and shelter. This is called mundane benefit. You help to establish them in a nice, comfortable state in this world. But if you can influence their attitude towards developing greater compassion and understanding, that is an even greater benefit which could be inexhaustible, because they can take those qualities along. The giving of material things is good, but giving protection against fear is an even greater gift. Greater than that still is the gift of the teachings, which helps their minds reduce disturbing emotions and increase compassion and knowledge. Giving the understanding into the nature of things is not a gift of temporary benefit: it is of lasting value.

Everything comes about through a connection between causes and conditions. Therefore, if we train in a way in which means and knowledge are in unity; if we train in a correct, pure way, we will realize a result which is equally pure and perfect. Perfect coincidence means accordance of causes and conditions. On one hand the perfect coincidence of causes and conditions seems very simple, but is not. Many factors need to synchronize for anything to happen. For example we need many items to make a delicious cup of tea. We need water, a cup and a clean pot. We need fire of some sort. Also, we need tea leaves, not to mention milk, sugar or honey, and maybe spices. Even for something as simple as a cup of tea, if one factor is missing it will not be perfect.

In the same way, without the means we do not have their outcome, which is knowledge. Of course, it would be much better to understand without using any methods. If food would simply be prepared spontaneously, without doing anything that would be wonderful. If we could arrive somewhere without traveling, it would be the best. But these things don't happen. Therefore, please don't frown upon the importance of taking refuge, taking the bodhisattva vow, purifying obscurations, perfecting the accumulations, the four mind changings, ngöndro, development stage, completion stage and so forth. Do not underestimate the value of these practices. A small method can yield a great result. Do not belittle the means, the methods. When we do not underestimate even a small method, that small method can help develop the eventual profound outcome of all these methods, which is the knowledge that realizes egolessness.

In all three vehicles in Buddhism, we practice in a way in which means and knowledge are combined in a unity. This is true whether we train in the knowledge that realizes egolessness, or in the profound emptiness indivisible from compassion that is the view of compassionate emptiness, or in the basic state of non-dual thought-free wakefulness. Whatever method helps you to progress in that, please use it. When something makes it more difficult, please avoid it. There are two helpful circumstances, *devotion* and *compassion*. These two methods are the best ways to purify obscurations and perfect the accumulations. Moreover, when it comes to overcoming obstacles, sidetracks and pitfalls in our practice, there are two practices that are very safe, simple and always efficient: devotion and compassion. Sincere devotion and sincere compassion overcome any and all hindrances.

I have also explained to you the purpose and benefits of precepts and vows. The heart of Vajrayana practice, the real purpose, is pointed out during empowerment. That is the wisdom which is the meaning and nature of the empowerment. To be truly empowered, to realize original wakefulness, traditionally requires a lot of preparation. This is the reason why the accumulation of merit, purifying the obscurations and perfecting the accumulations, are necessary. But just purifying and accumulating is not enough. It is important that we do not separate means and knowledge. As I mentioned before:

> *This coemergent wisdom, beyond description,*
> *Is recognized only through the practices of gathering*
>   *accumulations and purifying one's veils*
> *And through the blessings of a realized master.*
> *Know it to be delusion if you depend on other means.*

Now to summarize the vital points on mind nature: our mind is empty in essence and cognizant by nature. These two qualities, being empty and being able to know, are indivisible. This unity of being empty and awake did not come into being; it did not arise and it does not cease; it is naturally unformed. Please allow this unity of empty cognizance to simply *be,* without fixating on anything. Recognizing this unified empty cognizance automatically eliminates the views of eternalism and nihilism. It is said that the view in Buddhism is free from the two extremes of eternalism and nihilism. Please do not leave that as a mere intellectual idea. Bring it into your actual experience, by recognizing that the nature of your mind is beyond these two extremes.

Like untainted mercury, self-existing wakefulness remains unpolluted by thoughts. Be free from both viewer and something viewed. By retaining an observer and something observed, aren't we caught up in duality? We need to leave samsara behind, and we can do that by leaving clinging behind. Wherever there is dualistic clinging, there are the twofold obscurations and there is samsara. Unless the twofold obscurations are actually pointed out, they may not be so obvious. The first, the emotional obscuration, is stinginess and so forth — all the opposites of the six paramitas — while the cognitive obscuration means any way of conceptualizing the three spheres. When we practice meditation, we may be free of emotional obscuration, but the act of conceptualizing may still go on. Therefore, we may not have separated from samsara during our meditation training.

Meditation in the context of this book should not be a training in dualistic mind; it should be *a training in mind essence*. Is it okay to continue in samsaric experience while meditating? Is it sufficient to sit with a straight back and a fixed gaze, caught up in ordinary thought, and call that sustaining buddha nature? Meditation means not being caught up in an ordinary conceptual attitude, in the usual samsaric way of perceiving. Thinking that is caught up in the three spheres simply obscures. This is a state of obscured suchness that is the same as any other mundane sentient being's mind set. The only difference is that you are sitting looking like you are meditating. We practitioners should be different.

Please notice this sentence: *cognitive obscuration is any thought that conceives the three spheres*. When we are unpolluted by the thought that conceives the three spheres, you can rightfully call that sustaining the natural face of awareness. Like mercury poured out on the earth, no matter how much mercury you pour out and no matter how dirty the soil is, it never mixes with the mercury. The soil cannot possibly pollute the mercury; it is impossible for it to mix with it. Like untainted mercury, self-existing wakefulness remains unpolluted by thoughts that conceive the three spheres.

In short, if there is some way of mistaking the view, some way of going wrong, some sidetrack, pitfall, or error, it all comes from maintaining a conceptual attitude. The conceptual attitude is the source of all hindrances, all sidetracks. Therefore, recognize your natural face, your naked, empty awareness that is totally free from any conceptual attitude, and attain stability in that.

STUDENT: Could you explain a little more about samaya?

RINPOCHE: The Sanskrit word samaya in Tibetan is *damtsig,* and there are several ways of explaining the literal meaning of the words. To make this very simple, *dampa* means sublime, and *tsig* is a statement. Thus, *samaya* is a statement that is true, genuine, pure, real. To apply oneself in a way that is in harmony with how the truth is, is called keeping the *samaya*. Whatever we see is visible emptiness. This is how it actually is. This is also what we need to realize. The realization that all sights are visible emptiness is the vajra body of all buddhas. This is how it is proclaimed. That statement is real, true, and sublime. Keeping that is called keeping the samaya of vajra body. The same applies to all sounds being audible emptiness, and mind being aware emptiness. That is an unfailing truth.

When the samayas are described in detail, there are hundreds of thousands that can be listed. But all of them can be condensed in this way. The foremost samaya is when you compose yourself in a state in which you in actuality experience the fact that all sights, sounds and awareness are visible emptiness, audible emptiness and aware emptiness. That is the best. Next best is to have the conviction or the certainty that this is so: "Whatever is seen is visible emptiness. Whatever I hear is audible emptiness, the voice of all victorious ones. And mind is aware emptiness, self-existing rigpa, intrinsic wakefulness; it is really so." To have that certainty is called keeping all the hundreds of thousands of samayas.

The opposite of this is to regard whatever I see or hear as a solid reality that is permanent, has concrete attributes, is formed and really exists. With regard to the thoughts and emotions that move in our minds, failing to recognize the very identity of that which thinks or feels as self-existing wakefulness, is known as damaging to the samayas of mind. Being opposed to trusting that our nature could be dharmakaya or rigpa, having an opinion against that, is known as turning against the sublime samaya statements, against the unfailing truth of what is. As long as one keeps that orientation, one is removed from realizing what is true and real.

STUDENT: What is the best method for purifying the obscurations and perfecting the accumulations, to stabilize the recognition of the view?

RINPOCHE: As I said, there are a great variety of methods for purifying obscurations, perfecting the accumulations, and stabilizing the recognition of the nature of mind. But the two most conducive circumstances are *devotion* and *compassion*. You can also call them devotion and pure perception, compassion and loving kindness. Certainly whatever sidetracks and hindrances that prevent confusion from dawning as wisdom need to be removed and overcome. Also, there are ways to go wrong in meditation, by being overcome by sluggishness, by dullness and by lethargy. The best method to dispel all these hindrances is devotion and compassion.

The great master Jamgön Kongtrül wrote *Calling the Guru from Afar*. Here are two lines from it: "Whenever I engage in Dharma practice, I get more and more dull and my senses become unclear. When I engage in mundane activities I feel vigorous and awake; my senses are wide open." This is true; it happens like that! From the time I was small, I was taught *Calling the Guru from Afar*. It is also known as the prayer to pierce one's heart with devotion. I have chanted it many times and I find it very helpful. I would like to encourage you also to take up the practice of chanting *Calling the Guru from Afar*.

This chant makes it seem at first as if the guru is far away. We call from where we are over here, seemingly far from him. So we have to cry out with a lot of yearning and longing. Also the chant makes many requests, a whole list of requests of things we want and are asking for. We are asking blessings to get such-and-such, one thing after the other. What we really want is to realize the ultimate guru, the natural state. In a nutshell, *Calling the Guru from Afar* is a plea that we want to recognize our innate nature, our original mind. Until we do so, it doesn't matter what kind of practices we utilize. All practices converge at the point where we recognize the ultimate guru, which is our innate nature. Until we recognize this and stabilize this recognition, we have yet to meet the true guru. We have only met his resemblance. Devotion and compassion as enhancements are thus the best remedies to avoid being caught up in the dullness and sluggishness that afflicts meditation, and for dispelling all obstacles to remaining in mind nature.

We also need perseverance. There are many types, but the best is a sense of constancy while delighting in what we are doing. Sometimes we need to do a job that we don't like, and even one hour of work can feel like a really long time, because we hate every moment of it. But if it is something that we like, something we take great pleasure in, we can dance the whole night and not feel that tired. If one were forced to dance, one would probably hate it — even for one hour. What we need is to practice the Dharma with that sense of joy, taking delight in what we are doing. This is possible and it will happen. It comes from understanding the value of the Dharma, understanding what the benefit of practice is and the immense impact that even a short period of practice has. Once we have that appreciation, then spending even a few moments practicing is something we do with great joy.

Diligence, exerting oneself with perseverance, also has to do with a sense of renunciation, the will to be free from samsara. The root cause of samsara is the attitude that clings to a self; this creates attachment, aversion and further stupidity. Dharma practice is exactly what frees us from the root of samsara. Often we hear the example that samsara is like a filthy swamp and liberation is like a pleasant island. Try picturing not just a swamp, but one that is full of nasty creatures, poisonous water snakes, crocodiles and disgusting things floating around in the water. When you look out in the distance, you see a beautiful island with palm trees and gardens. All around you are dangerous animals about to bite and kill you. With that kind of scenery, people do not waste even a second; they immediately swim as fast as they can towards the island of liberation! This crude example is actually close to reality: When we appreciate not only the qualities of being free but also see ego-clinging and duality as the root cause of further entanglement in samsara, we will not waste a second. Instead, we joyfully practice the Dharma that makes us free. We take delight in it, happily practicing out of sincerity and joy. Thus, we need perseverance which has a sense of constancy with delight and joy.

The attitude of ego-clinging is a deeply ingrown habit. We may want to give it up from one moment to the next, but it does not simply happen all by itself. After being involved in Dharma practice for a couple of months or a few years, it does not help to think, "I am not free yet, I have not been liberated; practice doesn't work." That will not do. We need to persevere. This is not a small task that we have set about to accomplish. Enlightenment and liberation is a great task, a grand task.

It is like being in a battle. Our enemies are the selfish emotions. We may not notice all eighty-four thousand different enemies, but we can notice the six major ones. On our side to fight back with we have compassion and insight into egolessness. Yet our weapons are not that sharp and these two helpers are not yet that strong. So we should not give up too easily. At this point, we may have recognized the intrinsic wakefulness that is the nature of our mind — the self-existing awareness, rigpa, which is the awakened state of all buddhas — but we still need to persevere. That perseverance takes the form of mindfulness, either deliberate or effortless. In the beginning, we need to be deliberately mindful and remind ourselves. It's like learning to drive a car: at first it is not clear where to put our hands, where to put our feet, what to do in what order. We may make mistakes, and we need to constantly remind ourselves what to do. But after training for a while it becomes easier and easier, until at some point it does not require much thought; it becomes almost effortless. That is the example for effortless mindfulness.

In the beginning there is a need to deliberately remind ourselves to recognize. As we grow increasingly used to that, the reminding occurs effortlessly. Eventually, the yogi or yogini, the male or female practitioner, is thoroughly trained in this that the essence of mind is immediately recognized each time a thought occurs. That is when that the statements, "The more thoughts, the more dharmakaya" comes true. In other words, each movement of thought reveals the awakened state of all buddhas. When the training is at that level, progress through the paths and bhumis becomes as quick as a streak of lightning.

In this context, there are three stages of Dzogchen training: recognizing, perfecting the strength, and attaining stability. The first is when we recognize in actuality the view that the nature of our mind is primordial purity. "Innate suchness" refers exactly to this view, as do other impressive names like dharmakaya, self-existing awareness, intrinsic wakefulness, buddha mind, and rigpa.

Next comes the broadening of that recognition, strengthening it by means of training. As I mentioned earlier, this training is not an act of meditating; it is more the sense that one grows increasingly familiar, becoming used to the natural state in an ever more confident way. It is said, "It is familiarization, not meditation." This is the process in which at the beginning we need to be mindful, we need to be deliberately alert, we need to have a sense of being awake and aware, trying our best to recognize again and again.

Later this intentional way of training becomes effortless. During this process, the qualities of compassion devotion, and insight begin to manifest further and further. Moreover, the selfish emotions become less and less; they lose their hold on your attention. The negative qualities — the unfortunate or unwholesome tendencies of our stream of being — start to vanish. Conversely, the good qualities — the wisdom of knowing the nature as it is, the wisdom that perceives all possibly existing things, the immense loving compassion, and more — become increasingly perfected.

These enlightened qualities become more and more manifest, until one finally attains stability. At that point, there is no longer any need to try to be aware and mindful, because there is no parting from the primordial state of awakened mind. The view of the primordially pure Great Perfection is not left behind, even for an instant, throughout day and night. This totally uninterrupted state of realization is the attainment of stability, also known as supreme accomplishment, complete enlightenment and buddhahood.

A Permanent Vacation

Please understand thoroughly that the Buddha taught how things really are. When we correctly apply the teachings of the Buddha to ourselves, that training is itself the source of lasting happiness and well-being. Imagine what it would be like, even within this lifetime, to be able to reduce our disturbing emotions, our selfishness, through training. Wouldn't it be wonderful to not be caught up in so many disturbing emotions? We would definitely be happier, more joyful and more naturally at ease. As our selfish emotions connected with attachment, anger and dullness decrease, we are increasingly in harmony with and appreciated by whoever we are with. We are also able to benefit whoever we are with. As you all know, when someone is easy-going, relaxed and carefree, he or she may not actively benefit others, but his or her mere presence is still appreciated. People take delight in such company. When your mind is at ease, the words you speak and the actions you perform will automatically will be peaceful and gentle. On the other hand, it's disturbing to be with someone who is passionately caught up in rivalry, conceit or other ways of being emotionally selfish.

What really helps us, both right now, within this lifetime, at the moment of death, and in the bardo and the following future lives, is a sincere attempt to soften our rigid minds and be more gentle. Immediate as well as lasting benefit especially comes from the effort to recognize the wish-fulfilling jewel of our mind essence, and to not only recognize this, but to train and attain stability in mind nature.

As a beginner in Dharma practice, it may not be so easy to mingle everyday activities with the view of compassionate emptiness, the recognition of mind nature. Therefore, set aside time and make sessions, to train in bodhichitta, loving kindness and recognizing the true view. Between sessions, the rest of the time, you can involve yourself in other good and meaningful activities — this is not excluded at all. During daily situations we can remind ourselves to recognize the nature of mind. Even if this is difficult, we should still try to be loving, kind, considerate, mindful, and conscientious. At all times try to keep a relaxed, gentle frame of mind, in accordance with relative bodhichitta, the wish to be of help and assistance to other beings. As much as possible, avoid keeping a negative attitude. By doing these things, we grow closer and closer to the genuine, real practice, the actual bodhisattva mindset.

Additionally, remind yourself that everything you perceive is like a dream. Through this thought, which is a close facsimile of emptiness, we move nearer to realizing the true view of the profound emptiness of all things. Right now, whatever we perceive is a seeming presence, an illusion that seems to exist in a very solid and concrete way. But the moment we look closely, no phenomenon whatsoever is found to possess any independent existence. Yet at the same time it is perceived, due to the coincidence between causes and circumstance. This is how reality is: that all phenomena by nature are empty and beyond arising, dwelling and ceasing, even though they seem to arise and are perceived through dependent origination. This is why the great master Nagarjuna said, "When the formed cannot be claimed to exist, how can the unformed be claimed to exist?" In short, everything is perceived without having true existence.

Words like formed and unformed, concrete and inconcrete usually refer to material things. Space is unformed, inconcrete, and immaterial. But objects kept in mind possess no true existence whatsoever. Here I am talking about perceived objects. The perceiving mind as well, is not found to exist in any way whatsoever as a concrete thing. Mind the perceiver is also beyond arising, dwelling and ceasing. All phenomena, everything, is therefore totally beyond mental constructs. *This is how things are*. All the buddhas of the three times are liberated through realizing how reality is; all sentient beings are confused because of not realizing how it actually is.

Really there are only two options: to be confused or to be free. Confused means confusing the *reality of what is*. In the moment of perceiving, rather than simply seeing what is, one invents or superimposes something in one's mind and apprehends an existence that does not exist. This mistaken conclusion is the belief in the existence of a self, a personal identity where no such thing actually exists, and the belief in the existence of objects where real objects do not exist. That is called confusion, mistakenness. Both the sutras and tantras describe in detail how confusion initially begins, and also how liberation takes place. The difference is then between being confused and being free.

The onset of confusion or total freedom is described by all the buddhas and the great masters simply, in this way: "When our minds are occupied with the two obscurations, there is confusion. When free of the two obscurations, there is freedom." This is why meditation practice is essential: in order to be free of the two obscurations, especially the subtler obscuration of the belief in self.

We should compose our minds in meditation in a way which does not conceptualize at all. For example, Mahamudra means mental non-doing. Mental non-doing means not holding an attitude that conceptualizes, that forms thought. In other words, it is quite unlike the ordinary way of thinking that allows us to again and again be carried away. Meditation training in the Mahamudra and Dzogchen view is not simply an attempt to be calm. It means to be without clinging. This is the opposite of the samsaric state, the opposite of conceptual thinking. Rather than thinking *of something*, allow the identity of what thinks to be thought-free wakefulness. Milarepa said, "In the gap between thoughts, you risk discovering thought-free wakefulness." This is the same meaning as Chandrakirti's statement on the Middle Way: "The ceasing of thought is the actualization of dharmakaya."

All great masters agree on this point: the training is to recognize the nature of mind as thought-free wakefulness. However, the training is not just recognizing mind nature: we also need to become stable in that recognition. In order to become stable, we need to recognize repeatedly, over and over again. We need to recognize to the point where the strength of this recognition prevents us from straying from the continuity of being the innate nature itself. When there is no more distraction, when the continuity of mind essence is totally unbroken, that is the same as true and complete enlightenment, the thirteenth bhumi.

It is the tradition in Tibetan Buddhism to study, reflect, understand, and then engage in meditation training. Generally speaking, we study the meaning of the three vehicles of Buddhism. The purpose of study is to understand the correct view. When one has adopted the correct perspective and trains in that, one can arrive at the result, which is the perfect fruition. In order to train, it is necessary is to become totally clear about the nature of things, the natural state. A qualified master communicates this when connecting with a qualified and receptive student. When a situation of mutual trust occurs, the authentic instruction can be transmitted. The student must feel that he or she can trust the teacher, the master, and this situation must also apply the other way: the master must feel that he or she can trust the student. With this basis of mutual trust, the natural state can be pointed out so that the student can recognize it in actuality. The natural state can be called either Mahamudra or Dzogchen. Once it is properly recognized, it can be trained in and made part of one's personal experience. Through training in the natural state, it is possible within this very lifetime and body to attain accomplishment in the sense of complete realization. As I mentioned several times, there are two different ways of practicing in the Tibetan meditative tradition: the analytical practice of a scholar and the resting practice of a simple meditator. Through either of these, or through a combination of the two, it is possible to establish with certainty how the natural state of all things actually is. The ultimate result of the scholarly approach is to go beyond analysis. *The very heart of the eighty-four thousand sections of the Dharma is to realize that your mind is the awakened state of the Buddha. The purpose of practice is to realize that. Through training, we can fully actualize this.* Without knowing this vital point, to just study Dharma as a way of gathering information, learning different categories, details and so forth, is not enough to attain realization.

Another point I repeatedly mentioned is that the nature of mind is empty and cognizant, and that these are an unformed unity. Please understand, and again and again remind yourself of this phrase: *the unformed unity of empty cognizance*. This is very important; it is an essential point to know that our minds are naturally empty and always were. It is primordial original emptiness. At the same time, our minds are cognizant; they have the ability to perceive, to experience. This ability to experience is something primordial, original. These two qualities of emptiness and cognizance are a unity. They cannot be separated; they are indivisible. All formed things are produced and then perish; they arise and cease. But this unity of being empty and cognizant does not arise and does not cease; it is unformed.

The understanding that our minds are essentially empty automatically eliminates any belief we may have in eternalism, that something in our minds is eternal and permanent. At the same time, understanding that our nature is cognizant eliminates the belief in nothingness. Understanding that these are a unity eliminates duality. These points are very important. They prevent you from falling into the two limitations of eternalism and nihilism, as well as the belief that the nature of mind arises and ceases, is produced and then perishes. This is of such vital importance that I felt the need to mention it one more time.

Isn't it true that we all like to take a break; that we all like to take a vacation, we enjoy being free? But the real and the best vacation, the permanent break, is when we suspend fixating on something and do not hold anything in mind.

Here is another important point: at all times and in all situations we find ourselves in, no matter what we are doing, we have a good and a bad side in us that could become active. So, *always, and again and again, try to reduce the negative attitude and try to promote the positive*. When you are able to do so, you can keep a mindful presence and calm yourself down when upset, aggressive or emotionally disturbed. Calming yourself down is the basic shamatha practice, and it does reduce negative emotions. But the way to totally dissolve a negative emotional attitude is by recognizing the nature of mind. Trying to be kind and compassionate does shift our attitude from negative into positive. Basically there are so many methods: we should try to apply whatever we can, whatever is convenient, whatever works for us.

We need to do ourselves a favor and not fool ourselves. In fact, we are in charge of our own care, so it is a poor idea to work against our own well-being. Someone who takes care of himself or herself is intelligent. Someone who destroys his own chances is stupid, foolish. In order to be of service to yourself, try your best to be better in your behavior, speech and attitude. You can harm yourself by the opposite, by making a habit of being nasty in thought, word and deed.

At this very moment, we all have some capacity for being wise, loving and capable. Unfortunately, these innate abilities of wisdom, compassion and ability are limited by selfishness and by the obscuration of momentary thinking, which prevent these qualities from being fully manifest. When these two momentary obscurations are cleared away, our qualities of wisdom, compassion and capability can be revealed.

We are in a very favorable position right now; we are in a very fortunate situation. As human beings, we are able to meet many great masters. Moreover, there are numerous profound teachings we can choose from. We have the opportunity to pick the best of the best, and practice them. In a way it's like we've reached a crossroads in the stream of our rebirths: what we do now will determine where we will go in the future. At this point we can choose where we want to go, whether we want to go up or down. Please choose wisely.

Please also understand that approaching the profound view of emptiness, the view of Mahamudra and Dzogchen, does require some effort on our part. It does not happen effortlessly, naturally, or spontaneously. It requires effort in being present, in being mindful, in reminding ourselves how to recognize. That is the meaning of perseverance. In the beginning we need to persevere: eventually, because of reminding ourselves over and over again, this reminding becomes effortless. Fortunately, the view of emptiness becomes easier and simpler to recognize and maintain the more we train in it, and our joy and delight in training becomes greater and greater.

STUDENT: What are the signs that your practice is on the right track?

RINPOCHE: There is a famous saying: *the sign of learning is to be more gentle and disciplined. The sign of practice is to have fewer selfish emotions*. When we find that we are less emotionally disturbed, less aggressive, less attached, less proud, less competitive and so forth, then we are progressing in meditation practice. It does not matter what practice we are doing; it's clearly going in the right direction. On the other hand, we may think we practice Mahamudra or Dzogchen and that we are an advanced practitioner, yet if we are more hardened, aggressive, conceited and full of flaws, then we had better go back and check with our teacher. Maybe we misunderstood how to practice, or perhaps something else needs to be adjusted.

All the teachings of the Buddha are meant to soften and cure the eighty-four thousand kinds of disturbing emotions in the mind streams of sentient beings. This is something that we do know. But it is not enough to know this; we need to take it to heart and live it.

STUDENT: How do we cultivate bodhichitta in a correct way, not just as a nice conceptual thought?

RINPOCHE: This is the reason why bodhichitta is explained as two types: one is conventional or relative bodhichitta, the other the ultimate or absolute bodhichitta. The attitude of relative bodhichitta is a very pure attitude, a very good heart. It is to be compassionate in a conceptual way. Ultimate bodhichitta is to be compassionate in a way that is suffused with the true view, which is free of concepts. Conceptual trust and compassion are thought-states which are limited and impermanent. This is because those feelings are dependent upon the thought *of something*. Thoughts are formed in the mind, and thus are not stable, ongoing or reliable. Such conceptual trust and compassion is therefore by definition limited: it is confined, it excludes.

What we really need is devotion and compassion that are unconfined, unlimited, impartial and unbiased. We need to be devoted and compassionate in a way that goes beyond thought, in a way that is embraced by true insight. That is the quality of our inconceivable nature. Other qualities of our nature are unhindered activity, the knowledge that knows the nature as it is, the knowledge that perceives all possibly existing things. The compassion that is impartial and free of hope and fear is a natural quality of recognizing the view of innate suchness.

STUDENT: Is non-involvement in thoughts an action or a non-action?

RINPOCHE: Remaining uninvolved in thoughts can be understood in several ways. It is not good enough to merely remain without thoughts, to train in a state of being without forming thoughts. By doing so, one can succeed in being reborn as a particular type of god in the deva realms. But this is not good enough. That is why I called the ultimate state *thought-free wakefulness,* not merely a thoughtless state. In the Buddhist metaphysical explanation of how sensory perception takes place, the five sense faculties of seeing, hearing, smelling, tasting and touching are already thought-free. Each instance is a conscious yet thought-free event. But simply remaining like that – in the mindful presence of not conceptualizing sense impressions — is not good enough. Rather than just being thought-free, without thoughts, the gap between two thoughts is actually the opportunity for *thought-free wakefulness.* It is the wakefulness that does not conceptualize the three spheres. Otherwise we are constantly caught up in perceiver and perceived.

We need the experience of recognizing mind nature, our innate nature that is inconceivable. This is experienced without an experiencer and some object being experienced. Our wakeful nature that does not conceptualize subject, object and action needs to be experienced while being free of an experiencer and an object of experience. For this to happen it is necessary to let go of grasping, to be non-grasping. It does not help to grasp on to some new object.

STUDENT: The process of letting go — would you describe it a little more fully?

RINPOCHE: Normal grasping is grasping. Trying not to grasp is also grasping. The meditator has a basic problem here, and that is the thought, "I should not grasp." We may remain with that thought, which is merely another way of grasping.

I've mentioned several times the two different approaches: one for the scholar, the other for the simple meditator. In the case of the scholar's analytical meditation, we use our intelligence to try to determine exactly what *is,* to discover the ultimate true nature of things. We examine repeatedly, deeper and deeper, until we arrive at the point at which we are honestly at a loss for words and concepts that can adequately describe how reality is. *The reality of what is, is in itself beyond words and concepts.* The ultimate view the Buddhist scholar needs to arrive at is the true view that is totally free of making any philosophical claims. That is why there is a famous statement: "Being free from any philosophical position, I am impossible to fault." In other words, the view that does not claim anything cannot be faulted.

To reach noninvolvement in thoughts through practice is the approach of a simple meditator. You can also let go in a moment of devotion or compassion. In these moments of love, the empty essence dawns nakedly. Similarly, the empty essence can be vividly revealed in a moment of fear. In the moment of anger, desire or in any other state of mind, there is an opportunity to recognize the essence in these thoughts. Whether or not the empty essence dawns nakedly in the moment of dullness, we need to check that very carefully.

The tradition of pith instructions tells us: "Cut through the chain of perceiver and perceived." That chain is never interrupted as long as we continuously form thoughts that conceive of and discern the objects perceived. Rather than forming further thoughts of what you experience, *recognize the experiencing mind.* In that very moment of recognizing the identity of the perceiving mind itself, let go into uncontrived naturalness in a way which is one hundred percent uncontrived, one hundred percent natural. At that instant, the chain of perceiver and perceiver is naturally and completely interrupted, one hundred percent. This is not an act of meditating *on something*. You do not need to do anything to your mind. As Maitreya's famous statement says:

> *In this, there is nothing whatsoever to keep*
> *And there is nothing whatsoever to remove.*
> *Truly recognize the true,*
> *Since in seeing the true you are totally free.*

To conclude, I would like to restate a few things. The very heart of all the Buddha's teachings is to realize the nature of mind. The nature of mind is the unformed unity of empty cognizance. This is variously called Madhyamaka, Mahamudra and Dzogchen. Through recognizing and training in this strength, we attain stability in this recognition of mind essence. This is the real buddha. This cuts through the root cause of delusion, of karma and emotions.

First, we need to recognize it: we need to recognize, fully and truly, this unformed unity of being empty and cognizant. Empty means that it does not consist of any concrete matter, form, shape or color whatsoever; not even as much as an atom. Cognizant means that, at the same time, there is the ability to know, to perceive whatever is. These two cannot be separated; they are an indivisible unity. This unity is unformed: it does not arise, does not cease, and does not perish. The Buddha described this as "profound, tranquil, unconstructed, unformed, luminous wakefulness."

Once stability is reached in this, there is nothing more to train. True stability means never again parting from the continuity of the unformed unity of being empty and cognizant. Padmasambhava describes this as, "Though there isn't as much as an atom to meditate upon, do not waver for even as much as an instant." In mind essence, there is nothing that needs to be cultivated through an act of meditating. There is no mental doing required. What we need is to be undistracted from this state of non-meditation.

For a beginner, the duration of the state of knowing this empty cognizance does not last very long. This is fine. To keep a state polluted by dualistic fixation for a long time is not the real thing. We need the genuine, real thing. Hence, *short moments repeated many times*. Honestly, whether it is short or whether it long doesn't really matter. We should simply allow it to last as long as it lasts. It is not our job to either artificially stretch it out or to chop it short.

We also need renunciation, which in this context means renouncing the state of unknowing, the opposite of the natural state. We need to be free of the unaware clinging to duality. To progress in that, we need trust and pure perception; the trust in and pure perception of non-dual wakefulness. Where is that? It is in the nature of our own minds. When we really have this trust and pure perception with complete sincerity, then it is very easy to remind ourselves to recognize. Along with this renunciation, trust and pure perception, we need one more thing: perseverance. Generally speaking, this is presence of mind; here, however, presence of mind or mindfulness is the thought, "I must recognize the nature of mind, self-existing wakefulness."

In the beginning, this reminding is much easier to have when we sit in a mediation session, in a quiet, remote place. It is much easier to practice in retreat because there are fewer diversions and less laziness. But as we grow increasingly accustomed to deliberately reminding ourselves of recognizing the awakened state, it seems that it becomes easier, so that finally, it happens by itself. Without trying to, or forcing ourselves to be in the natural state, it just happens. When that effortless reminding takes place in sessions, it is also quite likely to happen during ordinary life situations. Then we can truly mingle this practice with daily life. When training through reminding ourselves to recognize mind essence, there comes a point where *every movement of thought becomes an opportunity for recognizing mind essence*. When that happens, thoughts are automatically liberated upon arising.

Finally, whether we as practitioners follow the Mahamudra or the

Dzogchen teachings, there are some common factors that prevent us from going astray onto a misguided path. These also help enlightened qualities to manifest and ensure that we progress very quickly. Those factors are loving kindness, compassion, trust and pure perception. Please keep them in your hearts.

ACTIVITIES OF
CHÖKYI NYIMA RINPOCHE

www.shedrub.org

DharmaSun.org

ryi.org

MonksAndNuns.org

Monlam.org

www.ingramcontent.com/pod-product-compliance
Lightning Source LLC
Chambersburg PA
CBHW050428240426
43661CB00055B/2309